SPACE OF DETENTION

SPACE OF DETENTION

THE MAKING OF

A TRANSNATIONAL

GANG CRISIS

BETWEEN LOS ANGELES

ELANA ZILBERG   AND SAN SALVADOR

DUKE UNIVERSITY PRESS *Durham and London* 2011

© 2011 Duke University Press
All rights reserved
Printed in the United States
of America on acid-free paper ∞
Designed by Amy Ruth Buchanan
Typeset in Quadraat by Tseng
Information Systems, Inc.
Library of Congress Cataloging-in-
Publication Data appear on the last
printed page of this book.

In memory of
Dorene Golin Zilberg,
Alicia Rivas de Baires,
and Begoña Aretxaga

CONTENTS

It's the most violent gang in America . . . It has 10,000 foot
soldiers in the U.S., spreading its brutal ways across 33
states . . . And now it's going international, fueled by migration across the Western hemisphere, leaving its bloody
mark from Central [America] to the American heartland . . .
Police in a half-dozen countries struggle to crack its code
and decipher its methods.

— *World's Most Dangerous Gang* (documentary)

On February 5, 2007, Attorney General Alberto Gonzales of the United States
and President Elias Antonio Saca of El Salvador announced a new collabora-
tive effort to combat the gang La Mara Salvatrucha (MS) and the 18th Street
Gang. This effort, named the Transnational Anti-Gang Unit (TAG), would
be made up of the Federal Bureau of Investigation, the Department of State,
and El Salvador's National Civil Police, along with an "embedded" prosecutor from the Salvadoran attorney general's office. It would also facilitate the
efficient implementation of CAFÉ (the Central American Fingerprinting Exploitation initiative). The day after TAG was announced, the chiefs of police
for El Salvador, Guatemala, Honduras, and Belize met in Los Angeles to draft
a proposal for the third annual International Gang Conference in San Salvador. The same year, the federal Interagency Task Force on Gangs (comprised
of governmental officials from five agencies including the departments of
Homeland Security, Defense, State, and Justice, together with the United

States Agency for International Development) launched its program titled United States Strategy to Combat Criminal Gangs from Mexico and Central America. These transnational security agreements derive their logic and form from the premise that these gangs operate as sophisticated transnational criminal organizations with elaborate communication systems and networks that span Central America, Mexico, and the United States (if not beyond).

In this book I examine the current obsession with the so-called transnational youth gang crisis from the vantage point of the political history that constitutes the very ground that obsession works to obscure: namely, the ongoing participation of the United States in the production and reproduction of violence in El Salvador. During the twelve-year Salvadoran civil war, intervention by the United States thoroughly penetrated and transformed Salvadoran society and was crucial to the Salvadoran government's ability to stave off a triumph by the leftist revolutionary force the Farabundo Martí National Liberation Front (FMLN). The strategy used by the United States of low-intensity warfare, developed in the wake of the defeats in Korea and Vietnam, involved a counterinsurgency war by Salvadoran proxy under the guidance of the U.S. military rather than through the direct introduction of troops.[1] In the postwar period, the United States exported and extended to El Salvador its War on Crime, first through the deportation of immigrant youth associated with gangs based in Los Angeles, then through the exportation of its zero-tolerance policing strategies, and now through the development of transnational security agreements.[2] In this sense, I consider the contemporary gang crisis to be a product of a long-standing regional political structure and pattern between Latin America and the United States — or in the words of Cecilia Menjívar and Néstor Rodríquez, the "U.S.–Latin American interstate regime."[3]

The circulation of Salvadoran (immigrant) youth gangs and of U.S. zero-tolerance policing models between the United States and El Salvador is embedded within dense transnational networks of communication and uneven flows of labor, goods, money, information, and ideas between the United States and El Salvador. It is, therefore, part and parcel of the underlying circulatory patterns of globalization in which the United States and El Salvador are enmeshed "from above" (the state, corporations, multilateral agencies and international nongovernmental organizations) and "from below" (immigrants and their families, small-time tradesmen and women, and grassroots organizations and activists). So while Salvadoran immigration and gangs are arguably at the heart of this book, neither gangs nor immigrants are ultimately the objects of this study. Rather, they are the lens through which I examine the production of and contestation over the contemporary manifestation of long-standing "securityscapes" through and in which both the United States and El Salvador are linked and complicit.

The concept of the securityscape was first introduced by Hugh Gusterson as a "polite corrective" to Arjun Appadurai's "globalscapes." The term has previously been deployed by anthropologists to argue that national security policy is also an important part of transnational or local life, and to bring the profound influence of militarism on our lives back into focus.[4] I extend this concept beyond the overtly militaristic to include the patterns of circulation that result from the effort of states to police and control the mobility of subjects considered to be dangerous, in this case gang youth and immigrants. The securityscape here is the transnational space produced at the nexus of youth, migration, and violence between the United States and El Salvador. This expanded concept offers a way of understanding the spatial patterns of policing, immigration, deportation, and reentry into the United States that connect Los Angeles and its Salvadoran immigrant community to El Salvador, and to see how gangs and immigrants have been woven into these ongoing entanglements.

A Dialectics of (Im)Mobility

My focus on the policing, incarceration, and deportation of Salvadoran (immigrant) youth is primarily concerned with the "friction" in these transnational flows.[5] The figures of transnational gangs and transnational police and the securityscapes in which they are embedded push us beyond that now much maligned metaphor of mobility, "flows," and its tendency to obscure, naturalize, harmonize, homogenize, and as such serve as the official legitimizing language of globalization.[6] Clearly, the deportee reveals that these flows are not unimpeded, and that globalization is better characterized by a dialectic of mobility and immobility.

While my argument does draw from and elevate the phenomenon of mobility, it does not focus on the categories of mobility routinely used to define a globalizing world—namely, the flows of finance, technology, media, and goods. Instead, it traces the effects that ensue from judicial, immigration, urban development, and penal technologies; how discourses, institutional forms, and practices themselves migrate between countries; and how features of the security state are imbricated with political subjectivities and spatializing practices.

But policing and deportation also work in the obverse direction, and this is one of my key arguments. These securityscapes, thought to entrench the nation-state and to arrest flows, also enable the globalization of violence, in this case through the formation of transnational gangs and the globalization of U.S.-style zero-tolerance policing strategies. In other words, securityscapes not only constrain but also fuel mobility—legal and illegal, licit and illicit.[7] Deportation as a disciplinary practice can act very differently, therefore, from its overt logic. Deportation is configured as a preeminent means of defending, enacting, and thus verifying state sovereignty, by defining who is disposable and who is not and rendering them immobile.[8] But my ethnographic rendering of deportation through a study of the experiences of a specific category of criminal deportee suggests otherwise. When a deportee is forcibly repatriated after incarceration, or when Salvadoran youth are made refugees by the combined effects of gang and state violence in El Salvador, these "flows" are induced by nationalism and the entrenchment or policing of national boundaries. This study is, therefore, concerned with the mobilities induced by such friction and the ways in which security policies and neoliberal trade agreements both rest upon and provoke flows across borders. This view in turn asks us to examine the relationship between neoliberalism and security policies.

Neoliberalism

While rooted in a longer history of United States–Latin American security relations, the transnational gang crisis and the securityscapes that produced it emerged during a period characterized by the consolidation of "neoliberal" structural adjustment programs in both countries.[9] Neoliberalism is a multivalent term used variously to describe an economic model, a political philosophy, and a mode of personal conduct.[10] As an economic model, neoliberalism promotes free trade, deregulation of the market, and the privatization of functions previously carried out by the state. As a political philosophy, it promotes the freedom of the individual over the power of the state, and private goods over public goods.[11] As a discipline or mode of personal conduct, it advocates personal responsibility over social welfare. While neoliberalism is not a totalizing system, it is widely understood that its governing logic of market fundamentalism has had repercussions for forms of citizenship, subjectivity, and sovereignty across the globe.

Clearly, what has come to be termed "neoliberal" predates the period addressed in this book (1992–2007). The late 1970s marked the emergence of a new global order, variously described as globalization, disorganized or late capitalism, and post-Fordist and flexible accumulation,[12] and now more commonly termed neoliberalism or neoliberal globalization. Nonetheless, from an ethnographic point of view the effects of these neoliberal policies, the changing role of the state, and the emergence of a new regime of the self all become highly visible in both Los Angeles and San Salvador during the period under examination here.

In the United States, the neoconservative Reagan revolution of the 1980s was extended through the embrace and consolidation of a neoliberal agenda in the 1990s under the Clinton administration. The Clinton era represented a dramatic inversion of the binary opposition between conservatives and liberals that had characterized official American politics on domestic issues since the Great Depression. Thus while the subsequent election of Bill Clinton may have marked, for the time being, an end to the "rightward drift in U.S. politics,"[13] Republicans had already successfully disorganized and inverted Democratic discourse precisely over the issue of state intervention and deregulation.

The passage of the North American Free Trade Agreement (NAFTA) in 1994 accelerated the deindustrialization of U.S. cities, the exportation of U.S. jobs through off-shore production, the weakening of the traditional labor movement, and the flow of cheap, unprotected labor for the new service economy—all characteristics of the 1980s. During the same period, the institutional apparatus of the capitalist welfare state was entering its last moments before the full onset of neoliberalism[14] in 1996 with the passage of welfare reform legislation.[15] The state, which had produced a social service industry upon which the underclass fed, was to be redesigned along entrepreneurial lines. The welfare-dependent culture of poverty in the inner city was to be transformed into a culture of enterprise, family, and self-help. Both the government and the individual were to be disciplined according to the logic of the market, and state agencies began to address citizens as customers. By the turn of the century, conspicuous consumption and casino capitalism had become the pillars of society in the United States.[16]

In El Salvador, well before the implementation of the Dominican Republic–Central America Free Trade Agreement (DR-CAFTA) in 2006, privatization had affected all aspects of life, including health care, education, banking, and public utilities. William Robinson makes the somewhat ironic and tragic argument that the FMLN unwittingly provided the United States its pretext for massive intervention—not only through military but, in fact, largely through economic aid and training. The latter involved cultivating a new elite, or what Robinson terms a "neoliberal polyarchy," that would challenge the old agricultural oligarchy as well as the more progressive "import substitution" economic model, and govern instead through a "market democracy."[17] While the Peace Accords did contain a limited land reform agreement, by war's end the Salvadoran government had removed all subsidies on agricultural products, thereby leaving the beneficiaries of land reform without technical and financial assistance. El Salvador shifted from being a net exporter to a net importer of basic foodstuffs such as beans and rice. The cost of the "basic [food] basket," the term of art in Salvadoran economic analyses, continued to rise each year.

By war's end, labor was El Salvador's primary export, and immigrant remittances exceeded coffee as the number one source of foreign revenue.[18] Needless to say, international migration did not abate with the end of the war but actually increased with rates of poverty and crime.[19] Informal and criminal economies actively exploited new zones of ambiguity opened up by deregulation.[20] In this new entrepreneurial and import-oriented society, these sectors of the economy became the only available alternatives to international migration for an increasing number of Salvadorans. Like immigrant remittances, extortion became a fundamental means of survival within El Salvador's neoliberal economy. In this sense, migrants, gangs, and criminals are mimetic of the normative ideological figures of the neoliberal era, the entrepreneur and the consumer. It is for these reasons that I choose to add the modifier "neoliberal" to "securityscapes." I argue that a critique of neoliberalism must also account for the place of security policies in that system, and that focusing on security policy can further our understanding of processes associated with neoliberalism.

Zero Tolerance

The growing severity and scope of law enforcement accompanied by an increasingly punitive criminal justice system would seem to contradict the neoliberal logic to minimize state intervention. Indeed, Michel Foucault's anticipation that American neoliberalism would be accompanied by a more tolerant penal justice system has not been borne out. Foucault argued that while eighteenth-century reformers sought to "eliminate all crime through the internalization of the gaze," neoliberals "only seek a degree of compliance—that is an acceptable level of return on society's investment." Zero-tolerance gang-abatement strategies and the accompanying legislation, however, depend on the creation of a limitless supply of crime by subjecting more and more actions to penalties, and increasing the penalties of actions already deemed criminal. As such, the neoliberal security under investigation in this book diverges from Foucault's expectations that neoliberalism would entail "a balance between the curves of the supply of crime and negative demand," where a certain degree of crime is to be tolerated.[21]

Instead, zero-tolerance strategies appear to be central to the neoliberal logics of deregulation and individual responsibility. For instance, take the case of gang injunctions. Certainly they involve state intervention into and regulation of the minute practices of everyday life such as walking, whistling, gesturing, and associating in public. Gang injunctions criminalize these everyday behaviors and automatically increase the prison sentences of the particular group of people named in the injunction. At the same time, they are form of fast-track justice. Like deregulation in the marketplace, zero-tolerance policing strategies are key components of mechanisms that "cut the red tape" and "streamline bureaucracy" by removing all sorts of state protections: standards for probable cause, access to legal representation and judicial review, and judicial discretion. They also severely weaken the guarantee of habeas corpus. The result is to "fast track" (not surprisingly now used as a verb, much like "to grow" the economy) youth and young adults into the criminal justice system, and as a result, immigrants into the deportation pipeline. Habeas corpus, on the other hand, belongs to an alternative moral or ethical framework that demands absolute certainty that the state is arresting, imprisoning, and executing the right person. It is a "Byzantine" and lengthy process precisely because it is a guarantee of the most fundamental protection—legal redress against unconstitutional imprisonment and execution. Habeas corpus, in the words of Ned Walpin, "is the most basic way that the judiciary can protect our life and liberty against government tyranny."[22]

This fast-track justice has done much to "grow the economy" through privatizing prison functions such as dining, janitorial, and maintenance services.[23] But more significantly, the production of new offenses and the felonization of nonviolent offenses has required extensive new construction of prisons, which involves large government contracts with private companies.[24] So, for instance, the single largest allocation in the Crime Bill of 1994 was for prison construction. The felonization of illegal reentry has also led to a vast and lucrative growth industry of detention centers all along the border between the United States and Mexico. The majority of these contracts have been filled by the private Corrections Corporation of America (CCA). According to the Web site of the CCA:

> As a full-service corrections management provider, CCA specializes in the design, construction, expansion and management of prisons, jails and detention facilities, as well as inmate transportation services through its subsidiary company TransCor America. The company is the fourth-largest corrections system in the nation, behind only the federal government and two states. CCA houses approximately 80,000 offenders and detainees in more than 60 facilities, 42 of which are company-owned, with a total bed capacity of more than 80,000. . . . Since its inception, CCA has maintained its market leadership position in private corrections, managing more than 50 percent of all beds under contract with such providers in the United States. The company joined the New York Stock Exchange in 1994 and now trades under the ticker symbol CXW.[25]

The CCA is a perfect sign of the encroachment of the corporation into the functions of the state. It offers "full-service corrections management," and it is a leader in the private corrections "market." Moreover, prisons and prisoners have achieved commodity status and are traded on the stock exchange. Between 2004 and 2008, Congress doubled its spending on these privately constructed and managed detention centers.[26] In 2007, Governor Arnold Schwarzenegger signed a Jail Construction Funding bill, which authorized the single biggest prison construction project in California, the United States, and indeed, the world.[27] It seems that prisoners are as essential to market fundamentalism as are consumers. There is clearly a market logic to this neoliberal justice.

The neoliberal philosophies of "just desserts" and "truth in sentencing," and the discourses that feed the construction of prisons and detentions centers, derive their moral framework from the liberal conception of individual responsibility that was radically revived under neoliberalism. The Illegal Immigration Reform and Immigrant Responsibility Act and the Personal Responsibility and Work Opportunity Act, both of 1996, are both deeply beholden to this notion of the "responsibilization" of the individual. Criminals refuse to "responsibilize" themselves.[28] This is not to say that gang youth are not agents in their own demonization, criminalization, and elimination; indeed, they are. However, neoliberal security discourses and practices displace all agency onto gang youths and their families, and do not account for the power of the law and law enforcement in producing and reproducing crime. Salvadoran (immigrant) youth gangs are produced and embedded in a complex web of forces. The people with whom I am in conversation in this book are neither demons nor heroes. Instead, they operate in complex and agentive ways within an overdetermined transnational terrain, while struggling to distance themselves from the competing narratives of gangs and law enforcement without being able to fully escape either one.

Just as germane to this study is how neoliberalism has been accompanied by what Sasha Abramsky identifies as the "return of vengeance culture."[29] Over the last three decades, Americans have given up on rehabilitation for a soul-killing punitive mandate that seems to value little more than revenge, and where vengeance becomes a form of public spectacle. Abramsky dubs this structure of feeling and its affect "American furies." The hard-line policing of immigrant and minority youth and young adults, combined with the deportation of legal permanent residents and the flourishing of prisons set aside solely for the incarceration of immigrants serving out sentences for "illegal reentry,"[30] are surely central to this dominant structure of feeling.

The prevailing structures of feeling in postwar El Salvador—extreme disillusionment, suspicion, unbearable levels of social uncertainty, and fear—contradict the widely held belief in U.S. government and international relations circles that El Salvador's transition to democracy was a success.[31] Nonetheless, the great majority of Salvadorans no longer had expectations that the state could provide for either their economic or physical security. The Right quickly blamed the postwar penal code and human rights reforms for the uncontained violence, and it proffered zero-tolerance gang abatement strategies as developed by the United States as the necessary antidote to the "liberal excesses" of postwar democratization.[32]

A great many championed the style of what Daniel Goldstein in *The Spectacular City* terms in the Bolivian case "flexible" or "self-help" justice, performed through private security patrols and vigilante lynchings. A public opinion poll from 1998 indicated that 46 percent of the Salvadoran population believed that people had the right to take justice into their own hands. While the new National Civil Police force (PNC) struggled to furnish its local and regional offices, private security agencies flourished. Numbering fewer than 10 in 1992, these private companies increased to more than 80 in 1995 and 265 in 2001. The number of private security agents more than tripled from 6,000 in 1996 to 18,943 in 2001, thereby far outnumbering officers in the National Civil Police.[33] Private security companies and thus benefited directly from the failure of the state to contain the violence.

The globalization of a certain kind of market fundamentalism at the end of the cold war also required, it seems, the spread of tactics of policing and discipline that sought to ensure the continuous production of marginalized bodies in the form of cheap labor and criminals. Labor migration served the interests of the marketplace, and incarceration furnished the means with which the nation-state could secure the basis of its sovereignty and legitimate its monopoly over coercion. And yet, it appears that nationalism was not as successful as capitalism in this regard. Despite the seeming contradictions between the political economy of free trade and the postdisciplinary regime of zero-tolerance policing, both seem to produce the spaces of circulation and interconnection associated with globalization, whether through sanctioned or transgressive mobility. The concept of the neoliberal securityscape thus is a way of mapping the simultaneous spread of zero tolerance and neoliberal reforms across the United States and El Salvador, and the spatial outcome of these discourses and practices.

The Social Production of Space

While this book is embedded in the macrophysics of neoliberalism it maps the microphysics of everyday life, including the very particular ways in which immigrants, activists, gangs, and police produce, control, use, and compete over the space of the barrio, be it in Los Angeles or San Salvador or both. Indeed, the urban barrio is an important stage for the production of and contestation over the neoliberal securityscape and its transnational geographies of violence. As such, it is space—its production, representation, and use of and arguments over; its affective and imagined dimensions—that serves as the primary interpretive thread throughout the book. The book builds upon the contention that history unfolds spatially, that space is central to the exercise and analysis of power and culture, and that every mode of production secretes its own space.[34] Consequently, each chapter focuses on a technology of spatial legislation (border patrols, curfews, gang injunctions, building design, etc.) or on the production of a particular kind of space.

My notion of the social production of space is derived from Henri LeFebvre's theorization in *The Production of Space* of the following spatial trialectic: representations of space, spaces of representation, and spatial practices. The first term "representations of space" is understood as the conceptual, abstract formulations of space as modeled by social engineers (urban planners, government technocrats, criminologists, etc.), and it constitutes the *savoir* (knowledge) of power. The second term, "spaces of representation," is taken as the space of inhabitants, users, and activists. It is the dominated space that the imagination seeks to change and to appropriate—the *connaissance* (knowledge) of the underground and clandestine side of social life. These two spaces combine with the third term "spatial practice," or movements and operations in physical space, to produce the space of a particular society and in this case, between particular societies, at a particular historical moment.

While LeFebvre distinguishes between dominant and resistant spatialities, in my analysis these spaces or systems are not separate from each other but rather deeply imbricated. For example, the spatial practices of law enforcement and what I term "gang peace activists" are strangely mimetic of one another.[35] Their strategies—violence intervention and prevention versus gang abatement—while distinct, are both deeply beholden to mimicking the structure and practices of the gang itself. The spatial practices and performances of the police and of gang peace activists both involved mimetic improvisations of their object of transformation, the gang. Thus LeFebvre's model, in which mimesis has its role and function in the domination of space,[36] is ultimately an unstable combustion of the trinity of these relatively coherent spatial forces. These relations of forces are always in the process of change, and are, in this case, made even more dynamic by their transnational reach.[37] In this regard Michel de Certeau's elaboration of "the practice of everyday life" through his vocabulary of practiced space and travel itineraries—spatial trajectories, vectors of direction, geographies of action, and velocity—also inform my elaboration of the production of transnational space.[38]

The concept of the social production of space is particularly germane to the nexus of migration, youth, and violence, for territoriality is an issue central to immigrants, gangs, and police. On the one hand, "migration has always had the potential to challenge our established spatial images" of, for instance, the notion of a bounded national territory.[39] Gangs and police, on the other hand, are both engaged in enforcing their control over territory. Spatial control is fundamental to the police's efforts to maintain social control.[40] Similarly, gangs have been described as the "impoverished architects of social space."[41] Representing and protecting the territory of the "neighborhood" (or "hood") is fundamental to gangs.[42] Moreover, refugee flight and forced repatriation are accompanied by feelings of geographical disorientation and spatial alienation.[43]

Given the centrality of the physical space of the barrio, the city, and the nation to all three actors, it is worth asking just how transnational are the spatial practices of these so-called transnational gangs. Certainly there were cases where gang members deported to El Salvador formed their own cliques once in El Salvador—often at the urging of those local youth. However, according to the earliest studies, gangs were not new to Central America in the 1980s, and El Salvador had its own school-based or student gangs as early as the late 1950s.[44] Through increasing contact with Los Angeles as a result of migration and deportation, existing Salvadoran gangs began to align themselves with either the MS or 18th Street gangs and to adopt the cultural codes of gangs based in Los Angeles. So what began as small, localized, and diverse bands became a broad-based confederation of cliques associated with the two large gangs.[45] Existing gangs began to imitate the style, cultural codes, and mores of Los Angeles–based gangs, as noted by José Miguel Cruz, thereby "leading to a gradual assimilation of identity." Cruz argues that "the origin of gangs as transnational networks is not only the product of direct importation [via deportation] of gang members: it is the product of the connection between two phenomena which emerged separately and in the early 1990s made contact as the result of migration and deportation of Central Americans."[46]

But researchers in the region question the extent of these transnational ties. Although by 1996, 85 percent of active gang members surveyed in the San Salvador metropolitan area claimed membership in either 18th Street or MS, only 17 percent of them had been to the United States, and only 11 percent of them had joined a gang in that country. Only 15.5 percent of gang members who had been to the United States admitted to maintaining periodic contact with gang members there.[47] Research conducted in 2006 indicated that only 8.5 percent of the Salvadoran gang members sampled had traveled to the United States or Mexico. The study concedes that global communication does enable the rapid and early exchange of information and that contact between gangs in different countries is probable, or at least that some decisions are mutually accepted. However, the study also argues that these circumstances have not yielded any substantial evidence that all factions of the same gang follow orders from any single country.[48] Researchers conclude that the extent of these transnational networks is highly questionable and that in fact the transnational character of the gangs in the region is limited primarily to the symbolic domain.[49] Thus the research suggests that while these gangs may have taken on transnational names, their activities and identities are still predominantly local.[50]

My own research indicates that the members of MS who are jumped into the gang in El Salvador are not automatically accepted into the gang in Los Angeles but instead must be reinitiated. This suggests that MS in Los Angeles does not recognize "transnational membership" status. This lack of recognition has caused political rifts rather than consolidated relations between Los Angeles and San Salvador. Even Homies Unidos, initially envisioned as a transnational violence prevention and intervention project with offices in San Salvador and Los Angeles, was not able to realize that transnational vision. Despite the intimate knowledge that both the San Salvador– and Los Angeles–based leadership had of each other's terrain, and their consciously articulated transnational connection, technical assistance, and funding (albeit limited), the Los Angeles office broke formal ties with the San Salvador office precisely over the inability to successfully coordinate their efforts.

Again, this is not to suggest that there is no communication, contact, or even coordination between gang members across borders, but rather only to say that its scope is limited and by and large not well orchestrated. That said, my research also indicates that zero-tolerance strategies only enable greater—not less—coordination and communication precisely through their various forms of spatial legislation. Limiting access to public space, mass incarceration, and increased deportation all induce closer ties by actively promoting association between gang members on local, regional, national, and transnational scales.

Criminal Type

It is not the work of social science to uncritically reproduce state discourse or the prevailing common sense.[51] This point is particularly salient for the time period addressed in this ethnography given the number of new categories of crime and of felonies that have been added to the rolls of criminal and immigration law, not to mention the mandatory sentence enhancements that bump up misdemeanors to felonies. We know from Foucault that categorizing and labeling practices are exceedingly effective in producing and reproducing "crime," and from Caldeira we have seen how "crime talk" also helps violence circulate and proliferate.[52] In this light, standard criminology and traditional gang studies are complicit in the reproduction of crime and criminality.

I have already stressed that this book is not about gangs or a particular gang. Neither is it a study of why young people join gangs or of how to get them out of gangs. Nonetheless, this book is inevitably engaged in a conversation with a number of studies that part from a traditional criminological perspective on gangs and the pathologies attributed to them. The authors of these works have contributed to what might be called critical gang studies or critical criminology studies that do not start from the perspective of law enforcement or view gangs as first and foremost criminal enterprises.[53] Moreover, rather than highlighting gang crime while ignoring other forms of criminal activity, a critical criminology perspective places gangland rivalry, policing, and war making on a continuum.[54] Similarly, it explores how the "everyday" violence of gangs is coproduced by "structural" violence, or political and economic disenfranchisement, and by "symbolic" violence, or the internalized humiliations and legitimations of existing social inequalities.[55] This is not to rationalize gang violence but rather to identify the relationship between political and economic disenfranchisement and violence.[56]

Not unlike researchers who reject stereotypes of violent gangs and advocate for critical criminology studies, many migration scholars also reject the term "illegal immigrant" by opting instead for the less value-laden adjective "undocumented immigrant." The illegal immigrant or "illegal alien" are, they argue, state-centric terms that naturalize the legal categories of the state. As De Genova writes, in using the term to "constitut[e] undocumented migrants (the people) as an epistemological and ethnographic 'object' of study, social scientists unwittingly become agents in an aspect of the everyday *production of* those migrants' '*illegality*' " (my emphasis).[57] I share in this suspicion of the terms "illegal immigrant," "illegal alien," and "criminal alien," and I seek to redirect the unquestioning reproduction of state discourse by researchers in both the domains of criminal and immigration law as well as in mass media.

In my effort to meet these aims, in this book I interrogate the emergence of the view of members of La Mara Salvatrucha and of the 18th Street Gang as a "new criminal type" in both the United States and El Salvador.[58] But this trope or stereotype itself has a career or a prehistory in the figures of the looter, the street hoodlum, and the criminal deportee, as well as a future trajectory in the figure of the terrorist.[59] All of these criminal types strike different registers of the master trope of the illegal alien. Together they signal a mounting anxiety over the transgression of what Michel de Certeau has termed "the law of place."[60] All four tropes of Latino territorial transgression are linked to the unsettling of identities in an era of global restructuring, and to the illicit flows that suggest the seeming irrelevance or impotence of national boundaries.[61]

According to this mode of analysis, these criminal types—the looter, the hoodlum, and the like—are culturally constructed political categories under which multiply determined debates about migration, race, the economy, and so forth have been subsumed. So for instance, while the trope of the "Latino looter" surfaced in the media coverage of the Los Angeles riots in 1992, it, like the other terms, is linked to a larger system of representation of boundary transgression and transgressive mobility.[62] In the case of the riots, the looting of private property by those of Latino and Latin American background came to stand in for the wanton and opportunistic pilfering of state coffers and the transgression of national sovereignty by Latino immigrants. Whereas the live national news coverage of the event framed the riot within a "Watts II" paradigm as a black event, in contrast, the local news coverage followed by the national news after the riot quickly reframed the story as an immigration story about an unguarded southern border.[63]

By saying that the term the Latino looter is constructed, I do not mean that Latinos did not loot. Neither am I suggesting that the debates around the Latino looter did not have historical foundations: namely, the evisceration of a unionized service sector dominated by African Americans during the 1980s that was made possible in part with imported cheap Latin American labor, and the inability or the ambivalence of the U.S. state in maintaining the borders between North and South. Myth is not a lie but rather a distortion and inflexion.[64] In both cases, the interlacing motifs of racism, inner-city violence, and poverty, as well as the economic decline attached to the end of the cold war, the downsizing of California's defense industry, and the growth of offshore production are all reorganized around the figure of the "illegal immigrant."

Dialectical Image

In this book I juxtapose political categories such as the "illegal immigrant" with a number of puzzling and unstable images that recast gang members as peace activists, cops as criminals, homeboys from Los Angeles walking the streets of San Salvador, civil police merging with soldiers from the Salvadoran military, tattooed gangsters wearing the insignia of the leftist guerilla turned political party, the FMLN, and purported meetings between La Mara Salvatrucha and Al Qaeda. Some of these two-faced images emerge from inside the field itself, and some are deployed by "moral entrepreneurs" pushing a particular political agenda.[65]

My own analysis of these criminal types extends to Walter Benjamin's aesthetic of engaging and working through the figures circulating in the public imaginary and its discourses to arrive at allegorical readings of those forms as "an act of political poesis."[66] As a result, this book is not so much a critique of representation as it is a study of disturbances in representation or the eruption of what is repressed in representation.[67] Benjamin's notion of the dialectical image proves central to the methodology I employ to look for these disturbances. The dialectical image, a construction of seemingly opposite or contradictory elements, interrupts the context into which it is inserted, thereby leaving the image's ideational elements in productive suspension and setting its semiotic content into question. Benjamin used this "image material" to blast the object out of the continuum of history's course in order to make visible a picture that the fictions of conventional historical writing cover over.[68]

Within the relations between the United States and El Salvador, however, the destabilizing potential of these dialectical images was reabsorbed into familiar plots of terrorism and counterterrorism. Just as cold war technologies of war and policing were animated by a substrate of fantasies about communists, more-contemporary shared fantasies were triggered by the menace of criminals and then, or yet again, terrorists. In this light, the War on Terror appeared as a disturbing continuation of the past in the present that was made visible in hauntingly familiar forms. Poised between the danger of gangs to the North and anti-neoliberal and socialist victories to the South in Venezuela and Bolivia, El Salvador once again became strategically placed within the interests of the United States, albeit with recourse to the dominant paradigm of the War on Terror. As with the cold war, the Salvadoran right wing succeeded in leveraging U.S. monsters to fight its own.

The George W. Bush era's geopolitics of disaster provided new opportunities for the ruling right-wing party, Allianza Republicana Nationalista (ARENA, or the National Republican Alliance), to resume its cozy cold war relations with the United States, and for the U.S. Southern Command to rationalize its renewed military presence in Central America. In this sense, the "newness" of the War on Terror was largely an invention.[69] Tellingly, that war drew directly upon the Latin American policy of the United States up through the cold war. El Salvador, which provided a school for the United States to execute imperial violence through proxies, is an iconic case of how Latin America has long served as a "workshop of empire."[70] It was no coincidence then that the "Salvador Option"—the use of local paramilitary forces, otherwise know as death squads—was proposed by Cheney as a successful model on which to base counterinsurgency operations in Iraq after direct intervention by United States troops had failed.[71] El Salvador was and then became once again an integral part of these geopolitics of disaster. The ARENA political party, which was founded by the known intellectual author of the 1980's death squads Roberto D'Aubuisson, was eager to throw its lot in with the Bush administration and its "coalition of the willing."

Prior to 9/11, the U.S. Southern Command had already begun to shift its focus to the "securitization" of "nontraditional" security threats that had previously been understood to fall under the domains of social policy or policing. These disparate threats—immigration and gangs alongside such criminal activities as human trafficking, document forging, money laundering, and drug production—lacked a unifying logic. The 9/11 attacks on New York and Washington by Al Qaeda and the ensuing War on Terror provided not only that logic but also the rationale that the U.S. military establishment needed to justify increased military aid to the region.[72]

These implied interconnections between gangs, immigrants, and terrorists were further bolstered by military strategists who argued that the division between gangs as a law enforcement concern and terrorists as a military concern could no longer be maintained where, in the words of Max Manwaring, "distinctions between war and crime are becoming increasingly blurred."[73] This "gang crime–terrorism continuum"[74] was popularized by the pundit Newt Gingrich in his documentary *American Gangs: Ties to Terror?*

In 2006, the Salvadoran government passed its anti-terrorist law, which was directed not only against gangs but also against leftists protesting the privatization of water and street vendors contesting restrictions to their access to public space. The ARENA administration deployed the gang crime–

terrorism continuum to repackage their internal enemies in terms of the governing security paradigm of the United States. As I demonstrate in the conclusion, El Salvador successfully leveraged the security paradigm of the War on Terror to reenter the "global military-gift economy" and become once again part of the U.S. "protection racket."[75] What we saw then was a rejuvenation of the collaboration of the cold war and civil war by the United States and El Salvador through the threat of the "gang crime–terrorism continuum," be it an effect or actual strategy.

In other words, collective representations of crime and terrorism reveal complicated intimacies and ongoing cultural contaminations that have long animated relations between the United States and El Salvador. The reigning common sense and bureaucratic discourses about transnational gangs are not opposed to social reality; rather they create a forceful intervention into this transnational political field and contribute to that reality. This is my argument to those who would read this book as an apology for youth violence and for the romanticization of gangs. I hold neither position, nor do I hold that gangs are fictions without material basis. If anything, I am concerned with the productivity of repression, which is to say the productivity of zero-tolerance gang abatement strategies in reproducing that which they purportedly set out to repress: gang violence.

Politics of Simultaneity

The inter-American obsessions with transnational gang youth, enlisted into the War on Terror, reveal more than just the ongoing duplicity between the United States and El Salvador in the reproduction of violence. The proliferation of interlocking images of terrorists and criminals guide the reproduction of relations between the two countries. Those resonances — mimetic correspondences, not equivalences — read like rearranged particles of social and political narratives of the United States and El Salvador. Through this deep structure of repetition, the United States and El Salvador emerge as a dense hall of mirrors, an endlessly refracted and warped time and space of connection and contact. The contemporary history of relations between the countries surfaces as endless repetition of this "mirroring paranoid dynamic"[76] and as a continual return of the repressed.

My own project is an attempt to perform and produce something of the effect of the politics of simultaneity at play in this particular inter-American securityscape. My fieldwork between Los Angeles and El Salvador was deeply influenced by the call for multilocale projects designed to produce the effect of simultaneity between places through their juxtaposition, and by mapping the complex connections and paths of circulation that bring together locations of cultural production previously blind to each other.[77] My plans to travel between El Salvador and Los Angeles proved difficult to conceptualize. I had initially envisioned several trips, each with a distinct category of intercontinental traveler. But the view from Los Angeles was a dizzying maze of people coming and going all at once, and I found myself exasperated with trying to track multiple travelers in one journey. While in Los Angeles my gaze was continually deflected south, and in El Salvador it was deflected north. It was as if I were struggling to be in two places at one time, and the effect was disconcerting. Still, as it turned out, I didn't need to orchestrate these connections and intersections myself. Instead, they happened quite serendipitously because they had become so commonplace in the experiences if not the everyday lives of Salvadoran immigrants, in spite *and because of* the enormous constraints placed on their mobility by U.S. immigration policy. From this ethnographer's vantage, time and space became increasingly compressed between El Salvador and the United States.

Certainly I set out to track this movement by developing a research methodology based on following the multiple paths of circulation as outlined by George Marcus, who urges the researcher to "follow the people, the things, the narratives, and the conflicts," or what de Certeau might term the ways or paths of operation.[78] But it was the uncanny coincidences, the unexpected (re)encounters and resonances across this expansive terrain that allowed the phenomenon to emerge from inside the story itself. El Salvador and Los Angeles became a dense intertextual field and a minefield of connection and contact.

The stories of dispersion and imprisonment in this book, and the terrain that they cover, do not fit neatly into the disciplinary domains of ethnic or area studies in general, or into American, Latino, and Latin American studies in particular. Instead, they challenge those boundaries.[79] The need to cross geopolitical lines between the Americas to grasp the blurred cultural zones that people inhabit has been a defining tenet and contribution of those working in border regions. While the primary geographic reference of this field is the border between the United States and Mexico, Salvadoran transnational migration and community formation allows us to see just how much further south that contact zone between the United States and Latin America extends.[80] Moreover, the immigration consequences of policing strategies and criminal law also point to how the borders of the nation-state are being policed on the streets of immigrant barrios or *barrios marginales* (low-income, marginalized neighborhoods) in cities like Los Angeles and San Salvador.

My choice to divide the first two parts of the book according to national boundaries might seem to belie my argument that Los Angeles and San Salvador exist in a relationship of simultaneity, or that one can't engage the spatial politics of one side of this social field without simultaneously accounting for those at play on the other side.[81] There is, of course, the physical reality that one cannot literally be in two places at once. But there is more than physical limitation at issue here. Despite the transnational spatial politics in which both Los Angeles and San Salvador are embedded, the "local" and the "national" contexts do matter. A transnational expression of place does not belie but rather creates an essential place for ethnographic knowledge,[82] and globalization does not contradict the continuing salience of the nation-state. In my case, I came to know San Salvador and other towns in El Salvador through Los Angeles. I also came to understand more about Los Angeles and the United States through my encounters in El Salvador and with Salvadorans.

That said, the seeming linearity of moving from Los Angeles to San Salvador and the chronological development from the wane of the cold war to the rise of the War on Terror is constantly interrupted precisely because both place and time are unstable and often look strangely familiar to one another, or appear as an effect of mutual contamination. Moreover, while the chapters of the book are organized more or less along these geographic and historical distinctions, in the third part of the book these spatial and temporal divisions dissolve into one another. Chronology gives way to simultaneity, the present to the past, and progress to the continual return of the repressed and endless recurrence.

Because this book is situated in a complex time and space, the chronology that follows the introduction is therefore intended as a guide or map with which to read the rest of the book. Beginning in 1992 and ending in 2006, the chronology situates "the Central American transnational gang crisis" in its larger historical and political context. As such it is a montage of geographic space, historical events, contemporary ethnography, world leaders, the central characters in the story and their ghosts, and my own political and research trajectory. With the exception of a long flashback to the 1980s, the chronology is linear. It foreshadows many of the events that occur later in the chapters. Thus while the book begins in Los Angeles, the reader will already have a sense of how many of these processes occur in San Salvador simultaneously, or will subsequently take place there too, and vice versa.

Ethnography and Advocacy

This book begins in the Pico Union district in Los Angeles in the late 1980s and early 1990s not because there isn't another place or a prior moment from which to begin but because that is when my relationship to both places and these politics began. The fact that this study is partial—in both senses of the term (incomplete and written from a particular perspective)—is both undeniable and inevitable. The recognition of knowledge as situated, and of the inescapable relationship between power and knowledge, are not only relatively recent feminist or poststructuralist claims.[83] As Charles Hale notes in his defense of activist scholarship, even Max Weber, the venerable founding father of the social scientific method and a fierce proponent of scientific objectivity, acknowledged that "any given notion of objective social science [is] culturally and historically particular, and shaped by provisional societal consensus rather than by universal standards of validity."[84] This book consciously rubs against the grain of dominant "societal consensus" regarding the origins, threats of, and solutions to transnational youth gang violence. Yet all knowledge about this topic is produced in political contexts and is actively aligned, even if not openly or knowingly so.[85] The key here is to name and to confront the partial (again in both senses) nature of the knowledge produced, and to critically reflect on one's own positionality as a researcher and on the intersubjective character of the research process. The most one can achieve, however, is a positioned objectivity.[86]

I have tried to be transparent about how my knowledge is situated, produced, and contaminated by particular complicities.[87] Yet I prefer to think of this as a recursive rather than a reflexive text. I draw here from Kim Fortun's discussion of the ethnographer as advocate: "Reflexivity calls for the ethnographer to position herself. Recursivity positions her within processes she affects without controlling, within competing calls for response. Reflexivity asks what constitutes the ethnographer as speaking subject. Recursivity asks what interrupts her and demands a reply."[88] Fortun sees recursivity as a way to hold ethnography responsible for advocacy. As she states further: "Attention to recursivity foregrounds how every articulation—whether ethnographic or in direct advocacy—operates on previous articulations, nesting every move and every work within multiple discourses and worlds. . . . What is said in direct advocacy [or for that matter the law or in the media] implicates what it is possible and necessary to say in ethnography."[89] To this end, the chronology that follows calls attention to me and to my small but agentive role in this history as collaborator, advocate, consultant, scholar, and friend, and to my willful, unwitting, and ambivalent participation in these overlapping and sometimes incommensurate and conflicting projects. In the chapters that follow, I struggle to balance on the one hand the methodological and analytical requirements of academic research, and on the other the political engagements and accountability of advocacy. I do not attempt to hide the tension. At times this "strategic duality" limits what can be said; at other times it demands that certain things be said; and still other times it enables what could not be said without the interplay between scholarship and advocacy.[90]

A Final Note on Names

I have used pseudonyms for my contacts in all cases except with those who are elected or appointed public figures, those speaking as representatives of organizations (unless they have asked me to take their comments off the record), and those whose stories have already been the subject of articles, television coverage, documentaries, or books. In the case where I include previously unpublished information in the latter category, to fullest extent possible those individuals have read what I have written about them, and I have either modified or excluded any information with which they were not comfortable. In the great majority of cases, these individuals requested only modest revisions if any at all. In addition, because I write as both scholar and advocate, the material in this book along with previously published material has been shown to the successive directors of the Central American youth violence prevention and intervention organization Homies Unidos in Los Angeles and in El Salvador.

Many Spanish speakers will flinch at the spelling of particular names, and English speakers will flinch at others. For instance, "La Huera," which is usually spelled "Güera," is spelled with the English transliteration of the soft or silent "g" in Spanish. The same is true for "Pansa," which is spelled "Panza" in Spanish where the letter "s" mimics the actual pronunciation of "z" in Spanish. It is not unusual for Spanish names to be spelled differently by immigrant youth and youth in El Salvador. This is both due to a relative lack of formal education in Spanish as well as the influence of English on Spanish. The same principle works in the opposite direction. The name "Lonely," which in English is spelled with an "e," is printed in Salvadoran newspapers as "Lonly." The Spanish name "Camaron" (shrimp) appears as "Cameron" in FBI documents. While this is not a linguistic study, I have kept these spellings in the text to mark how these names migrate across linguistic, geographic, and political boundaries. Finally, I make a distinction in writing the name Homies with a capital "H" when referring to members of and participants in the organization Homies Unidos as opposed to "homies" for gang members.

1992

In the plaza of San Salvador's main cathedral, a red banner soars in the foreground of a bright blue sky. White doves of peace open their wings to take flight. It is February 1. The United Nations-brokered Salvadoran Peace Accords were signed two weeks earlier at the Chapultepec Palace in Mexico City. Twelve years of civil war between the leftist guerrilla forces of the Salvadoran National Liberation Front (FMLN) and the right-wing Salvadoran government are now officially over. Inside the cathedral, Archbishop Monseñor Oscar Romero's body lies entombed in a crypt beneath the sanctuary.

On March 24, 1980, shortly after sending a letter to U.S. President Jimmy Carter begging him to cease military aid to El Salvador, Romero was assassinated. He was shot after giving a sermon imploring Salvadoran soldiers not to kill their fellow countrymen. Carter, however, did not heed Romero's call. During the funeral Mass in front of the cathedral, tens of thousands of mourners who had gathered in front of the cathedral in San Salvador to pay homage to Romero fled in terror as government security forces on the rooftops around the square opened fire. The FMLN launched its first major offensive the following year on January 10, 1981. Over the course of the war, between 75,000 and 100,000 Salvadorans died, and approximately one million (a sixth of the country's population) fled the country. The United States funded the Salvadoran government with $6 billion to defeat the FMLN military and to lay the ground for neoliberal structural adjustments to the Salvadoran political economy.[1]

The cold war had been symbolically drawn to a close with the fall of the Berlin Wall in 1989. That same year the FMLN launched its final offensive. While the FMLN did not succeed in taking over the state, the offensive did make clear that the ruling right wing would not be able to defeat the FMLN militarily. The electoral defeat of the leftist Sandinista government in Nicaragua the following year, however, also signaled the success of the U.S. strategy that included the overt, then covert, funding of the Contras, the right-wing counterrevolutionary forces. Nonetheless, the FMLN offensive of 1989 marked a turning point, and soon thereafter the U.S. government gave up on its policy of pursuing the military defeat of the FMLN and began to support a negotiated solution to the civil war. The assassination of six Jesuit priests along with their housekeeper and her daughter by the Salvadoran military during the offensive was finally a human rights violation to which the U.S. government could not turn a blind eye as it had done with one brutal murder and massacre after another.

But on this day in 1992, peace is finally at hand, and it is a heady and hopeful moment in El Salvador. The Peace Accords instigate the construction of an entirely new police force, the National Civil Police (PNC), which is to be grounded in a culture of human rights. This will involve dismantling the previous security apparatus of the state by delinking the police from military and intelligence functions and promoting its "modernization" and "professionalization" as a civilian police force. The sense of siege is over. The opposition has been legalized and civil society is flourishing—a characteristic of post–cold war social movements across the globe. Peace brings with it a proliferation of nongovernmental organizations.[2] The (re)construction of Salvadoran civil society coincides with the globalization of discourses on human rights in general, and the rights of children and youth, women, and indigenous peoples in particular.

Ironically, during the war most Salvadorans fled to the belly of the beast. As a result, Los Angeles, California, is now home to the second-largest Sal-

vadoran population outside San Salvador. On the day the Salvadoran Peace
Accords are signed, ten thousand Salvadorans now living in exile gather at
MacArthur Park in the Pico Union District to celebrate. Home to nearly every
Salvadoran community and political organization, Pico Union has become
the symbolic center of the Central American disapora in Los Angeles. It is
also home to several immigrant-dominated labor unions and their local af-
filiates, and to many Central Americans working in Los Angeles's service and
informal sectors: janitors, hotel and restaurant workers, day laborers, street
vendors, and domestic workers.

MacArthur Park, located as it is in the heart of Pico Union and opposite
the Salvadoran consulate, has served as the proscenium stage and privileged
site of political protests over U.S. aid to El Salvador, the assassination of Salvadoran Archbishop Oscar Romero, the struggle to win refugee status and
legal permanent residence, and the fight by street vendors and day laborers
for the right to the streets. During the 1980s, MacArthur Park was a place
where Salvadorans would reencounter friends and enemies who, like them,
had fled across three international borders to seek refuge from the war.

When the park was built in the 1880s it was called the "Champs-Élysées
of Los Angeles," and its lake and fountain, both fed by springs, were surrounded by luxury hotels. Yet little more than a hundred years later it is in sad
disrepair. Now it is associated with violence, drug dealing, and false documentation; and the lake is the site of drownings and the dumping of corpses
and weapons. Each of the four corners of the park is territory to a different
gang, which include the archrivals the Colombia Lil Cycos clique of the 18th
Street Gang and the gang La Mara Salvatrucha (MS). In the imaginary of
most Angelinos, the park functions effectively as a sign for the "inner-city
jungle" with all its attendant pathologies.

The 18th Street Gang has been around since 1959 in the Pico Union area.
La Mara Salvatrucha has existed since the early 1980s. At first 18th Street was
part of the Clanton 14 gang, but those living on or around 18th Street decided to form their own clique and become an independent and rival gang.
The 18th Street Gang was a Mexican immigrant rather than a Chicano gang,
and it opened its ranks to newly arrived Salvadoran and other Central American refugees. La Mara Salvatrucha started out as a loose-knit social group
for young Salvadoran immigrants who had settled in the neighborhoods surrounding the park.[3] Many were homeless, alone, and without a means of survival. At first they were into marijuana, heavy metal, and long hair, identified
by making the sign of the devil with index and pinky fingers up. But after

members started to experience incarceration, they began to assimilate into the contemporary gang style with shaved heads and goatees slicked back with Tres Flores hair grease and a palm comb. Calling each other "homies," they sported the brand-name clothing of Dickies and Dockers as their new uniform. The real fighting didn't start until 1985, when a homeboy was shot and killed by a rival gang. After that incident, MS went to war with Crazy Riders, another gang in the MacArthur Park area. At first 18th Street and MS were not rivals, but their loose alliance unraveled in 1992. Then it was all-out war, a war within a war.[4]

Many Salvadoran youth had lost family members to the Salvadoran civil war, or were left by parents on the run from political persecution or for reasons of mere economic survival. They had seen tortured corpses and severed body parts on their way to school. While in school or out on the streets, boys no more than twelve years old were forcefully conscripted into the army. Children joined the guerrillas — in the early years, sometimes by force.[5] Some learned to make Molotov cocktails, to kill and to torture. This was the history that followed them to the Los Angeles, a history funded by the United States.

Today, MacArthur Park is a place of hope and celebration. But will the end of the war and the signing of the Peace Accords mark the end of Salvadorans' sojourn in the United States? Will they go home to rebuild their war-torn country to fill the political spaces that the Peace Accords have opened up, or will they stay in the United States?

These questions were already at the forefront of the strategic planning sessions of El Rescate, the Central American refugee advocacy and service agency where I had worked since 1989. My engagement with the agency was nothing compared to those who had worked alongside Salvadorans all through the war, but it was intense work nevertheless and I had been fundamentally changed by my association with Salvadoran activists and their allies and by the immigrant rights movement in the United States.[6]

Salvadoran political activists, who had come to United States specifically to organize an opposition movement to military aid to El Salvador and to support a socialist revolution in El Salvador are — in the aftermath of Berlin and Managua — left without a governing paradigm.[7] Many hope to return to El Salvador to careers and educations long put on hold for the struggle. Indeed, after years of military occupation and closure due to earthquake damage, the Salvadoran National University is open again.

Temporary Protected Status (TPS), granted to Salvadorans through the 1990 Immigration Act, was later extended as Deferred Enforced Departure

(DED). Under TPS, Salvadorans entering the United States before September 19, 1990, were finally recognized as refugees and provided with legal work permits. Ironically, TPS was only granted after the political context that had spawned the Salvadoran refugee crisis in the United States—the civil and cold wars—was beginning to fall apart.

During the 1980s and the Salvadoran civil war, there was an intense fight over the representation of Salvadoran migration at national and international levels. Were these Salvadorans political or war refugees or were they economic immigrants? The Salvadoran and U.S. Left, together with a host of international organizations (such as the United Nations High Commission for Refugees), world church bodies (Church World Service, World Council of Churches, etc.), and nongovernmental organizations, rallied behind the representation of the Salvadoran expatriate as the "essential refugee." The governments of both the United States and El Salvador, on the other hand, stood behind a quite different representation: namely that of the "economic immigrant" at best, and the "communist" or "terrorist" at worst.

The U.S. State Department did not recognize the "refugeeness" of these Salvadorans. Given the U.N. definition of the term refugee, to do so would be tacit admission that Salvadorans were being persecuted by their own government. To grant the "refugeeness" of Salvadorans would, therefore, also concede that the U.S. government was supporting a repressive regime and violator of human rights. Indeed, during this period, only 2 to 3 percent of Salvadoran political asylum claims were granted, a figure notably lower than for those fleeing communist regimes. Salvadorans were thus left out of the refugee policy of United States and its system—a kindness calculated firmly within cold war interests.[8]

Controversial or not, for the Salvadoran solidarity movement based in the United States, the term "refugee" provided a useful conceit and code for discussing political injustice and instability, particularly in the absence of the political space to counter U.S. policy more directly.[9] Indeed, for Salvadoran activists and those in solidarity with them, the trope of the refugee—as victim of a misguided U.S. foreign policy and an unjust Salvadoran regime deserving of sanctuary and charity—had served as a powerful political text for their work. As one Central American leader put it to me in our conversations about the post-riot political climate, "We had learned how to play that violin string of the refugee real well."

I knew only too well to what he was referring, given my own participation in representing and reproducing that narrative as a fund-raising tool for

El Rescate in the 1980s. Indeed, the solidarity movement had leveraged the representation of the Salvadoran refugee crisis in Los Angeles very skillfully and powerfully in its work with the Hollywood liberal Left. El Rescate, for instance, had successfully partnered with Reebok's Human Rights Project to produce video segments about the refugee crisis for the organization's annual benefit—an Academy Awards after party. In addition to working with the event committee and its Hollywood-oriented members, my job was to brief celebrities. For those long committed to the cause and deeply knowledgeable about the genesis of the crisis, I would address the current conditions impacting Salvadorans at home and in Los Angeles.[10] For those who were new to the scene or who were there primarily for publicity, I would provide them with a sound bite to ensure that when they were tackled by the paparazzi with questions about their evening attire and latest love interest they would be able to throw in something about the "Salvadoran refugee crisis in Los Angeles."

The trope was also essential to the Sanctuary Movement and its daring refugee rescue projects as well as to the refugee asylum projects of the ecumenical communities in general.[11] In the early to mid-1980s, Central American activist organizations invariably centered their fund-raising trips around the "God Box"—a building on Riverside Drive in New York that housed most of the denominational grant-giving projects—and it was an important stop in our fund-raising trips to the East Coast.

During this same period, at the end of the 1980s and the beginning of the 1990s, it became increasingly clear that the majority of Salvadorans living in the United States, no matter what the conditions behind their flight— political or economic—were in the United States to stay. There was an attendant shift in community agencies and media representations of the Salvadoran from "refugee" to "immigrant."[12] Even the liberal Left no longer depicted Salvadorans as temporary sojourners in the United States living in a painful limbo but rather as a permanent population and a new "minority" within U.S. racial and ethnic politics, and among the newest and fastest-growing constituency of the Latino population in the country. Thus while these organizations were now devoting their resources and energies to the available legal remedies—TPS and the American Baptist Church settlement also required representing Salvadorans as war and political refugees respectively—they did so with their eyes firmly on the ultimate prize of citizenship via legal permanent residency.[13]

Today it is apparent that most Salvadorans must remain in the United

States in order to continue to support family in El Salvador with the hard-earned cash they manage to save from their meager jobs in the service industry and the informal economy. Indeed, by the war's end remittances from Salvadorans in the diaspora had overtaken coffee exports as the single-largest source of foreign income in El Salvador.[14] Not surprisingly, the streets of Pico Union are now lined with businesses offering transnational services (money wiring, courier, cargo, and travel) specializing in handling the flow of money, goods, information, and communication between Los Angeles and El Salvador.

Pico Union, like most neighborhoods in Central Los Angeles, is one more casualty of the neoliberal reforms of the 1970s and 1980s. At the state level, Proposition 13, the tax revolt of California homeowners in 1978, has taken a particularly hard toll. White residents have long since fled the inner-city neighborhoods for the security and racial homogeneity of the suburbs and the separately incorporated cities that did not have to share their tax base with the populace at large. But with the end of the cold war, the downsizing of the defense industry, and the outsourcing of formerly unionized jobs, members of all hues of the American middle class are on insecure ground. By 1992, however, George H. W. Bush and Margaret Thatcher are promoting the New World Order's "peace dividend." The massive cuts in defense spending, they argue, will work to build the economy, create jobs, and fund social programs.

It is a time of hope. Two wars have ended and two battlefronts are closed. Globalization is in the air.

Three and a half months after the signing of the Salvadoran Peace Accords, a riot breaks out in Los Angeles. Sparked by the Rodney King verdicts, at first it looks like a reenactment of the earlier Watts riots of 1965.[15] But it quickly bursts beyond the black and white frame of the Watts riots to include the Mexican, Central American, and Korean diasporas. The face of the urban core of Los Angeles has changed radically.[16] Salvadoran refugees living in Pico Union and the surrounding neighborhoods of Central and South Central Los Angeles now find themselves caught in the midst of the riots as innocent victims and peace brokers, looters and thugs. But it is the figure of the Latino as looter that dominates local media coverage. During the riots, or quemazones (fires) and disturbios (disturbances) as Latino immigrants call them, seventeen thousand Latinos are arrested, most purportedly for looting, and at least one thousand are subsequently deported before the ACLU or immigrant rights groups can intervene.[17]

During the riots and in the aftermath, Central American advocates are hard at work trying to counter the image of the Latino looter that is quickly coming to stand for not only trespassing on private property and stealing goods but also for the larger trespass of entering the United States without documents and of taking American jobs (the figure of the Latino looter will quickly be successfully deployed as a political text by the anti-immigrant movement). I spend the months following the riots working with Salvadoran activists organizing press conferences and putting together a public forum for the Central American residents of the affected areas.

As the "world community" makes commitments to partner with Salvadorans to reconstruct their war-torn country and to lift it out of its "third world condition," a delegation of the Geneva-based World Council of Churches visits post-riot Los Angeles and calls for "nothing less than a Marshall Plan" to rebuild the underdeveloped inner city. Even some of the areas of South Central Los Angeles, burned in 1965, have still not been rebuilt.

As the U.N. Truth Commission investigates human rights violations in El Salvador, and as the country's new National Civil Police is being constructed independently of the armed forces, Amnesty International sends a delegation to Los Angeles to investigate the Los Angeles Police Department (LAPD) on charges of "disturbing patterns of abuse and impunity." The report issued that same year, "Torture, Ill-Treatment and Excessive Force by Police in Los Angeles," finds that in Los Angeles human rights violations of low-income minority populations, including immigrants, are a systematic feature of the "war against crime." The American Civil Liberties Union also finds that it is ethnicity and not the commission of a crime that is the basis for arrest.[18]

1993

On March 15, 1993, the U.N. Truth Commission for El Salvador issues its report "From Madness to Hope: The 12-Year War in El Salvador." In its general overview of cases and the patterns of violence, the report registers more than twenty-two thousand complaints of serious acts of violence. Over 60 percent of these complaints concern extrajudicial executions, over 25 percent disappearances, and over 20 percent complaints of torture. Armed forces personnel are accused in almost 60 percent of complaints, members of the security forces in approximately 25 percent, members of military escorts and civil defense units in approximately 20 percent, and members of the death squads in more than 10 percent. The complaints registered accused the FMLN in approximately 5 percent of cases.[19] The report also includes specific findings on thirty-two notorious or representative cases, and it implicates virtually the entire High Command of the Salvadoran Armed Forces in the murder of six Jesuit priests, their housekeeper, and her daughter in November 1989.[20]

Less than a week after this report appears, the Alianza Republicana Nacionalista (Nationalist Republican Alliance, or ARENA) government issues a declaration of a general amnesty for all through the National Reconciliation Law. President Alfredo Cristiani urges Salvadorans to "forgive and forget" and to turn the page to "continue forward."[21] When the FMLN and ARENA had agreed to the proposal by the United Nations to form an Ad Hoc [Truth] Commission, both political parties had also agreed that a broad amnesty would follow.[22] Perhaps it was the concession that the FMLN needed to make in order to be legalized as a legitimate political party after being labeled as a terrorist organization by both Salvadoran and U.S. governments. Certainly, its leadership also did not want to face prosecution. Human rights groups immediately call for a reversal of the amnesty law, but to no avail.

In the United States, the election of the Democratic candidate Bill Clinton in late 1993 seems to signal an end to the rightward drift in U.S. politics, but the result remains to be seen.[23]

On December 8, 1993, the North American Free Trade Agreement (NAFTA) is signed by a trilateral trade bloc composed of the United States, Mexico, and Canada. It represents Mexico's intention to shift from a protectionist policy and import substitution model and with the country's final concession to the neoliberal globalization model required for funding from the International Monetary Fund and the World Bank. In the United States it signals more outsourcing of jobs, and the labor and environmental protections called for are not included in the signed document.

In El Salvador, the ARENA government is already eagerly complying with the NAFTA model even though a similar free-trade agreement between the United States and El Salvador is still years away. Moreover, although the Peace Accords has succeeded in opening up new political spaces for the opposition, the FMLN has all but conceded to the ruling party's neoliberal pact with the United States. In many ways the Salvadoran civil war has provided the destabilizing conditions for transforming El Salvador's elite from a landed oligarchy into a new transnational elite or "polyarchy," and the governing economic system from Import Substitution Industrialization (ISI) to a free-trade model.[24] In the aftermath of the cold war, the collapse of Cuba as a regional power and the Sandinista defeat, the alternatives—be they Marxist Leninist, socialist, or even a pact between capitalism and labor—are no longer on the negotiating table.

The shocks administered to the Salvadoran economy over the next fifteen years will be cushioned by the massive influx of remittances from Salvadorans working abroad. This flow of capital from immigrants will prove to be an important safety net for Salvadorans affected by the postwar neoliberal structural adjustments initiated by the IMF and the World Bank and put into effect under the ARENA government.[25] The much valorized figure of *el hermano lejano* (the far-away brother), a hardworking responsible individual who migrates abroad to secure the maintenance of his or her family in El Salvador, becomes a perfect sign for the neoliberal subject—at least in El Salvador.

In the meantime, Central Los Angeles is the site of intensive intervention by redevelopment projects. In the wake of the riots, one report after another appears with recommendations for how to rebuild the city. The Labor Community Strategies Center releases its report demanding that Los Angeles be rebuilt "from the ground" up by grassroots organizations and substantial reinvestment by government. The African American gangs the Bloods and the Crips sign a truce after the riots.[26] They issue a call for the city to give them the "hammer and nails" and they will rebuild Los Angeles. The proposal also calls for them to shadow the LAPD and to work in collaboration with the police to make their neighborhoods safe, and it promises to match the city dollar for dollar in a public-private partnership. However, Mayor Tom Bradley appoints Peter Ueberroth (former head of the committee constituted to prepare Los Angeles for the 1984 Olympics) to head up a new organization, Rebuild Los Angeles (RLA).

In Washington, Democratic proposals converge in unexpected ways with Republican discourse: the logic of the market, deregulation, enterprise zones (a domestic counterpart to the free-trade zone south of the border), welfare reform that encourages privatization, and a new culture of enterprise and self-help rather than dependency on government intervention. Ueberroth's RLA does much the same, but it also elevates the needs of consumers in the central city population.

1994

Between 1994 and 1996 the wars against crime and immigrants both in California and in the United States not only gain considerable momentum but also combine in ways that have enormous consequences for immigrant settlement, most notably for youth. The Violent Crime Control and Law Enforcement Act of 1994,[27] otherwise known as the Crime Bill or "The Beast," makes sixty new offenses punishable by death. The bill allows the use of evidence acquired through illegal search and seizure to be included in criminal proceedings. These warrantless searches are sanctioned under the "good faith" rule in cases where the police think they could have obtained a warrant.[28] The bill's largest single allocation is for Grants for Prison Construction Based on Truth in Sentencing (Title V).

Moreover, the riots are followed by two initiatives on the California ballot of 1994: Proposition 187, also known as the "Save Our State" anti-immigrant initiative, and Proposition 184, the "Three Strikes and You're Out" anti-crime initiative. While Latinos organize against Proposition 187, they are strangely silent about the draconian anti-crime measure of Proposition 184, which is generally understood to be an African American issue.

The terrible irony is that the politics fueling the three strikes initiative is a Latino issue too. After all, as the anti-immigration backlash deepens and public attitudes toward juvenile offenders become more punitive, the Immigration and Naturalization Service (INS) launches its Violent Gang Task Force targeting immigrants with criminal records for deportation to their countries of origin. Latino immigrant youth, alongside African Americans, become fodder for the flourishing prison industrial complex, fed as it is by the everyday microphysics of the drug war and the aspects of that war as it plays out on the streets of inner-city neighborhoods.

While laying bare the cultural politics of the Latinization of Los Angeles, the riots also mark the growing Americanization of Salvadoran Los Angeles. Central American community leaders are publicly reformulating the refugee status of Central Americans within the discourse of rights to permanent and full inclusion in U.S. society—as American citizens. This language of settlement and permanency finds its way into proposals to turn the refugee center into the community center: indeed, CARECEN, formerly the Central American *Refugee* Center, changes its name to the Central American *Resource* Center. The "language of settlement" in the United States becomes all the more important in Los Angeles's post-riot politics.[29] At the end of the day, it seems clear that Central Americans are here to stay.

The language of settlement regarding the natural and inevitable course of the full legal integration of Salvadorans into the U.S. nation-state proves misleading, particularly with respect to the deportation of immigrant gang affiliated and alleged youth. Many of these youth are already legal permanent residents and have grown up culturally Americanized, albeit as Latino, yet they become the most vulnerable sector of the immigrant population to deportation.

1996

Although Proposition 187 passes in the ballot race, most of its provisions are declared unconstitutional. However, key aspects of the measure's nationalist politics subsequently find legal teeth in the federal Illegal Immigration Reform and Immigrant Responsibility Act of 1996 (IIRAIRA). Meanwhile, Proposition 184, which was approved and enacted, feeds into the federal Anti-Terrorism and Effective Death Penalty Act of 1996 (AEDPA). These acts combine to make it considerably more difficult for immigrants to acquire legal permanent residency and citizenship.

Under IIRAIRA, offenses that are neither "aggravated" nor "felonies" under criminal law now constitute "aggravated felonies" within immigration law. These include nonviolent "crimes of moral turpitude" such as driving while under the influence of alcohol, simple battery, shoplifting, and selling small amounts of drugs.[30] This expanded definition of aggravated felonies is applied retroactively and sets into motion "expedited removal" proceedings, through which immigration officials may remove unauthorized entrants without a court hearing as long as these individuals do not express a credible fear of persecution.[31]

At the same time, AEDPA exacerbates the effects of IIRAIRA because it allows the government to activate "alien terrorist removal procedures" without having to give even a nod to due process. Under this act, noncitizens can be accused, tried, and deported without ever appearing in court. It also relaxes electronic surveillance laws and grants the president sweeping new powers to selectively target unpopular domestic groups as well as to arbitrarily criminalize activities determined by the president to be a threat to national security.[32]

The two interrelated acts of IIRAIRA and AEDPA represent the formalization and expansion at the federal level of what is already taking place in Los Angeles in the aftermath of the riots. In 1997 alone, according to the INS, nearly fifteen hundred Salvadorans with criminal records will be deported from streets and prisons in the United States. And these figures do not reflect the many more expulsions that occur as so-called voluntary departures rather than formal deportations.[33] Many Salvadoran gang youth opt for this alternative form of removal under the misguided understanding that in so doing they will be allowed to return to the United States after a set period of years and that their passports won't be marked "deported." Many also choose "voluntary departure" to speed up the deportation process. Most have been released from long prison sentences only to be re-incarcerated in facilities designed as temporary holding tanks.

This anti-crime agenda, which severely curtails rather than increases the protection of those accused of crimes (including trying minors as adults), combines with anti-immigrant policies to create the conditions for gang violence in El Salvador. In the Salvadoran case, the refugee "forced out" of one country is then forced back, this time as "criminal deportee."[34] Whereas the former refugee fled the Salvadoran civil war, the latter is pushed out of the United States by the wars on crime and against immigrants.

In San Salvador during November 1996, in collaboration with Magdaleno Rose-Ávila—a long-time Chicano and human rights activist now living in El Salvador—a group of twenty-two gang members join together in an effort to a construct a peace accord of their own between the members of the arch-rival gangs 18th Street and MS. The group is to be called Homies Unidos. Most of its members have grown up in Los Angeles and its surrounding areas and have been deported to El Salvador after serving sentences for criminal offenses. The new law applies not only to undocumented immigrants but also to immigrants with permanent legal residence. Some have been "deported" by their parents who thought that they were sending their children away from gangs, and others have returned of their own accord, in some cases to flee a vendetta from a rival gang or to evade the police. For many of these youth and young adults El Salvador is a strange new country, and a dangerous one too. After all, they are now a U.S. export and without local street smarts.

This same year, I have my first face-to-face encounter with deported gang youth.[35] I am in the state of Usulután working as a field researcher for the Salvadoran think tank the National Foundation for Development (FUNDE) in a study on the impact of remittances on youth. Until recently, FUNDE has traditionally focused on agrarian reform, but in 1996 it has added a migration component to its work on development. In towns where agriculture has come to a virtual standstill, construction and consumption are, nonetheless, on the rise. Remittances rather than agricultural production are fueling the economy.

I take off for Santa Elena, a town and a municipality in eastern El Salvador with heavy out-migration to the United States. Santa Elena had been a conflict zone during the war as well as the site of a student massacre by the military, which had a base nearby. With a considerable portion of it residents now living in the United States, Santa Elena has active immigrant hometown associations (HTAS) in Los Angeles, San Francisco, and the Washington, D.C. area. There is a local committee in Santa Elena that receives money from the HTAS and oversees construction projects such as a children's playground and a sports facility. The committee also provides medical assistance and receives the bodies of Salvadorans who have died abroad for burial in their hometowns. This committee, my sponsor, has expressed the need for a study of the effects of remittances on youth and their attitudes toward education and work. There is a discourse circulating in El Salvador that remittances have made Salvadorans lazy, and its youth vulnerable to all sorts of vices and the loss of traditional mores.

In my work at this time I do not intend to study deportees or gangs. Yet, each time I explain to people in Santa Elena the purpose of my study, they interpret it as such. That is, they point me in the direction of the same three young men, all gang members, who have been deported from the United States.[36] As an immigrant rights advocate in the United States, this is a subject that I have intentionally avoided for its sensational qualities and out of respect for the Salvadoran immigrant community in Los Angeles. Like immigrant advocates, I am concerned about the association between the illegality of the undocumented immigrant and the illegality of the criminalized inner-city gang youth turned criminal deportee. Many in the immigrant rights movement considered it a "boutique" issue. Further, I did not think I was the person to conduct such a study, and I certainly had no particular research interest in gangs. In fact, I am suspicious of the term "gang." Yet I find myself drawn to these young Salvadorans, and they in turn are drawn to me because I "come from Los" (Los Angeles) and I know the cherished territory of their barrios. For other youth in the town—because I do not have the expected and requisite blonde hair and blue eyes, and because I am also an immigrant to the United States—I am called a *gringa chaveliada* (fake gringa) behind my back. While they no doubt intend this as an insult I am pleased that they can discern the difference—problematic as their criteria may be. I decide to extend my own dissertation fieldwork to include criminal deportees as yet another set of actors, alongside small-time couriers, entrepreneurs, and political activists, forging transnational connections between Los Angeles and places in El Salvador.

1997

On November 19, 1997, President Clinton signs into law the Nicaraguan Adjustment and Central American Relief Act (NACARA), which grants the American Baptist Church (ABC) class of Salvadorans exemptions from certain provisions within the immigration act IIRIRA of 1996. However, Salvadorans and Guatemalans face the same discrimination they experienced in the 1980s. Nicaraguans, who fled from a "communist" country, are automatically eligible for relief, but Salvadorans and Guatemalans must prove that they and their families will face "extreme hardship" if they are deported back to El Salvador. The burden of proof rests with each individual application for "withholding from removal" or "suspension from deportation" under NACARA.

1998

A year and a half later I return to El Salvador, this time to the nation's capital of San Salvador. I am in El Salvador as part of a delegation sponsored by the Salvadoran Association of Los Angeles (ASOSAL). We have come to document conditions of "extreme hardship" faced by deportees in order to support individual Salvadoran claims for permanent residency under NACARA. Homies Unidos is on our meeting schedule. Two of the delegation participants are the California state senator Tom Hayden and his legislative assistant Silvia Beltrán. Hayden is currently heading up the Gang Violence Prevention Task Force of the California State Assembly, and he is a supporter of the African American gang truce in Los Angeles. Several of his aides are formerly active gang members, now working as what he terms "inner-city peace makers" in Los Angeles. Silvia Beltrán is herself a Salvadoran refugee who moved to the Pico Union area as an adolescent. Though she never joined a gang, she lived in 18th Street Gang territory and had a boyfriend in the gang.

After the delegation leaves I stay on with the express intention of exploring the stereotype fueling an imaginary about youth and migration: namely, the contamination and Americanization of the Salvadoran cultural landscape through inner-city immigrant Latino gang culture, infused as that culture is with Chicano and African American cultural codes. This is when my connection to Homies Unidos in San Salvador begins.

In 1998, the United States deports 5,348 Salvadorans—a significant increase from the figure of 2,493 in 1996. Only about a third of those deportees were "criminal" as opposed to "administrative" deportees, and only a small percentage of criminal deportees were gang members. Nonetheless, in stark contrast to the heroic figure of el hermano lejano, the appearance of the deported gang member as a "new criminal type" in postwar El Salvador serves effectively as a packed sign for the failed promise of peace.

In pointing to an annual homicide rate of 136.5 per 100,000 individuals, the PNC claims that post–civil war El Salvador is purportedly experiencing higher levels of violence than it did during its bloody twelve-year civil war. El Salvador is said to be the most violent country in the hemisphere (including Colombia), and the most violent in the world at large after South Africa. The country is in a "state of hysteria." Many Salvadorans now perceive the post–civil war period as worse than the war. Crime, which did not even appear as an official category during the war years, is now considered the most important issue facing the new democracy for 46 percent of the population. Moreover, a national study reveals that 45 percent of the country supports "social cleansing" of those elements deemed responsible for the violence—even if that means the recurrence of the paramilitary death squad activity of the 1980s and vigilante-style justice.[37]

The paramilitary group La Sombra Negra (the Black Shadow) has been operating in the state of San Miguel since December 1994, carrying out social cleansing operations against gangs, criminals, and homosexuals. By April 1995 La Sombra Negra had claimed responsibility for killing seventeen people. Amnesty International, among others, suspects that these groups include former soldiers with "some tacit support from the PNC." The group argues that their actions are justified given that the "laws of the country were not working" and that the PNC "did not have sufficient resources to combat crime." In addition, there are reports of five additional death squads in operation.[38]

The study also reveals that 80 percent of the population wants to see the military step in to suppress delinquency. In a country that has only recently demilitarized its police forces—a hard won post–civil war reform—these sentiments are disturbing. Salvadorans may have achieved peace, but it is a violent peace without security. Needless to say, they feel deeply disillusioned and cruelly duped.[39]

Ironically, the reappearance of the death squads and the anti-crime agenda coincides with the rewriting of the Salvadoran penal code in accordance with the postwar judicial and human rights reforms. These changes, which have just come into effect, include new protections for juvenile offenders, assurance of due process for those accused of crimes, and the elimination of the use of forced confessions as evidence in trials, among other things. The new Penal Code Reform of 1998 includes drafting modern criminal procedure with sentencing codes, as well as shifting from an inquisitorial procedure where the judge has complete authority to an adversarial process that gives greater power to the prosecuting and defense attorneys. It also disallows forced confessions or those given without counsel present.[40] As early as one year later, ARENA will introduce the reform of these reforms.[41]

The Los Angeles branch of Homies Unidos is founded in November 1998. Magdaleno Rose-Ávila, now the transnational director of the organization, flies back and forth between the two countries. He has a vision of building a transnational equivalent to Barrios Unidos, a grassroots Chicano gang intervention and prevention program in Northern California. The person working on the ground in Los Angeles is Alex Sanchez. Alex is a veteran leader of the Normandie Street clique of La Mara Salvatrucha. After serving a sentence in prison, he had been deported to El Salvador in 1994, but returned in 1996 without authorization after more than one encounter with death squads. I first meet Alex in 1998 shortly after my trip to El Salvador, when Magdaleno invites me to join them for dinner.

Under the guidance of Magdaleno, Alex is beginning to develop a counterpart program in Los Angeles. This is no small act for someone who is likely to be deported if he gains a public profile. The location and the timing of the founding of the two branches are considerably different. Whereas Homies Unidos in San Salvador emerged in the context of the conflicting projects of postwar reforms and death squads, the Los Angeles branch faces zero-tolerance policing strategies and the increasing severity and intersection of criminal and immigration law. Moreover, the Los Angeles riots in 1992 had overshadowed the police reforms called for by the Christopher Commission as a result of the Rodney King beating.[42] Sparked by a case of police brutality and immunity, the riots actually added fuel to the harsh policing that characterized the war against crime and drugs. More pointedly, Pico Union and parts of Koreatown are under the thumb of the Rampart Division of the LAPD's anti-gang unit Community Resources Against Street Hoodlums (CRASH), and thus subject to its "paramilitary culture . . . of total suppression . . . by any means necessary."[43]

1999

Rampart's CRASH unit becomes the subject of an investigation for police corruption. While officers in the unit have been under investigation since 1997, the investigation becomes a public scandal in late summer 1999. Seventy officers are charged for unprovoked shootings and beatings, planting evidence, framing suspects, stealing and dealing narcotics, bank robbery, perjury, and covering up evidence of these activities.[44] Their primary targets had been gangs in general, yet they were particularly interested in Latino immigrant youth and young adults affiliated with gangs. At the same time, however, some of the officers were also purportedly working as security guards for businesses associated with the African American gang the Bloods.[45]

Over the course of the scandal, 106 prior criminal convictions are overturned and investigators travel to Central America to look for immigrants who might have been deported as a result of Rampart's corruption. The settlements eventually involve more than 140 civil suits and settlement costs of approximately $125 million.

2000

During the ongoing Rampart scandal, Alex Sanchez testifies before a hearing on police abuse convened by the Gang Violence Prevention Task Force of the California State Senate. In January 2000, Sanchez is picked up by Rampart officers and handed over to the INS for an immigration warrant for illegal reentry. While in an INS detention center, Sanchez files for political asylum on the grounds that he has a reasonable fear of persecution and bodily harm if he is returned to El Salvador. Meanwhile, a coalition of Homies Unidos supporters form the Free Alex Sanchez campaign, arguing that the harassment against Alex and other Homies Unidos members is a continuation of the same misconduct under formal investigation, and proof that the police corruption was ongoing during the scandal itself.

After Alex is detained, Silvia Beltrán, former aide to Senator Hayden, takes on the directorship of Homies Unidos in both San Salvador and Los Angeles and begins to fly back and forth between the two projects. I return to Los Angeles that summer to work on Alex's trial with his attorney Alan Diamante and a team of people pulling Alex's case together. Alan wants me to build an argument for conceptualizing gangs as a social group. I am not a gang scholar, so I call Susan Phillips, an anthropologist who has worked closely with gangs and knows the literature on gangs. She in turn brings in Rosemary Ashamala, an anthropologist who runs a tattoo-removal program. I serve as a backup witness on the experiences of deported gang members and on conditions in El Salvador based on my encounters in 1998 and 1999 with Homies Unidos in San Salvador.

2001

On January 1, 2001, the U.S. dollar replaces the colon as the currency of El Salvador. Many resent the loss of the colon as a national symbol. The official dollarization of the Salvadoran economy in 2001 is the formalization and co-optation of what even Salvadoran children have long known about the value of the dollar. In 1990, a Salvadoran woman wrote from San Salvador to her husband in Los Angeles to thank him for the dollars he had sent the family. When she gave the five-dollar bills to her children, they exclaimed: "Bravo, Papi is making a pile!" As she wrote, "I don't know how they ascertained the value of the dollar but they said to me: 'Mama you can sell the five dollars, but only at eight colones a dollar. If not, we won't sell it.'"[46] Given the centrality of remittances to many Salvadoran's household economies, Salvadorans were not only acutely aware of the exchange rate, but also had long paid attention to trends and shifts in Californian and U.S. politics and economics.

In Los Angeles, the Rampart scandal is beginning to wind down; CRASH has been officially dismantled and the LAPD is put on notice that its conduct from here on will be under close scrutiny. The City of Los Angeles agrees to a Consent Decree with the federal Department of Justice that subjects the LAPD to federal oversight by the U.S. attorney general, the Department of Justice's Civil Rights Division, the U.S. District Court of Jurisdiction, and an independent monitor. The decree is formerly entered into law on June 15, 2001.

Things are shifting on the immigration front too. The "Fix '96" campaign succeeds in restoring social security insurance and health benefits to documented immigrants with permanent residency, who had lost them as a result of the immigration legislation of 1996. In June 2001, the U.S. Supreme Court revisits and ameliorates some of the worst deportation abuses.[47] George Bush is negotiating a new immigration program with Mexican President Vicente Fox, who is greeted in Washington with a festive firework display.

Less than a week later, Al Qaeda attacks the Pentagon and the World Trade Center; the political landscape changes overnight. As was the case with 1989, the year 2001 marks another major paradigm shift: in 1989 it is the end of the cold war, and in 2001 it is the rise (although by no means the beginning) of the War on Terror.

On October 26, 2001, President Bush signs into law the USA PATRIOT Act (Uniting and Strengthening America by Providing Appropriate Tools Required to Intercept and Obstruct Terrorism). Among many other things, the act enhances the discretion of law enforcement and immigration authorities in detaining and deporting immigrants suspected of terrorism-related activity. The act also expands the definition of terrorism to include domestic terrorism, thus enlarging the number of activities to which the expanded law enforcement powers can be applied.

In November 2001, I submit a proposal for postdoctoral research to the Global Security and Cooperation Program of the Social Science Research Council. I want to know what impact 9/11 will have on Salvadoran youth in Los Angeles and in San Salvador as well as on Homies Unidos's transnational vision. While many of the changes in the laws on immigration, crime, and anti-terrorism have been in effect since 1996 and in some cases since 1994, there is no doubt that they will gain considerable force after 9/11. What will the reforms to fix IIRAIRA mean in the aftermath of the attack? Will immigrants be subject to renewed harassment? What kind of impact will a national security agenda make on human rights and civil rights? How will it affect police and penal reforms in El Salvador? What will it signal for relations between the United States and El Salvador, particularly in the realm of regional security? How might it shape the application of the consent decree and law enforcement in Los Angeles? Until now I have studiously avoided focusing solely on the question of "transnational gangs." I have been a most reluctant ethnographer of this subject, loath to participate in the production of this "crisis." But I can no longer ignore where my research has been leading me.

Two and a half years after Alex Sanchez's arrest by Rampart officers, he wins his political asylum case and is free to stay in the United States with his family and to continue his work with Homies Unidos. But by now Homies Los Angeles is worried about the implications of the growing conflation of immigrants, gangs, and terrorists for their work in Los Angeles and in San Salvador.

I secure funding for my postdoctoral research proposal, and I go back to El Salvador in August 2002.

On November 25, 2002, President Bush forms the U.S. Department of Homeland Security to protect the territory of the United States from terrorist attacks and natural disasters. Homeland Security absorbs the functions of twenty-two federal agencies, including the INS and its immigration functions.

Also in 2002, William Bratton is appointed chief of the LAPD. Bratton was chief of the New York Police Department from 1994 to 1996, where together with Mayor Rudolph Giuliani he implemented the Broken Windows or Zero-Tolerance strategy to "clean up" New York.[48] Subsequently, both Bratton and Giuliani market their respective interpretations of zero-tolerance policing globally through private consultancy firms. Bratton has also just finished serving as a consultant for Kroll Associates, the independent monitors of the LAPD charged with ensuring the implementation of the federal Consent Decree. He begins his first term as LAPD chief by conflating gang activity and terrorism under the term "homeland terrorism." Not only does this reinforce the aforementioned connection between gangs and national security but it also feeds into an emerging discourse that theorizes links between gangs and terrorists.

2003

The following year, on March 1, 2003, the INS is dismantled and its functions are divided between two new agencies within Homeland Security: U.S. Immigration and Customs Enforcement (ICE) and U.S. Citizenship and Immigration Services.[49] Like IIRAIRA, ICE also focuses on the intersection of immigration and crime. Building on the Immigration and Nationality Act of 1996 (a result of IIRAIRA), Homeland Security and ICE are authorized to enter into agreements with state and local law enforcement agencies that permit designated officers to perform immigration law enforcement functions under a Memorandum of Agreement (MOA).

This development unleashes a debate in Los Angeles over the validity of the city's Special Order 40, which prohibits the LAPD from performing immigration functions. After considerable contentious debate, Bratton stands by the order. The Los Angeles County Sheriff, however, is quite happy to enter into an MOA with ICE.

The same month that ICE is formed, the United States invades Iraq. Salvadoran President Francisco Flores joins Bush's "Coalition of the Willing." El Salvador is one of only three Latin American countries to join the thirty-member coalition.

El Salvador once again tops the list of recipients in Latin America of U.S. military largesse, with almost $23 million received since 2002. It is also the second-largest recipient of military training, and it is eleventh on the list of arms sales recipients, having purchased a total of $46.8 million in weaponry between 2000 and 2003.[50]

In July 2003, a month after my return to the United States from El Salvador, my intuitions and suspicions materialize in dreadful ways. Out-going President Flores declares a state of emergency in El Salvador and unleashes a police campaign named El Plan Mano Dura (the Firm Hand or Iron Fist Plan) and proposes new anti-gang legislation. Not only does El Plan Mano Dura represent a major blow to the postwar human rights agenda in El Salvador, it also signals the successful transnationalization of the zero-tolerance gang-abatement strategies of the United States. Moreover, it brings the Salvadoran military back into policing functions by establishing joint police and army patrols. Soldiers are thus back on the streets of San Salvador for the first time since the end of the civil war.

2004

A year later, the newly elected president Antonio Saca follows Flores's plan with El Plan Súper Mano Dura, which includes even stiffer penalties for gang membership and leadership. Saca's plan further undermines post–civil war reforms to the penal code and makes minors under twelve years old subject to the same tough provisions established for adults. Between July 2003 and July 2005, thirty thousand youth accused of being gang members are arrested.

Both plans have a boomerang effect. Homicides and extortions increase considerably and more Salvadorans, youth in particular, flee for the United States. Many Salvadorans on the run from violence in El Salvador apply for political asylum in the United States. The civil war refugee thus returns to U.S. immigration courts as the gang war refugee.

In September 2004, newspapers erroneously report that a top Al Qaeda lieutenant, Adanan G. El Shukrijumah, was spotted in a July meeting with leaders of La Mara Salvatrucha in Honduras in an effort by the terrorist network to seek help infiltrating the U.S.-Mexico border.[51] The U.S. federal officials subsequently report that they have not found any evidence to support these claims made by Honduran security officials and Salvadoran President Saca.[52] Nonetheless, these purported "ties" continue to pepper the political imaginary in the conservative news media and on Internet blogs.

At the end of 2003, Weasel, a former director of Homies Unidos in San Salvador, attempts to return to the United States. After living in Los Angeles for twenty years, Weasel had been deported back to El Salvador in 1998 — a country he had not seen or thought much about since he was seven years old. I first met Weasel shortly after his return when I was in El Salvador participating in a delegation charged with investigating conditions in the country in support of Salvadoran NACARA applications. Weasel's first two attempts to return to the United States fail. First he is turned back in Guatemala and then in Mexico. On his third try he makes it across the U.S.-Mexico border, only to be apprehended by the Border Patrol.

2005

In February 2005, ICE launches its Operation Community Shield. At its inception, the operation brings together federal, state, and local law enforcement agencies in the United States and abroad to apprehend and deport members of MS. In its first operation, ICE arrests 103 purported members of MS in seven cities in the United States. By July, it extends its operation to include 18th Street and other Latino gangs. Gangs from different ethnic groups, be they Asian, Caribbean, Armenian, or Jamaican, are all targets as the operation continues. By September 24, 2007, ICE claims to have arrested 7,655 gang members and associates, representing over seven hundred different gangs, but MS remains the poster child of the operation.[53] As part of its strategy ICE works in collaboration with its attaché offices in Latin America and with foreign law enforcement counterparts in the region. The globalization of the U.S.-style zero-tolerance policing strategies is morphing into transnational policing.

In San Salvador, the United States opens up a Latin American office of the International Law Enforcement Academy (ILEA) in San Salvador. Most Salvadoran human rights organizations oppose the agreement, saying that ILEA is the new School of the Americas (SOA)—a U.S. military academy that was the training ground for many of the Salvadoran military officers accused of gross human rights violations during the civil war.[54] Others, however, argue that ILEA is the last hope to realize the Peace Accord's goal to construct a civilian police force truly independent of the military in order to counteract state tyranny. After all, they argue, it was the ineffectiveness of the PNC that had been leveraged to justify the need for joint army and police patrols.

On December 18, 2005, Evo Morales is elected as Bolivia's new president. Morales ran on an anti-neoliberal platform and promises to enact an ambitious and radical agenda remaking the state into the prime actor in a national developmental project. This includes nationalizing gas resources, the telephone company, mining corporations, and so forth, thereby reversing the trend of the neoliberal years.[55]

2006

In 2006, Venezuelan President Hugo Chavez is reelected for a third term. Chavez has consistently acted against the Washington Consensus and in support of alternative models of economic development to neoliberalism. Chavez is, according Bush, a threat to democracy in Latin America. Chavez in turn denounces Bush as "the devil" at the U.N. Assembly General.

Weasel, former director of Homies Unidos El Salvador, is deported back to that country after spending fourteen months locked up in the California City Corrections Center for illegal reentry.

El Salvador signs the Dominican Republic–Central American Free Trade agreement (DR–CAFTA). It thus reaffirms its commitment to the next phase of the U.S. neoliberal economic agenda in El Salvador, in stark contrast to the so-called Pink Tide (the renewal of the Latin American Left in countries like Bolivia and Venezuela). The U.S. government's Millennium Challenge Corporation (MCC) awards $461 million to El Salvador.

In August 2006, the Salvadoran legislative assembly passes an anti-terrorist law, which labels both gang members and activists against neoliberal policies as terrorists. A year later on July 3, 2007, sixty protestors rallying against the privatization of water are arrested. They are charged as "terrorists."

By the end of 2006, ICE has deported 10,588 Salvadorans. A year later, the figure will climb to 20,045.

PART I | **LOS ANGELES**

LAW OF PLACE

Where do we put the Chicano fathers who forced their
mischievous children to return stolen articles to a Sears
store in East Los Angeles? The article in *US News and World
Report* on the riots skipped that piece of drama, opting
instead for a picture of a desperate Salvadoran, loaded
with food and detergent, standing in a grocery store. The
caption tries to say enough: Latino looter.

—Ruben Navarrette Jr.
  "Should Latinos Support Curbs on Immigrants?"

In the film *Falling Down* (1993) the main character, William "D-Fens" Foster,
an unemployed Anglo American who is angry and about to get even, is depicted sitting with his briefcase on graffiti-covered cement stairs that once
served as an entryway to a structure that is no longer there. From the vantage
of this ruin, he surveys the skyline of downtown Los Angeles through a hole
in the sole of one of his shoes, then turns to look through the want ads in
the newspaper he is carrying. As he tears off some of the paper to cover the
hole in his shoe, a shadow emerges on the ground in front of him. Two Chicano gang members approach him and begin to circle the cement structure.

LATINO GANG MEMBER 1 [LGM1]: What you doing mister?
D-FENS [DF]: Nothing.
LGM1: Yes you are. You're trespassing on private property. You're loiter-
     ing too, man.

LGM2: That's right. You're loitering too.

DF: I didn't see any signs.

LGM2: What you call that? [He points to the gang taggings on the cement structure.]

DF: Graffiti?

LGM1: No, man, that's not fucking graffiti. That's a sign.

LGM2: He can't read it, man.

LGM1: I'll read it for you. It says, "This is fucking private property. No fucking trespassing." This means fucking *you*.

DF: It says all that?

LGM2: Yeah.

DF: Well, maybe if you wrote it in fucking English, I could fucking understand it.

LGM2: Thinks he's being funny.

LGM1: I'm not laughing.

LGM2: I'm not either.

DF: Wait a minute. Wait a minute. Hold it. Hold it, fellas. We're getting off on the wrong foot here. OK. Um. This is a gangland thing, isn't it? We're having a, a territorial dispute, hmm? I mean, I've wandered into your pissing ground, or whatever the damn this is, and you've taken offense at my presence. I can understand that. I wouldn't want you people in my backyard either.

Why begin the history of the production of the "transnational gang crisis" with media coverage of and reflection upon the 1992 Los Angeles riots and Hollywood's mediation of the racial, social, and economic tensions brought to the fore by those riots? To be sure, both examples bring into view images of mischievous youth and violent gang members. But it is to the other two figures, the Latino looter and the unemployed Anglo American, that I wish to draw attention. The juxtaposition of these two seemingly disparate figures involves more than the same contemporary moment or the empirical fact of the riots. It also invokes a prior historical connection. Together, they bring into view Los Angeles at the end of the twentieth century and its reconfiguration in the aftermath of the cold war and the Salvadoran civil war as funded by the United States.

Let's accept, for the moment, the more sympathetic depictions of the Latino looter as a Salvadoran refugee desperate for basic necessities, and the angry American as a middle-class white guy who has recently lost his job to the downsizing of the defense industry and who has become an exile in his own country. Building on the notions of contrapuntal histories and complex patterns of cultural interagency, both the Salvadoran refugee and the unemployed Anglo American defense worker live within, albeit at different ends of, the same global and local processes.[1] Although they occupy different levels of displacement at the wane of the cold war, both are migrants whose everyday movements—life paths through time and space—have been disrupted, the Salvadoran's by militarization and the Anglo American's by demilitarization. Both journeys are produced and undone by the instrumental spatiality of the cold war and the defense industry.

The journeys also mark a particular historical juncture when the primary threat to national security is no longer encoded in communism but rather in the intersection of criminality and immigration. This moment marks a new stage in the production of the securityscapes in and between the United States and El Salvador. The project of law enforcement (by police and immigration officers) now has primacy over global defense (by the military and weapon manufacturers). The triumphant project "to make the world safe for democracy" gives way to the more timely project "to protect and to serve." This shift signals the subsequent convergence of immigration and criminal law that will prove so central to the production of the "transnational gang crisis."

The Latino Looter

When the movie cameras on the set of *Falling Down* shut down during the riots, those of the nightly local news were working overtime to capture and give name to what was unfolding in the streets of central Los Angeles (including downtown, South Central Los Angeles, Pico Union, Koreatown, and Hollywood) that were, for the moment, off limits to the movie's cast and crew. The sections following offer a composite of that coverage as drawn from fourteen hours of home-taped video footage of the local news coverage of the riots. The local viewer who taped the footage during the riots employed the typical contemporary viewing practice of surfing between channels.[2] The resulting video footage of the riots, which is broken up absurdly and jarringly by commercial advertising and sitcoms, actually comes close to the viewing experience of many who frantically shifted from channel to channel to try to make sense of the events unfolding around them. Television viewers, who were taken out into the streets and up into the air with

the media, were encouraged to see from the point of view of the media, reporters, and news anchors. Not only was this coverage framed in a law-and-
order narrative but also as a direct appeal and demand for the deployment
of law enforcement. What follows is my composite of excerpts from that
coverage, compiled after the event and with a narrative frame not available
to the viewer at the time of watching.

WHERE ARE THE POLICE?

The not-guilty verdict in the Rodney King beating case was pronounced less
than two hours ago. The television set is tuned to local live coverage of the
Los Angeles riots. The screen switches from one image to another and from
one channel to another. The action unfolds through this series of images:
First, on the ground in front of Los Angeles Police Department's headquarters (LAPD), a peaceful political demonstration turns into a violent flame-
and rock-throwing protest. Next, the camera soars high above this scene,
travels several miles south to the intersection of Florence and Normandie,
the famous flash point of the riots. This is the corner where Reginald Denny
is soon to be pulled from his truck and severely beaten by an angry mob
in an eerie replay of the brutal beating of Rodney King by LAPD officers.[3]
National networks already have crews covering the unfolding events out of
the First American Methodist Church in South Central Los Angeles, and
from the intersection of Florence and Normandie. A panoramic view of
the geographic path of the riots is being fed unedited by Skycam 5 Live,
Telecopter 4, and Newscopter 7, among others. These newscopters fly over
one burning shopping center after another, while their mobile newscasters
shout out a running commentary over the whir of the propellers: "I can see
one, two, three . . . eleven, twelve . . . I can see about fifteen fires from this
location."

The camera pans across the monotonous grid of the asphalt parking lots
bordering commercial establishments yet to be torched. The viewer's attention is drawn to small groups of people "just walking into the Payless [the
Thrifty, TJ Maxx, the Korean liquor store, the Boys Market, the Pep Boys, the
Circuit City] . . . and taking whatever they want." Some of them are even
stopping to try things on for size . . . and others actually leave to fill their
cars and then come back in for more merchandise. "There're no police down
there . . . There is no police presence at all." The media has deployed its forces
where the police have not, and between the newscopters in the sky and the
cameras on the ground, the viewer has a near panopticon view of these ac-

tivities—rioting and looting. Inside the newsroom, far away from the scene, the anchormen and women comment upon the "this" (hand gesture)—the events that have not yet been named. They are unaware perhaps of the power that they will have, not only in representing but also in producing the "this" as riots and as media spectacle.

Newscasters, groping for words, struggle to frame and to contain the raw footage within the law-and-order narrative generally employed for nightly crime news. This is all the more ironic, and indeed necessary, given the noticeable and curious absence of police on the streets for the first several hours of the riots. Early on, the fire captains deploy the newscopters to scan the horizon for new fires. Fighting alongside firefighters in this way, the newscasters begin to speak for them and, indeed, for everyone. The "fire officials are just looking so disgusted and so angry—something that everyone is feeling right now." Without recourse to the routine techniques of editing, the language seeping in from the streets through the television is rough, heated, and filled with expletives. The news anchors are clearly uncomfortable with the emotional and political tone of their footage and with their relatively unmediated engagement with the streets. Disconcerted, they clear their throats to apologize to the viewing public for the "foul language" over which they "have no control."

The audience is told that the "this" is "senseless violence." To the images of everyday folks darting in and out of the stores, the newscasters explain: "These people are gangbangers, thugs, and hooligans" who "have nothing to do with what took place in the Simi Valley courtroom." An African American man shouts at the camera, with his arms full of stolen goods, "We're doing this for Rodney." The news anchors respond, "These people are absolute criminals, lawless people who have chosen to take advantage of a terrible situation." A young black woman shouts with tears of anger, "The system doesn't care about us black people . . . Black people have no rights in this country . . . This is about the extinction of the black male." The news anchor turns away from the footage, toward his coanchor, and states: "We have, after all, a system of justice in this country, and it's called being judged by your peers. That means that the four officers were judged by what were said to be twelve of their peers, and the decision was rendered, and that's the way it works." The cameras turn back to the crowd scenes, "These people have absolutely no fear of us or the authorities. There's a traffic jam of looters here." In comes more aerial feed from the newscopters, "There's no border to it anymore. . . ."

"Where are the police? There are no police down there." Reports come in that chief of police, Daryl Gates, is at a fund-raiser in the exclusive Westside neighborhood of Bel Air. "You've got to wonder," responds the newscaster, not wanting to judge the authorities or police too quickly. Still the insinuations grow. "Why the police have not been deployed. . . . Why it's taking so long. . . ." It is not until the next day that the business of newsmaking shifts to normal. Television cameras take their positions at a press conference in front of the talking heads of Los Angeles leadership, Daryl Gates included. Questions fly about the delayed police response and whether the National Guard will be brought in. The media begins to frame the action in more insidious ways. Reporters begin to infer culpability and cause and effect with seemingly innocent speculations such as, "I don't want to make any comments about the group we see here in front of us, but, um, coincidentally, that's when it [the damage to Parker Center] started."

Once the police are deployed, on this second day of the riots, the cameras on the ground relinquish the frontline to the police and retake their positions behind that police line. At the same time, however, the cameras in the sky continue to film what is not visible to the police in front: looters coming into the buildings from the back. The news coverage is increasingly punctuated with remarks such as: "One of our helicopters just spotted someone coming out of a flaming mini-mall, and they followed him to his residence, and the police are now headed in that direction" or "He was in full view [of us] . . . I think that video is going to surface somewhere—in court and with the police no doubt." As the riots progress, the newscast audio begins to mix intermittently with the interference of the police audio.

Finally, the police, along with the assistance of the National Guard and its armored tanks, start taking back control of the streets. While in the earlier footage, people came in and out of the stores with seeming impunity, now the streets were beginning to fill with other images: lines of black and brown bodies lying face down (or in a "prone-out" position) with their hands cuffed behind their backs. By this time, the television crews have resumed their roles as observers, crouching behind the black-and-white squad cars of the Los Angeles Police Department.

But something new has entered this frame. Just beyond the police cars is a sport utility vehicle belonging to the U.S. Border Patrol. Not far up the street, at Vermont and Third, the parking lot of a Vons supermarket is now filled with an entourage of Immigration and Naturalization Services buses— "waiting to give these folks a free ride back to [their] country."[4]

With the riots unfolding onscreen, the KABC reporter Linda Mour is back in the television studio discussing with her anchor whether or not the looters are "illegal aliens." In KABC's rendition of the riots, Latinos quickly become interchangeable with illegal aliens. As the *Los Angeles Times* television critic Howard Rosenberg later mused: "Perhaps Mour was able to identify them as illegal because some of the looters had that stamped on their foreheads. Or—a much better bet—perhaps both she and [news anchor] Greene were predisposed to believe that illegal immigrants automatically commit crimes. If so, their predisposition was transmitted across the airwave as fact."[5] It is precisely at this point that the association between the terms looter, Latino, and illegal is sealed in the viewer's imaginary as the *Latino looter*. The Latino looter becomes a packed sign through which immigration from the southern border becomes an increasingly dominant narrative frame for explaining the riots in much of the subsequent local media coverage and some of the national coverage.

While local news channels babble on in the moralizing law-and-order narrative of nightly crime news, the more liberal, analytical national news coverage frames the event within a "Watts II" paradigm and thus racializes the event as black.[6] For instance, Ted Koppel of the ABC news show *Nightline* locates his television coverage out of the First American Methodist Church in South Central Los Angeles, and at the intersection of Florence and Normandie. Ted Koppel's forays into South Central Los Angeles and his town meeting inside that venerable African American institution from the civil rights era casts African Americans as "event insiders."[7] Koppel frames the events as a consequence of the Rodney King verdict only, thereby ignoring other causes for the rioting: namely, the impact of post-Fordist structural adjustment programs and the globalization of inner-city communities, along with the unacknowledged fact that Latinos were covictims of racist policing.[8] It is certainly true that the media, particularly at the national level, took the 1992 riots as time to reflect on what had indeed been and not been achieved with race relations since 1965. But the riot coverage rendered Latinos "voiceless, but not invisible," and it could not blot out the obvious difference between Watts and 1992—"the appearance of Latinos on TV screens as looters."[9] Neither could it suppress scenes like the one that was featured in an op-ed published in the *Los Angeles Times* about a week after the riots died down. Writing from the same church from which Ted Koppel conducted his riot coverage, Niels Frenzen, a local immigration attorney and law professor, and Frank Acosta, then director of the Coalition for Humane Immigrant Rights of Los Angeles (CHIRLA), offered a very different perspective: "The sight of one our city's leading African-American churches converting its basement meeting room into a temporary shelter for displaced people who were majority Latino and mono-lingual Spanish speaking was on the one hand, striking evidence that the face of our city has been changed irrevocably, and on the other hand, a powerful symbol of the common issues and problems which tie together the Latino, African and Asian-American communities."[10] That is, the riot revealed that the historically African American area of South Central Los Angeles—the epicenter of the Watts riots in 1965—was majority Latino by 1992. More than that, the rioting very quickly spread beyond even those geographic borders to neighborhoods like Pico Union, Koreatown, and East Hollywood. These neighborhoods were also now heavily populated by Mexican and Central American immigrants. The riot coverage thus may have "rendered Latinos voiceless," but not invisible. It could not blot out, as pointedly stated above, "the obvious difference between Watts and 1992—the appearance of Latinos on TV screens as looters."

Héctor Tobar, a crime reporter for the *Los Angeles Times* at the time of the riots, recalled the unfolding of events in an interview with me several years after the event. We talked over lunch in a restaurant on Sunset Boulevard—which had, seven years earlier, been the northern front, if you will, of the riots. I had asked to meet with Tobar after reading his novel *The Tattooed Soldier*, which was set in the same transnational urban geography of my ethnographic research. Tobar responded to my question about the Latinization of the riots, as follows: "It was in fact the African American riot that started first. And I lived this personally because . . . I remember that night I was assigned to do a rewrite on a story about the police reactions to the Rodney King verdict, and we started to see it unfold on TV. Florence, Normandie, etc., etc., the protest downtown—that was the first part. Then later the next morning, I was sent out to go to the area where things had burned down and talk to people. So I started off in South Central Los Angeles." But as Tobar explains, the geographical progression from south to north marked the progression of an African American event to a Latino one:

> They [the *Los Angeles Times*] thought the riot was over. As we all know, the riots started up again and really got going the second day. I ended up following the progression along with the photographer I was with, the progression of it northwards.

I think we started out by Washington, south of Washington, like Vernon, and I ended up following it up north, and at the end of the day I ended up in Echo Park. Yes, I ended up on Sunset Boulevard. Yes, because it spread from East Hollywood, all the way up to Santa Monica Boulevard, the real Central America in East Hollywood, where KCET is . . .

That progression of the riot northwards was parallel to the progression of the riots from an anti-police, African American echo of Watts in 1965 to sort of the modern-day poverty riot in a city that had become a Latin American city, and that was having this Latin American vent take place . . . [with] masses of people storming the markets.[11]

There is no question that Latinos, immigrants in particular, were victims, bystanders, and participants in the events unfolding in front of them. The point here is how this Latinization of the riots was interpreted through the trope of the Latino looter. That trope was eventually absorbed into national post-riot coverage in quotes such as "Over 61% of arrested looters were Latino" and "Nearly one-third of riot suspects were illegal aliens."[12] It was as if in these two statistics lay the real explanation for the riots: an unguarded southern border.[13]

In the full-length articles on the riots that emerged in national magazines in the following months, the riot story quickly became an immigration story, with titles such as "Blacks vs. Brown: Immigration and the New American Dilemma" by Jack Miles, a liberal *Los Angeles Times* editor. Peter Brimelow, a right-wing journalist and English immigrant to the United States, referred to these riot statistics in his essay "Time to Rethink Immigration," in which he urges the reestablishment of Anglo American cultural hegemony. While Miles's story about the riot quickly becomes a story about immigration, Brimelow's story about immigration ends with the riot story. In either direction each writer constructs a powerful frame, which successfully naturalizes the association between the two stories. Thus both liberal and conservative depict Latino immigrants as a threat to American national sovereignty. Miles argues that "because the world has shrunk, [these] emigrants . . . don't have to cut all ties to home and cast their cultural and economic lot with us as they once did." Indeed, he sees within the reluctance of Mexican immigrants to choose American citizenship the potential for foreign interference in domestic political affairs. With so many Mexican citizens living within U.S. borders, "some future Carlos Salinas de Gortari could become a factor in U.S. domestic affairs as the powerful extraterrestrial leader of millions of non-citizen residents in the U.S."[14] Similarly, Brimelow argues that "the idea of the American nation-state as a sovereign structure" that is the "political expression of a specific ethno-cultural group" is in eclipse. The "American Nation" is being threatened by the "Anti-Nation" within the United States: namely by "so-called Hispanics," who are being "encouraged (by the likes of the Ford Foundation) to assimilate into and build a Latino Nation across national boundaries, beyond the United States' sovereign borders."[15] The later injunction contains an explicit fear of the Latinization of the United States as colonization. The transnational nature of Latino migration, settlement, and cultural patterns threatens the established boundaries of the nation-state and, with it, hegemonic conceptions of American national identity.

The American "inner-city crisis," laid bare by the Los Angeles riots, fed into a vicious anti-immigrant politic and was taken as an urgent call for "new enclosures."[16] Indeed, the fixation on and mounting paranoia over constraining the mobility of the Latino immigrant took on the dimension of a "national moral panic."[17] This fixation culminated in the Californian initiative Proposition 187 "Save Our State" and in the federal Illegal Immigration Reform and Immigrant Responsibility Act (IIRAIRA) of 1996.[18] The "visible, if silenced" participation of Latinos in the riots, therefore, fed into the reassertion of a particular moral geography designed to curb and criminalize Latino mobility through arrest, incarceration, detention, and deportation.[19]

No matter how pejorative the coverage of African Americans rioting and looting, even the local news anchors had to acknowledge, if only to negate, the narrative frames of police abuse, the Watts riots, and the long, hard struggle for civil rights. Latinos, however, emerged from the same coverage as thoroughly dehistoricized and unsympathetic subjects and were denied any moral or political ground for their actions. They were judged as purely criminal opportunists taking advantage of black rage to rob American businesses. The only available narrative frame with which to explain Latino participation was the "prominent theme of borderlands media coverage— Latinos as law-breaking foreigners."[20] The Latino looter thus became a folk devil judged guilty of transgressing "the law of place" on two counts: private property and national sovereignty.[21]

This representation of the twofold transgressive mobility of the Latino during the riots, ironically enough, brings to mind the video of the Rodney King beating. Thomas Dumm in his treatment of the video re-presentation of the Rodney King beating in the Simi Valley courtroom argues that the defense positioned Rodney King's mobility—driving at an excessive speed on the freeway (that sign of free circulation) and his refusal to be still while being beaten—within a larger system of representation, which characterizes the dangerous person as hyperactive and subversively mobile. Similarly, the transgressive mobility of the looter was linked to a preexisting and larger system of representation of boundary transgression. The brazen looter—under the eye of the camera, in the full light of the helicopter's nightscope, and even in view of the police—took the time to try on his or her loot for size, or to make several runs to the store until his or her car in the parking lot or on the street was full to capacity. This brazen looter comes to stand as a sign from the "brazen border crosser," who dares to sneak across the border without papers, *sin permiso* (without permission).[22]

Indeed, on my first trip to the California-Mexico border in 1989 I accompanied a border patrol officer down into a gully called the "soccer fields." It was dusk. From the vantage of the van, we could see the Mexican side where people were gathering to cross. The fires of the taco and corn stands were burning. It was a lively social scene. Suddenly, there was a cheer from the crowd. The border patrol officer explained the uproar to me this way: "They're cheering the group that just made it across. It's like scoring a goal. That's why we call it the soccer fields." Whether this depiction of what was really behind that cheer was accurate or not, I don't know. But the image of that "brazen border crosser" was clearly fixed in the imaginary of this officer, or in the imaginary he wished to impart to me.

CHAINS OF BLAME

What does the Latino looter as brazen border crosser have to do with Salvadoran migration per se? After all, the Latino immigrant population in Los Angeles is still largely Mexican. At the time of the riots, all Latinos, immigrants or not, were presumed by the general population to be of Mexican origin. While the term Latino may not capture the specificity of Salvadoran or even Central American migration, the trope of the Latino looter came to do just that, at least within the context of local Latino politics.

Through a perverse chain of blame, whites pointed at blacks, who pointed at Latinos, who in turn pointed at Central American immigrants. Much of the looting took place in neighborhoods heavily populated by recently arrived Latinos, a growing number of whom were Central American and, primarily,

Salvadoran. To quote from the *Economist*: "Tellingly, when the riots swept through the city, Latino East Los Angeles remained relatively untouched. . . . The worst-hit Latino areas were those such as Hollywood, where most of the immigrants were new arrivals from Central America. They appeared to make up a high proportion of looters, but a much lower one of burners and killers."[23] As illustrated at the opening of this chapter, journalist Rubén Navarrette Jr. argued that when Mexican Americans saw photo captions such as the Latino looter in media coverage of the riots, they began to question their political strategy of aligning Latinos of various countries under a single ethnic label.[24] The Latino looter caption, he suggested, led to a frantic effort by Mexican Americans to distance themselves from the "desperately poor Central American and Mexican immigrants depicted in the photograph."[25] Thus the Latino looter was, at the local level, further inflected as a Central American immigrant.

In the same article, "Should Latinos Supports Curbs on Immigration?" Navarrette writes: "A week after the riots, Jesse Jackson addressed a Senate subcommittee considering an urban-aid package. Overnight polls showed that the object of America's moral outrage had, in 48 hours of mayhem, shifted from the verdict in the Rodney G. King beating trial in Simi Valley to arsonists and looters in South Los Angeles. Jackson strained to absolve African-Americans of total responsibility for the lawlessness. He pointed fingers at another ethnic group: 'Fifty-one percent of arrested looters were Latino.'"[26] Once again, the point here is not that Latinos or Central Americans did not loot but rather that these facts were emphasized with a particular political agenda in mind.

Navarrette goes on to make a similar move to Jackson's attempt to deflect criticism away from African Americans: "Yes, Central-American immigrants and Chicanos might both be termed 'Latino.' But the ethnic link between the two groups is thin—no more pronounced than the one joining dark-skinned African Americans with dark-skinned Haitian."[27] His effort to unpack the term Latino as a homogeneous entity, while certainly justified, is also an attempt to redirect the public gaze away from the sympathetic Other (Mexican American) toward the offending Other (Central American immigrant). Finally, given the degree of racial profiling conducted by police, it is highly unusual for African American and Latino public spokespersons to assume that arrest is proof of actual culpability.

The Angry Anglo American

The production of the film *Falling Down* resumed after the rioting stopped, and the film was released the following year. There is ample evidence that its reception was colored by the post-riot climate, particularly given that the riots brought to the fore the issues of racial, social, and economic tensions portrayed in the film and vice versa. In a post-riot interview with the film's director, Joel Shumacher, a journalist wanted to know if Shumacher didn't consider the riots to have been a lucky break for the promotion of his film.

Falling Down is a sophisticated allegory about an angry Anglo American, D-Fens, who is mad as hell with the state of things, in Los Angeles in particular and with the United States of America in general, and is about to get even. The Latinization of Los Angeles is subsumed with discourses on the "third worlding" and "browning" of the face of the city and the nation. D-Fens has had all he can take of the city's democratic promiscuity and its clash of formerly distinct cultures. While Latino immigrants feature in the film's backdrop, as with the live coverage of the riots, their mute but visible presence nonetheless does the ideological work of pointing to the Latinization of Los Angeles as a particularly marked aspect of discourses on urban blight, moral decay, and national decline.

The film is a dramatic reenactment of the vigorous attempts then underway in Californian cultural politics to reterritorialize this disorderly and disruptive cultural flow by remapping the boundaries of what constitutes the official and legitimate public sphere. This entails reasserting the cultural and racial hegemony of the Anglo American male over a disconcerting proliferation of multiple counterpublics. This filmic manipulation of the face of the nation mimes an important aspect of the national project: to topographically reform the civic body. The following composite is drawn from the opening scene of the film.[28]

Begin with a sharp intake of breath, the sound of life hooked up to a ventilator. Fill the screen with a man's parted lips, beaded with sweat. Move like a fly along the bridge of his nose.

Stare into the eye, which stares out through a foggy lens at steam rising from car's engine. The outside world comes first as noise filtered, its base tones heightened, through water. The objects in the landscape come into view, one by one: a Latina child clutching blonde bombshell doll, her empty stare fixed on the viewer; a woman painting her protruding exaggerated lips scarlet red; a school bus of screaming children — multiculturalism wrapped in American flag; Hollywood hustlers, smacking chewing gum, clinching a deal loudly by cellular phone.

You are imprisoned amidst all of these fragmented worlds of the metropolis in this impossible space—the hardened arteries of the Los Angeles freeway. The air conditioning fails. A fly buzzes, invisibly but insistently, around your head. Repeat, close-up and frame by frame, at greater and greater speed—Garfield's barred teeth; "Jesus Died for Our Sins"; the American flag; "DELAY . . . DELAY . . . DELAY"; "How's My Driving? call 1–800 Eat Shit"—to this music, a Cagian urban cacophony, an unbearable, shrill crescendo.

The car door flies open. The protagonist, D-Fens, abandons his car to the highway. "Hey, where do you think you're going? Hey! Hey!" an angered man parked behind D-Fens's car shouts, fist in air, horn honking. Running for the embankment, D-Fens returns the volley, "I'm going home." Disengaging from the high ground of the highway, his normal life path through space, D-Fens enters the low ground of the inner city on foot to begin his epic journey across the postindustrial wasteland of Los Angeles.

Falling Down begins thus, with an assault on the nervous system and with a powerful evocation of the sensory and emotional tone of Los Angeles at a particular historical juncture. In so doing, the film draws us in with an exploration of the psychic disturbances associated with the contemporary recomposition of space-time-being in post–cold war and fin de siècle Los Angeles.[29] Signifying chains have snapped, and D-Fens is left without a frame of reference with which to make sense of this changed grammar of urban life. He temporarily loses his capacity to organize his immediate surroundings perceptually and to map his position in relation to the external world.[30]

The earlier modernist frame, which gave meaning to action in this Los Angeles context—the freeway commute between the bourgeois private sphere (the nuclear family) and the capitalist public sphere (the Fordist-era workplace)—has been disrupted. As the film unfolds, we discover that D-Fens's odyssey is set between two receding horizons. He navigates between a job lost to the downsizing of the defense industry and a home broken by domestic violence and divorce. D-Fens, in truth, has nowhere to go: he is a migrant in postmodernity. The film offers a potentially insightful exploration of a specific phenomenology of late capitalism, its changed structures of feeling, and one level at which the economic and social transformations of regional integration are being felt by the downsized worker.[31]

D-Fens could well serve (and does to some extent) as an intriguing foil for the examination of a distress and unease that some would argue as being particular to the late twentieth century: namely, place-panic or an insecurity of territory.[32]

In the opening scene, D-Fens, "a white guy in a white shirt and tie" (so described in the film), is caught in a traffic jam on the Los Angeles freeway. The standstill traffic and the shocking diversity of barbarous commuters are all symptomatic of decline and fragmentation. This grotesque social body clogs the arteries of progress and individualism that the freeways once represented—at least, to our protagonist.[33] That American dream—so thoroughly propagated by the Hollywood dream machine—is now re-presented as having come to a careening and inelegant halt. Los Angeles is falling down and apart.

D-Fens's transformation from commuter to pedestrian, his disengagement with the highway and engagement with the urban landscape of Los Angeles, mark a potentially powerful encounter with the changed cultural cartography of Los Angeles. By mounting the concrete barrier that separates the highway from the lived spaces hidden on the other side, D-Fens brings into our field of vision the spatial apartheid of Los Angeles.[34] The unfamiliar cultural landscape that D-Fens enters is littered with the signifying scars of the inner city: gang graffiti, "Homeless, will work for food," "We are dying of aids," Latino street vendors selling oranges and peanuts, "economically unviable" African Americans, and the like. D-Fens's journey maps Los Angeles and its "ecology of fear" as deconstructed by Mike Davis: a downtown financial core surrounded by a ring of barrios and ghettoes that give way to wealthy gated communities "on the distant metropolitan frontier."[35] In this regard the film is what it claims to be, "a tale about urban reality."[36]

By turning his world upside down and entering its reverse side D-Fens has the opportunity to come into free and familiar contact with people who in life are separated by impenetrable barriers, and to explore a new mode of interrelationship between individuals.[37] But the disruptive potential of the foregoing destabilizations is lost on these fronts: the reassertion of white male power and authority; the failure to account for the role of the defense industry; U.S. foreign policy; economic restructuring in transforming the face of Los Angeles; and the film's redemptive law-and-order narrative.

As an urban folktale of sorts, Falling Down serves as an ideologically orienting framework for the production, reception, and interpretation of "middle-class folk" discourses about "inner city" and "third-world folk."[38]

Or to draw upon Clifford Geertz, it is a tale that middle-class folk tell themselves, not simply about others but about themselves and their fear of falling from their privileged race-class position, a metaphorical fall into this black hole, the abyss that the inner-city jungle is taken to represent. As a result, the important class subject of the downsized worker is recast as the angry Anglo American male.

D-Fens's tragic journey from a job to a home that no longer exists employs the inner city of Los Angeles as a contemporary Hades. Our hero, like countless Western heroes beginning with Odysseus, must traverse a dangerous territory filled with lost and desperate souls in order to prove his strength and cunning. In making his way through the immigrant neighborhoods that comprise the inner city, D-Fens reasserts his hierarchical race-class position and his authority over greedy Korean grocers, irrational and violent Chicano youth, and undeserving homeless poor. Here, the inner city is little more than a macabre hyperviolent world through which D-Fens roams freely, shooting at the obstacles in his way.

The inner city is thus a symbolic frontier for the reconstruction of the white masculine norm threatened with extinction. As such, *Falling Down* merely shifts the ethnic marking of Hollywood's convention of the urban jungle from Chinatown and South Central Los Angeles to Koreatown and Little Central America. These "inner-city folk," therefore, serve as little more than a textured backdrop to the Anglo American protagonist's journey. Their fallen state is an underprivileged but necessary backdrop to the central tragedy of the privileged fall of the middle-class Anglo American.

NATIONAL DEFENSE

After D-Fens leaves the freeway, his first stop is a convenience store run by a Korean immigrant.[39] He needs change to make a phone call to his ex-wife to inform her that he intends to come home for his daughter's birthday. The storeowner insists that D-Fens buy something if he wants change for his dollar. D-Fens chooses a can of Coke. When he discovers that it will cost him eighty-five cents, leaving him without sufficient change to make his phone call, he goes ballistic.

> ANGRY ANGLO AMERICAN (AAA): You don't got no "Vs" in China?
> KOREAN IMMIGRANT (KI): I'm not Chinese, I'm Korean.
> AAA: You come to my country. You take my money. You don't even have the grace to speak my language. You're Korean?

KI: Yes.

AAA: Do you have any idea how much money my country has given your country?

D-Fens is, of course, referring to the Korean War and central role played by the United States in warding off communists in North Korea from taking over South Korea. D-Fens grabs the baseball bat that the store owner has picked up to protect himself from D-Fens's ire and begins to destroy entire shelves of merchandise, while taunting the man to turn his prices back to the 1950s (ironically enough, the era of the Korean War, when Koreans began to come to Los Angeles in large numbers). After getting what he wants, a Coke for fifty cents and fifty cents in change, D-Fens leaves the now-destroyed convenience store. With baseball bat in hand, he begins to roam through a world he doesn't recognize as America. How is it, he wonders, that this country has come to look like the third world?

Falling Down is a complex example of a middle-class defensive reaction to the changing cultural cartographies of continental American landscapes and its concomitant phobic representations of the mass migration stream from South to North. It is a piece of popular culture that springs from and feeds into the cultural movement afoot to reterritorialize its place in the new global world order. But it fails to interrogate the role of the project to defend American "national security" in the "third worlding" of the American city. As a result, the film misses the opportunity to fuel what Edward Soja argues is urgently needed in mapping (postmodern) geographies—namely, the "awareness of our personal political responsibility for the social production of space as something we have collectively created."[40]

What might U.S. foreign policy in the cold war have to do with this changed landscape? And what does the Korean War have to do with Salvadoran refugees? Indeed, the defense industry is a subtext that never comes fully into view and is never located in the urban ecology through which D-Fens travels to his fateful end. This is a glaring omission in the landscape of a city like Los Angeles—a city built on two industries, the military-industrial complex and Hollywood, and one in deep economic crisis over the apparent dismantling of the former in the post–cold war era.[41] Perhaps the most under-read signs in the movie, and yet surely a most compelling empirical residue, is "D-Fens," the license plate and my pseudonym for the protagonist as well as the NOTEC parking permit on his windshield. The latter is an obvious abbreviation of Nortech, a Los Angeles–based engineering company that has, to quote from its current Web site, provided forty years of service to the defense and aerospace industries. Foreign intervention by the United States has played a large role in producing refugee and immigrant flows to cities such as Los Angeles.

The role of the defense industry in the production of the Salvadoran refugee could not be more pronounced. As I outlined in the introduction to this book, during the twelve-year Salvadoran civil war, the United States funded the Salvadoran government with $6 billion in economic, military, and covert aid. That war resulted in over seventy-five thousand deaths and the flight of one-sixth of the Salvadoran population. Yet D-Fens is unable to reconcile his work to defend American national security with the alien environment in front of him. He fails to understand the role his work in that industry has played in reshaping the spatial, economic, political, and personal geographies of the city in which he is now an exile. In fact, if anything D-Fens misrecognizes his role when he threatens the Korean immigrant grocer with his baseball bat while saying, "Do you know how much money this country gave your government?"

Thus, while *Falling Down* does engage the contemporary recomposition of space-time-being through D-Fens's dislocation from the economy and his disorientation in the cultural and physical landscape, this "tale about urban reality" ultimately veils the reality of (de)militarization. D-Fens does not recognize the synchronism of the urban crisis in the world that surrounds him with the global crisis in the world out there, and thus the relationship between his exile in his homeland and the exodus of Central Americans from their homeland. D-Fens and the Salvadoran refugee are expendable surplus labor in the wasteland of industrial capitalism and the post–cold war era. The film's refusal to bridge the gap between the urban geography and the cultural landscape with the political economy of the military industrial complex masks the "changed look of things" as an effect of immigration and crime rather than the effect of militarization and demilitarization. Indeed, the biographies and spatial journeys of both the downsized defense worker and the Salvadoran refugee are linked precisely around the cold war and the role of the United States in the Salvadoran civil war. But *Falling Down* fails to bring these subject positions into an empathetic relationship to one another because of the defensive cognitive map that undergirds its narrative.

While *Falling Down* depicts a world falling apart, the problem is how it attempts to put that world back together. The film reframes a polyphony of contemporary discourses on immigration, economic decline, inner-city violence, racism, capitalist greed, and government waste into an ordered law-and-order narrative. The film's neglect of global militarization is carried through to its concomitant notion, the militarization of the local landscape. The low-intensity warfare tactics of the cold war have found their way to the criminalized inner city.

While *Falling Down* is one more installment in a long tradition of the white male journeying across a terrifying landscape to get home, D-Fens isn't the hero upon arrival. *Falling Down* is billed as a story about a "man at war with everyday life [who] is about to get even." But it is as much a story about a cop, Detective Prendergast, who regains his agency and the courage to restore law and order. He does so in a shootout with D-Fens, in which D-Fens is eradicated and falls into the abyss of the sea. It is, in fact, the cop who is ultimately reconstructed as the white masculine norm.[42]

At the same time, polyglot Los Angeles and the diversity of the inner city are mirrored in the composition of the staff at the local police headquarters. It is only there, within the boundaries of law enforcement, that the possibility of a new mode of interrelating between groups formerly separated by racial and national hierarchies is realized. The operative mode is policing. D-Fens's triumphant but now defunct project "to make the world safe for democracy" is conceded to the cop's more timely project "to protect and to serve." Discourses about immigration, racism, and inner-city violence are all subsumed within this ideological frame of criminality. The project of local law enforcement (Prendergast) now has primacy over global defense (D-Fens). National security is encoded in a new dominant mythology that is no longer communism but criminality.

The nostalgic portrayal of local law enforcement as the kindly and gentle grandfather figure of Prendergast is a remarkable one for a city that is home to the likes of former police chief Daryl Gates and convicted police officers Stacey Koon and Mark Fuhrman, and a city that had only recently come under the critical gaze of international human rights and local civil rights monitors alike. The film reads rather like a redemptive narrative for the bruising that the police force took in the wake of the beating of Rodney King, and as such it is an erasure of King's baton-bruised body. However, given the period of its production (post–Rodney King beating) and the timing of its release (post–1992 riots), the choice to frame *Falling Down* within a cops-and-robbers genre, and Los Angeles within a law-and-order discourse, invokes those events. Rodney King is an absent presence.

Let's return to those events and to the figure of the Latino looter, whose arrest was taken even by African American and Chicano spokespersons as proof of actual culpability. In fact, the Los Angeles riots in 1992 had provided a particularly instructive moment to observe the deployment of law enforcement against Latinos. Both the American Civil Liberties Union (ACLU) and the Central American Refugee Center (CARECEN) released reports denouncing the widespread civil and human rights abuses against Latinos during the riots. The reports charge that law enforcement failed to protect city residents without regard to ethnic or national origin and violated constitutional protections that mandate that interrogations and arrests be made on probable cause and not on ethnic appearance. This situation was further inflamed by the chief of police and the U.S. attorney general, who singled out Latino and Central American immigrants as a major cause of the uprising.[43]

Moreover, the same year a report by Amnesty International, "Torture, Ill-Treatment and Excessive Force by Police in Los Angeles," found that in Los Angeles human rights violations of low-income minority populations, including immigrants, were a systematic feature of the "war against crime." The full deployment of these multiple agencies of law enforcement (LAPD, LASD, INS, Border Patrol, National Guard) during the riots was thus only a hyper-intensification of activities that occur under normal conditions.[44] D-Fens thinks America has come to resemble the "third world" by virtue of its "changing demographics," code for "immigration crisis" and "browning of America." The Los Angeles police department's "disturbing patterns of impunity" with regard to frequent police abuse of black and Latino residents suggests resemblances with the "third world" at another level, a police force itself exempted from law and order. The inner city in *Falling Down* stands as the "free fire zone" that it is,[45] but absent from this portrayal is an interrogation of how the violent social body is violently produced as a criminalized third world by a local low-intensity warfare—the war on the racialized poor and immigrants.

Whereas D-Fens enters the inner city from the high ground of the highway, the buffer zone of the apartheid urban order, the Salvadoran refugee enters Southern California from the low ground of places, such as the subterranean and rat-infested sewer between Tijuana and San Ysidro, and more recently the killing fields of the desert.[46] These disparate vantages persist in the inner city where their journeys collide. There, where race or ethnicity and not the commission of a crime is the basis for arrest,[47] D-Fens's mobility, across the inner city at least, is unfettered by the constant and visible police presence on the ground and overhead. At the border and in the city, however, Salvadoran refugees must dodge a veritable "armed response" to their illegal presence: a full constellation of law enforcement agencies mobilized to arrest, detain, charge, and deport them. Images of benign police officers and depictions of harmonious multicultural police forces belie the lived reality of Salvadoran refugees before, during, and after the riots.

As with the media coverage of the riots, the "visible, if silenced" presence of Latino immigrants, the film *Falling Down* fed into the reassertion of a particular moral geography and to a program of topographic reform. Both the film and the live coverage offered particular representations of the space of the inner-city immigrant barrio as a lawless place in need of a greater presence of law enforcement, be it the police or the police in concert with immigration.

WE CAN'T HELP OTHERS UP, IF WE ARE FALLING DOWN

As a filmic representation of a particular historical juncture in the development of the American city, Los Angeles in particular, *Falling Down* hit a raw nerve and entered a zone of heated cultural debate about crime, urban decay, and immigration. The conservative populist radio talk show host Rush Limbaugh, a fierce proponent of the anti-immigrant and anti-crime legislation proposed in the aftermath of the riots, was repeatedly likened to D-Fens. Limbaugh felt compelled to defend his "good name," which had been "besmirched countless times in discussions and reviews of the movie *Falling Down*."[48] Electronic mailing list discussions on Proposition 187 picked up on the question haunting the film, "Are we falling apart?" with retorts like, "We can't help others up, if we are falling down."

In the aftermath of the riots, the image of D-Fens looking through the want ads as he sits on a ruin of an old cement structure against the backdrop of downtown Los Angeles, only to discover that he is trespassing on gang territory, captured a feeling of radical instability. In this post–cold war and post-Fordist landscape, both D-Fens and the Chicano gang members who confront him, demanding a toll in the form of his empty briefcase, are scavengers of a "future already looted,"[49] by the immanent forces of an emerging neoliberal regime and its attendant securityscapes. If in this chapter I have tried to evoke something of the affective dimensions of this historical juncture and its politics of fear and enclosure, in the next chapter I consider how this new mode of production secretes a new kind of space in the ruined landscape of the inner city of Los Angeles and its immigrant barrios.

STREET HOODLUM ———— **TWO**

TOPOGRAPHIC REFORM

In August 1992, three months after the Los Angeles riots, the city's Central American immigrant leadership, which had emerged from the solidarity movement of the 1980s, held a press conference in front of the ruined minimall at the corner of Pico and Alvarado streets. As discussed in the previous chapter, in the aftermath of the riots, the media and the anti-immigrant movement had been mining ruins such as these for nationalist narratives, for which the body of the Latino looter was fast becoming a powerful political text. The Central American leaders at the press conference hoped to construct something else out of the loosened building blocks of the ruin, and to very different ends.

Standing between the ruin and the cameras, these activists offered the following rereading of the production of the ruin. Against the media-generated image of the Latino looter that was burned into popular (televisual) consciousness as illegal Central American immigrants, these spokespersons produced affidavits testifying that law enforcement and immigration officers had taken advantage of the confusion and the generalized suspicion of looting to collaborate in rounding up and raiding the apartments of Latinos, all under the guise of looking for stolen goods. On the streets and inside these densely populated apartments, when no loot was to be found, immigration papers were sought instead. These Central American leaders argued that the vast majority of Latinos turned over to the Immigration and Naturalization Services (INS) were either never even criminally charged or were, in fact, arrested for violating a vague and confused curfew policy upheld unevenly and disproportionately in immigrant neighborhoods—and not, as imagined, for looting. These leaders and advocates gave very different testimony before the cameras, insisting that the residents of Pico Union were hardworking, law-abiding citizens who only wanted the right to make better lives for themselves and their children. They were not looters or rioters, and they were not illegals in the country to take advantage of the welfare state.

The actual pretext and news angle for the press conference that day was a complaint: The city had done nothing to clear the rubble and to begin rebuilding. Pico Union and its Central American population were, they lamented, the last to receive the attention and resources galvanized by the riots. The sudden arrival of the bulldozer on the very morning of the press conference threatened to upset the photo opportunity that the group's press communications staff had choreographed. They desperately attempted to keep the gaze of the few reporters in attendance away from the bulldozer, just long enough to imprint the image of the ruin on film before it was leveled. The camera operators were ushered into position with their backs to the machine, but the drone in the background was unmistakable.

Standing between the ruin and the cameras, the speakers issued an impassioned call to rebuild the neighborhood. They closed the press conference with an announcement of an upcoming community forum organized to insert the needs of the area and of the Central American community into the agenda of Mayor Tom Bradley's and Peter Ueberroth's post-riot redevelopment initiative, Rebuild Los Angeles (RLA). Only the Spanish-language media responded to the press releases and came out to record this deconstruction of the Latino looter and call for the development of the Pico Union area.

Fast forward to 1999 and to the rebuilt environment of Pico Union. The ruin of the mini-mall is now gone, and so too is the tall wire fence with a "for sale" sign that had surrounded the empty dirt lot—one of the 250 properties registered under the Vacant Lot Revitalization Project sponsored by Rebuild Los Angeles. For years the only trace of the mini-mall's demise was the blackened wall of the lone remaining brick building, which served as its backdrop. Then in 1999 the corner of Pico and Hoover became the site of a brand-new Jack in the Box. The corner also fell under the 18th Street Gang injunction enforced by the Rampart Division of LAPD's elite anti-gang unit Community Resources Against Street Hoodlums. The ruined mini-mall, which had served as the central prop to a seemingly failed media event, came to be a target area—indeed, the epicenter—for both RLA's redevelopment program and LAPD's crime prevention strategies. What kind of social spatial harmony were these distinct techniques of managing the inner city and its immigrant population attempting to restore or to build anew?

Both projects sought to restructure the topography of the inner-city immigrant barrio at the level of its built environment (its buildings and streets) in order to redirect or constrain the transgressive mobility of the Latino immigrant. Whereas RLA envisioned, in the frenetic and disorderly crowd of looters, a new market ripe for consumer capitalism, LAPD's anti-gang abatement unit saw in that same crowd the figure of the "street hoodlum" (aka gang member) ruling and administering over a countervailing and illegal economy that strangled legitimate local business.

In the post-riot era the space of these immigrant barrios were reshaped by these multiple and contradictory pressures: the representations of space emanating from redevelopment and law enforcement agencies; and the spaces of representation emanating from labor, immigrant entrepreneurs, immigrant rights advocates, youth gangs, and the immigrants themselves; and the "spatial practices" of both. The inner-city immigrant barrio thus serves as a key ethnographic site through which to view the nature of contemporary urban restructuring, the authoritarian limits of democracy as it combines with neoliberal policies, and how both combine to manage the pressures of globalization.

Rebuild Los Angeles

Let's return to the rebuilt Jack in the Box on the corner of Pico and Hoover and to RLA's Vacant Lot Revitalization Project.[1] Pico Union and the Central American community did, in fact, enter RLA's agenda. One of the Central American leaders present at the press conference in 1992, Carlos Vaquerano, was invited onto RLA's community board of directors. Moreover, Pico Union became "Cluster Area no. 1" in the Vacant Lot project, and the intersection of Pico and Alvarado was termed "Site 1" in the project's investment package portfolio. The corner, the neighborhood, and the community thus became the site of intensive intervention for redevelopment.[2]

The spatial discourse of RLA constructed Pico Union as a particular kind of object of knowledge: notably, a "neglected area," a "zone of need," and the "ignored poor, isolated inner city."[3] This discourse about the undeveloped inner city was not new, of course, but rather derived from the Johnson administration's War on Poverty in the 1960s.[4] What was new, however, was the privatization of the development function, not to mention the focus on retail and commercial enterprises and on consumption rather than production. The problems of the inner city, which once required state action, were now seen as the results of state activity. Activist social policies such as welfare, public housing, and community block grants once posed as the solution had now become the problem. The state was now depicted as an unproductive agent in development, a function that was to be returned to the marketplace and to the private economic arena.[5]

The discourse of RLA was, of course, a locally and historically contingent manifestation of shifts in federal policy. Two post-riot reports were indicative of this turn to the neoliberal. The first emanated from George Bush Sr.'s presidential task force on the Los Angeles riots and the second from the Democratic Party's think tank, the Progressive Policy Institute. The discourse of both the Republicans and Democrats, party affiliations not withstanding, revealed a remarkable and unprecedented convergence in their proposals for the redevelopment of inner-city Los Angeles. In each case, the role of the capitalist welfare state had become the crucial focus. While Democrats blamed the plight of the inner city on "twelve years of Republican neglect," Republicans attributed the condition of the inner city to the "failed programs of the Great Society."

On the surface, the positions of the parties regarding the interventions and the role of the state appear to be considerably different, with one calling for more state intervention and the other for less. The proposal by the presidential task force merely reemphasized Republican strategies of the 1980s to "cut the red tape" and provide "regulatory relief" in order to promote corporate investment and "indigenous entrepreneurship." Republican discourse remained grounded in an ideology of deregulation that argued for the further dismantling of entitlement programs and government intervention in private affairs and market forces. The riots did not rupture Republican common sense.

The Democratic position was more complex but, in the end, not markedly different. The proposal by the Progressive Policy Institute began its report with a call for an alternative to the "traditional Left-Right schism" and then proceeded to "demythologize" both Left and Right interpretations of the riots. However, the alternative it posited actually moved the debate closer to the discursive boundaries of the opposition and to the governing logic of the market. At the outset, the document repositioned the Democratic Party in the center of the Left-Right schism. This involved bringing its policy recommendations closer to the Right. What was needed to replace the "social service industry" upon which the underclass fed was a "new kind of governmental action" and a "redesigning of government along entrepreneurial lines." The state was invoked as an "entrepreneurial government" as well as a "public enterprise." These rhetorical plays might be read as a successful absorption of the oppositional Republican discourse to serve a Democratic agenda and Bill Clinton's bid for presidency in the upcoming national elections. However, much as Stuart Hall has argued about the effects of Thatcherism in Britain, one could claim that the collapsing of state and private sectors into one another turned out to represent the final victory of the Reagan/Bush agenda, where the logic of the market now governed the state and society.[6] The subsequent election of Bill Clinton did not represent a break from but rather a firm embrace of "Reaganomics" formalized as the "Washington Consensus" during the Bush Sr. administration.[7]

The proof of this inversion and convergence is in the recommendations of both parties. With the exception of Clinton's jobs incentive program,[8] the programmatic agendas of both the Democrats and the Republicans were better characterized by a series of deregulations in the form of welfare reform and regulatory relief (from taxes, planning codes, environmental emission standards, and the minimum wage) in order to encourage businesses to invest in the inner-city "enterprise zones." While Democrats were less willing to speak of enterprise zones as "panaceas," these zones together with regulatory incentives also occupied a central place in their agenda. Welfare reform emphasized the transformation of bureaucratic state agencies into mini-malls of "one-stop shopping centers," which promoted "competition in social services." Thus while Democrats were not yet calling for the complete eradication of welfare, social services were to be privatized and governed by market forces and the urban poor would be freed of their dependency on welfare and reeducated through a new culture of enterprise, family, and self-help. Like the government, the individual was to be disciplined according to the logic of the market.

Rebuild Los Angeles fit squarely within these ideological and programmatic shifts in national policy. The program was a compelling example of the privatization of functions formally attributed to the state. It is instructive to compare RLA after the Los Angeles riots of 1992 to the Community Redevelopment Agency (CRA) instituted after the Watts riots in 1965. Both entities were set up by Mayor Tom Bradley in order to address the post-riot needs of the inner city. But whereas the CRA was a city agency RLA was a privately incorporated organization. The literature produced by RLA was filled with pejoratives about government. Indeed, it boasted that "RLA is not government, it is not laws, taxes, courts" but rather "the only *predominantly private-sector* response to civic crisis in history" (italics mine); and, further, that where "government [has] failed . . . thankfully corporate America has responded."

This is not to say that government did not have a role to play, albeit subordinated, in redevelopment.[9] To quote the designer of RLA's three-ringed logo, the rings represented "the tripod of the Community, the Government, and the Private Sector." Government was certainly present—albeit reenvisioned as an entrepreneurial venture. My concern here is with the role that "community" was meant to play in redevelopment and what this discursive move obscured. First, who was this "community"? As I mentioned above, RLA did open its doors to the Central American "community" with a seat on its board. And indeed, RLA cannot be faulted for its lack of representation of the official African American, Latino, and Asian community leadership— many of whom were relatively new voices in Los Angeles, and had never sat at the same table with the likes of the governor or the CEOs of Bank of America, ARCO, and GTE. Indeed, this position was no small feat for Carlos Vaquerano, who first came to Los Angeles to work with the Central American solidarity movement against the Salvadoran state and the U.S. corporate interests therein. At the time of this writing, Vaquerano heads the Salvadoran American Leadership and Educational Fund (SALEF). This organization draws much of its support from corporate contacts, which Vaquerano would argue he made through RLA.

Second, what did the language of "community" displace? The "*positive power* of community" (italics mine), to use the language from RLA's organizational brochure, excluded labor and inner-city residents themselves. One can arguably infer the indirect representation of inner-city residents in the board membership of city council members, church leaders, and agency directors—the official representatives, albeit invariably not the residents of the inner city. But where were the official representatives of labor on the eighty-member board of RLA? The previous social contract of the Ford-Keynesian era between business, government, and labor—dismantled in the 1970s and 1980s—had been rewritten as private sector, government, and *community*. To be sure, the discursive shift to "community" implied that a "continuing recognition that some degree of inclusiveness was necessary to ensure stable growth of capital."[10] However, it would appear that if business were going to be "persuade[ed] to come back to the inner city,"[11] it was going to have to be without organized labor. Certainly in the case of the Central American immigrant "community," this was a remarkable exclusion. To elide the historical fact that Central Americans comprised a significant sector of the low-wage immigrant labor pool that was vital to the contemporary restructuring of Los Angeles was also to avoid the centrality of their role in a newly invigorated labor movement, a movement that was building strength at that very moment in the history of Los Angeles.

THE JUST JANITOR

Indeed, less than a month after the riots the project Justice for Janitors of the Local 399 of the Service Employee International Union held its second annual march to commemorate the beating in 1990 of a pregnant union member by Beverly Hills police—that is, their equivalent to the Rodney King incident. The marchers, many who resided in Central Los Angeles and the vast majority who were immigrants and mostly from Latin America, gathered in Century City Plaza. Dressed in militant red-and-black *justicia* (justice) T-shirts and with red bandannas wrapped around their foreheads, and some with faces covered by monstrous masks inscribed with the letters LAPD, they all held up placards with the campaign slogan "L.A. must work for everyone." This invisible workforce—the members of which ordinarily are in and out of the Century City towers after and before regular business hours—gathered on a grassy inner circle between the four corners of glass and steel—towering monuments to corporate America. In contrast to their nightly routine they stood in broad daylight, clashing with the three-piece suits pouring out of their executive suites for "power lunches." The march began with the transnational rallying cry "¿Qué queremos? ¡Justicia! ¿Cuándo queremos? ¡Ahora!" ("What do we want? Justice! When do we want it? Now!). Neither the colors nor the chant had changed with the journey from Central America to Beverly Hills.[12]

The confrontation in 1992, however, was not with law enforcement. The gray-suited labor detail police stood off at a safe distance on the balconies above. The lower echelon of the police force, uniformed, took to the streets on motorbikes. Since the beating of the pregnant union member and the incidents surrounding Rodney King, the police were on their best behavior. The union had won a contract as a result of the press coverage from the last beating. This time the officer in charge shook hands with the union organizer as they discussed the route for the march. This year the police were a helpful escort.

Instead, the confrontation was with the developers and with RLA in particular. While over the last year Justice for Janitors had made ground with law enforcement, they had yet to be invited onto RLA's community board. That board, according to RLA's leader at the time, Peter Ueberroth, was "representative of every sector of our society." Not so, said Justice for Janitors, which later took its protest to RLA's offices. Ueberroth refused to meet with the demonstrators outside his office as requested, asking them instead to make an appointment to see him in private. But Justice for Janitors would not back down. They would make their demands heard in the public arena, not in the private sector.

The director of the project later wrote to follow up on the demonstration outside RLA's office. Justice for Janitors wanted an opportunity to discuss their "Workers' Bill of Rights"—out in the open, of course—and to challenge Ueberroth's statement that "minimum wage jobs bring dignity to those who labor." The letter to Ueberroth argued that RLA's economic plan for "fast-track incentives" to bring business back to the inner city was flawed by its very nature. Further, RLA had failed to recognize the real problem of the inner city: namely, "the misery of people working a 40 hour week and still living below the poverty level." Justice for Janitors redefined the problem of the inner city as not too few but rather too many dead-end minimum-wage jobs. "LA should work for everyone," that is, the *working poor* alongside the "lawless corporate class." The complaint thus was twofold: not only did RLA not have any membership from labor on its community board but its twenty-two-point list of "What can companies do?" did not make a single reference to quality of jobs or labor practices. As such, Justice for Janitors argued that RLA failed to serve its professed goal to address the causes of the riots and to alleviate poverty. The focus by Justice for Janitors on economic justice issues effectively shone a light on the larger economic restructuring processes associated with the shift from Keynesian to neoliberal labor practices.

A COMMUNITY OF CONSUMERS

If RLA's spatial discourse failed to recognize or to acknowledge the Central American "community" as "the working poor," that discourse worked actively to represent them as an untapped community of consumers. The redevelopment strategies of RLA in Pico Union focused on the "shopping cluster concept," and the intersection became a featured "investment package" therein. Using the Atlas Mapping Programs of the city's Geographical Information Service, RLA matched the vacant lots at Pico, Alvarado, and Hoover with a number of geographical variables. The site was photographed, its title reports obtained, property owners contacted, and zoning information gathered. Potential investors were to be sold on the idea that this immigrant neighborhood represented an as yet "untapped consumer market," and that "businesses were likely to yield high profits because of the large degree to which [this] neglected area [was] underserved." These claims were backed up by "community needs assessment surveys," which in documenting consumer retail and commercial needs were in effect marketing research surveys. The interests of capitalist expansion were expressed therein as the fundamental and essential material needs of the community. This call for private enterprise to meet the "underserved community's . . . pent-up demand" was, to say the least, ironic in the aftermath of the riots.

Or was it? Hadn't looters behaved like consumers par excellence? Isn't the looter, the ur-form of the consumer, an objective emblem of commodity fetishism and of consumerist culture in late capitalist society? For the immigrant working poor, might not looting represent a spontaneous fantasy of realizing this aspect of the American dream as yet unrealized? From this vantage, looting might be understood as a mimetic improvisation of the capitalist exhortation to buy and buy, and this newest stratum of immigrants viewed as a "dreaming collective of consumers" cultivated by global media capitalism.[13] The looter who takes off with a designer pair of Nikes appropriates these commodities as fetishized wish images of the unrealized and broken dreams of El Norte as a place of luxury, wealth, and excess.[14]

As Héctor Tobar, the novelist and Los Angeles–based Guatemalan American reporter and later columnist for the *Los Angeles Times*, put it to me:

I was a professional witness to the riots and to the masses of people storming the markets. The looting was a metaphor for people who felt cheated. It's almost a subconsciousness; a class subconscious I think is the way to look at what was happening that day. It was all very visceral, you know. People were just really acting from the most personal, almost childlike motives—you know, "I wanna get some," "Everybody else is getting something" . . . I was outside this store on 3rd Street, this grocery store that was being looted, and this kid runs out. I asked him, "What did you get?" And he shows me the bag . . . it was all the candy.

The grandest irony was how the looting was further induced by the contradictions of consumer capitalism. Toward the end of the riots the newscasters began to nod their heads in shame and denial as callers to the station begged them to consider their role in fanning the flames and further inciting the looters and rioters. "What role is media playing?" asked one such caller: "People see the looting [through] . . . all the broadcasting . . . You've got to consider their psychological mindset. They're going to run out and to do the same." Although much of the footage was filmed from the air and not on the ground, media did not merely cover the event from a distance but actually participated in it by adding fuel to an already inflamed setting. Helicopters making runs for TV news shows also served as reconnaissance for the populace below. TV coverage provided viewers with unprecedented visual access and the rioters and looters with the intelligence to conduct further strikes and raids.[15] Mike Davis, with a tongue-in-cheek appropriation of George Bush's phrase "a thousand points of light," describes how, like the fires in Los Angeles, the riots spread from Los Angeles to Las Vegas and beyond. The riot coverage parodied local network television's everyday practices—the promotion of law, order, and consumerism. Now television was advertising fire sales of a different law and order; the looting sites were like liquidation sales where "all merchandise must go" and "prices have been slashed to rock bottom."

Tobar, pointing to the interactive nature of media coverage, explained the phenomenon to me as follows:

I was outside of a market that was being looted, and it was clear to me that people were coming from as far away as [the primarily white, upper-middle-class neighborhood of] Santa Monica to take part in the looting. So they had seen it on TV and decided to drive out and take advantage. In the same way that a few years later, when O. J. Simpson was involved in that car chase. People saw it on TV, decided to run out, and even had time to make signs to show O. J. as he headed towards his home.

As a mimetic improvisation of the capitalist edict to consume, looting was the active reproduction of television's technical production and the vehicle through which desire and need were expressed, realized, and enacted.[16]

Members of the Situationist International,[17] writing about the Watts riots in 1965, argued that those events were

> a rebellion against the commodity, against the world of the commodity in which worker-consumers are *hierarchically* subordinated to commodity values. Like the young delinquents of all of the advanced countries, but more radically because they are part of a class totally without a future, a sector of the proletariat unable to believe in any significant chance of integration or promotion, the Los Angeles blacks take modern capitalist propaganda, its publicity of abundance, *literally*. They want to possess immediately all the objects shown and abstractly accessible because they want to *use* them. That is why they reject their exchange-value, the *commodity-reality* . . . The looting of the Watts district was the most direct realization of the distorted principle, "To each according to his false needs" . . . But since the vaunting of abundance is taken at its face value and immediately seized upon instead of being eternally pursued in the rat race of alienated labor and increasing but unmet social needs, real desires begin to be expressed in festival, in playful self-assertion, in the *potlatch* of destruction . . . The flames of Watts *consummated* the system of consumption . . . Looting is the *natural* response to the society of abundance—the society not of natural and human abundance, but of abundance of commodities . . . What is a policeman? He is the active servant of the commodity . . . whose job it is to ensure that a given product of human labor remains a commodity with the magical property of having to be paid for . . . The Watts youth, having no future in market terms [no buying power], grasped another quality of the present . . . By wanting to participate really and immediately in the affluence, which is the official value of every American, they demand the egalitarian *realization* of the American spectacle of everyday life.[18]

The fears expressed by journalist Jack Miles in his article, "Black vs. Brown," discussed in the previous chapter, were thus not altogether un-

Looters = sign of consumer culture gone awry.

Buildings being burnt = Failed material of late capitalism

founded. Miles, the "worried Roman," watches the looters, the "Goths at their sack" on television.[19] If the looters were a sign of its consumer culture gone awry, the buildings going up in flames on the screen represented the "failed material of [late] capitalism." After all, these ruins were overwhelmingly commercial establishments and not domestic residences, schools, or even government buildings. The target was, in effect if not in intention, consumer capitalism. The ruins in Los Angeles, much like the shopping arcades of Walter Benjamin's writings, were not only emblems of the transitory nature and fragility of capitalist culture but also of its destructiveness and inherent contradictions.[20] Looting was thus not divorced from consumption but instead was a particular, indeed a parodic, mode of consumption, which subverts "culturally and legally approved paths of exchange."[21] But the looting was also part of the madness borne of consumer excess, its accumulated energy, its cultural bomb.

WINDOW SHOPPING

Interestingly, not even labor remained untouched by the logic of the neoliberal market. It, too, internalized a consumerist inflection. Let's return briefly to the Justice for Janitors march in 1999. I was there with camera in hand; in my capacity as official observer, I was to take photographs and statements if any problematic incidents with the police arose. Since the march proceeded smoothly, I took photographs of a different sort. The crowd of union members walked up Rodeo Drive past its exclusive shops and restaurants, and then ascended the staircase of an internationally celebrated postmodern revival of a European street. Continuing past the dramatic wrought-iron gates of the Beverly Fairmont Hotel, the crowd filed through the service entrance at the back.

Two men brandishing placards made for the march—one, a photograph of the beating from two years before with the slogan "Never Again," and the other, a red-and-black graphic of workers marching with the slogan "L.A. must work for everyone"—stopped in front of a Rolls Royce showroom. Their images, together with the reflection of the First Imperial Bank building behind them were refracted on the sleek body of the Rolls Royce on view. At the next corner, they stopped in front of a men's fine clothing store of the sort where the salesmen evoke the bygone era of haberdashers. By now they were hot from marching and had placed their LAPD monster masks on their heads like caps. They stared with bemused looks at the window display and at the cardboard silhouettes of gentlemen in top hat, coat, and tails mounted in front of a penny-farthing.

Let's pull to the fore the image refracted in the windowpane of a Rolls Royce showroom. The image is a montage of the exclusive stores lining Rodeo Drive, the reflections of the Just Janitor holding his sign "L.A. must work for everyone," and the marquis on the building behind him, "First Imperial Bank." Like Benjamin's emblem, the photo is a "concept imagistically constructed out of a montage of visual images and linguistic signs . . . from which one can read, like a picture puzzle." And like the image in the previous chapter of the Latino looter lying face down on the pavement in front of the ruined mini-mall, this image—rising up against the backdrop of the towering high-rises of downtown Los Angeles—is yet another "intellectual spectacle" through which to reread history.[22] The centerpieces in both of these before-and-after images are commercial establishments. The disparities contained within and between both photographs bring two spheres usually separated from one another through a spatial apartheid into critical engagement. These distinct fields of action, a mini-mall in a Central American barrio, the glass towers in the international financial centers of Los Angeles, and the exclusive storefronts of Beverly Hills, combine with two modes of action—looting and marching.

When the Just Janitor, while marching, pauses to look through the display window, is he gazing upon the Beverly Hills Rolls Royce dealership with a critical smirk that comes in recognition of how perfectly the relationship between labor and capital is condensed into an emblem by the refracting glass? Is he filled with the desire to acquire the images that were dangled in front of him from afar about El Norte? Shouldn't the anthropologist pause to wonder—in the ambiguity of this gaze—if the trade unionist isn't also gazing upon his wish image of El Norte, now a private broken dream? Did he imagine that in El Norte he would be patronizing these specialty stores and silver service restaurants on Rodeo Drive rather than the 99-cent store and El Pollo Loco on Pico Boulevard? Indeed, as far as commodities and consumer choice go, Pico Union is closer to Central America than Rodeo Drive. Its swap meets are filled with the same cheap assembly-line goods produced in and dumped on the third world market. Is the Just Janitor feeling outrage at the disparity between these cityscapes? Or is he hankering after the promise for a better life lost on two fronts? After all, he's still shouting the same chant, "¿Qué queremos? ¡Justicia! ¿Cuándo queremos? ¡Ahora!" that got him booted out of Central America. With his right to bargain for a fair wage still quite tenuous and fair wages being 50 percent of their value in the 1970s,[23] it appears that the Central American immigrant isn't going to get a Rolls Royce or a fine Italian suit from either looting or marching.

The next time I joined the janitors in their annual march was in May 1999. This time the route led from Beverly Hills up the Avenue of the Stars and into the Plaza on Century Park East—a shopping mall filled with restaurants and movie theaters below a quadrangle of high-rise corporate towers occupied by lawyers, real estate tycoons, and the like. As we entered the mall, the chant changed from "¿Qué queremos? ¡Justicia!" to "Se ve presente, la unión está presente" ("The union is present."). And what a visible presence, indeed. The roughly one thousand marchers filed down two sets of stairs cascading on either side of the open shopping mall to the left and to the right against the background of a marquis announcing the latest Hollywood releases, including *Free Enterprise*. We continued our march down the four parallel passageways of the lower level, passing the lunchtime crowd of executives and secretaries, and then cascaded down the remaining set of stairs into the plaza below.

This year Latino- and labor-friendly city, county, and state politicians joined the Janitors in full. The Janitors had come a long way in winning wide respect and recognition. One speaker after another placed their moral and political weight behind the Janitors' campaign for 2000 entitled Principles for a Responsible Real Estate Industry. Behind this performance of labor's demands, the plaza gave way to a bizarre set of contradictions. On one half of its circular grounds, there was a luncheon buffet in session. The theme was a Hawaiian luau, complete with a musical trio and hula dancers. A gleaming-red Porsche was being raffled on one side of the plaza, while the other side was taken over by the Janitors. The philanthropic charitable discourse of the raffle sign, "Win a Porsche. Help change a life," mingled with the trade unionist slogans of the Justice for Janitors campaign placards. Some janitors wore white mops on their heads and carried their brooms and blue buckets with Local 1877 printed thereon. A few gay pride activists also were present with placards reading "pride at work, OUT and organizing" to show their solidarity for this "coming out" of the janitorial cleaning supply closet.

Strangely, the union's demands and wishes began to incorporate the backdrop of the Porsche for raffle and the Hawaiian luau. Alongside the usual call for salary increases, vacation, sick leave, and health care coverage, the union leadership turned to the unanticipated props behind them to acknowledge directly the desires of their members to join the ranks of the middle-class consuming public. "Why not say it?" boomed a member of the *junta directiva* (board of directors). "Yes, to buy a nice new car. To take vacations without worrying about how to cover one's daily living expenses." Even this "¿Qué queremos? ¡Justicia!" call of the radical Latin American Left had, after years of organizing in the United States, taken on an overtly consumerist inflection. The Just Janitor has been mobilized on two fronts—as radical trade unionist and as consumer. His "mobilized gaze" as window shopper, however, speaks to his lack of and desire for empowerment in the marketplace.

While the juxtaposition of the Porsche and the unionist had not been intentionally staged, such stagings are, in fact, commonplace in the photographs that families in El Salvador and elsewhere receive from their immigrant families in the United States. The cover of Sarah Mahler's ethnography of Salvadoran and South American immigrants is a vivid portrayal of this phenomenon, something she calls immigrants' "material fetishism." Against the stark black-and-white reality of the immigrant's makeshift bedroom in what is more than likely a living room in an overcrowded one-bedroom or efficiency apartment, with clothes hanging on wires that extend along the ceiling, is a photograph that manufactures the immigrant's material success in El Norte. In this "constructed illusion," the immigrant is posing next to a flashy red sports car against a backdrop of an upper-middle-class building complex. He has gone in search of these props to send an image back to his family in El Salvador that conveys his successful realization of the American dream. As Mahler notes, "Material fetishism . . . erupts when people from commodity-poor societies enter consumptive, industrialized ones." As with the cargo cults in the South Pacific during the Second World War, "the material goods migrants send or bring home have fostered a fetishism that mystifies the human efforts which produced them."[24]

In the Justice for Janitors campaign of 1999–2000, the increased buying power of immigrant labor appeared, albeit by serendipity, alongside the negotiation package for better salaries, benefits, improved working conditions (including the immigrant's right to work without fear of INS raids), and wage exploitation. Was this consumerist inflection simply, to quote Mahler, "a fetishism that mystifies the human efforts to produce"? Does consumption only act to mystify the social relations of production? If realized, the platform of the janitors' group would bring immigrant labor into consumer capitalism and closer to the realization of the materiality and luxury of the

American dream. To quote from the docudrama featuring Justice for Janitors, *Bread and Roses*: "We want bread, but we want roses too!" In expressing this view, they registered their inequality as laborers and as consumers of luxury goods too.

In the aftermath of the riots, that "pent-up demand" for goods unleashed by the frenetic disorderly crowd of looters had now been absorbed into RLA's discourse of redevelopment, which refashioned looters and laborers alike as a potential docile consuming public. Indeed, another of the Central American leaders present at that press conference went on to earn a master's degree in business administration, after which he began to give PowerPoint presentations on the Central American consumer at venues such as the exclusive downtown Los Angeles City Club, the long-time home of the city's business elite. The Central American population's settlement and consumption patterns had made the agenda. Indeed, as the body of the Latino looter was being circulated as a political text for the anti-immigrant movement, in the business realm Central Americans were being discovered as something more than a cheap labor force for global capitalism. They were now also ripe subjects for consumer capitalism.

As a project, RLA did not last long; indeed, it closed its doors two years after the riots, and by all accounts it was relatively ineffectual.[25] Nonetheless, RLA was a sign of its times. Its redevelopment strategy for Pico Union mirrored broader economic restructurings and was embedded within the wider periodicity of late capitalism on these three fronts: the privatization or devolution of the welfare state, the post-Fordist reneging on the social contract with labor, and the emphasis on consumption rather than production.

The Los Angeles Police Department

While the ambivalent critique of consumption by Justice for Janitors recognized the power of the Latino immigrant as a new class of consumers in the emergent neoliberal order, it failed to account for the production of a new criminal class. Surely a critique of neoliberalism must also account for the place of security policy and for the combined spatial practices of consuming and policing. I turn now to the second project of topographic reform under investigation in this chapter—policing and the spatial discourse of LAPD's special gang-abatement unit, Community Resources against Street Hoodlums (CRASH). The notion of the street hoodlum was to the rebuilt environment of Pico Union as the Latino looter was to its ruined environment. On the same site that RLA proposed its Vacant Lot Revitalization Project, the LAPD proposed a court injunction against the 18th Street Gang. The litigation maps prepared for the district attorney's gang unit by the city's Geographic Information Specialist (GIS) took into their domain the very same neighborhood geography as RLA's GIS investment maps.

Passed in 1997, the 18th Street Gang injunction leveraged public nuisance and loitering laws to legally enshrine and formalize severe restrictions on the freedom of movement and the right to free association between gang members, thereby criminalizing everyday behavior. It also gave LAPD's special CRASH unit a very nearly idealized exercise of disciplinary power over the rebuilt environment in question. Gang injunctions, much like the media splashes by the INS at the border between the United States and Mexico, are spectacular performances in spatial legislation designed to retake command over a politically marked space. Building on the Street Terrorism Enforcement Prevention Act (STEP) and combined with anti-loitering laws, this injunction banned all forms of association and communication between two or more gang members—be they standing, sitting, walking, driving, gathering, appearing, whistling, or gesturing anywhere in public view. The net effect of the STEP Act was to designate a profile of young persons whose rights and prospects were statutorily different from others in their cohort and to transform any kind of youthful stepping out of line into major confrontations with the system. The STEP Act combined with the injunction enabled the LAPD to finesse the standards of "probable cause" or "reasonable suspicion" by "rendering suspicious anyone who looks like a gangbanger or has been fingered by an informant. If the frisk reveals little evidence, the officer still can write up a suspect as a "gang associate," despite the fact that there simply is "no such membership category in the gang world."[26] Moreover, "enhancements" were added to the already-established sentencing guidelines, which resulted in increased sentences and fines for alleged gang associates. In the event of any future encounters between those alleged associates and law enforcement, additional enhancements would be applied yet again.[27]

A TROUBLED CORNER

Like the INS campaigns at the border such as Operation Gate Keeper,[28] gang injunctions are exaggerated reenactments of practices and procedures already generalized over a much larger territory such as racial profiling of youth of color. The 18th Street Gang injunction took as its field of operation the architecture and geometry of the barrio of the Hoover Street Locos, one of five 18th Street cliques operating in the Rampart division, and the intersection of Pico and Alvarado was identified as a strategic site therein. Rampart's six-volume case file constructed Pico Union not as a "neglected area" ripe for redevelopment but as a violent topography in which a countervailing and illegal economy strangled legitimate local business. A three-part series in the Los Angeles Times on the 18th Street Gang, which was included as supporting documentation in the case file and which mirrored much of the testimony therein, devoted considerable attention to The Pico Fiesta mini-mall at the southeast corner of Pico and Alvarado—just one short block east of the Jack in the Box.

The architectural rendering of the mall, titled in bold "Troubled Corner," was introduced with the words: "Burned to the ground during the 1992 riots. Rebuilt, it now faces a more insidious danger: dope dealing orchestrated by the 18th Street gang." The article broke down the topography of this violence play by play in and around the three structures that comprise the mini-mall, as follows: (1) The Street: Gang members patrol Pico Boulevard to protect their drug-dealing partners; (2) King Taco: An armed guard, a veteran of the Nicaraguan National Guard, eyes illicit activity; (3) La Casita de Don Carlos: Gang members and dealers drink beer inside the restaurant, watching the activity and coming outside to make sales. The owner stands by helplessly; (4) El Pavo Bakery: Dealers line up in front of the bakery, selling to walk-up traffic; (5) The Fiesta Parking Lot: As a lookout watches for police, dealers loiter on the sidewalk and sell to customers who drive through the strip mall.[29]

The reader is left with a most vivid picture of the mini-mall as an occupied territory: a resistant space of significant strategic importance to the 18th Street Gang and, therefore, in the war for and against drugs. The gang has successfully superimposed its countervailing economy on the rebuilt mini-mall by using its architecture to tap into a consumer market quite distinct from that targeted in RLA's strategic plan. Here we have a clash between two competing ideologies of entrepreneurship and their respective niches in the market: dangerous and docile consuming publics. The signage on the built environment is testimony to this mixed economy of the neighborhood. Graffiti is visible on the wall behind the barbed wire fences and iron gates bearing "no trespassing" signs, and under and above the signage for the local businesses advertising their productos Latinos—carne, lengua, pupusas, and the like, defacing even the occasional cultural-heritage board signs in the neighborhoods. Once "consumed" by looters, this area rebuilt is now a thriving commercial zone for the street hoodlum.

Like the looter, the hoodlum was a mimetic improvisation of its normative counterpart, in this case the minority entrepreneur.[30] Both looting and drug dealing were the more visible and heightened aspects of a countervailing set of economic practices wherein certain "interested parties" engineered diversions to remove things from an enclaved zone to one where exchange is less confined and more profitable. This diversion of commodities from their prescribed and customary paths, and I include here the mix of economic practices commonly referred to as the informal or underground sector, always carries a risky and morally ambiguous aura.[31] These openly illegal exchanges are a parody of formal capitalist relations of exchange and the neoliberal logic of conspicuous consumption. They are also parodic of the quasi-legal economic coping practices of subaltern groups marginalized within capitalism by relations of production and consumption.

ENCLOSURE

The 18th Street Gang injunction equated gang-identified youth with organized crime, albeit at its lowest echelons, and their very presence in public as transgressive. As with the transgressive mobility of the brazen Latino looter described in the previous chapter, the injunction's criminalization of youth's most minute and banal movements brings to mind the relationship explored between mobility and freedom through comparisons drawn between European enclosures and African American mobility. In the seventeenth century, authorities attempted to control the movement of, according to Thomas Dumm, "master-less men" through the establishment of "poor laws to criminalize vagabondage—the state of being in transit." In the contemporary context of the United States, large segments of African American and Latino male populations are subject to this operation of enclosure through "internment" or incarceration.[32]

Injunctions draw upon the highly localized geopolitical knowledge of city officials and the intense scrutiny of the everyday practices of particular individuals. Indeed, a crucial phase in the development of an injunction is the identification of the dangerous individual, who he is, where he hangs out, how he is to be characterized, his gang affiliation, his moniker (or his nom de guerre), and how surveillance is to be exercised over him in an individual way. This analysis of the massive plurality of the gang, not unlike the techniques and procedures that Foucault discusses as the "principle of enclosure," attempts to break up collective dispositions and their distribution, circulation, and dangerous coagulation.[33]

The injunction's first and foremost principle is therefore to ensure that these gang members have no opportunity to combine.[34] In 1997 sixty such individuals were named within Pico Union's 18th Street injunction and were prevented from "combining" therein—although the effects were generalized to all neighborhood youth. Oddly enough, according to the spatial arrangements of the injunction, these gang members were theoretically not prohibited from "combining" outside their barrio. As Rebelde, a member of 18th Street's arch rival, said to me: "The injunction doesn't really matter anyway, because as soon as you cross over the border, say it's Normandie, then the injunction doesn't apply to you anymore, and the police in the next division don't know you, because their CRASH units only work with the gang in that neighborhood." In this respect, the injunction would seem to have worked quite differently from other well-known forms of spatial legislation such as the U.S.-Mexico border or South Africa under apartheid.[35] The injunction was not directed at the borders between territories, nor does it entail confinement to the barrio, and it did not focus on violence produced by trespass of another order—that is, gang members crossing over into rival neighborhoods.

Clearly, policing these boundaries was in full force for gang members or presumed gang members and youth of color as they traveled through the city and its surrounding neighborhoods. Moreover, the rival gang was hard at work policing the borders between the barrio and the territory of their rivals. However, the injunction itself was directed at the territory within and integrally tied to the geometry of the barrio as it was mapped out and produced by the gang structure itself. In so doing, the anti-loitering ordinances effectively struck at the heart of the gang, its raison d'être and modus operandi: hanging or "kicking it with [one's] homies in the barrio," an activity often referred to as el vacil. This term, derived from the verb vacilar, is the flipside of loitering, and both are integrally tied to the pedestrian quality of the barrio—the everyday use of its built environment.[36] Indeed, the barrio is one of the few spaces in the contemporary built environment of Los Angeles where pedestrianism exists outside the postmodern theme-park shopping malls of City Walk or the Third Street Promenade in Santa Monica, and in a city that is otherwise intimately associated with the "death of the street."[37]

Until recently, in urban theory Los Angeles has been taken as the extreme demonstration of the decline of public space and of the destruction of any truly democratic urban space.[38] The corner at Normandie and Eighth was, however, a vivid site for viewing what Mike Davis theorizes in his manifesto *Magical Urbanism* as "the redemptive power of *Latinidad* for the preservation and revitalization of public space."[39] The policing of the barrio was very much about the disciplining of new subjects for particular kinds of spatial orders. The gang was only one site (albeit the most publicly acknowledged and sanctioned) for punishment. But even those more palatable and overtly progressive social movements of street vendors and janitors have met with similarly heavy-handed police reactions to their attempts to take over and use public space. Given the centrality of the street to life in the barrio, it was nearly impossible not "to combine" under the terms of the injunction. If the gang member was to avoid incarceration for violation of the injunction, he had two options: to stay off the streets entirely or to leave the barrio. Anti-loitering laws on the streets of the barrio effectively placed the gang member under house arrest, at least within the boundaries of the neighborhood, or forced the gang member into exile by essentially evicting him from his barrio.[40]

Interestingly, the injunction rested on and derived its moral authority from a similar trinity of social forces as that employed by Rebuild Los Angeles: private enterprise, the state, and the community. The name of the case file was, after all, "The People vs. the 18th Street Gang," and the concept of community was built into the acronym CRASH: *Community Resources against Street Hoodlums*. As Deputy District Attorney Lisa Fox, author of the injunction, explained to me, the injunction was intended to "help the community take back their neighborhoods." Indeed, gang injunctions are generally framed within the tradition of community policing and are pitched as a strategy to engage community involvement with law enforcement and thus improve the quality of life in neighborhoods.[41]

The question thus arises once again: who was this "community," the purported agent in and benefactor of the restoration of this former social spatial harmony? By CRASH's own account, the Pico Union Neighborhood Watch, the only representative body of the community's concerns included in the case file, drew few people to its gatherings. Community residents, we are told, were fearful of retaliation by gang members. I don't want to disregard this fear, but the relative weight given to declarations submitted by police, government employees, security guards, and business owners, on the one hand, versus that given to community residents, on the other, is overwhelming. And the community residents included therein were, with one exception, property owners—a rare breed in Pico Union in the 1990s where the housing stock was given over almost exclusively to rental units. Absent from community testimony were the renters of those properties: street vendors, day laborers, janitors, maids, gardeners, and nannies and their "at-risk" children, be they actively or allegedly affiliated with gangs. The original acronym of CRASH was, in fact, TRASH (Total Resources against Street Hoodlums), but the ring of it did not sit well with the "community." The spatial-cultural discourses of the injunction thus rested on a similar social exclusion as that of RLA's redevelopment strategy: Pico Union's working-poor inner-city residents and their children.[42]

Inside the Jack in the Box

It's the summer of 2000, and I am eating lunch in the Jack in the Box at the intersection of Pico and Hoover. My lunch companions are Magdaleno, a long-time Chicano and civil rights activist, and Melly and Cristina, sister and wife respectively to Alex, the former leader of the Normandie clique of 18th Street's rival gang, La Mara Salvatrucha. It's my treat, but it's Melly and Cristina's choice. The fast-food veneer, indistinguishable from any other Jack in the Box on the outside and from the street level, reads quite differently on the inside. My companions and I order through a Plexiglas buffer, which shields the counter help and cash registers from its neighborhood clientele. All legitimate transactions—the exchange of money for food—are conveyed though drawers that can only open out to one side of that exchange at a time. The chance of the illicit use of bullets, knives, money, or drugs is thus carefully curtailed by the architecture of this Jack in the Box, which on the inside looks more like a high-security bank or prison. Inside the Jack in the Box, it would seem that development and policing have combined to control the spaces of consumption in this barrio and to order the act of consumption along acceptable paths of circulation in the face of that "pent-up" demand for, among other things, intoxicating goods.

My companions and I have just come from a hearing at the Los Angeles County Criminal Court in downtown Los Angeles. Sitting on yellow and red plastic stools, eating burgers and fries and drinking shakes, our conversation about the morning's convoluted legal arguments and the complex relationship between criminal and immigration law is repeatedly interrupted by Melly's and Cristina's cell phone chatter with boyfriends, homegirls, and homeboys: Where did I get my cool new red, sporty book bag with cell phone pocket? Where can Cristina get her nails done like Puppet, who just got out of "juvy" (juvenile hall) and is looking "hot"? When can we go to Universal Studio's City Walk, to see a movie and to be seen? Can Magdaleno, who is bound for El Salvador, take them to a swap meet in South Central Los Angeles to buy Dickies clothing, hair combs, and Three Flowers hair oil for their homeboys deported to El Salvador? Can I give them a ride for their Father's Day weekend plans to visit Cristina's child's father, who is in prison, and Alex, who is being held in an INS detention center? When Magdaleno asks to borrow the phone to check in about his next meeting, Cristina chides him to be quick, adding in a gleeful gloat over this latest acquisition, "No es público. Apúrate! Apúrate!" (It's not a public phone. Hurry! Hurry!). Their excited chatter about consumption, laced as it is with signs of incarceration and deportation, rubs against the backdrop of redevelopment and policing as they combine in the architecture inside the Jack in the Box.

Perhaps it is not all that surprising that RLA and the LAPD would converge at this corner and in this fast-food joint. I am not suggesting here that RLA's Vacant Lot strategy was written in direct consultation with the 18th Street Gang injunction, or vice versa. I would argue, however, that both were written in conversation with a broader set of assumptions ushered in by the same larger field of cultural and political transformations that have come to be called neoliberalism. The architecture of the Jack in the Box and the excited chatter of its young immigrant customers are a vivid manifestation on the ground of those transformations, framed as they are here by these "bifurcated technologies" of neoliberalism, redevelopment, and law enforcement.[43]

As with RLA, the 18th Street Gang injunction was also linked to larger networks and structures of national trends. Two law enforcement projects in particular come to mind: the Federal Weed and Seed program and Broken Windows, as popularized and indeed globalized by then chief of the New York Police Department, William Bratton (who would later become chief of the LAPD), and then mayor of New York Rudolph Guiliani in the redevelopment of Times Square. The federal initiative, the Weed and Seed Program, was set up to funnel urban renewal monies through the Justice Department. After the tour of Los Angeles by George Bush Sr. in the aftermath of the riots, the president responded to the "malign neglect" of the inner city by offering to extend the national pilot project to Los Angeles. Weed and Seed was a redevelopment model that rested on the premise that neighborhood weeds (that is, its criminal elements) must be eradicated before anything else, such as enterprise zones, can take seed. The City of Los Angeles actually rejected the Weed and Seed money offered to them by Bush.[44] The Broken Windows model, as it enabled gentrification and commercialization of whole neighborhoods and developments in Manhattan, was yet another model that tied urban revitalization to zero-tolerance policing strategies.[45] Crime prevention was, therefore, key to laying the conditions for stable economic development.

Certainly, with respect to crime prevention, RLA was a much more subtle agenda for redevelopment. After all, "security" was the last item to be included in the "investment packages" of RLA's Vacant Lots Revitalization Project. The Vacant Lot strategy was aimed at cleaning up the lots whose "deterioration," it was argued, "breeds illegal dumping and accumulation of trash and crime." Nonetheless, the conflation between enterprise zones and "weeding" was made explicit in an editorial in the Los Angeles Times that argued strongly that RLA's work to encourage greater investment could only succeed if the "federal government also . . . promot[ed] public safety by supporting urban police forces."[46] In both cases of redevelopment and policing there was no illusion that the market could govern by itself. As Patrick O'Malley writes, this was particularly true for "those sectors of the population not connected to the market, and certainly not where the demand for commodities rarely follows meekly down the paths convenient to government and good order."[47] The 18th Street Gang injunction put into effect in the neighborhood surrounding the Jack in the Box and the Pico Fiesta minimall is a case in point.

While RLA did acknowledge structural issues such as poverty and unemployment, the LAPD's zero-tolerance strategies acknowledged no such root causes, except a "moral deficit in the individual."[48] Nonetheless, RLA's entrepreneur, like the street hoodlum in CRASH, was an autonomous subject of responsibility utilizing his or her freedom. And the relation between the responsible individual and his or her self-governing community came to substitute for that between social citizens and their common society in both institutional agendas.[49] Redevelopment and law enforcement thus shared the governing strategies of advanced liberal societies as discussed by Nikolas Rose. This political rationality is, according to Rose, a form of government that shapes "the powers and wills of autonomous entities: enterprises, organizations, communities, professionals, individuals," and, I would add, alleged criminals.[50] Finally, it is no coincidence that both RLA and the LAPD derived their moral authority from the language of "community." Community, as a referent to an outside origin of power, conveniently transcends the ongoing political and contested nature of urban space over and within city neighborhoods.[51] Both RLA and the LAPD invoked the depoliticizing language of community to rebuild and retake the vacant lot on the corner of Pico and Alvarado.

CRIMINAL COP ——— **THREE**

SPATIAL JUSTICE

In late summer 1999, Officer Rafael Perez of the LAPD was arrested for cocaine possession. Perez made a deal for a lighter sentence in return for informing on what he described as "a cancer [of corruption]" in the Community Resources Against Street Hoodlums (CRASH) unit in the Rampart neighborhood. Its officers patrolled the rebuilt environment of Pico Union, and their declarations had been used to support the 18th Street Gang injunction, as described in chapter 2. Just as they did in the post-riot climate, during the Rampart crisis law enforcement officials once again invoked the language of "community" to restore order and to silence resistance and contradiction precisely at the level of "community." A *New York Times Magazine* article on Officer Perez, entitled "LAPD Confidential," claimed that "the predominantly Latino community of Rampart has been supportive of the L.A.P.D." That claim was bolstered by the concluding statement that "after the Perez disclosures, police supporters staged a well-attended pro-Rampart rally [in the community]; a protest rally scheduled for the following day never came off."[1] This broad brushstroke of generalized Latino support for Rampart did the LAPD's bidding by wiping out all resistant spaces inside the neighborhoods surrounding Rampart. Similarly, both redevelopment and law enforcement worked to suppress community protests over urban space in the post-riot climate. The problematic construction of "community" as an unconditional social unity and as a homogeneous unanimity shut down the available spaces of representation for alternative views.

In this chapter I counterpose the dialectical images of the criminal cop with the gang peace activist. Whereas the criminal cop is simultaneously the law and its transgression, the gang peace activist leverages his status as *veterano* (veteran) of the gang to recruit neighborhood youth for peaceful rather than violent endeavors. The gang peace activist, another figure obscured in the language of "community," offers a particularly compelling lens by which to repoliticize arguments over urban space. Whereas in the previous chapter I looked at the representations of the space of the barrio imposed by Rebuild Los Angeles and LAPD, in this chapter I turn to the spaces of representation in the barrio opened by immigrant rights advocates in general, and by Homies Unidos, in particular. The Los Angeles branch of Homies Unidos is a youth advocacy and violence prevention organization that focuses on Central American immigrant youth and Latino youth living in Pico Union and the surrounding areas.

Homies Unidos was actually founded in San Salvador in 1996 by members of the archrival groups the 18th Street Gang and La Mara Salvatrucha (MS), most of whom had been forcibly returned to El Salvador after serving sentences for criminal offenses.[2] The Los Angeles branch of Homies Unidos was founded two years later, in 1998. The point person for the local office, Alex Sanchez, had been a veteran leader of the Normandie Street clique of La Mara Salvatrucha. In this chapter, I shift away from the ethnographic setting of the previous chapter to a barrio in Koreatown, just west of Pico Union, and to another street corner, still within Rampart's jurisdiction.[3] The intersection at Normandie and Eighth was home (or barrio) to Alex Sanchez and the Normandie clique of La Mara Salvatrucha. While there had been a loose alliance between MS and 18th Street, they became archrivals in 1992. As the name connotes, MS was made up almost entirely of undocumented Salvadoran and other Central American immigrant youth.[4] However, by virtue of its geography, the gang was by 1998 a mixture of other Latinos, be they immigrant or born in Los Angeles, and even an occasional African American or Asian American. Even so, the gang remained closely identified with the history of Salvadoran mass migration to Los Angeles during the United States–funded Salvadoran civil war in the 1980s.

In the early days of its founding in Los Angeles, Homies Unidos held its organizational meetings in Los Comales, a Salvadoran *pupuseria* on the corner at Normandie and Eighth.[5] In the late 1990s, the architecture of this particular intersection—the restaurant, the parking lot behind it, the surrounding tenement apartments, and the arcade across the way—was heavily worked on and over by the three competing forces of Homies Unidos, the Rampart CRASH unit, and La Mara Salvatrucha.

The central device in chapter 2 was the destruction and redevelopment of the ruin. In this chapter, the figure of the street and the struggle to win the right to it and to take control of it, is at the heart of this chapter. In this light I consider how the organizing strategies of Homies Unidos, which relied heavily on the pedestrian quality of the barrio, ran against the grain of the spatial discourses of law enforcement and countered CRASH's techniques of representing and managing the inner city and its immigrant population. The refusal by Homies Unidos to relinquish the barrio and its streets as its space of representation was, in fact, an argument over space and for the equality of mobility through space—that is, a political project of spatial justice. This struggle to win back their neighborhoods from the gang and from law enforcement led to the arrest and detention of Alex Sanchez, two community protests outside the Rampart station, a political asylum trial, a hunger strike, and a lawsuit.

Alex Sanchez's case was not a Rampart case in the literal sense, as it was not one of the cases officially under review by the LAPD. But it was a case that unfolded in the Rampart division during the Rampart scandal, and it was certainly read as a Rampart case by Homies Unidos. In other words, Homies Unidos saw the harassment against its members as a continuation of the same misconduct under formal investigation, and proof that the police corruption was ongoing even during the scandal itself.

Our Place

In September 1999—right around the time of the "well-attended pro-Rampart rally" and the failed counter-rally mentioned in the *New York Times* as cited above—members of Homies Unidos and leaders in the Latino, Asian, and African American "community" in the Rampart division gathered in the basement of the Immanuel Presbyterian Church. The church, which was just a few blocks north of the Homies Unidos "office" at the corner of Normandie and Eighth, had become home to the group's weekly creative writing and poetry workshops. This week, in place of the poetry workshop, Homies Unidos was hosting a special panel convened by the California state senator Tom Hayden, chair of a special task force on preventing gang violence established by the president of the state senate. Hayden's "citizen panel" included lawyers and representatives from fifteen of the leading civil and immigrant rights groups in Los Angeles. Among those present were the Reverend James Lawson, Connie Rice, Angela Oh, and representatives from the Central American Resource Center, the Mexican American Bar Association, and the Coalition for Humane Immigrants Rights–Los Angeles.[6] The panel is of interest here on two levels: first, with respect to the kind of space of representation it opens up to those so-called dangerous classes;[7] and second, for its participants' alternative views of gang members: their transformative potential, how they get transformed, and the parties whom the panelists deem the proper and correct agents for their transformation.[8] To these panelists, Alex Sanchez, the gang peace activist, appeared as a positive counterweight and a legitimate alternative to Rafael Perez, the criminal cop.

Of course, this body was not necessarily any more representative of the Latino "community" than was the pro-Rampart rally, but it did represent a dissenting voice, the competing strategic discourse of the Left. All of the panelists were clearly vocal critics of "the hard side" of neoliberalism and its "punitive technologies."[9] Hayden opened the session explaining that the purpose of the panel was, as was the purpose of his committee, to "bring to light conditions and problems in the inner city . . . that might give rise to gang behavior and to give a voice to people who are invisible, who are voiceless . . . give a voice to people who are powerless." Senator Hayden had come to the meeting with an agenda gained through his experience with the Crips and Bloods gang peace process, a process that began before the Los Angeles riots in 1992 but gained strength in its aftermath.[10] Indeed Hayden is an interesting figure here because he is simultaneously a politician, an advocate for the gang peace process, one of the founders of the Students for a Democratic Society in the early 1960s, and prolific author of writings about—among other topics—street gangs.

Sanchez also had a history. He was deported to El Salvador in 1994 after serving a sentence in federal prison, but he returned to Los Angeles in 1996 without authorization in order to be "a father to his son" (as he put it).

Alexito (Little Alex) was born while his father was still in prison. Upon his return to Los Angeles, Alex started out as an informal courier delivering letters from his "homies" in El Salvador to their family and friends in Los Angeles, and as a counselor-cum-social worker visiting parents estranged from or worrying over their deported sons. This work brought him in contact with Magdaleno Rose-Ávila, who began to mentor Alex in the nonviolence training techniques he had learned through his work with César Chavez.

Hayden opened the proceedings by stating, "If nothing is done quickly to create space for individuals working for peace in Los Angeles, some of those individuals will surely be lost to us through incarceration, deportation, injury or death. It is with that gravity that this meeting has been called." Hayden was likely referring to the three Homies Unidos members who had already been killed after their deportation to El Salvador.

Before Alex's testimony that evening, he was introduced by Hayden's chief of staff, Rocky Rushing:

> We're in Mr. Sanchez's neighborhood right now . . . Last winter, Mr. Sanchez was in one of his neighborhood restaurants talking to some youngsters, passing out some leaflets and buttons, discussing primarily the benefits of peace when the discussion was interrupted by an LAPD officer . . . He ordered Alex outside, claiming that Alex matched the description of a rape suspect. Said it loud enough for everyone to hear . . . [Alex is then] taken to the Wilshire station, where he is interrogated for several hours. After the police realize they have no grounds to hold him, they offer him a ride home . . . They drive Alex around the neighborhood, giving the appearance that he's cooperating with police. After several hours they finally drop him off. The policeman yells loud enough for everyone to hear, "Thank you. If you have any information, you know where you can get hold of me." They've confiscated Alex's literature. They know full well that he works for a gang intervention organization. Despite that, he's been photographed, handcuffed, and had several encounters with law enforcement right up to, I believe, yesterday [Alex leans over to him], and even today.

I had first met Alex shortly after the incident in the neighborhood restaurant, and it was the topic of conversation between him, his homeboys, and Magdaleno Rose-Ávila. Magdaleno talked about the need to sit down with the police and get the credentials to be out in the streets doing this work, but also the difficulty involved convincing them that the "Homies" were "really down for the work." Certainly Alex's looks—his heavy weightlifter build, the mark of time in the prison yard; his arms tattooed with his MS affiliation, the prison guard tower, the laughing-clown smile now, cry later motif; and his still closely shaven head—together with his criminal record and illegal reentry were not reassuring.

Alex began his testimony with the history of Homies Unidos in El Salvador and how he became involved in organizing a branch in Los Angeles. Referring to the space where we were sitting, he explains:

> This is Homies Unidos' Arts Expand program. This is where we meet every Thursday at 7:00 to 9:30, and this is where we do our poetry, our arts, our theatrical works with the help of Arts Expand.
>
> This is our place, and as I was told, the police also know, and they were here today. I don't know if you saw them. I don't know if you had the chance to see Mr. Amezqua and Mr. Marquez today, two officers of the Rampart Division. Well, they don't really believe this is happening and I don't know why. But our mission is to continue our peace work as you've been hearing [from] the experiences of all of us today.

As I was to learn from the pastor of the Immanuel Presbyterian Church, Frank Alton, Amesqua and Marquez had actually come by earlier that day to ask the custodial staff if there might be a place they could hide to spy on the meetings of Homies Unidos.

Alex continued by stating:

> I have the experience of going through a lot of this harassment by the police officers. Currently, we have one of our youth that was one of the most active in the program incarcerated [for an alleged murder]. He was with us during the time that the incident [the murder of which he had been accused] took place. Now he's arrested . . .
>
> I guess our word is not of much value to the courts and not being reliable witnesses, so the youth is now in jail, and he was here [in a Homies Unidos poetry workshop] at the time [of the murder]. But this is something that has brought some attention out in the streets because they know that I'm testifying for the youth, that he was here that day and so is Héctor Piñeda [former president of Homies Unidos in El Salvador] that works with me in this program. They know that we're involved in the case, so they're coming around looking for us and really trying to get something on us.

Last time I got a ticket for jaywalking, and they also gave me a ticket for not notifying the DMV of my address change within ten days. Now, I don't know how petty you can get . . .

Alex had shown me the jaywalking ticket the week he got it. The officer had scrawled "Big Al, gangmember" in large letters on the ticket. As Alex continued his testimony to the panel, I was transported back to another meeting, three days earlier. It was in the home of José, or Sleepy, a fifteen-year-old member of Homies Unidos and the youth that Alex referred to who was being held for murder charges despite his alibi witnesses. The judge had just determined to try José as an adult; this being the year that state Representative Pete Wilson—friend to Propositions 187 and 184—had authored a new proposition to, among other things, try juveniles as adults and make juveniles subject to the death penalty. José had been picked up by the Rampart CRASH unit in his barrio—but his parents now lived in the rapidly Latinizing area of South Central Los Angeles. They had opened their home that evening to talk, and several other concerned parents were present: The mothers of two other program participants, Happy and Clever, along with Héctor and me. Héctor was a founding member of Homies Unidos in El Salvador. Although he had been a leader in MS in Los Angeles in the 1980s, he was never deported and so could return legally to Los Angeles.

That night, I was deeply moved by Sleepy's parents, who were still stunned by the terrible shock of this turn of events. Sleepy's father began the discussion by saying: "One never knows what's happening. We have got to wake up. They, what they want is to destroy our children. We have got to organize to stop what they are doing to our children. They are objects of brutality." Héctor, who had organized this meeting, interjected: "They put a ticket on me for nothing. It's just a method to keep us off the streets. They know we can't pay. We don't have good communication with our parents. We've got to wake up our parents so that they become aware of these abuses. We are jailed, deported unjustly. Mothers, what you have not suffered with your children!" As we continued around the room, Happy's mom, who herself was having difficulty with the police for street vending,[11] voiced her concerns. Rampart officers had entered her apartment without a warrant and taken photos of her nephew. Sometimes her daughter was coming home with three tickets a day; she had an appointment to appear before the judge the following week.

Clever's mom began to talk about nights in the barrio and a mother's fears for her children. Every night, she explained, she would go out onto the balcony of her five-story apartment building—the elegant and gracious urban architecture of the Los Angeles of the twenties now turned inner-city tenement building—and look up at the helicopter hovering above, looking down at her. "They must know my face by now, have a picture of me," she said, framing her face with her hands and cocking it to one side: "Whenever I am *balconeando* [out on the balcony], they're always there above me. They must have a close-up photograph of my face peering up into the sky with that worried look, wondering, always wondering: Who are they looking for? Where is my son? What terrible thing has happened or is about to happen?" These thoughts and images were at the forefront of my mind as I sat at Senator Hayden's panel, listening to the senator and Alex discuss the group's poetry reading. The event had to be delayed and shortened from two nights to one, because half of the participants had been ticketed and taken in by the police over the previous month. "Where did they go?" Hayden asks. "Juvenile hall and the county," Alex replies.

Again, my mind wandered back in time to the poetry reading held just two weeks earlier. That performance ended with a tribute to all the Homies who were not there. A dedication was also printed in the evening's program: "Homies we wish were here: José, Laura, La Laffy, Happy, Bitcho, Bandit, Sleepy, Clever, Funny. All the homies incarcerated." From his incarceration at the Youth Authority, Clever had sent in an entry for the poetry reading. Entitled "Not Even Worth a Dime," it spoke about doing "dead time" and offered a warning to all the Homies to be careful on the streets and to stay out of jail.

Pulling myself back once more to the proceedings in front of me: I watched as Hayden pointed to Arlene Alvarado, whose poetry was printed in the program booklet. Arlene, a woman of no more than twenty years of age, introduced herself to the senator as a coordinator for the girls program run by Homies Unidos. Hayden, pointing to the child she had in her arms, asked her wryly, "Is that the baby that the police stopped?" "Yes," responded Arlene. Hayden shook his head and commented with sarcastic wit, "He looks like a real troublemaker." Arlene then recounted the experiences she had with the police putting both her and her baby against the wall to conduct searches for no apparent reason. They had done this to her child three times she says; the first time he was only six months old. Last week, she relates, CRASH descended on the barrio. The streets were flooded with CRASH officers wearing helmets and black shirts and pants, going through the streets searching every car. "Who were they looking for?" Hayden asked. "They're looking for anybody they can get," she explains, and adds, "Tonight, when we came in they [Officer Amesqua et al.] were here, and they said they'd be waiting for all the Homies when we came out." "Is there an injunction in this neighborhood?" asks Hayden. "No." He presses further, "Is there a curfew?" Arlene replies: "Just for the minors." Alex takes back the microphone from Arlene to answer questions from Reverend Lawson, a nonviolence pioneer from the heyday of the civil rights movement: "So you think the police are out to get you?" Alex confirms: "Yes I would say so." "Are the police at war with you?" Lawson wants to know. Nodding his head again, Alex elaborates: "Yes, it's a question of who'll win the war, either my 'gang' or your 'gang.' I'm putting my life in danger as much as everyone else. I'm as much afraid of the police, of the CRASH division, as I am of other gangs."

Then Angela Oh speaks up. She calls attention to the stark reality that makes the programs of Homies Unidos illegal in principle and thus criminalized from the start, be they poetry readings or prayer inside the church. Probation prevents any youth who has graduated beyond the "at risk" category from any form of association with other known gang members. I won't repeat here the very loose criteria by which "gang membership" is defined; the point is laws targeting affiliated and alleged gang youth gut the right to freedom of association.

Oh is intent on emphasizing this matter to Alex. "Until you get clear with probation, you're in a position of violating. If they [the probation officers] are not aware of your program, you can't be in this church, even if you're just praying together." As I listen, I'm wondering to myself if holding this meeting here is an enormous oversight or intentional resistance on the part of Homies Unidos. I am shocked into recognition of how dangerous these benign meetings might turn out to be for some of these young people, and how risky the enterprise of peacemaking, of nonviolence, is in practice. In response to Oh, Alex states: "But they [the police] have the choice to do it [i.e., ticket them for violation of probation]," and Hayden backs him up by noting "It's discretionary, not mandatory."

Then Hayden invokes the big picture. "All this goes to the issue: How can you make this peace process legal? How can it be protected when by definition it includes people who are vulnerable of being picked up?" Oh nods in agreement, saying, "To be . . . be effective on the streets you have to have been in [the gangs, the criminal justice system]. Once you get in you've probably been tagged. Once you've been tagged, you've got to stay away or no association. So the very people who are in a position to do the peace work can't freely associate."

Hayden turns to Alex, "You've got a rap sheet?" "Yes," Alex replies, "I've done my time." "Have you sat down with them—the CRASH unit?" asks Hayden. "No. They don't believe; they don't want to believe in this work. They want to do it their way and their way is to lock everybody up." Alex may not have spoken to the police, but other people, including Hayden, have done so on his behalf in an effort to get him the immunity he needs to do his peace work in the streets.

In fact, the first time I heard about Alex was in El Salvador in November 1998, when I was with Hayden on an investigative delegation sponsored by the Los Angeles–based immigrant rights organization ASOSAL (Association of Salvadorans in Los Angeles). During our meeting with the U.S. ambassador to El Salvador, Hayden brought up Alex's case, and about the lack of political support for gang peace activists like Alex:

> The odd thing is, the anomaly is that if you're an informant with a lifelong criminal record and you turn informant, you can get a paper from the INS allowing you to stay in this country as an illegal person, but you can't get a piece of paper if you ask to be supervised as a peace activist. There's a political will issue here, and I think that the police attitude is a problem, but even if you get through it you're going to have to create a . . . mechanism that allows the police to stay back from this process so that they won't be held liable if something happens. That's the big legal argument.

The result of Hayden's efforts was a wild goose chase, with LAPD deferring to the INS, and the INS deferring back to LAPD. Meanwhile, Alex continued to be vulnerable on the streets.[12]

Back at the panel hearing, Alex's testimony ended with a question from the immigration attorney Alan Diamante: "Do you know of any members of Homies Unidos that were on probation and whether the probation officers reported them to the INS or police officers reported them to the INS?" Alex asks for clarification: "Directly from Homies? . . . No, we haven't had a case like that." The hearing continues, but Alex and the members of Homies Unidos leave to gather in the smaller adjoining room. I accompany the Homies as they leave—as do Rocky Rushing, Silvia Beltrán (Hayden's legislative assistant and community liaison), and Rana Haugen (the assistant director of the poetry-reading group Arts Expand)—because we are worried about the police presence inside and outside the building. The Homies, as they are collectively called and call themselves, are chattering with nervous energy, fearful yet excited. Many of them had been startled to walk into their normal meeting space to see it occupied by cameras and politicians and to discover that their weekly poetry workshop had turned into a very public political battlefield. They worried about this public exposure and the dangers of speaking up. Even though they had wanted to give their affidavits, they would have preferred to do so in a safer and more private space. The arts program director is indignant. She has worked so hard to build a safe house for these young people to come off the streets. "The youth weren't even warned," she protests.

Alex is clearly nervous but also full of bravado: "Let them come find me." He kind of likes that the police are asking for "Big Al," he says. He knows he is in the limelight and that there is no going back. He knows he is in danger, but the danger is intoxicating. It reminds him of his gangbanging days, the excitement of war, and the "us" versus "them," or so he claims. The immediate problem at hand, however, is how to get the Homies out of the building safely without being stopped by the police. Earlier that evening, the police had ordered one of the Homies to vacate the premises immediately, and warned another that more police would be waiting for him outside when he came out. We organized a convoy out to the cars, and gave rides home for everyone as a buffer between them and the police. It was all well and good, but we wouldn't be with them on the streets the next day.

After that evening, Alex was very much on edge. Things were coming down on all sides: in El Salvador, certain informal and intermittent gang truces between rival barrios were unraveling. In Los Angeles, Alex was stopped by CRASH officials, who threatened that he and Homies Unidos would be gone in six months. Alex was also nervous because of Sleepy's murder trial. There was a disturbing pattern of official intimidation, indeed of state-federal collaboration, that had not yet emerged in the press coverage of the Rampart scandal. It was a pattern that Alex knew all too well from his street-level experience. The numbers in reports released later were to corroborate his concerns: the LAPD had targeted ten thousand gang members for deportation, and the INS and Border Patrol agents maintained a regular presence in LAPD booking and charging-out facilities. As a result of this collaboration, even when the criminal charges against gangs and purported gang members were overturned, the INS still maintained a deportation hold on them. According to the Public Defender's office, this tactic had been employed by the LAPD to push many key hostile witnesses into and through the deportation pipeline, thereby hindering the efforts of defense attorneys in pending cases against immigrants, as well as the efforts of those seeking to prosecute rogue officers in the Rampart case itself. It was Alex's fear that the Rampart CRASH officers would use the process of deportation to eliminate him as a hostile witness in Sleepy's trial.

The Barrio as a Space of Representation

Why did the members of Homies Unidos and their work with immigrant Latino youth affiliated with gangs and those impacted by them meet with the same heavy-handed gang abatement strategies that targeted criminals and gang members? While there are many ways in which the behavior of the gang peace activist is not subject to the polite negotiation of civility, the relationship of Homies Unidos to the space of the street is a key here.[13] As I have shown in previous chapters, the topographical reform of the barrio focuses on the space of the street—be it to shut down that space or to preserve and expand it. Without recourse to a court injunction, CRASH employed very similar tactics at the corner of Normandie and Eighth, then the organizing ground for Homies Unidos. The injunction was de facto if not de jure in place. Moreover, CRASH appeared equally intent on identifying and targeting the leadership of Homies Unidos and breaking up the organization's collective dispositions and pedestrian practices as it was on those of La Mara Salvatrucha and the 18th Street Gang.

As indicated by the testimonials above of Homies Unidos's leaders and program participants, CRASH's microphysics of constraining everyday movement on the streets of the barrio had enormous implications for organization's work. Its "outreach" occurred on the streets, outside these buildings and on the sidewalks. We have seen that this mode of "community organizing" was criminalized as "jaywalking" by CRASH, and that members of Homies Unidos were coming home with sometimes multiple tickets a day for jaywalking, blocking the sidewalk, and improper association. As Alex explained, "If you don't pay [the jaywalking ticket], you eventually get a warrant, and then you go to jail, and then you get placed on probation, and then you wait for them to catch you and put you behind bars."

Furthermore, members of the organization's leadership were often frisked by police officers on their way to their weekly poetry workshop. In trying to preempt this harassment, the program director of Arts Expand decided to pick up the younger members outside their homes en route to the church hall. But even this strategy proved problematic. While waiting for her on the streets outside their apartments, program participants would once again be ticketed. Thus, alongside the poetry and games, meetings came to include strategizing about where the youth could wait without being subjected to police scrutiny. At one point, the police even stopped the Arts Expand staff and questioned their presence in the neighborhood, and I myself began to worry that my participant-observation would include such interrogations.

From start to finish, the work of Homies Unidos relied heavily on the pedestrian quality of the barrio. The group's strategy of organizing in the streets was actually a refusal to relinquish the barrio as their "space of representation." As such, Homies Unidos and the gang peace process ran up against the grain of acceptable social programs precisely because they failed to withdraw from the streets. This is an argument over spatial justice: the right to organize and to leverage their barrio as a "third space" that is neither that of the gang nor of the police, but instead is a "space bearing the possibility of new meanings, a space activated through social action and the social imagination." [14] Even once *calmado* (calm), no longer *activo* (active), gang peace activists refuse to shed those aspects of their identity that are not subject to polite negotiation: their relationship to the streets foremost. Thus, gang peace activists remain "dangerous" insofar as, in the words of Thomas Dumm, their "oppositional energy reanimates [the public space of] civil society." [15]

Criminal Cop

During the Rampart scandal, much was said about how the LAPD was perhaps "the biggest gang of all." [16] The material archive on how Rampart officers played at being gangsters and interiorized their enemy is a rich one. The testimony of Rafael Perez, criminal cop turned informant, speaks eloquently to the ways in which CRASH functioned as "both the law and its transgression." [17] From all accounts, Rampart's CRASH unit was an "especially tight-knit group" [18] — a veritable gang. The officers in CRASH embraced this gangster identity corporeally. The photograph on the cover of the issue of the *New York Times Magazine* cited above is case in point. Officer Rafael Perez—posing in his prison sweats with his tattoo exposed and his hair shaved close to his head—looked just like any other "gangster," at least according to the overly broad definition used to place alleged gang members on the CAL/GANG list.[19] Perez's tattoo exposed the insignia of his unit, his clique, his gang: namely, as Lou Cannon writes, "a skull with a cowboy hat and a poker hand of a pair of aces and pair of eights, the dead-man's hand that the frontier outlaw Wild Bill Hickok was holding when he was shot to death."[20] Neighborhood residents complained that CRASH officers would confront them, showing off their tattoos as if they were saying, "This is my gang. This is where I come from."[21] The CRASH officer used his tattoo to mimic the territorial identification and barrio mentality of the gang member to mark his territory, Rampart, and to signify his gang affiliation, CRASH.[22]

The dialectical image of the criminal cop goes well beyond these expressive forms. According to Perez's testimony, he and his cohorts — homeboys, if you will — organized and took part in bank robberies, drug dealing, and prostitution rings for officers. They wounded and killed unarmed gang members, and planted guns and drugs on their victims. They appropriated gang members' pagers, answered incoming calls, took drug deals in the name of gang members, and resold drugs they had repossessed from those very same gang members. Indeed, the Rampart scandal first broke when Perez was caught with cocaine; he was checking out repossessed cocaine ostensibly as exhibit items for pending trials, but then he failed to return it because he was dealing in the stuff. These CRASH officers literally took on the drug trade in the Rampart division through a "hostile takeover" of their competitors' market share. The Rampart scandal hinged on the degree to which Officer Perez's and his cohorts' ganglike practices were structurally embedded within the police department and to what extent they constituted institutionalized practices and strategies for the "pacification of the dangerous classes."[23]

We see this structural logic at work in Perez's tearful public confession. In referring to the slogan over the door of the Rampart CRASH office, "We will intimidate those who intimidate others," criminal cop Perez offered these words: "Whoever chases monsters should see to it that in the process he does not become a monster himself."[24] Perez's confession rested on the idea that police violence is mimetic and therefore derivative of the gang; that is, the ur-source of violence is not the state but the gang. But the Rampart scandal undid dichotomies of good and evil and of heroes and villains, and it demonstrated instead the reciprocal nature of gang and police violence.[25] It is far from easy to say who was the imitator and who the imitated, which was the copy and which the original.[26] Indeed, some argue that the scandal was not about "cops who became criminals," but rather about "criminals who became cops."[27] A year before the Rampart scandal broke, an investigation into the murder of one cop by another had uncovered evidence that police officers were operating within the Los Angeles Police Department both as members of the Bloods gang and as security for the gangsta-rap kingpin Suge Knight, president of Death Row Records. These officers were charged in the unsolved murder of one of rap music's biggest stars, Biggie Smalls. The investigation was subsequently delayed, diverted, and finally shut down, and the proceedings of a related wrongful-death suit were suspended and called a mistrial. Nonetheless, the case file documents one bizarre incident after another in which, simultaneously public and secret, Rampart CRASH was often both the law and its transgression.[28]

Gang Peace Activist

Not unlike CRASH, Homies Unidos in Los Angeles was also, albeit differently, beholden to the structure of the gang. As a veteran of the gang La Mara Salvatrucha, Alex Sanchez occupied a position of respect and authority within his clique and within the gang at large. In this position he recruited, trained, and led a group of "soldiers" to protect the territory of the Normandie clique. It was this status as veteran that afforded him the authority to lead and to direct Homies Unidos and that enabled him to be an effective recruiter of younger members — this time for a gang violence prevention program rather than for the gang itself.

One day, I met Alex in the parking lot behind Los Comales. Silvia had pulled up with a trunk load of donated men's clothing, used but very elegant. She was planning to take the clothes with her to El Salvador for the Homies there, but she thought she'd let the Homies here look them over first. Although Alex was in the process of fixing his car, he stopped to try to convince his buddy Laughie into taking one of the tailored jackets to wear for public presentations. Laughie, however, was unenthusiastic. He always sported the baggiest of pants held up with rope and finished off below with white sneakers and laces tied into enormous bows. Silvia left, and as I waited for Alex to confer with the neighborhood mechanic, a Salvadoran with bloodshot eyes called Werewolf, one of the Homies pointed to the tenement apartments above that looked abandoned — at least from this angle. He started reminiscing about the days when MS "soldiers" had occupied the basement of that building. They would pay the landlord as they could with the things that they stole. One month they paid their rent entirely in Tupperware. He laughed at the absurdity.

This very terrain or turf in which Alex was an *activo*, an active gangbanger, was precisely the same geography of action where he now worked as a gang peace activist. Similarly, the participants in Homies Unidos programs were "homeboys" and "homegirls" to one another, thus mimicking the territorial basis for gang identification. In fact, because Homies Unidos had been, in its early days, based in the neighborhood and organized around the highly localized geography of a particular barrio, it was rare to see youth or veterans from other gangs at their meetings.[29] For such outsiders to "hang" or "kick it" with its leadership at the corner of Normandie and Eighth would be even less feasible. Linked as it was to the space of the barrio, the organization provided a place of deeply affective and emotional (familylike) relationships, where young people came to feel a sense of family belonging not unlike that which they derived from their actual gangs.[30] The organization was a bit like a halfway house (without the physical facilities) for "recovering gang members," who could "fall off the wagon" or "become lost in action" at any time. While they may have strived valiantly to give up *la vida loca*, it lived on all around them in the underground social and political economy of the barrio and beyond *and* in the productive apparatus of the police and the criminal justice system through injunctions, gang lists, petty violations, and the like.

Then there was desire. Take, for example, a fourteen-year-old participant in the arts program of Homies Unidos. Not long after attending a youth violence prevention conference, he was picked up for possession of a firearm, "packing a weapon." Upon hearing of his arrest, I found myself slipping into a "discourse of sobriety,"[31] expressing my dismay to a program volunteer at the contradictory scripts at work in this case—war and peace. She came back with this: "It's the excitement of being out there on the streets." She said it almost as if it were understandable child's play, and indeed, children do play at being "soldiers"—in this case "soldiers" for La Mara Salvatrucha. This young woman, who was a mentor to these youth and who had herself grown up close to these streets, reminded me, "You have to be patient. It's a very slow process with lots of steps backwards." Pastor Alton of the Wilshire Presbyterian Church put it best when he explained that "Alex's work, like any transformational or restitutive approach, is just slower. It just is. It's a lot faster to put them away."

The transformational, or restitutive, strategies of Homies Unidos in organizing gang youth and youth at risk into a program for nonviolence was based precisely on its ability to mirror the gang—its hierarchy, structures of solidarity, and the architecture of its barrio. Consider the fact that the working definition of "gang member" by law enforcement was already overly broad, and add to this Homies Unidos's manipulation of the gang's spatial practices to perform its own work. Police patrolling the area could well have misrecognized this repetition with a difference as mere repetition.

The war and peace efforts of Rampart and Homies Unidos respectively both required mimetic improvisations of their object of transformation. In both cases, these doublings, be they police with gang member, or peacemaker with gang member, constituted highly unstable unions. Perez and his cohorts, gangster cops, spoke eloquently to this instability. So too did the members of Homies Unidos. And the desires and intentions of both Homies Unidos and Rampart converged on the same object: La Mara Salvatrucha and its recruiting ground.[32] But while both forces might have wanted the same object, one wanted the gang member in order to lock him or her up, and the other wanted the gang member in order to calm him or her down. Herein lies perhaps the more serious point of contention between Rampart's CRASH and Homies Unidos: namely, their strategies for the "pacification" of immigrant gang and at-risk youth, transformational and restitutive versus belligerent and punitive.

Pacification through incarceration and deportation, based as it was in right-wing criminology, did not allow space for the transformative potential of gang youth. In contrast, for the gangbanger transforming or transformed into peace activist, pacification was invariably expressed by the adjective *calmado*, derived from the verb *calmar*, to calm down or to become calm or peaceful. Whereas civility is the outcome of normalization, or as Patrick O'Malley puts it, the " 'correction' of the individual in the direction of a standard social form,"[33] the peaceful state, calmado, is not the normalization or pacification of the "dangerous classes" in a straightforward sense. Through the peace process, activos were to become calmados, but in the transformation from active gang members to peace activists, their oppositional energies were not to be pacified but rather redirected.[34]

Homies Unidos did not ask youth to renounce their gang membership in order to participate in its programs. The intent was to convince them to renounce violence through participation in the organization's programs. Indeed, the retention of "gang culture" was highly visible and audible in the aesthetics, style, language, and gestures of both the leadership and participants of Homies Unidos, who sported the full costume of shaved heads, baggy pants, tattoos, cell phones, beepers, and palm combs. The task, said Magdaleno Rose-Ávila, was "to transform the gang culture from within . . . to use those networks of solidarity to change the gang mentality from violence to an understanding of human rights and human potential." As Alex wrote in a statement delivered by his brother Oscar, "We are all 'soldiers' fighting for peace in the streets." There it is again, the wedding of the structure of solidarity of gang to that of a nongovernmental organization with a mission to build a social movement for nonviolence and human rights. "Consciousness-raising" (concientización) was, not surprisingly, a key trope in Homies Unidos's violence prevention and intervention project. It was also the means by which these "dangerous classes" were to come to "recognize themselves under disciplinary regimes" [35] — that is, as a class in and for itself. The political philosophy of nonviolence, therefore, was not just directed at gang members and youth at risk but extended to the police and to society at large. In this sense, the gang peace activist strove to redirect the energies of the gang into a social movement for change. [36]

The Deportation Pipeline

Perhaps it is not all that surprising that three and a half months after Alex Sanchez testified before the hearing convened by State Senator Hayden, he was banished from the streets after being arrested on an immigration warrant by two Rampart CRASH officers outside the arcade at Normandie and Eighth. Alex was taken to Rampart headquarters for processing. According to Alex, the arresting officers told him that he, Alex, could take "Homies Unidos and shove it . . . and start it in El Salvador" if he wanted." "So I knew then," he continued, "that they had gone beyond their investigative work and were actually now dealing with immigration. They knew they could get rid of me through immigration. I asked them, 'I don't owe anybody anything.' They said, 'Immigration you do.'" Alex was then handed over to INS, who placed him in the San Pedro detention facility on Terminal Island where he was held for eight months. Immediately after Alex's arrest, Homies Unidos launched their Campaign to Free Alex Sanchez, and not long after there was a community protest outside Rampart. [37]

At the protest on the steps of Rampart headquarters a crowd gathered to demand Alex Sanchez's immediate release, and to file community complaints against the police for their violation of their own Special Order 40, a department policy that ostensibly prohibits police officers from making arrests on immigration charges. Senator Tom Hayden was at the helm of this gathering too. In the background was Oscar, Alex's younger brother, holding a bigger-than-life-sized poster of Alex. Oscar, who lived in a single apartment in the Rampart division, was an art student at Cal State Los Angeles. He worked for Tree People, a nonprofit organization dedicated to the reforestation of the city. The first time I met Oscar, at a Homies Unidos Christmas party, I didn't make the connection between Oscar and Alex until he made it for me. I admit to being thrown completely off course by Oscar's dreadlocks and rainbow reggae knit cap. The contrast with Alex's tough gangster look could not have been more pronounced. Standing there in the rain some three months later, holding the cardboard cutout of his brother in his arms, Oscar's look is as soft as his brother's is tough.

Oscar stepped up to the microphone. We were in the midst of the events surrounding the deportation of the young Cuban boy Elián, and Oscar astutely draws the parallel.[38] Alex, who changed his life around after his son was born and reentered Los Angeles illegally to be reunited with him, is now being painfully and irrevocably separated from his American-born child. Oscar had just come back from Washington where he and a delegation had hoped to meet with head of INS, Doris Meissner. Meissner had explained that she was terribly sorry that she couldn't sit in on the meeting because she was overwhelmed with the Elián case, and her deputy would have to stand in for her.

Another figure at the protest was Maria, a resident of one of the apartment buildings of faded 1920s elegance not far from the corner at Normandie and Eighth. Maria, a militant Salvadoran poet from the civil war era, was active in the Bus Riders Union in Los Angeles.[39] It was something to see this icon of Salvadoran revolutionary politics chanting "¡Libertad Alex Sanchez! ¡Libertad Alex Sanchez!" These kinds of slogans always disoriented me by throwing me back to the early 1980s, the period that originally made refugees of Alex and his family.

After Oscar speaks, Angela Sambrano, executive director of the Central American Refugee Center (CARECEN), took the microphone to protest the illegal use of an INS warrant by CRASH to pick up Alex Sanchez and the effect of the collaboration between the INS and LAPD on "the Latino community" at large. "The community," she argued, "will not report crimes to police because they will be afraid of the immigration consequences." This was also an ongoing lament within the undocumented immigrant community, but the last time it received any significant airing was during the riots. In the past, immigrant rights advocates had argued from the perspective of victim's rights. How could undocumented immigrants, victims, or witnesses of crime approach the police for protection or to assist in investigations if they feared being turned over to INS? Indeed, the Rampart scandal drew attention to an insidious intersection between the LAPD and the INS in the barrio.

Specifically, the scandal led to an internal probe of allegations that INS agents from the agency's Organized Crime Drug Enforcement Task Force "had helped anti-gang officers in the LAPD Rampart Division have more than 160 immigrants deported and 40 others prosecuted for illegal reentry into the United States." That same investigation noted that "incriminating allegations reported by Rampart anti-gang officers were included in immigration files."[40] But with the immigration act from 1996, this collusion now went well beyond Special Order 40 and the spatial practices of the LAPD. The immigration consequences of criminal law were now formalized at the federal level. In addressing this issue Sambrano brought together the real crux of the matter—the ways in which the LAPD and INS collude to silence the community—something not accounted for in the depiction of the "Latino community" in the article in the *New York Times Magazine*.

After the press conference ended, Hayden led the crowd into the police station. They repeated after him, "We are here nonviolently to exercise our legal rights to file a complaint against Officer Amesqua and Rampart CRASH." As the people wait in line, filling out their complaints forms, an African American began to chant in hip-hop rhythm: "Listen what the people say, Free Alex Sanchez, Free Alex Sanchez; Listen what the people say, Free Alex Sanchez."

Over the next year or so, the efforts by Homies Unidos in Los Angeles shifted to freeing Alex Sanchez and winning political asylum for him. Alan Diamante, the immigration lawyer present at the senate hearing, took on Alex's case. Together, Homies Unidos in Los Angeles and in El Salvador along with their supporters mounted a very effective campaign both in the media and in the courts. But with his prior felonies, Alex would not qualify for political asylum. The only alternative, Withholding from Deportation—a provision under the Convention against Torture—required a much higher standard of proof. So while Diamante prepared his case for withholding, the criminal attorney Mark Geragos worked on vacating Alex's prior felonies.

Although the judge agreed to reduce the felony charge for his illegal reentry in 1996 to a misdemeanor, Alex still had another felony from his prior criminal record. While Geragos worked on that matter, Homies Unidos pulled together for the immigration case an enormous amount of supporting documentation on conditions in El Salvador, as well as a distinguished cast of expert witnesses, some of whom flew in from El Salvador. These included Mirna Perla, a Salvadoran judge, Eduardo Linares, the chief of the San Salvador Metropolitan Police, and a former police officer from the Salvadoran National Civil Police. The Los Angeles–based witnesses included Senator Tom Hayden, Magdaleno Rose-Ávila, Gilbert Sanchez of the LA Bridges Project, Silvia Beltrán, a former aide to Hayden and later director of Homies Unidos, the photojournalist Donna Decesare, and three anthropologists: Susan Phillips, Rosemary Ashamala, and me.

The immigration case was mounted on two fronts. Alex Sanchez had a well-founded fear of persecution upon return to El Salvador. On the one hand, as a gang peace activist Alex would face opposition from the police, the gangs, and death squads. Moreover, the Salvadoran state was incapable of or unwilling to protect him. Four members of Homies Unidos in El Salvador had been killed in the past two years, and there was ample documentation in the Salvadoran press to suggest that deportation was effectively a death sentence for gang members or those mistaken for gang members.[41] Thus Alex would be unsafe both on the basis of his political opinion (his work as a gang peace activist) and as a member of a "recognizable social group" (a gang).

In the meantime, Alex languished in the San Pedro detention center for eight months. Even while suffering from acute depression, he managed to mount a hunger strike during the Democratic National Convention to protest the poor conditions inside the facility. After considerable outside pressure, he was released halfway through his immigration trial. A year later, the judge ruled on his case. On the same day of the ruling, Diamante was successful in clearing Alex's last felony. As a result, he was finally now able to file a claim for political asylum. The judge ruled favorably, granting Alex political asylum in the United States. The ruling was unprecedented; it was the first case in which a gang member had been granted asylum. But it would be, at least up until the writing of this book, the only such case. And its success was only partial. The judge ruled on the "political opinion" argument but not on that of the "social group."

As Diamante put it in a conversation with me after the event:

I knew all along that the social group argument would be a hard pill for the court to swallow, because that would open up the flood gates to gang members. But nevertheless, I invested so much energy into it because that was the most important issue. I truly believe that was the strongest argument. But the judge ruled on the political opinion [argument] because it was an easy way . . . without touching the other issue. And in her opinion, she specifically said that she would not touch the other issue. She granted him asylum based on future persecution, based on political opinion. [She said that] it was likely that if Alex was to continue his activism in El Salvador that he would be persecuted like similarly situated members of Homies Unidos. It was a clear that he had a reasonable fear of future persecution.

We stressed his role as a political activist against police corruption. [Police] impunity—was a thread through our case . . . We had a judge testify to that effect and had clear documentation of human rights violations by police and of judicial abuse by days of the month for the last couple of the years. That report also referred to death squad activities, gang members murdered in extra-judicial style killings with hands tied behind their backs.

Alex's case would not set a precedent on any formal level, not even for the political opinion argument, because it did not have to be appealed. And it certainly offered no precedent for gang members in general. On that ground, the immigration consequences of criminal law remained unchallenged. What it did achieve was Alex's right to stay in this country, and to be a father to his son. Yet even this victory was hedged. While the case brought some critical attention to the issue, it did not stop the build up of zero-tolerance strategies in Los Angeles or prevent their adoption in countries like El Salvador.[42] Neither did it give Alex immunity on the streets. For that, Homies Unidos had to file a lawsuit.

On June 2, 2000, while Alex was still in detention, Homies Unidos filed a federal civil rights lawsuit against the city of Los Angeles, LAPD Chief Bernard C. Parks, and two Rampart officers, Mario Marquez and Jesus Amezcua. The lawsuit charged that the civil rights of Homies Unidos and those of its members were violated by Rampart officers. Their complaint alleged that the LAPD engaged in the systematic practice of harassing members of the organization in violation of the plaintiff's First Amendment right to association and Fourth Amendment protection from excessive force, false arrest, and detention. In short, Homies Unidos was seeking a "mirror image" of the gang injunction. "We want the police to stop acting like gangs," said the lead attorney Paul Hoffman. "It's as if it's Los Angeles' dirty little secret that we treat certain people as if they're outside the Constitution." As Magdaleno Rose-Ávila put it, "You can call a Doberman pinscher a Chihuahua, but it's still a Doberman."[43] This lawsuit sought spatial justice for Homies Unidos.

Beyond the Street Corner

While the case was eventually settled out of court, the truth is that Homies Unidos never really went back to the streets. While Alex was in detention, Homies Unidos took its office and its operations off the streets and away from the corner of Normandie and Eighth. The organization moved into the La Curacao building—the twin towers to Central American commercial, legal, and civic life in Los Angeles—located in the Pico Union district, the symbolic center of Central American Los Angeles and 18th Street Gang territory. This move out of and up from the street level was in part about Homies Unidos formalizing its operations as a community organization (and to have a base from which to fight Alex's case), but it was also intended to give the organization a breathing space off the streets and away from the police.

Despite the challenge made by Homies Unidos, the harassment had worked. As Alex explained of the period leading up to his arrest, "They [the police] harassed the guys coming over to the program, more than those hanging out over on the street, [and I was] harassed to the point that everywhere I went to speak I would tell people that, 'Look, I'm worried I'm going to get arrested.' I felt it, but there was nothing I could do about it." "And I even told *you*," he said to me as I nodded thinking back to the period just before his arrest. "I had all these kids that I was responsible for now, that were in some ways blaming *me* for the trouble they were in. Some of them didn't want to come into the program anymore."

By the time Alex was awarded political asylum, his work at Normandie and Eighth had all but dissipated. And while Alex was still waiting for his immigration papers, he was effectively banished from the streets. On one level, it appeared that Rampart had succeeded in undermining the spatial practices central to the organizing strategy of Homies Unidos, thereby subverting the role of the street in the public life of the barrio.

In Alex's absence, Silvia Beltrán, former aide to Senator Tom Hayden and a Salvadoran immigrant herself, had taken over the position of director. Alex diverted his efforts from the streets to working with kids and their parents in neighborhood schools. This was no small feat for an ex–gang member to be invited back into the system that had failed him. And so one could also say that Homies Unidos no longer needed the space of the street because it had succeeded in challenging a major institution to open up space for it. There the group focuses on violence prevention and parenting classes. While the organization's transformational strategies had arguably been pacified by the inclusion of the neoliberal philosophy of individual responsibility in its training models, Homies Unidos continued to protest zero-tolerance police strategies and deportations and to raise awareness of conditions in Central America. Nonetheless, in the case of Alex Sanchez, the combined forces of LAPD and INS, and of criminal and immigration law, had at least for the time being limited the organization's challenge to the spatial politics of neo-liberal security.

This was my understanding of the situation, but Alex Sanchez argued otherwise when I showed him the original conclusion to this chapter: "We were not defeated. We won almost everything that we wanted. Formalizing our agency. Keeping me here with my son. We managed to settle our lawsuit against LAPD and continue serving our community." So although it is true that they were no longer based at the corner of Normandie and Eighth, as Alex explained, "It was about Koreatown. It was about Pico Union. It was about the Westlake area. It was about all these other gangs that needed our services." So their stage was now much larger, their notion of community and neighborhood much broader. "Once I saw all those people from different neighborhoods, gangs, and organizations protesting outside that Rampart station, I realized then that it wasn't just about Eighth and Normandie. It was a much bigger issue." Alex argued forcefully that if it hadn't been for Homies Unidos's fight to protect the space in Immanuel Presbyterian Church for the youth and for the Arts Expand Program that the collaboration between Rampart and INS might never have been brought into the Rampart investigation.[44] So without Alex's case, Rampart might never have become an issue of concern to immigrant rights agencies. Even though Rampart officers were not technically in violation of Special Order 40 in arresting Alex, his arrest "ultimately opened up [that] can of worms."

The "Free Alex Sanchez" campaign and the lawsuit against LAPD, therefore, added to the impact of the Rampart scandal. Alex mused further, "Did it stop the attitude of law enforcement? It made them more careful, more cautious. They couldn't mess with our program any more . . . they couldn't get away with what they were getting away with before." In the end, Homies Unidos had successfully opened up a space of representation much larger than one street corner.

PART II | SAN SALVADOR

Each week, up to three U.S. Marshal aircraft fly into El Salvador's national airport bearing planeloads of handcuffed deportees. Anywhere from two hundred to six hundred Salvadorans are forcefully repatriated in this manner each month, and among them gang members who have completed their time in prisons in the United States.[1]

Speaking from San Salvador, Weasel, a deportee from Los Angeles, explains his situation this way:

> I've got this document right here. It says my full name and it has a little box right here that's checked and it says deportable under section blah blah blah. Removed from the States. Anyways, the bottom line is that I've been banished from the United States, you know, like they used to do in the medieval days, they used to banish "fools" from the kingdom . . . people who did something that was considered a threat to the crown

(in my case society). Anyway, that's how I felt. They kicked me out of society [the United States] and sent me into the jungle [El Salvador] to live alone in my own solitude.[2]

But Weasel is far from alone. He is surrounded by "fools," "homeboys" from "Elay" also "banished from the kingdom." Indeed, El Salvador is now host to a new social formation built on this puzzling relationship between space and identity. Deported Salvadoran immigrant gang youth—banished from the United States after spending the better part of their young lives in this country—are returned "home" to a place to which, in their memory, they have never been. As Bulldog exclaimed five days after his rude return to El Salvador: "Shit, homes, I've never been here. I mean, I know I'm from here, homes, but I've never been here." And then with disbelief, "You from here too?"

Weasel, who left El Salvador for Los Angeles when he was five years old, continues thus: "Ey, you know [a little laugh] . . . I went to kindergarten in Elay, elementary school, junior high school, high school. Man, I grew up singing—you know—my country 'tis of thee [he laughs again] . . . the song 'America the Beautiful' . . . and—you know—pledging allegiance to the flag. Well, I grew up with all of that . . . and here they are, you know, twenty-something years later, kicking me out." When these Salvadoran immigrant gang youth deported from the United States run into each other in the busy, congested streets of El Salvador's capital, San Salvador, or in the cobbled streets of its dusty pueblos, the first thing they ask one another is, "Where you from, homes?" This is a multiply determined question about origin, geography, affiliation, and identity, which takes this much in common—the territory of the Latino barrio in the United States.

This chapter, the first of part 2, crosses three international borders to El Salvador; to the landscape from which Alex Sanchez had fled, first as war refugee and then as a criminal deportee. This is precisely the geography that I argued in chapter 1 was obscured and yet coproduced by the anti-immigrant politics expressed in the downsized worker D-Fens. His critique of Los Angeles's crumbling and hyperviolent urban geography failed to account for the impact that both the foreign and domestic policy of the United States have had in changing the face of Los Angeles. Similarly, the landscape that comes into view in this chapter is also an effect of the cold war, played out as it was through the United States–funded Salvadoran civil war and the war on crime as it impacted Latino immigrants in the United States.

This transnational space is produced through the collusion of U.S. criminal and immigration law and is made visible through the figure of the criminal deportee and the reappearance of La Mara Salvatrucha and the 18th Street Gang in El Salvador. Transnational formations such as La Mara Salvatrucha and the 18th Street Gang are a somewhat ironic result of nativism and its work to criminalize immigrants. Indeed, in the case of deported Salvadoran immigrant youth, it is on the streets of the urban barrio that the United States is most effectively policing the boundaries of the nation-state. The local police beat in cities like Los Angeles has thus become both a staging ground for managing the pressures of globalization and for producing the "transnational gang crisis."

As the journalist Peter Boyer explained, "The [Rampart] investigation was a messy process, because it had no precedent. [Rampart CRASH officer] Perez [the key defendant and informant in the case] would tell the task force about a bad case, and the detectives would fan out to . . . village[s] in Central America" in search of wrongfully deported immigrants.[3] While Rampart was described as LAPD's worst scandal in sixty years, I would argue that Rampart was an unprecedented scandal largely because of its transnational dimensions. While Rampart police officers patrolled a very limited and highly localized beat, their actions on the streets of Los Angeles's urban neighborhoods had a transnational reach.

In part 1 of this book, I focused on the immigrant barrios in Los Angeles, where many of these deported youth are "from," and I tracked the spatial politics behind the expulsion of "fools" like Weasel "from the kingdom." Yet as the emergent subjectivities of these transnational protagonists suggest, any such study must be able to traverse local, national, and global scales and to track flows—material, discursive, and affective—between the immigrant barrios of Los Angeles and barrios populares (working-class neighborhoods) of San Salvador. Certainly, the inner-city barrio in Los Angeles is a complex articulation of local forces. As I discussed in the previous three chapters, it is a space acted on by the contradictory pressures of media coverage, urban redevelopment, and law enforcement agencies and social justice organizations, as well as by the enabling and disabling everyday practices of residents themselves.[4] But there is still more at stake. There is the spatial politics of forced repatriation on the other side, in Central America. Indeed, the barrios in Los Angeles are haunted with voices from and banished to El Salvador.

Youth deported from Los Angeles walking the streets of San Salvador calling themselves "homies" are the shock effects of globalization as it clashes with nationalism. They are the embodiment of what I term forced transnationality. While the literal mobility of these deported youth may have been arrested, contained, and reversed by the forces of nationalism, their narratives—which leak beyond the bounds of the nation-state—tell us volumes about the complex relationship between space and identity. They reveal a painful rupture between culture and nation, where cultural identity does not correspond to but rather is excluded from national citizenship. It is to those narratives that I now turn to examine the ways in which the geographies of violence, belonging, and exclusion, in the immigrant barrios of Los Angeles have been relocated and reinscribed within the post–civil war landscape of San Salvador's *barrios populares* or *marginales*.[5]

Gato's Story

I met Gato in Modelo, a *barrio popular* in San Salvador and territory to a *clika* (clique) of the gang La Mara Salvatrucha (MS). In Los Angeles, Gato was a veteran of the MS archrival the 18th Street Gang. We began our conversation in English sitting outside his home, a modest concrete apartment attached to a small liquor and convenience store run by his mother. Gato was fully conversant in both Spanish and English. However, as is clear from the transcription below, he was not a native speaker of English. His speech—a mixture of street English, the Spanglish of Chicano gangs, and the caliche of Salvadoran colloquial Spanish—still marked him as Salvadoran and as immigrant to the United States.[6]

Gato is originally from Modelo. I am confused and curious about how he navigates living inside enemy territory and with the enemy. He begins to explain:

G: First they told me, "Don't write on the walls." You know, write 18th Street . . . And I told them, "I won't do that."

E: So you came to an agreement with them?

G: Yeah, we came to an agreement. I told them, "If you guys don't bother me, I'm not going to bother you guys." But, if they do . . . planning to do something, do it good. You know, kill me.

E: So nothing's happened?

G: No, that's because I don't . . . I'm working. I have my life together. If they know I'm still gangbanging, of course, they could kill me man, you know.

E: But this is your barrio, where you're from?

G: All these guys, they were my friends when I was a little kid, and they get mad because [they say], "Why don't you be jumping in an MS neighborhood?" You know, I told 'em, "Hey, when I went to California I grew up at Sixth and Junior." That was PBY [Play Boy] territory, now it's 18th Street. You know the hangout for my neighborhood? Of course, they all go in Normandie . . . or other streets that was from MS. I would jump in MS because I love my country, but . . . it's not that.

Back in his neighborhood in El Salvador, Gato must now explain why he did not join La Mara Salvatrucha, the gang associated with Salvadorans, at least not at its inception. I look at the barrio around us and wonder at how its territorial identifications have been reshaped by the war and by United States–bound migration. Gato and his benevolent enemy hosts grew up together in the same barrio in San Salvador—Modelo. But by virtue of their relocation to adjacent inner-city neighborhoods in Los Angeles—Pico Union versus Koreatown—they are now from different neighborhoods in Los Angeles and, therefore, inside El Salvador. While they hail from the same home, they are not homeboys to one another but instead are enemies. Salvadoran geography has been remapped by this migration, inner-city politics in the United States, and deportation.

As Gato explains later, "The problem is that we came deported from the States. Someone . . . they're bringing the neighborhoods down to my country . . . That thing of the neighborhood [is] from California." It was common for Salvadoran youth who had not stepped foot on American soil to implore deported gang members to jump them in, or to form their own cliques based on the information that they could glean from media coverage of stories about and encounters with California gang culture. Gato launches into a critique of the naive transposition of the political terrain of Los Angeles onto El Salvador by Salvadoran "wannabes" and poor copies of the real thing in the United States. I have heard this critique from one deported gang member after another.

Whoever brought my neighborhood back here in the '90s, they fucked up, really fucked up my country. Because, man, you really see the writing on the walls in the streets. That came in the '90s . . . It's like you're seeing the freeways from LA, and they don't even know how to write on the walls. They write real stupid, you know. They put "Westside 18th Street" or "Northside MS," and we're not really on the Northside or Westside here. We're in South Central. Or they put area "213." Man, that's a telephone call from downtown California; or put "818." That's El Monte, you know. They get me real mad because they don't even know about the South-side thing, or the Northside thing. They just know enemy 18th Street, or enemy MS.

And so it is to the "real" landscape of California that our conversation wanders. Gato's vivid account of the globalization of his *sureño* (South-side) identity politics demonstrates how deeply linked San Salvador is to the spaces inside Los Angeles and vice versa. As Gato begins to explain the geography and genealogy of his criminalization, he guides us through the familiar landmarks of Pico Union's built environment. Gato was a student at Belmont High, "right there on Wilmont and Lucas." He was jumped (ini-tiated) into his neighborhood gang when he was fifteen or so as a means to seek revenge against "a guy from Rockwood" who stole a gold chain from him. His father, who was killed in El Salvador for his political involvement, had given the chain to Gato before he died. His gang life culminated in an arrest for two attempted murders of two members of Crazy Riders, who had driven into his neighborhood and pulled out an AK-47, hitting his homeboy. "It happened right there by a Jack in the Box, on Sixth and Bonnie Brae, by what used to be the Hotel California (infamous first stop for many a newly arrived immigrant), next to a place called La Barata." He was chased down Westlake, close to MacArthur Park—the symbolic center of Pico Union.

Like so many in his situation, in order to get a lighter sentence Gato ac-cepted a deal with the judge and pleaded guilty to the felony counts. Gato be-gins to talk about the minefield of cultural politics inside prison, which jump between these scales of identification: neighborhood (the gang), nationality (El Salvador vs. Mexico), geographic orientation (Southsider vs. Northsider), and racial identification (Latino vs. black, white, and Asian).

Every time the door opens and you step out, you don't know if the prob-lem's going to be with a Blood, a white boy, or Japanese, and you got to react because you're Latino man, you are Hispanic. Inside prison, believe it or not, we're united man. We are united as Southsiders, *sureños* . . . It would be cool if . . . neighborhoods could get along like in prison man. Not because you're Mexican, you're from Peru, or you're from El Salvador. No. We're all Hispanic man, we're all brown, we all speak the same language. Just because I'm a Salvadoran, you're going to feel better than me? No. We're all equal, man. Some of my homeboys, and the guys from MS, they don't think that way.

Once inside the prison, the city's geography seemed to lose some of its primacy. The relationship between space and identity now transcended the borders of the urban barrio that were so crucial to identity formation prior to incarceration. Local barrio identities gave way to racial, ethnic, regional, and national differences. The prison thus became a crucial site for the remediation of urban identities, and deportation took this reidentification one step further. Gato's discussion concludes with an elaboration of an intricate geography of belonging: a continental American and pan-ethnic identity as Latino. But upon deportation to the streets of San Salvador, this *concientización* (consciousness-raising) as Latino and as *sureño* is more often than not overwhelmed by the reproduction of divisions between barrios in San Salvador, reworked as they are by those in Los Angeles.

Gato's words weigh heavily as I write. He was killed not long after our interview by an MS gang member. The burden of representation looms large. Gato's attempt to be from one barrio and live in another, to marry across barrios, to stake claim to his childhood territory—all proved fatal. Gato was shot and killed in front of his infant son for his past affiliation with the 18th Street Gang in the very same spot where his father was killed in front of him for his political involvement with the FMLN (Farabundo Martí National Liberation Front) guerrilla forces.

Weasel's Story

Weasel, the "fool banished from the kingdom" as he refers to himself above, captured my anthropological imagination from the start. Unlike the deportees I had met up to that point, Weasel bore no traces of his Salvadoran identity. I was thrown by his style and his speech. The latter—filled as it was with the stylistic markers of Chicano and Californian youth culture, as well as playful appropriations of African American linguistic forms, was unmistakably American English. Indeed, Weasel described his reencounter with his "native" country as a "complete culture clash."

Neither did Weasel fit into the dominant configuration of gang affiliation among Salvadoran immigrants in Los Angeles: MS or 18th Street. I asked him about his gang. "My gang was called the Westside Los Crazies, and we're in Echo Park." I tell Weasel that I live in Echo Park. His eyes light up, and he jokes about me being his homegirl, and from there on out Weasel always introduces me as "Elana, she's from my ex-barrio."

w: The members are mostly Chicanos, or if they've got any Salvadoran or Cuban background, Puerto Rican, whatever, you know they're born there, they're born in the States, you know.

E: So it's not an immigrant gang?

w: No, no, not at all, not at all. I mean, they're all born there. I mean their parents could've been immigrants.

E: Or you were an immigrant?

w: Yes, but I didn't even recognize that word "immigrant" you know until I got a little older. You know, I just . . . I grew up like, I guess you could say like, naive to the fact that I came from another country and I was living in the States, and I just, I never thought about you know like . . . backgrounds . . . because everybody around like me spoke Spanish or English and you know they were Latino in general, the majority was Mexican, and Chicanos, very few blacks. But I did grow up seeing black people, and so it wasn't a total Latino neighborhood.

E: Do you remember what you said to me the other night over dinner? You said, "I guess you could say I am, or I was, a Salvadoran living in America living a . . ."

w: Living a Chicano lifestyle! Yeah, that's what I said.

. . . The funny thing, is that everyone thought I was Mexican, 'ey. I kept on telling them, "I'm not, you know, I was born in El Salvador, 'ey." You know, everytime they would ask me, I'd say, "I'm Salvadoran. I was born in El Salvador." But uh . . . after a while they'd forget about it because they're so used to you and you're so much like them that it doesn't even matter, you know.

. . . Like I was telling you, you know, I had like a Mexican upbringing. And in Los Angeles they [the schools] have this, like, this multicultural uh, uh . . . I guess, they teach you, about other cultures, and since there's a lot of Mexicans there, they teach you a lot about that, you know. They teach you about Cinco de Mayo and stuff like that.

Our conversation turned to the shock of deportation and his complete lack of preparation for such an eventuality. He was, after all, a permanent resident.

w: Well I thought I was a permanent resident you know . . .

E: Because you thought permanent resident meant permanent?

w: Yeah, permanent, and plus I never paid much attention to that legal status too much, you know. It was just something that was . . . I mean I thought I was at home, you know. I thought . . . that was me forever.

E: You had no idea that that was a possibility—that you would be deported?

w: I thought that was just for illegals, you know, and since I was legal, you know, I was a resident, and meanwhile my brothers [and sisters] were becoming citizens.

Of course, Weasel couldn't have known that he was vulnerable to deportation because the law—which was applied retroactively—was only put into effect in 1996, once he was already in prison and the year before he was deported.

E: When did you find out that you were coming back to El Salvador?

w: Well, the first time I went to prison, an immigration guy, agent, came to talk to me, but I was still lost, you know. I was a kid, you know.

E: What did he tell you?

w: He just told me, you know, "Where were you born," and this and that. He goes, "You better be careful, you know messing about. They'll send you back . . ." But I thought he was just, you know, joking or something. I said like, "How're they going to send me back? All my family's here." I didn't even think of anything like that. I'm here growing up thinking I'm this (American) when, in reality, I'm this (Salvadoran) because I was born here, you know . . . When I got out [of prison] the INS [Immigration and Naturalization Services] agent came to visit me. I didn't think nothing of it. Thought that he just wanted to see my green card and papers. The INS officer was trying to prove that I was a Salvadoran. He kept asking me questions like what was the biggest river in El Salvador. I kept trying to explain that I didn't know nothing about El Salvador. I mean I hadn't been there for twenty years. I mean the biggest river around here is the LA River. I grew up in LA, you know. Anyhow, he said that given my criminal history, he didn't see no chance for me, couldn't see me changing . . . Now I know that the biggest river here [in El Salvador] is the Rio Lempa.

Weasel then recounted his arrival scene, an amusing—if not intended— parody of the ethnographer's first encounter with a strange culture.

w: I arrived with a lot of rumors in my mind about there's like this death squad that's going to kill you if you're all tattooed.[7] So I'm a little nervous and scared. Then the police come and snatch you and put you in a little room, and I said, "Oh fuck . . . that's it, forget it. They got me. They're going to kill me." They started asking me like where I live, and where I'm going to live, and took pictures of me, of my tattoos, my fingerprints, looked through my stuff, you know . . .

E: How did San Salvador feel to you? What were your first impressions?

w: It was like they were sending me to Mars or something. I hadn't been in the country for twenty-something, twenty-two years. And then I come back and I'm completely lost, man.

As it turned out, Weasel began his new life in San Salvador in San Jacinto, not far from Gato's barrio, Modelo. He went on to describe his shock at his new surroundings.

It was like real dirty to me, and I was like, "G-d man, where am I?" you know. "What am I going to do here?" They had trees everywhere and, you know, a lot of shacks. So I was like, "What did I get myself into man. Where am I?" And to my sister, "Hell no, hell no, I ain't staying here, I ain't staying here . . . I tried to go get my passport and they, uh, denied me a passport because they didn't think I was from here, 'cause I couldn't speak Spanish that well. And if I did speak Spanish, I spoke a different Spanish.

Like Modelo, the local geography of San Jacinto had also been transformed by Los Angeles's territorial conflicts. Unlike Gato, however, Weasel occupied a much different relationship to that geography. Indeed, local gang members, although initially suspicious, did not in the end know where he was from, which is to say they did not recognize his barrio since it was neither MS or 18th Street. This afforded Weasel a modicum of autonomy and space in relationship to the Salvadoran gangs, although to Salvadoran society at large he was just another *marero* (gang member).

In El Salvador, Weasel entered into an identity crisis.

Yeah, I was telling you about the crisis I had. I'd been in a crisis. It goes back to the same thing too. People look down at you because, you know, the way you dress, baggy clothes . . . they call it marero here, and that's like something real low to call a person.

When I first got to San Jacinto, I couldn't really relate to nobody in the house, so I started going out a little bit, hanging out in the front of the house, and the neighborhood kids they would see me. [But] talking to those people is like, you know, whoever talks to them is part of 'em . . . so you're scum, you're trash, whatever. So I didn't really want to be classified with [gangs], you know, even though I could relate to them.

In an effort to reinvent himself, Weasel started to go to punk concerts.

E: This is you moving from your *mara* (gang) to your punk stage?
W: Gangster.
E: Cholo? Is that how you would describe your look?
W: Gangster.
E: Is that different from cholo?
W: Not really, but gangster's like, I feel it's a step above cholo. Cholo's . . . anybody could be cholo. Okay, I started going to concerts. I liked it. These guys were cool . . . I started going out with them. Found a place called La Luna [he laughs], started going there a lot.
E: La Luna is a very different scene . . .

I was astounded at the cultural fusion here. La Luna was one of those places where I would retreat to when I needed to escape the assault of being a foreign woman on her own in a conservative society. So I'm curious that Weasel, a self-described "gangster" from Echo Park, sought refuge there too. But there is a spatial logic at work here, globalization, which brought both Weasel and me into the same space. La Luna caters to middle-class liberal-Left Salvadorans, many of whom fled El Salvador as political exiles during the civil war, and expatriates working with nongovernmental organizations (NGOs), many of whom forged links to El Salvador through the solidarity movement during the same period. It also attracts unconventional middle-class Salvadoran youth drawn to experimentation with the global cultural flows of punk, rock 'n' *español*, rap, spoken word, and so on. Both Weasel and La Luna are produced and enabled by the spatial logics of globalization — albeit in and through markedly different registers of transnationalism: bohemianism and youth gangs.

Thus, while the focus of this chapter is on transnational geographies of violence, the presence of spaces like La Luna in Weasel's narrative demonstrate that these global flows are not simply about violence. If anything, La Luna, which is dedicated to opening up alternative performance spaces in a socially conservative society, has a utopian dimension. Weasel, who was an accomplished tattoo artist, was able through his contacts made at La Luna to employ gang expressive culture to build an "art tattoo" business for himself, catering to middle- and upper-middle-class Salvadoran youth. As such, Weasel comes to embody the fusion of both of these dimensions of globalization—dystopic and utopian.

E: You [said you] had a mohawk?

w: Yeah, I did.

E: Here in San Salvador?

w: San Salvador. That really tripped people out. Nobody's ever seen stuff like that here. In a way I was . . . I wanted to make a statement . . .

E: You were still living in San Jacinto at the time?

w: Yeah . . .

The absurdity of a punk rocker with a bright-green Mohawk hairdo in a popular barrio in post–civil war El Salvador will be lost on those unfamiliar with that landscape. Weasel said that being deported to El Salvador felt like being sent to Mars. And once in El Salvador, Weasel refashioned himself as the Martian, the alien he is made to feel by the stares, reactions, and disapproval of the people around him. In a follow-up e-mail to me in Los Angeles, Weasel modified his initial description of himself as "a Salvadoran living a Chicano lifestyle in the United States" to the following: "Now [I'm] more like a deported gang member from LA living a mixture of a Chicano, Gringo, weirdo lifestyle."

Geographical Disorientation

The cultural history and geography of Weasel's criminalization was different from that of Gato. Gato remembered his old barrio, and despite his pan-Latino discourse he retained his identity as Salvadoran. Gato migrated at a different age and a different epoch—at the height of the civil war in the early 1980s—and into a gang politic specific to that era and to that migration. Nonetheless, his geographical knowledge, the old maps, no longer worked for him upon his return to El Salvador. The barrio's designation, its geography, had changed on him, even as he was changed by it. Both Gato and Weasel were transnationalized, and their transnationalization left them on different sides of the war, a new civil war.

Gato's migration story began and ended in violence. Weasel, on the other hand, moved to Los Angeles in the mid-1970s, well before the Salvadoran civil war and the attendant massive influx of refugees. As a result, Weasel had no social or geographical memory of El Salvador and no attachment to a barrio in San Salvador or mental maps thereof. He knew nothing of the place from where he came. The test that the INS officer gave him on Salvadoran geography was a perfect manifestation of his geographical disorientation—his reference point is the Los Angeles River not the Rio Lempa. It was not until two years after Weasel's return to El Salvador that he was able to construct a mental map of the geography of this tiny country. As he put it, "I feel like a tourist, a permanent one."

Despite their different legal status and cultural claims to "the kingdom" (Weasel had permanent residency, whereas Gato did not; Weasel was recognizable as an "American," and Gato as an "immigrant"), after 1996 the distinctions between undocumented and documented immigrants were no longer recognized by immigration law for those with criminal records. Gato and Weasel would eventually meet through the Salvadoran branch of Homies Unidos, tellingly, also established in 1996.

Several forces came together to bring Homies Unidos San Salvador into existence. In 1996 Donna DeCesare, a photojournalist from the United States, exhibited her work on the deportation of gang members from the streets of Los Angeles to the streets of San Salvador, in San Salvador. She invited several gang members who appeared in her photographs to that exhibition, and then asked them to speak at a related conference on youth in El Salvador. The Permanente Committee on Youth Violence that emerged out of that conference included the participation of the gang members present that day, local and international NGOs and government agencies. Just days after the conference, Magdaleno Rose-Ávila relocated to El Salvador with his wife Caroline, who was to take on the regional directorship of the United States branch of the NGO Save the Children.[8] Given Magdaleno's experience with youth violence and human rights issues, his wife asked him to represent the NGO at the forum's meetings. As Magdaleno put it, he had come to El Salvador to be a househusband and to write a book, but he "fell in love" with the homies. Indeed, he spent his retirement funds and used up his credit on start-up monies for the organization.

Magdaleno then linked forces with DeCesare to take the issue of transnational youth gangs to audiences in the United States, and he started to contact and build credibility with leaders in MS and 18th Street in San Salvador and in Los Angeles. This was no easy feat. As a Chicano, Magdaleno faced much suspicion and resentment, particularly from MS. The first president of Homies Unidos, Negro, explained his initial reaction to Magdaleno this way: "I thought to myself, 'Damn what's this Chicano guy doing in my country, trying to help us. Those Mexicans, those Chicanos, those are the ones who were hitting on us.'" He was very suspicious, but Magdaleno took a huge risk and invited him and his homies over to his house, where Negro met his wife and his young daughter in this "big beautiful house." When one day Magdaleno left them in his house so they could finish up a project on the computer, Negro thought, "Damn, damn what an idiot this guy is leaving us with his stuff. Leaving us with his computer." Then he thought again, "No man, this guy's not stupid, he's doing this to show us he trusts us. And man I'm not going to let anyone touch his stuff. We're going to be *firme* (cool)."

Working in tandem with Rädda Barnen (Save the Children–Sweden) and with the consent of key gang membership, Negro of MS and Pajaro of 18th Street, Magdaleno approached Miguel Cruz, then director of the University Institute for Public Opinion (IUDOP) at the University of Central America with the idea of conducting a demographic and needs assessment survey of gang youth in the San Salvador area. Despite the reluctance of the leadership of the Jesuit-run university, Cruz agreed. He and Magdaleno started training the gang members, recruited by Negro and Pajaro, to conduct the survey. Given the violent animosity between the two groups, the training had to be conducted separately for each gang. Magdaleno would pick up one group in the morning and then the other in the afternoon. At the end of the study Magdaleno and Cruz brought both gangs together at University of Central America to hear the results of the study.[9] It was a great risk, and the meeting was very tense, but as Magdaleno put it, "Gang members were finding out that 18th Street was answering the questions the same way as MS, that there was no difference. They had more in common than they knew."

In the meantime, the homies were still attending the committee meetings, but they were getting tired of the endless talking. They wanted action. Concerned that they would be used by the other groups and their competing interests with one another, Negro and some of the other homies such as Night Owl, Diablo, and Hüera decided that they wanted to build their own organization. According to Magdaleno, the other members of the permanent committee went crazy, insisting, "You've got to do it under us. You need us. You're not prepared." This only made the homies more resolved to do it, and so Homies Unidos San Salvador was born. As they put it in their early brochures: "Twenty-two young men and women, eleven from MS and eleven from 18th Street came together and put aside their differences to say 'No, to violence!'"

Their different orientations to their Salvadoran identity notwithstanding, both Gato and Weasel sought out Homies Unidos San Salvador precisely as a means of reorientation to their "homeland," and both drew upon the organization to teach them how to navigate hostile and foreign terrain, or to derive a sense of place and a familial bond. While the writing may have been on the wall in San Salvador in the form of gang tagging, the meanings were not the same as in Los Angeles. Both deportees depended on Homies Unidos for the translation of these deceptively familiar codes.

As Gato told us:

> For us, it's kind of hard for us to live in our country. Wherever we go, we're always watching our back, our necks. I thank Homies because they showed me my country, man. From them, I learned where my enemies were, because when I came here I didn't really know where I was going. When people would say, "Let's go out, or let's go buy something," shit, I'd only go to the corner and come right back. Magdaleno and Huera [Güera][10] [of Homies Unidos] would take me out for coffee, and would tell me [as they drove through the city of San Salvador]: "They are MS, and this corner, this is 18th."

Weasel started coming to the office after he had seen Bullet, the rap composer and performer and member of Homies Unidos, at concerts. He explained:

> I came down and checked it out. I liked it, you know. I felt like that bond was there again—the one I left in LA . . . where I felt comfortable . . . Plus to top it off, I came to the office one day, and I see this guy walking down the street. And I said, "Damn, that guy looks familiar, 'ey." I got closer and closer, and then I said "Damn, I know that fool!" "Hey fool!" I say, "What's up?" And it was Grumpy. And me and Grumpy had been locked up together, so that even . . . so that even made the bond stronger . . . I ran into other guys I knew from prison . . . Alex, Frank, Rabbit. It was like I'd found my family again.

This reencounter scene happens outside the formal arena and in the everyday. Bullet told of encountering "homeboys" from Los Angeles before his affiliation with the organization: "I was walking along and I heard this voice. It was like music to my ears—my homeboy from Los Angeles."

But in addition to happy "family" reunions, these reencounter scenes can have a dark and insidious side too. It is not unusual to encounter a former enemy who carries a vendetta from the streets of Los Angeles to those of San Salvador. Tattoos and other identifying marks can also lead to the re-emergence of old conflicts or precipitate new ones. As Alex Sanchez put it, "I thought I'd have some time to relax, but the war [that he thought he had left behind in the United States] started up again [in El Salvador] two days after I got there."

Homies Unidos was an organization born of and devoted to countering the alienating forces of globalization as they combine with nationalism. Certainly Gato's and Weasel's narratives speak to a need to mediate a jarring and troubled relationship between space and identity. Beyond the generalized destabilizing effects of contemporary urban life, deported gang youth must contend with the effects of zero-tolerance policing tactics as they are deployed on the streets of the inner-city immigrant barrio and with the subsequent transnationalization of the geographies of gang violence between Los Angeles and San Salvador.

I have already shown in chapters 2 and 3 the ways in which gangs provide an important sense of place and are in many senses the impoverished architects of space.[11] In San Salvador, as in Los Angeles, Homies Unidos worked to provide an alternative "way-finding" function to the gang for these deported gang youth by providing them with a map of the ways in which the geographies of violence of Los Angeles have been rewritten into, and altered through their encounters with, San Salvador's urban landscape.[12] This geographical reorientation is intended to avert the reproduction of violence itself. Gato's story, alongside the many other deaths within the organization's membership, is, sadly, testimony to just how complex a task this is and to the fact that in many instances these navigational maps help to prolong but may not ultimately save lives and stop the violence.

But nonviolence is not simply an individual choice made to change one's lifestyle. In San Salvador, Gato was forever marked by "where he is from," which is to say his territorial affiliations in Los Angeles. No longer an active gang member, in El Salvador Gato remained a target for gang vendettas. Moreover, active gang members might have misrecognized or misconstrued the organization as a rival gang or viewed its outreach into their barrios as an encroachment and violation of their territory. So, for instance, Weasel, who hailed from territory in Los Angeles unknown in San Salvador, became more vulnerable to gang violence through his subsequent participation in Homies Unidos as a gang peace activist. Beyond gang violence, as the Alex Sanchez case shows, there have been cases of death squad and police violence directed at gang youth and at deported gang youth in particular.

Deportation narratives demonstrate how the Latino immigrant barrio and the Salvadoran barrio popular have both come to occupy the space of the global moment. Granted, Weasel may have experienced El Salvador as the primitive past—a veritable jungle of mud huts. But as a result of his deportation, he became an agent in and a foil for (and offers an immanent critique of) transnational spatiality. Indeed, the cognitive mappings of deported immigrant gang youth involve constructing legibility, not only within but between cities of formerly distinct hemispheres that have, as a result of migration and forced repatriation, become intimately connected, their geographies inextricably linked and complicit.

A Spatial Politics of Simultaneity

This chapter ostensibly marks the division between the United States– and Salvadoran–based chapters of this book. But these narratives of deported immigrants speak eloquently to the futility of engaging with the spatial politics of one side of this social field (Los Angeles) without simultaneously accounting for those at play on the other side (San Salvador).[13]

Imagine, for instance, riding buses through the streets of San Salvador with two deportees from 18th Street territory in Pico Union. The stories of these young men and of the geography of their everyday lives in Los Angeles, captured by my tape recorder, are filled with the booming sounds of the street life in San Salvador. Back in Los Angeles, I would drive through Pico Union and its surrounding barrios trying to relocate these narratives in their original geographies of action. Echo Park Lake and its gang-graffiti-covered walls by now had become enlivened by Weasel's stories and disturbed by his absence. As I drove by MacArthur Park, the Hotel California, the corner of Berendo and Eighth, Belmont High, and the Jack in the Box, pieces of these narratives would flash into consciousness: This must have been where Gato's friend was shot, this is where Ringo lived, that's where Gato's father's necklace was stolen, and that's where Weasel was last picked up. The urban landscape of Los Angeles became saturated with the narratives of these people whom I had encountered in El Salvador, and even more hauntingly by those who had since died in the streets of San Salvador. I felt this not just as time warp but also as a space warp—the "time-space compression" of simultaneity.[14]

The terrain in between was also marked by this migration. Driving south to the U.S.-Mexico border, heading for El Salvador and elsewhere in Central America, one begins to note, alongside the border patrol cars, caravans of three to five used cars, pick-ups, and yellow American school buses—all invariably filled with cargo for Guatemala and El Salvador. These vehicles and goods would be sold or left with family in their country of destination. I traveled this route with Magdaleno Rose-Ávila. We had purchased a used car in Texas to import overland into El Salvador for the San Salvador office.

In Tapachula, at the Mexican-Guatemalan border, we stopped at the Albergue Belén, a safe haven and shelter for Central Americans heading north to the United States. There I ran into a young Salvadoran man whom I felt sure I had met before. As we spoke, it came to me. I had met him just one month before in the Comalapa National Airport at the welcoming office for deportees in-bound from the United States, another key site for my ethnography. Yes, he corroborated, he had been through the office about a month ago, and was now heading back north, hoping to make it back across the Mexico-U.S. border. He was with another deportee, an older man, who had lived in the United States since 1991 and was on his way back to his wife, from whom he had been separated by his recent deportation.

In the transnational narratives of deportees, Los Angeles and San Salvador, and even the space in between, have been compressed into the same field of view. The Latino immigrant barrio and the Latin American barrio popular now overlap in crucial ways—not only from the privileged perspective of the traveling ethnographer but also from the vantage of Salvadoran immigrants themselves. Indeed, these narratives of forcible return do not simply function as haunting memories or as residues of past lives. They do more than refer back to or recollect their barrios in Los Angeles. Banished though these "fools" may be from the "kingdom," they remain linked to that landscape through, among other things, ongoing ties with family—be they actual or fictive kin.

Take, for instance, Doña Ofelia, who lives in a one-room apartment in the Pico Union district. I initially went to visit her at the urging of her son Pajaro, a deported member of the MS gang. Pajaro had asked me to look his mother up upon my return to Los Angeles from El Salvador. During our first meeting, Doña Ofelia and I talked as she readied herself for her evening janitorial shift in one of Century City's towering glass executive suites. When our conversation turned to Pajaro, she began to cry, "He can never come back, and now, I cannot go back to El Salvador to retire as I had planned, because I must work to support him there." Doña Ofelia's story was just one of the many mournful tales I heard from mothers who, separated from their children once by civil war, were reunited in Los Angeles only to be separated once again, this time through the forced repatriation and deportation of those same children.

Every three weeks or so, Doña Ofelia sets out from her apartment to catch the bus at Pico and Union bound for a neighborhood close to the University of Southern California in South Central Los Angeles. On her way to the bus stop, she traverses a streetscape cluttered with signs of Central American and Mexican diasporas—the pupuserias, street vendors selling green mango with lime and chile, and the *bótanica* windows filled with plaster-of-paris figurines of saints popular to Central Americans. She continues past Transportes Salvadoreños and Cuscatleco Travel and an array of other delivery and travel services that transport people, goods, money, documents, and letters back and forth along those now well-worn travel routes between Los Angeles, Mexico, and Central America. Doña Ofelia is herself on her way to drop off clothing and money for her deported son with a personal courier. The courier is Doña Leti, who travels back and forth between Los Angeles and her hometown in El Salvador, navigating the transnational space for those Salvadoran immigrants who cannot themselves travel but who must find a means to maintain a transnational household. Many of her Salvador-based clients, who once received packages from their families in Los Angeles, in turn become her Los Angeles–based clients who now send those packages.

On my first visit to Doña Leti's Los Angeles–based operations (her brother's house just west of USC) a young woman there recognized me from El Salvador. Amalia and I had met the year before in Doña Leti's house in Santa Elena, where she had come to pick up letters and money sent from Los Angeles. She had since migrated overland with a *coyote* (migrant smuggler) to Los Angeles, and now was sending things in the opposite direction.[15] I spent time with her family and cousins, who lived in an apartment complex with other immigrants from Santa Elena in the Koreatown area, close to Alex Sanchez's old stomping grounds. The next time I went to El Salvador, I visited their families in the rural settlements surrounding Santa Elena, and found myself bringing back photographs of homes built with their hard-earned remittances, in addition to emotionally charged taped messages from mothers to their daughters and sons.

On that particular trip to El Salvador, I drove with Doña Leti and her husband, Francisco, to San Miguel. They wanted to show me the rapid expansion of this city, which was moving from its status as third-largest Salvadoran city to second largest. There was some debate as to whether its boom could be better attributed to remittances from the United States or from drug-money laundering. Outside the city, Doña Leti and Francisco stopped the car so that I could take a photograph of a volcano, the beautiful, if always threatening, backdrop to so many Salvadoran scenes and literary works. As I snapped my camera, a pickup drove by honking. It stopped and reversed. It was Manolo, whom I'd last seen in his MacArthur Park apartment in Los Angeles, but who I had first met in Santa Elena the year previously when he had driven a truck in from Los Angeles, and decided to run for mayor of Santa Elena while he was in town. Ninety percent of the funding for the FMLN candidate that year came from a "group of Tabudos living in a foreign land [the United States],"[16] and who, in a public letter to the townspeople, called themselves the "FMLN diplomatic commission of Santa Elena."

I'd encountered a similar phenomenon with the annual beauty pageants hosted by the Comite de Amigos de Santa Elena, a philanthropic hometown association with committees in Santa Elena, Los Angeles, San Francisco, Maryland, and Houston. That year's La Reina de Santa Elena (Queen of Santa Elena) was from Los Angeles. One of the entrants, Lourdes, had run in the Los Angeles–based pageant, but couldn't raise sufficient funds to win the contest.[17] So, while she was in Santa Elena visiting her grandmother for the Christmas holidays, she decided to enroll in the local pageant, knowing that she had a better chance of competing for the prize here, drawing as she could on money from the United States. I would bump into Lourdes again in the San Fernando Valley, a collection of suburbs just north of Los Angeles, two years later. The occasion was a fund-raiser for Santa Elena's FMLN mayoral candidate in the municipal elections of 1999.

Deported gang youth, banished though they may be, are an integral part of this transnational network. They are, after all, the children of immigrant parents who toil in service to global capitalism as janitors, pieceworkers in the garment industry, cooks, nannies, gardeners, and day laborers, and who sometimes run against the grain as longtime community organizers and labor activists. Their brothers and sisters—often college students, police officers, or schoolteachers—might well be lauded as exemplars of successful incorporation into the nation-state and its institutions. These same dualisms are expressed in the legal language of naturalization and deportation cases. Candidates for citizenship must demonstrate "good moral character," whereas criminal deportees have been irrevocably marked by their crimes of "moral turpitude." Weasel's brother, for instance, worked for the Los Angeles Sheriff's Department, and his sister was an elementary school teacher. The banishment of gang-affiliated youth from the United States thus stands in contrast to but also in relationship with their parents' and siblings' naturalization as United States citizens.[18]

Gang-affiliated young adults who are deported also leave behind their U.S.-born children, wives, and girlfriends. Moreover, in fearing Gato's fate many of these deportees reenter the United States illegally even though they risk re-imprisonment followed by deportation if they are caught.[19] Alex Sanchez is a case in point. Far beyond this literal return of the repressed— the illegal reentry of those excluded from the nation—the absence of the deportee is a strongly felt presence in the neighborhood. Deported gang youth remain an integral part of the "structure of feeling" of the barrio,[20] of its internal relations and the everyday practices of its residents. In this sense, the identity formation made visible in these deportation narratives bears a relationship to the postcolonial narratives.[21] Although El Salvador was never literally colonized by the United States, I would suggest that these Salvadoran narratives of forcible return reveal a structural interdependence and complicity in identity formation between the United States and El Salvador in general and between Los Angeles and San Salvador in particular.[22] In the North-South relations under consideration here, deported Salvadoran immigrant gang youth oscillate between "home" and "abroad," where both home and abroad are themselves unstable locations.

At the same time, Salvadoran gang youth who have never been to the United States construct their identities around imagined urban geographies of cities like Los Angeles. Places in Central Los Angeles where the Salvadoran offshoots of the cliques with names like Tiny Locos of Shatto Park take on the romantic gloss of Disneyland or the sacredness of original ground. Some travel just to see and experience this landscape at the center of the tales passed on from the original homies—the land of their founding fathers. Others, who are more skeptical, go to verify that the place that deported gang members have painted for them in Hollywood Technicolor really exists. As one young man who was deported from the United States but originally had been jumped into 18th Street in San Salvador said to me five months after his forced return to El Salvador, "I did the impossible and I succeeded in getting there . . . It's like a extraordinary film that only a rare few get to experience." Others who couldn't go would spend hours surfing the Internet looking for their homeboys on sites like "America's Most Wanted"—their equivalent to the celebrities in *People* magazine.

Salvadoran girls, reading teen magazines or while surfing online, might respond to pen-pal requests placed by homies in U.S. prisons. A young woman from 18th Street told me of her smoldering transnational passion for an 18th Street member in Los Angeles whom she had fallen in love with eleven years earlier after seeing his photograph in the pen-pal section of a magazine. She cut out the picture and kept it in her wallet for all those years. He was from the founding clique, which had spawned hers in El Salvador. On the two occasions when she visited Los Angeles, she went in search of him—asking the homeboys from her clika to take her to Columbia Street in Hollywood. She never did meet him there since he was invariably locked up when she was in town. It wasn't until he was deported for the last time that she finally met him. He introduced himself with another *apodo* (nickname), but she caught him off guard when she said, "No you're not. I know you very well." That's when their brief and torrid affair began, and when she briefly realized her slumbering dream of becoming her idol's *heina* (woman). Deported gang members are deeply seductive figures. To many Salvadoran youth and young women, they are a window into, and a strange realization of, the American dream.

Salvadoran deported gang youth point out a "representational ambivalence" between Latino and Latin American identity. This "Central American–American" hybrid subject, as Arturo Arias writes, "cannot be designated univocally as either Latino or Latin American, but—to draw on Juan Flores—speaks rather of life lived 'off the hyphen,'" where the hyphen is a sign of both conjunction and disjunction.[23] Their narratives speak eloquently to the need for interpretive maps, which interrogate the relationship between space and identity and the blurred boundaries between the local and the global.

Shortly after the deportation of Alex Sanchez to El Salvador in 1994, a political cartoon depicting a U.S. Marshal plane loaded with deportees appeared
in a Salvadoran paper. As Alex recalled in a conversation with me, "[In the
cartoon] a plane was flying over El Salvador trailing a cage, which hovered
over the country by a rope. The cage was filled with six hundred tattooed,
mohawked child molesters, rapists, and serial murderers." Alex's return also
coincided with the birth of La Sombra Negra, a paramilitary group that redirected the social cleansing apparatus of the death squads of the 1980s at
a new enemy—no longer the guerrilla, the clergy, or the student activist but
now the *delicuente*, *mara*, or gang youth. As Alex explained:

> We thought of them as just another gang, another enemy to arm ourselves
> against and to fight. We didn't hide from them like the *guerrillas*, because
> they were afraid of death. All gang members expected to die, so why be

frightened of it, if you're going to die, you're going to die. . . . A lot of kids that we personally knew were killed. They were killing innocent kids, getting rid of people they didn't want—on the guise that they were gang members. We just took the attitude "come and get us" [and] armed ourselves. We got notice that they were coming for us. They would send us death threats. We wouldn't allow vehicles with tinted glass windows up in our barrios . . . We got set and ready for war again. You go down there to live a different life, but you can't. You get put in a position where you have to defend yourself. If not you get killed . . . and then there's the situation there about work . . . you can't get jobs, you can't go to work or to school if you've got tattoos . . . the news makes it seem like we're terrorists, so all the people who don't know nothing about us are scared of us. So you get put in a spot.

Upon their arrival, deported youth and young adults, like Alex, would find themselves walking into and contributing to a complex force field of violence and social discrimination and new forms of poverty unleashed by neoliberal economic reforms.

The deportation of gang members to El Salvador was to combine with the flourishing of organized crime, the incomplete disarmament of a highly militarized society, the reemergence of the extralegal social cleansing practices of the death squads of the 1980s, the uneven progress of police and of judicial reforms, and finally, the adaptation of the zero-tolerance gang-abatement strategies used in the United States.[1] Together these elements would provide fertile ground for the reproduction and articulation of the patterns of violence of both El Salvador and the United States.

It was within this constellation of forces—peaceful and violent, local and global—that Homies Unidos San Salvador came into being, began to flourish, and then, as I will argue, flounder. Indeed, the period under investigation in this chapter, 1996 to 2003, marks the founding and, ostensibly temporary, shutting down of Homies Unidos's San Salvador program. Be it the organization's brief history or the first phase of a longer organizational trajectory, the fortunes of the organization correspond to a particular historical trajectory within El Salvador: namely, the rise and wane of a post–civil war human rights and police reform agenda, on the one hand, and the rise, or one could say return, of the security state through the globalization of the zero-tolerance strategies of the United States, on the other. The following chapter offers an analysis of the struggle of Homies Unidos to open up alternative and neutral spaces of representation in this complex transnational force field.

The Gang Peace Activist Revisited

Homies Unidos was from the beginning an assimilation of contrary elements; its very name, for example, is bilingual (English and Spanish).[2] But the English is itself an assimilation of African American gang terminology reworked by Chicano gangs prior to any Salvadoran presence therein. Gangs are, among other things, about uniting against a common enemy, another gang, based on highly localized territorial claims—the barrio. In embracing the *unidos* in its name, the group was (in principle if not always in practice) an organized effort to assimilate enemies—notably the better-known archrival transnational gangs La Mara Salvatrucha and the 18th Street Gang but also smaller gangs from the United States and even those indigenous to El Salvador—across vast and disjointed territorial claims.

As in Los Angeles, Homies Unidos San Salvador was founded upon the principle of youth protagonism and dedicated to redirecting toward nonviolent ends the agency that youth derive from their gang involvement. Indeed, the organization sought to wed the structure of the gang to that of an emergent nongovernmental organization (NGO) with a mission to foment a youth movement for nonviolence and to make demands on the state—both that of the United States and of El Salvador. As an articulation between two social movements—namely, seeking to enjoin the movement for social justice with that purportedly organized for crime—Homies Unidos was a controversial project, to say the least. Their work to carve out a space of representation for deported gang youth and to advocate for their transformative potential would meet with resistance on all fronts—the gang, civil society, the state, and even within the organization itself.

Again, like its offshoot in Los Angeles, Homies Unidos was beholden to the structure of the gang. The program's discourses and practices set out to redirect, not dismantle, the gang structure or its disciplines and solidarities. To quote from the group's promotional materials: "We do not preach. . . . Our task is to transform the gang culture from within . . . while acting as positive role models in order to change the gang mentality from violence to an understanding of human rights and human potential."

The organization sought early on to transform the patriarchal nature of the gang by changing its original name of Homeboys Unidos to the more inclusive Homies Unidos. Nonetheless, its leadership in San Salvador would still be dominated by men, and for that matter, by deportees from the United States rather than "native" gang members. The relative power of the deportee in the organization only augmented the male-dominated nature of its leadership, since deported gang members were overwhelmingly men. The latter had much to do with the different ways in which criminality is gendered as male in the United States.[3]

Homies Unidos has described itself as an "organization of, for, and by gang members." Hanging out at the San Salvador office, as well as coming and going with the organization's leadership, was unlike any experience I'd ever had with an NGO. It was more like "kicking it with the homies." As I described in chapter 3, the retention of "gang culture" was highly visible and audible in the aesthetics, style, language, and gestures of Homies Unidos's leadership and program participants. Its leaders derived their authority not from their nonprofit management skills but from their status as veterans of their respective gangs and from their criminal records—prison time, deportation, and so on. One member confided to me that he felt discriminated against because the other homies didn't consider him "criminal" enough.

While inside the office the very modestly paid staff would be learning the business of an NGO (reporting, accounting, proposal development, and so forth), outside on the stairwell and in the courtyard there was always a contingent of homeboys and homegirls just hanging around. Other members might be inside using the weight equipment, watching gangster movies or rap videos, and surfing the Internet for sites on gangs, hip hop culture, and on "America's Most Wanted."[4] As would be true in Los Angeles, the San Salvador organization mimicked the solidarity of the gang. Participants in Homies Unidos programs were homeboys and homegirls to one another. It was a place of deep affective relationships where people came to feel a sense of belonging, not unlike that which they derived from their actual gangs. As one deportee explained of his first visit to the Homies Unidos office: "I found a group of people [in Homies] who respected me and who knew where I was coming from."

According to the study noted in chapter 4 by the University of Central America (in which Homies Unidos collaborated), 43 percent of male respondents join gangs for *el vacil*.[5] El vacil is understood as a combination of actions that can include going out for a walk or an outing, going out to drink and to parties, having sex, meeting in parks, consuming drugs, breaking the law,[6] and anything that alludes to diversion, pleasure, or entertainment.[7] El vacil, in the sense of going on work-related outings, was an everyday practice at Homies Unidos, and it combined with the administrative and programmatic functions of the NGO in intriguing ways. I made many trips with Weasel, Homies Unidos San Salvador's director, who was in charge of the organization's vehicle. Weasel's job as director of Homies Unidos often extended to picking up members from their homes and dropping them off again later. Initially, it struck me as an odd and inefficient distribution of tasks for a director of an NGO to be the organization's chauffeur until I recognized us, the two women in the cars, as homegirls in a gang, crammed tightly in the back seat with a tattooed *vato* (dude) on either side of us and two homeboys with the higher status in front, music blaring between X-rated rap, soft soul, golden oldies, and Queen. These trips, which often involved a bank transaction, picking up office supplies, or paying bills for the office—all of which might be accomplished just as well by one or two members of the staff— were always opportunities to *salir* (to go out) and *vagar* (to cruise) in the city for the whole, dare I say, gang. Long-time organizer Magdaleno Rose-Ávila co-opted el vacil and these outings as opportunities to organize: "Chauffeuring was a technique I used as a farm worker organizer and which I extended to Homies Unidos. You make sure that folks get to the meeting . . . I normally used car time to do lessons and to set the tone for where ever we were going. I used car time for miniworkshops when we [Homies Unidos] first started, since no one could pay attention for over ten minutes, and we continue to use the car time to make sure that folks know *what time it is!*" "Hanging out" at the Homies Unidos office also had something of the feeling of an Alcoholics Anonymous twelve-step program. As I was told by one of the Homies who, like so many, had gone in and out of drug (crack and glue) use: "I always know that Homies is there when I'm ready to clean myself up." Although Homies Unidos does not claim to be a drug rehabilitation center, it was perceived as something of a safe house to withdraw from the street and la vida loca for those who struggle with addiction.

There was also the economic element with which to contend. As an aspiring NGO, Homies Unidos became a channel for small change by providing gang members with jobs and very modest per diems. One gang member explained that he joined his gang in Long Beach because he needed "a hustle"—an inside track on fast cash. The cash provided by Homies Unidos was hardly fast or even that much money; its funding came through foundation grants with reporting requirements and through an umbrella fiscal agency in the United States. Nonetheless, there was a "hustle" attached to

Homies Unidos. There were economic and material perks for hanging out at Homies Unidos, especially when the foreign visitors were in town—free meals, gifts, the possibility of a loan. Visitors from the United States were asked to bring care packages of Three Flowers hair oil, palm combs for closely shaven hairstyles, Dickies brand clothing, and tattoo equipment and supplies.

For all their valiant efforts at building a program for violence prevention and intervention, Homies Unidos was still vulnerable to claims that its members were "transgressing the line" between violence and nonviolence.[8] Their work, after all, was positioned precisely at that line—the border between gang peace activism and gang activity—and as such, the goal was to transform that *activity* into *activism*. The organization's recruits and constituency, some of whom were still active gang members, sometimes confused the organization for a gang (their gang), and thus might transgress the line between gang and NGO. Indeed, learning to hold that line was an ongoing struggle, and part and parcel of a gang member's rehabilitation. Homies Unidos's members were subject to being threatened, beaten up, and worse still, killed. Gang members had on occasion attempted to secure *viaticos*, the per diems offered to committed volunteers, through extortion. At one point, rumors circulated that there were plans afoot to kidnap the organization's director "just to talk" about the organization's budget.

There was also an ongoing struggle for leadership within Homies Unidos between the two major gangs, MS and 18th Street. In 1999, these tensions culminated in an incident where active members from a disgruntled gang first threw a grenade and then shot into the courtyard in front of the office. Shortly thereafter, Homies Unidos members from MS retreated from active participation in the organization. While there was concerted effort to mitigate the effects of polarized gang politics by recruiting participants from smaller, lesser-known gangs, there was always the need to ensure that the resources of Homies Unidos were not co-opted by one of the dominant gangs.

Well beyond explicit ideological statements and positions, there were myriad ways in which Homies Unidos's organizing "strategies" for social change were built around established "tactics" and "ways of operating" among gang members.[9] And the reasons for "joining" Homies Unidos may not be all that different from the reasons for joining the gang: el vacil, solidarity, protection, an economic channel, and the aesthetic dimension of gang identity formation.[10] The organization's genius—to leverage the structure of solidarity of the gang and to mimic its practices for nonviolent ends—could also, however, lead to dangerous contradictions among its participants as well as misrecognition by other NGOs and state institutions.

Given its work as a youth violence prevention project, Homies Unidos developed strategies to enter the fray of formal identity politics, but it was not yet what Michel de Certeau might have termed a "proper institutionalized location."[11] Indeed, Homies Unidos did not have *persona jurídica* (legal status as a nongovernmental organization) in El Salvador. Despite the protests of its San Salvador–based members, the decision was eventually taken to seek nonprofit status in the United States first, in the anticipation that their application would be protracted if not denied in El Salvador. Members of Homies Unidos said that when they met with then-President Calderon Sol through a contact with the United States Embassy, Calderon Sol said that to grant Homies Unidos persona jurídica would be to legalize gangs. In 1997, the Salvadoran legislature had passed a bill to increase the oversight of NGOs and their sources of foreign funding. This was generally recognized as an attempt to shut down the spaces of civil society that were flourishing in the post-1992 climate of the Peace Accords and that marked the most outstanding achievement of the peace negotiations. The measure was a continuation of the ruling right-wing's long-standing historical suspicion of these organs of Salvadoran civil society, and the discourse of *doble cara* (two-faced). In the 1980s, this discourse had been leveraged to accuse NGOs and popular organizations of operating as fronts for the FMLN. Similarly, in the 1990s Homies Unidos was often viewed a front for gangs.[12]

Moreover, Homies Unidos enjoyed a somewhat tenuous place among those NGOs, the organs of Salvadoran civil society. Undoubtedly, to quote a Salvadoran researcher on youth violence who spoke with me, they were recognized as "the best channels for access [to gang youth] and those who can best ensure that [the] linguistic codes [of surveys and programs] are compatible, *but not beyond that*" (my emphasis). Homies Unidos was consistently invited and its members recruited to do the groundwork for surveys of gang members by other NGOs and research organizations. Homies Unidos was loosely affiliated with an extensive network of organizations involved in issues relating to youth, gangs, migration, and health, but their inclusion therein was largely utilitarian or cosmetic and their impact, as I have already indicated, was dismissed as "minimal."

Homies Unidos was only very loosely attached to El Foro Permanente de Migrantes (Permanent Forum on Migrants) and it was not among the NGOs included in the Bienvenido a Casa (Welcome Home) project managed by Catholic Relief Services and based in the Salvadoran national airport. The latter exclusion was sorely felt by the organization, whose members felt that they were, in some sense, intellectual authors of the project. It is by no means surprising that as deportees with criminal status in the United States they would not be asked to oversee a U.S. government–funded project. However, neither were they among the organizations that participated in the project directly through conducting the intake interviews of deportees at the airport, although they were eventually added to the referral sheet handed to deportees in their orientation packet. While deportees are by no means all gang members, it is interesting to note that the specific needs of deported gang members were not accounted for in the initial design of the Bienvenido a Casa project. As a former member of the Foro Permanente de Migrantes put it, "Homies Unidos has not succeeded in making the click with organizations working on youth and migration." Far from clicking with them, the representative of Homies Unidos to the Foro Permanente de Migrantes felt marginalized and disrespected within that network.

The project "Towards a Society without Violence" by the United Nations Development Program had been asked by Catholic Relief Services to develop a program for deported youth within their local juvenile delinquency prevention project. The project, however, had been removed from their agenda because, to quote its director, there was "no interest on the part of the communities" and they "could not locate deported youth." The director's explanation that they did not want to create a problem where the community, in contrast to the police, did not see one seemed both strategic and politic. However, the fact that Homies Unidos, well known to the program through the Central American University gang study, was not consulted before the project was dropped was also telling.

Indeed, to a certain extent it may in fact have been Homies Unidos's international solidarity (some to Europe but, at the time, primarily to the United States) that more than anything afforded Homies Unidos its entry into Salvadoran civil society. As one of the Salvadoran-based program leaders complained during a conference call with the United States–based office, "Everyone suddenly wants to talk to us when you send a delegation down. But as soon as you're gone, they don't have no time for us. They don't care." In this sense, Homies Unidos bore traces of another moment in United States–Salvadoran solidarity politics during which "internationals" provided cover and contributed to opening up political spaces for the Salvadoran Left—be they political refugees criminalized as illegal aliens, grassroots organizations criminalized as guerrillas, or guerrillas criminalized as terrorists.

Take, for instance, the skepticism of a San Salvador–based researcher who writes on youth violence in Central America. He was not convinced of the successful assimilation of these contrary elements in Homies Unidos but instead saw evidence of "contradictory practices." While he felt strongly that those youth who had left gangs should become involved in the work to engage gang youth in their communities in positive ways, he nonetheless did not believe that former gang members had the capacity to be the "operators" and "executors" of *programas de inserción* (programs for social insertion). For this researcher, these programs were best directed by those structurally ordained spaces for the exercise of popular interests such as the churches, their parishes, international aid organizations, and perhaps even select government agencies.[13] If as Alvarez and others suggest that social movements must not only draw on networks of everyday life but also must construct or configure new interpersonal, interorganizational, and politico-cultural linkages with other existing movements, then the success of Homies Unidos in San Salvador was still indeterminate.

The Space of Civil Society

By 2002, public forums held in posh San Salvador hotels had become the primary stage for the performance of civil society and democratic debate in postwar El Salvador, and Homies Unidos, despite its controversial status, had become a ubiquitous presence at these events. One day in August of that year, I arrived late to the Hotel Transcontinental, the location of a forum for seeking solutions to the phenomenon of student youth violence. The event was sponsored by the Salvadoran legislative assembly and the University of Texas, Austin, the latter of which had been providing technical assistance to the assembly through its Modernization of the State project. When I entered the room housing the forum, the Salvadoran attorney general was speaking very broadly about the causes behind youth violence. As I surveyed the room to find a seat, Luis Ernesto Romero (aka Pansa Loca) of Homies Unidos signaled to me to come over to sit with him and his "homies."

The first time I saw Homies Unidos members in a setting like this was in November 1998 at a presidential candidates' debate on migration held at the exclusive Hotel El Salvador. I remember then being taken aback by the contrasts at play there. In the back row of the elegant and plush salon were eight or so gang members—most of them deportees from the United States sporting shaved heads and tattoos designating their affiliations with U.S. Latino immigrant gangs. Some wore the expected baggy attire. Most startling in this context was a young woman, La Smiley, whose spider-web tattoos climbed up her neck and onto her face. It was difficult not to stare, and to look past the distracting lines, to engage the face behind. Needless to say, the entrance of these young people against the sea of tailored suits was enough to turn the heads of the crowd. These unlikely members of Salvadoran civil society had come to the debate as members of Homies Unidos in San Salvador and as loosely affiliated participants in this social movement for migrants' rights.

Four years later at the Hotel Transcontinental, members from Homies Unidos were in attendance as participants of a social movement for youth rights. Some of the faces from 1998 were again present in the room; others, however, had since been lost—killed on the streets of San Salvador. Some of the faces were new, recently arrived courtesy of U.S. Marshal planes. The topic of the forum in 1998 was migration, but crime and youth gang violence surfaced as a powerful interpretive thread running throughout the candidates' presentations. Although the topic of the forum in 2002 was youth violence, migration to the United States, and the subsequent deportation of gang youth from that country, surfaced as a key explanatory concept behind youth violence. In each case, youth violence and migration had become integrally linked.[14]

PRESIDENTIAL DEBATE ON MIGRATION, AUGUST 1998

The 1998 presidential debate was sponsored by El Foro Permanente de Migrantes, a consortium of churches, research institutes, and NGOs organized for the defense of migrants' human rights.[15] With 20 percent of the Salvadoran population living abroad, primarily in the United States, the Salvadoran economy was already heavily subsidized by immigrant remittances. As a result, there were tremendous anxieties and expectations surrounding migration, including how to leverage those remittances productively, how to ensure the Salvadoran diaspora's continued attachment to the homeland, and how to cope with family disintegration and other social stresses caused by migration.[16] This presidential debate on migration was the first of its kind. I was interested in the presidential elections insofar as they pertained to Salvadoran state policy on Salvadorans abroad and those in the United States in particular.

The debate on migration issues included, among others, a cast of characters that I had met in Los Angeles—some during the war and some only very recently. There was Salvador Sanabria, a former FMLN diplomatic representative in Washington, D.C., during the war, and Jesus Aguilar, a founding member of the Central American Refugee Committee (CRECEN) in Los Angeles, the political counterpart to Central American Refugee Center (CRECEN) that would subsequently direct CRECEN International in San Salvador.[17] Both Salvador and Jesus had been political refugees themselves, and they had shared their border-crossing stories with me. They had returned to El Salvador after the war to participate in the rebuilding of El Salvador and its transition toward democracy. Jesus was working directly with the Foro, and Salvador had cofounded a new NGO and think tank—Fundación Centroamericana para el Desarrollo Humano Sostenible (FUCAD) (Central American Foundation for Sustainable Human Development). In El Salvador they would come to focus on hometown associations, and several years later Salvador would return to Los Angeles to further develop these links as director of El Rescate. There were others, too, that I recognized from Los Angeles; Werner Marroquin, for example, who worked in the Immanuel Presbyterian Church just up the street from the MS Normandie clique and where Homies Unidos held their poetry groups in Los Angeles. Sitting in the same hall was Carlos Martínez, whom I had interviewed in Los Angeles about his role in the terrestrial and maritime trade between Los Angeles and El Salvador. His very successful business, Transportes Salvadoreño, was located in Pico Union, a straight shot up from the Jack in the Box at Pico and Hoover streets. I had met Carlos though at the Salvadoran Chamber of Commerce, which was housed at the Curacao building—the twin towers of Central American commercial, legal, and civic life in Los Angeles where Homies Unidos had relocated after Alex Sanchez's arrest by Rampart CRASH officers.

The debate on migration issues began with the FMLN presidential candidate and former guerrilla commander Facundo Guardado. He chose *inseguridad* (insecurity) as the theme of his speech on migration and used it as an analytical blade to dissect the history of Salvadoran migration, which he partitioned into the three historical waves of the periods before, during, and after the civil war. According to this schema, Salvadoran insecurity prior to the civil war was (as were the reasons for migration) economic—that is, the insecurity of not being able to earn a living. Leading up to and during the civil war, Salvadoran insecurity was (as were the reasons for migration) political—namely, the insecurity of not being able to exercise one's political rights or to enjoy one's human rights. Finally, in the post–civil war era Salvadoran insecurity is (as are the reasons for contemporary migration) crime.[18] As in the case of most analysts and policymakers at the time, Guardado's speech was based on published PNC statistics that put the homicide rate at 136.5 per 100,000 individuals.

Guardado was followed by the candidate for the right-wing party, the League for Democratic Reform (LIDER), who offered his own theory about the relationship of migration and violence. He warned against the dark side of El Salvador's migration story by explaining the phenomena of wanton sexuality, drugs, gang violence, and AIDS in terms of migration and "Americanization." These, he concluded, were all "cultural contaminants" that Salvadorans had brought back with them from the United States. The direction and object of his scorn—the young men sitting in the back of the room—couldn't have been clearer. What, I wondered, were they thinking? I would return to El Salvador in 2002 to investigate how deported gang youth had becomes foils for and agents in the fearful reality of post–civil war violence in El Salvador and the practices and imaginaries that surround it, along with the placement of Homies Unidos therein.

FORUM ON YOUTH VIOLENCE, AUGUST 2002

Back at the forum and workshop for seeking solutions to the phenomenon of student youth violence, I made my way across to the group of members from Homies Unidos, who greeted me with both the formal Latin American kiss on the cheek and the gang-style handshake. I took a seat between Chamaco, a deportee from the United States, and Huera. While Huera had traveled to the United States, she had never lived there. Unlike the other homies present that day, she was jumped into her gang in El Salvador, albeit into a clika (clique, group, or cell) started in El Salvador by deportees from the United States. Nonetheless, she spells her name, which means "blondie" or fair skinned, according to a Spanglish version (Huera) rather than the Spanish equivalent (Güera). By the time I sat down, the attorney general had finished speaking and relinquished the floor to the next speaker. It was Mauricio Sandoval, then-director of the PNC, who explained that gangs were not new to El Salvador but appeared in the 1970s. Back then, however, they were not considered violent, and were even thought to be of service to their communities by working in their defense. But in the 1990s, Sandoval said, these groups turned violent, a condition that was aggravated by the deportation of delinquent youth from the United States and the associated process of "transculturalization." Sandoval suggested that the responses to youth violence must include all sectors of the state (the police, the attorney general, and the prisons, as well as broader sociocultural conditions), but he narrowed in on the justice system on two counts. First, he called for a revision of the law governing juvenile offenders, and second, he decried the use of "human rights as a defensive strategy" on behalf of these juvenile offenders. And herein lies the crux of what was at stake in El Salvador—namely, the *reform* (some would say dismantling) of post–civil war *reforms*. Sandoval wanted to gut these protections. Chamaco leaned over to me and says, "Man, that guy just wants to put us all away."

Up next was Salvador Samayoa, president of the National Council for Public Security. Samayoa offered very different solutions to those given by Sandoval: "I don't believe that this problem will be solved by police, but rather by social prevention." Chamaco liked this last comment: "That's cool. What this guy is saying is *good*." Samayoa then began to talk about the programs he has seen in operation in New York. He listed them off one after the other as models to emulate, painting a rosy picture of success stories in Latino immigrant communities in the United States, New York in particular. Given the lack of resources available in El Salvador, the New York model might look progressive, but I was sitting in the midst of a group of young people whose presence was a product of zero-tolerance strategies not unlike those instituted in New York.

The last speaker of the morning was Padre José Pepe Morataya, a Spanish priest of the Salesian order. He was speaking in his capacity as general manager of the El Poligono Don Bosco, a church-based program that operated a very impressive complex of cooperative bakeries, carpentry workshops, and alternative schools. Don Bosco was invariably the example cited alongside Homies Unidos as one of the only programs in the country focused on the needs of gang youth. Yet Don Bosco and Homies Unidos had a mutual disregard for each other's programs. Was this, I wondered, due to their respective organizing strategies of Catholic hierarchy versus youth empowerment. Perhaps the European disdain for the role and influence of the United States in El Salvador was also at work here?

Padre Pepe's charismatic and inflammatory speech brought into sharp relief the points of contention between the organizations. Organized violence, he asserted, comes from migration. After noting that El Salvador received five hundred deportees from the United States each month, he claimed that on their arrival, with the help of other deportees, they take a tour of the entire country to survey the terrain and to assess the existing networks of crime in order to set up their base of operation. The priest continued in this vein by stating that the deportees successfully create regional networks throughout Central America and that Salvadorans have become well known as the regional leaders.

His discourse created a stir around me. Up until now, Chamaco, seemingly bored by the drone of talking heads, had been doodling the name of his gang, CV Amigos Westside Los Angeles, under the legislative assembly's logo on the notepaper provided in the event packet. But Padre Pepe had caught his attention: "*Solo paja* [what bullshit]" say Chamaco and Travieso to each other, shaking their heads and laughing.

The picture of the deportees' supposedly privileged tour through and bird's-eye view of El Salvador was very different from the experience and geographical disorientation of those who came through the doors of Homies Unidos. As I described in the previous chapter, Homies Unidos did provide orientation to deportees to help them with the shock and alienation they experience upon their return to what for many of them was an unknown "homeland." Deportees invariably expressed fear at having to go as far as the corner store, and just getting on a bus can be a traumatic and dangerous experience. Many of them approached Homies Unidos to learn how to navigate hostile and foreign terrain, or to derive a sense of place and forge a familial bond.

Pepe came to the end of his speech, and the MC retook the stage to initiate the question-and-answer period. He started to read a long list of questions, turned in on index cards, including: How is it that the PNC can be struggling to diminish organized crime and drug trafficking and so on if there are police involved in these problems? Would you define a gang member as a delinquent? Is being a youth becoming a crime in itself? Is the PNC saying that youth should be punished as adults? Why hasn't the legislative assembly approved the Ley de Juventud (Law of the Youth)? Is there a problem providing alternative education to gang members? Why are there no opportunities to study for deportees who have completed ninth grade in the United States? The last was Travieso's question.

As the first respondent began to address the questions, Huera got up, signaling to the Homies to join her. She then moved to the side of the room where a group of young people were unfolding banners that read, "Youth is not synonymous with violence nor drugs" and "Youth is not a crime." The leader of the group tried to get the attention of the MC, who responded by asking them to respect the established order of things: this was not the time or the place for this sort of action. But the audience intervened once again by admonishing the MC to let the group speak. After he conceded, the group made the following statement: "We are trying to build a youth culture with the object of contributing to our community. So far all we have heard are the negatives. We have not heard you say anything positive about us. Here we are conducting national consultations working to develop La Ley de Juventud. We have heard you speak, but the needs of Salvadoran youth have still not been fulfilled. You want to silence us, but why should we let adults speak for us?" As the audience members applauded, a group representative continued: "We don't use any violence or drugs. What we want is for you to listen to us truthfully and not to leave us on the sidelines, or as a question on a little piece of paper [the index cards]. We want answers." And with that, the youth returned the floor to the panelists, who resumed taking the questions one by one.

Sandoval's call for reforms to the juvenile offender law was linked to a post–human rights agenda and to the zero-tolerance and gang abatement strategies of the United States. In contrast, the youth's call for La Ley de Juventud was linked to an international movement for human rights and youth rights. In addition to these vastly divergent strategies, there were also very different notions of the category of "youth" at stake. Sandoval would try minors as adults and increase prison sentences; Huera's group of youth advocates would extend the category of youth up to the age of thirty to provide rehabilitation programs to those tried as juveniles but released as adults. El Salvador's contemporary politics surrounding youth, globalization, and law enforcement were thus situated between these two poles, albeit leaning heavily in Sandoval's direction.

In the months following the forum on youth violence, La Ley de Juventud would flounder in committee with post-electoral changes in the composition of the legislature.[19] Sandoval's agenda, on the other hand, would gain considerable momentum and culminate in his successor's implementation of El Plan Mano Dura (the Firm Hand, or Iron Fist, Plan). As a result, Chamaco's disconcerted commentary during Sandoval's address, "Man, this guy just wants to put us all away," would be proven correct.

The members of Homies Unidos present at the forum on youth violence that day in 2002 did not, in fact, join their homegirl Huera and the group of youth in their public petition to be seen and heard through La Ley de Juventud. I asked them why. "Na," they shook their heads. "We don't like to do that kind of stuff. We're already visible enough. As it is, every time we walk into places like that, people always turn and stare." Huera, however, was not appeased by this response. She felt very let down by the Homies and by their refusal to stand up and be counted in the movement. But I discerned from this situation that while Homies Unidos may have become fixtures at these events, its members were uneasy participants in civil society.

The disquieting place of Homies Unidos in Salvadoran civil society would become all the more apparent the next day at a seminar sponsored by the UNDP. I discovered there that my own positionality at the forum "smack in the middle of Homies Unidos" had been duly noted, with eyebrows raised, by the director of the National Council for Public Security, Oscar Bonilla. Bonilla was the right-hand man to the council's president, Samayoa. Laughing off his remark about my sitting next to Homies Unidos, but feeling labeled, I asked Bonilla in a subsequent meeting at his office if the council had worked with the organization. Bonilla responded that he did not find the organization particularly "credible."

Indeed, within Salvadoran civil society, Homies Unidos was ultimately a disconcerting and untenable blend of what the literature would dub "distasteful" movements with those sanctioned as "progressive" social movements.[20] The group's tattooed young men and women—many with a criminal record of one sort or another—were unlikely contenders alongside the "candidates of choice" in the "approved" marginalized groups of indigenous and ethnic peoples and members of movements for women, gays, and the environment.[21]

A week after the forum on youth violence, Homies Unidos met to talk about, among other things, an invitation by the PNC to present their gang violence prevention program at the office of Homies Unidos. The discussion was heated. One of the Homies claimed that the PNC had invited some gang members to a meeting in the past where they were ostensibly going to talk about their programs, but arrested them all instead. "Just to know them? What for?" "I don't want them to know where our offices are so they can come and spy on us." Weasel added, "We already have problems working in the communities as it is. I don't want to be seen as no snitch. What they want from us is information." Another member was adamant, "With so many homies in Mariona [prison] right now" why would they want to work with the police?[22] Pansa and Huera, who had introduced the PNC proposal to the group, were defensive. Pansa insisted: "I'm no snitch. I'm not working for the police." Huera brought the discussion to a close, "We'll leave it tentative then." "Okay," said Weasel, "We'll put it down as tentative."

This tentative relationship with the police marked a shift in Homies Unidos. Early on in its formation, the San Salvador program had succeeded in building working relations with both the PNC and the central office of San Salvador's metropolitan police force Centro Area Metropolitana (CAM). Over the following months, with the explosion of a very public and gruesome murder attributed to deported gang members, the relationship of Homies Unidos to the PNC became even more "tentative." That case, dubbed the "Case of Rosa N.," turned out to be just the first in a series of macabre mutilations and decapitations attributed to members of the 18th Street Gang. Between December 2002 and March 2003, Sandoval, the director of the PNC, launched a major media campaign around these *descabezamientos* (beheadings/decapitations) that involved mass arrests of gang members and a call for the passage of special anti-gang laws.[23]

One morning in January 2003, I walked into the office of Homies Unidos, which was abuzz with news on the media coverage of the recent mutilations attributed to 18th Street and the police reaction to it. There was a mixture of fury and fright in the air. Some of the accused were among those who had passed through Homies Unidos's doors, and were known to members there. The Homies were fearful of the inevitable guilt by association that would be made between the organization, the gangs, and the scandal. The neighbors in the complex were growing suspicious of and hostile toward the organization, and everybody felt that it was time to move the office to neutral ground. As Weasel put it, "Getting a new office is like starting over, a fresh start." This would be the organization's fifth move in its six-year history.

There was some discussion as to whether Homies Unidos would express public indignation at the mass arrests of gang members and Sandoval's proposed new law targeting gang violence, but some members wanted the organization to lay low and to avoid press coverage. They did not want to come out in the press and thus be associated with the current events. Still others were concerned as much about the reaction of the gangs as they were about those of the public and the police.

Homies Unidos had long been the place where journalists—Salvadoran and international—went to set up interviews with active gang members in the field. But recently this was causing repercussions for the organization. Gang members, often quite willing to perform their gangster identities in front of the camera, were becoming more camera shy as the media and police mounted campaigns against them and Homies Unidos was struggling with its mediating role. "We must ask in advance and get the permission of the clika. Please Homies, let's respect the law of the street." But the problem had already gone beyond the organization's control. Apparently, journalists from one of the major national newspapers had started going into gang territory using the name of Homies Unidos to secure interviews with the gang members. As a result, some of Homies Unidos's bridges with the gangs had been damaged if not broken. The outreach coordinators were becoming more reluctant to take people out into the field or even to go themselves. Homies Unidos's field of operation—the barrios on the outskirts of San Salvador—were becoming increasingly tense and difficult to enter. The gangs were suspicious, and the police presence was daunting. Word was that they were picking up anyone on the streets under the vague and all-encompassing infraction of *asociaciones ilicitas*.

During this time I was gone for a week, and I returned to San Salvador only to learn that Homies Unidos's newest office had been broken into. All of the equipment had been stolen: TVs, computers, and videos. The word was that it was an "inside" job; perhaps by disgruntled program participants. Regardless, the staff felt that they couldn't return. They recovered what they could and abandoned the location. It had been only four months since they felt compelled to move from the last location to start anew, and needless to say the mood was heavy and spirits very low. "Imagine," Huera exclaimed, "that this would happen to us. We who used to do such things ourselves!" Shut out of the barrios—the ground of the field operations of the organization—by the combined heat of gang politics and the heavy police presence, Homies Unidos was now also without an office. This organization, first conceived of as providing an alternative space of representation for gang affiliated youth and young adults and a safe and neutral space for those willing to try to give up la vida loca, had turned first into an impossible space and now into a nonspace. One month later, the ruling right-wing party Alianza Repulicana Nacionalista (ARENA), in concert with the PNC, unleashed its zero-tolerance strategy, El Plan Mano Dura.

El Plan Mano Dura

In July 2003, just one year after the forum on youth violence, then-President Francisco Flores declared a state of emergency and unveiled the police campaign named El Plan Mano Dura, along with an accompanying legislative proposal, *La Ley Anti-Mara* (the Anti-Gang Law). Both became central to the ruling right-wing's political platform in the ensuing presidential elections, and together they represented a victory for the post–human rights agenda of the Right.

The Left came out against the plan. In the aftermath of the Peace Accords, however, the FMLN's position on crime was not markedly different from that of ARENA. Just days after the Foro's presidential debate on migration in 1998, the FMLN candidate Guardado made "crime" his key campaign issue with his *La Tarjeta Roja* (the Red Card) proposal. La Tarjeta Roja promised to reduce violent crime by putting repeat offenders behind bars for life. This indistinction between the Left and the Right in regard to crime was not peculiar to El Salvador. With the exception of Brazil, in the aftermath of their military dictatorships and dirty wars, the Latin American Left in general did not extend its human rights agenda for political prisoners to the domain of common criminals or to prisoners' rights in general.[24] As the Salvadoran researcher Mauricio Chavez elaborated in a presentation given at the University of California, Northridge, in 1999, the anti-crime discourses and legislation in El Salvador elided the complex historical relationship that El Salvador bears to violence: namely, a class system based on the outright coercive force of power; the absence of postwar reconciliation efforts as a result of the suppression of the human rights record and the generalized amnesty for violent offenders (on the Right and the Left); and, of course, its relationship with the U.S. government. "One would expect," he said, "given that they were a *revolutionary* party, that the FMLN would have a different understanding of these issues. But it's not there. They have entered into a competition with ARENA over who's tougher on violence."

Interestingly, this post–human rights agenda drew upon the analysis of a former military commander of the FMLN, Joaquin Villalobos (albeit who subsequently was persona non grata with the FMLN). Villalobos, who turned to advising the Salvadoran government on security issues in the postwar period, argued that the human rights agenda had spawned legislation in post–civil war El Salvador that was more appropriate for European countries such as Switzerland, where crime is low and its citizens have long been educated in the responsibilities that accrue to citizens in a democracy. Human rights as enshrined in the Penal Code of 1988 were thus *leyes para los suizos* (laws for the Swiss), not for Salvadorans.[25] El Salvador, however, was in need of a firmer hand until its population had been disciplined (in the Foucauldian sense) as governable democratic citizens. While Villalobos as well as the FMLN spoke out against Mano Dura when it was unleashed in 2003, in the postwar years the Left alongside the Right deplored the ways in which human rights had come to serve as "privileges for bandits"—to use Teresa Caldeira's phrase for a similar twist in Brazilian culture and political life.[26]

The reforms of the reforms deemed more suitable to this "weak" and "immature" democracy were derived from the laws that had purportedly worked for the gringos (the United States). El Plan Mano Dura represented the successful transnationalization of United States zero-tolerance strategies in El Salvador, or *los leyes para los gringos*. This is not to say that the United States and its policing models did not already have considerable influence over the PNC. But that influence—technical assistance and funding—was structured, at least initially, around the implementation of the Peace Accords rather than post–civil war violent crime.[27]

During this period, the primary task of the United States turned from aiding the Salvadoran military in its fight against the leftist guerrilla forces to aiding in the construction of a new National Civil Police in collaboration with other countries such as Spain and France. This process, overseen by the United Nations, involved disbanding the existing public security system that had been composed of the National Police (PN), the National Guard (GN), and the Hacienda (Plantation) Police (PH), all of which were part of the Salvadoran Armed Forces and, as such, operated under the Ministry of Defense. In addition, paramilitary organizations functioned as militias under local military commanders and provided a network of political intelligence throughout the country. The primary function of these combined forces was to maintain internal order and to control the population.[28] In their place, a new civilian police force was to be established that would be entirely independent from the military, free of all partisan activity, function as a service provided by the State to its citizens, and dedicated to defending the human rights of all citizens.[29]

Given the role of the United States in training the Salvadoran military in counterinsurgency strategies and the troubling record of human rights violations by Salvadoran officers trained at the School of the Americas,[30] the FMLN was understandably suspicious of the involvement of the United

States in this reconstruction effort. While the United States maintained an office in the PNC headquarters, its role in the construction of the PNC was, according to the terms of the Peace Accords, to be limited to technical training in the investigation of crimes. This technical assistance was provided through the U.S. Department of Justice's International Criminal Investigation Technical Assistance Program (ICITAP).[31] The new recruits, as well as the Salvadoran SWAT and the anti-riot police (GOPE), were trained by the Spanish and the French respectively. At the same time, the United States's role increased in the area of the drug war through collaboration with the Salvadoran attorney general's office, and through trainings in the United States with the FBI and the DEA.

Still, under the sponsorship of the U.S. embassy, most senior police officers had already been introduced to zero-tolerance models through their visits to police departments in New York, Boston, Chicago, Los Angeles, Houston, and elsewhere. The walls of their offices were invariably lined with certificates from the U.S. Justice Department to commemorate these trainings and exchanges. Moreover, a number of crime prevention models from the United States, including 911, DARE, Bratton's CompStat crime-mapping computer systems, the Field Interview Card, and the San Jose version of community policing in the form of Community Police Intervention Patrols (PIPCOM), had been introduced into El Salvador directly by ICITAP, which, as I mentioned, maintained offices in both the U.S. embassy and the PNC headquarters. However, unlike other countries such as Mexico, Venezuela, and South Africa, these exchanges took place between the United States and Salvadoran governments through "international cooperation" and not through private consultancies with the Manhattan Institute and the Giuliani Group.

El Plan Mano Dura was by no means the first attempt to introduce zero-tolerance policing strategies in El Salvador. Indeed, Guardado's La Tarjeta Roja plan was governed by the same punitive logic as the initiative "Three Strikes and You're Out" (Proposition 184) introduced and passed in post-riot Los Angeles. Following Three Strikes as it does by four years, La Tarjeta Roja read like an attempt to translate the same principle into Salvadoran cultural terms. The reference in each case was drawn from sports—Three Strikes from baseball in the United States and the Red Card from soccer in El Salvador. The intimate relationship between sports and nationalism resonated in both United States and Salvadoran policy initiatives. In El Salvador, this relationship between sports and nationalism also had a powerful precedent with the infamous soccer war over border skirmishes between that country and Honduras. (Indeed, it was the poetic resonance, so to speak, between Three Strikes and La Tarjeta Roja that first drew me to look at the traveling of crime prevention strategies as one more component of the dense transnational networks of circulation between the United States and El Salvador.) While Guardado's anti-crime platform did not target gang members or deportees per se, it nonetheless mirrored the cultural politics of the United States, the very sort that fed into the criminalization and subsequent deportation of a key sector of Homies Unidos's leadership and membership sitting in the back row of the conference room where Guardado had presented his thesis about migration and crime.

The ARENA government had already explored the possibility of instituting a quasi-transnational probation system for criminal deportees and had twice introduced emergency crime legislation, in 1996 and again in 1999, in the form of the Social Defense Law. If it had passed, that law would have jailed upon their arrival Salvadorans deported from the United States for criminal offenses. Under this proposal, that is, a deportee would have received triple punishment for his offense: jail time in the United States, deportation to El Salvador, and reimprisonment in El Salvador.

As René Dominguez, vice-minister of citizen security, put it when I met with him in May 2003, "the project [to introduce anti-gang legislation] was already developed but was put on hold, because it did not have the necessary resonance in society." He explained this to me as we leafed through a booklet of anti-gang abatement legislation from the United States (curfews, injunctions, the felonization of graffiti, the limits on free association, the criminalization of gang membership, the use of cell phones by alleged gang members, and so on) compiled from the National Youth Gang Center's Web site for the ministry by the National Council on Public Security.

Certainly, as a study conducted by IUDOP suggested, there was sufficient resonance in society by 1998.[32] Perhaps what Dominguez meant by "resonance in society" was resonance in *civil society*. Indeed, it was the human rights agenda of post–civil war Salvadoran civil society more than anything else that had put the brakes on zero-tolerance strategies—a point stressed by Sandoval in his address to that forum on youth violence. As Miguel Cruz, then director of IUDOP, explained to me in 2002: "What we have in the post–civil war era is *una ensalada* [a salad or mixture] of progressive and regressive laws, an incoherent, disordered, and contradictory set of laws." He noted further that over the last three years, since the passage of the 1998 [progressive] penal reforms, we have seen a backslide in those reforms with various amendments. After the war there was a huge effort to reform, then came the discourse that behind the level of violence is the liberty that comes with human rights discourse. So the progressive spirit is in danger. [This backlash had] not yet actually affected youth. Despite the attempts to reform the juvenile offender laws, there has been strong support for it especially from the family tribunals, even though there has been pressure to criminalize all sorts of activities. This could change, of course.

The introduction of El Plan Mano Dura did precisely that. It changed juvenile offender laws to criminalize a whole category of youth between the ages of twelve and eighteen.

Mano Dura and the anti-gang laws drew from models like the California Street Terrorism Enforcement Prevention Act (STEP) and anti-loitering laws.[33] As with the anti-gang legislation in the United States, El Plan Mano Dura worked actively in the name of prevention to build a record against and criminalize youth through petty infractions and hence channel young people into the criminal justice system before serious crimes could be committed. The goal was to get young people into the system by giving law enforcement probable cause to arrest them. While many of these practices were already in effect under the catch-all category of "illicit association," the supporting legislation increased fines and prison sentence for minors, as well as made illicit a range of additional activities previously legal. The plan made gang membership itself illegal and also prohibited the association of two or more gang members. As with the CALGANG list in Los Angeles, the Salvadoran law had a very broad interpretation of what constituted gang affiliation and thus probable cause for detaining alleged gang members. Silvia Beltrán, then-director of Homies Unidos in Los Angeles, argued that El Plan Mano Dura "practically makes being young and poor a crime . . . The police and army are targeting youth who congregate in poor communities."[34]

A Dream Deferred

The implementation in 2003 of El Plan Mano Dura was the last straw for Homies Unidos San Salvador. If the organization had been weakened before Flores's announcement, its tattooed peace workers were completely immobilized and their already fraught association with and outreach to their constituency—gang and poor youth—was now "illicit." Indeed, like its counterpart in the United States, under El Plan Mano Dura police officers made no distinction between gang peace activists and nonactive and active gang members. Moreover, under changing conditions, including the increasing radicalization of the gangs as a result of the all-out assault against them by the state, individuals within Homies Unidos in El Salvador found it increasingly difficult to draw that already fuzzy line between the NGO and the gang. As El Plan Mano Dura put the screws on the gangs, the organization came under increasingly intense pressure from the barrio politics of the 18th Street Gang, which only served to further marginalize them from civil society. Being from a smaller, lesser-known gang, Weasel was particularly vulnerable; one of the staff members there told me that he had already had to intervene more than once to save Weasel's life. Not long after the implementation of El Plan Mano Dura, Weasel tried to reenter the United States with the help of a coyote. He was turned back twice in Mexico before making it across the U.S.–Mexico border, but he was quickly apprehended by the border patrol on the other side. When he turned up in the San Diego County Jail in January 2004 I was not exactly expecting him, but I was not surprised that he had tried to make a run for it. What else could he be expected to do if he felt that death was chasing him? Indeed, even I was warned to stay away from the organization and El Salvador in summer 2005 when I intended to do follow-up research on El Plan Mano Dura. People in Los Angeles felt that they could no longer vouch for their homies down there because things had spun completely out of their control.

The last time I had seen Weasel in the United States was behind a Plexiglas partition in the California City Corrections Facility (one of many facilities owned by the government but operated by private security companies and occupied, according to Weasel, exclusively by "criminal deportees" now doing time for "illegal reentry"). Weasel had completed his fourteen months in federal prison and was waiting to be transferred to an INS detention facility, where he would be processed for deportation.[35] Despite our urging he had decided not to fight his immigration case, because he wanted to be reunited with his wife and with his daughter, who was born just months before he left for the United States, rather than languish in a detention center waiting for his case to be heard.

Meanwhile, the Los Angeles–based directorship of Homies Unidos had cut its institutional ties with its El Salvador operations. The Salvadoran-based office changed its name to Hombres y Mujeres Inserción Social de El

Salvador (Social Insertion for Men and Women of El Salvador, or HOMIES) and found a fiscal agent through which they were able to channel support in CORTAID (a Dutch NGO). When last I met with Luis Ernesto Romero in September 2009 to review with him the contents of the Salvadoran chapters of this book, he was expecting the organization's application for nonprofit status to come through any day. HOMIES had moved into spacious offices in a large condominium complex with a security guard. The building was located right across from a PNC station and in the heart of a commercial district. At the time, the organization had seven paid staff members on its books.

Nonetheless, the utopian project begun a decade earlier by bringing together deported members of both MS and 18th Street gangs to stop the violence had all but come to a halt. The dream of a transnational organization between Los Angeles and San Salvador created by, for, and on behalf of gang members seeking an alternative path to violence and globalization had been crushed on multiple fronts: by the state, civil society, the gangs, and the enduring inequities in capital and power between North and South.

SOLDIER COP | ────── **SIX**

REMILITARIZED SPACE

In El Salvador three years after the implementation of El Plan Mano Dura, the picture was bleak. The homicide rate in 2006 had, according to available statistics, increased by 45 percent since the implementation of zero-tolerance policies in 2003. Everyone I came into contact with felt strongly that *manodurista* policies or *manodurismo* had made their community-based work impossible and had only served to radicalize the gangs by turning them into much more sophisticated and now clandestine operations.[1] The violence was so crushingly close. As Silvia Guillén, the director of Fundación de Estudios para la Aplicación del Derecho (or FESPAD, an NGO focusing on the application of constitutional law), described it to me—"the violence is in our face every day now." There was so little room to maneuver, and the political space seemed to be shutting down in every direction. The phenomenological effects of the violence on my long-time Salvadoran informants, friends, and colleagues were palpable. The pressure was reaching unbearable levels, even within the relatively sheltered urban, professional middle class. Hysteria about post–civil war violence was not new in El Salvador, but the discourse seemed to have shifted from "it's worse than war"[2] to "it looks like the precursor to another civil war" or "another Colombia." By all accounts ARENA's manodurista policies were a *fracaso* (disaster).[3]

If the Peace Accords had succeeded in delinking the military and the police, manodurista policies enabled their reconnection through the figure of the soldier-cop. The green uniforms of the army and the blue uniforms of the police began to blur into something not unlike camouflage. The soldier-cop configuration harkens back to an early moment in Salvadoran history when the police were a division of the Salvadoran Armed Forces. Indeed, the plan's introduction of joint patrols of police officers and of soldiers threatened to bring the military back into politics and thus strengthen the hand of *los señores de la guerra* (the warlords),[4] whose power had diminished considerably since the signing of the Peace Accords in 1992.[5]

The fieldwork that I had conducted three years earlier, as well as prior to that in the 1990s, was no longer feasible. Going into the neighborhoods and the prisons had only become increasingly difficult and dangerous and required clearance not only from the gangs (who were more and more reticent to give it) but now also from the police, who were not only considerably more militarized in their own tactics but now had the backing of the military. After massive prison riots in 2005, all NGOs had been barred from entering the prisons (with a few exceptions for religious organizations). By 2006 the NGOs were only just trying to regain permission from the prison wardens *and* the gangs to reinitiate their programs in the prisons.

Given the conditions in El Salvador and the retreat of Homies Unidos, I decided to take a more cautious (that is, institutionally backed) path into the neighborhoods. So I tagged along with the violence prevention workers attached to the constellation of organizations now focused on gang and criminal justice issues. Several of these groups and individuals had worked in collaboration with Homies Unidos in the mid-1990s, in those heady days when human rights were high on the agenda and when there was an unprecedented degree of open political space for such initiatives. By 2006, the space for such initiatives had diminished considerably—although President Saca's renewal of Flores's El Plan Mano Dura in the form of El Plan Súper Mano Dura included two concessions to civil society's critique of the former's sole focus on repression. El Plan Súper Mano Dura, somewhat ironically given its name, now included a plan for violence prevention, Mano Amiga (Friendly Hand), and a plan for gang rehabilitation, Mano Extendida (Extended Hand), and the creation of La Secretaría de Juventud (Secretariat of Youth) to oversee the coordination of such initiatives. It was these sorts of initiatives that the youth behind La Ley de Juventud and then-president of the National Council for Public Security (CNSP), Salvador Samayoa, had called for at the conference on youth violence in 2002 discussed in chapter 5.

Given the vastly unequal distribution of funds and the number of youth impacted, the latter two programs appeared as mere window dressing. Indeed, the Secretariat of Youth had no autonomy from the president, and it was focused only on violence prevention rather than on intervention. Moreover, despite the addition of Mano Extendida it was evident that there was still much more effort and money being devoted to repressive measures. Whereas over the first two years of its implemetation Mano Extendida had reached about thirty-five gang members, between Mano Dura and Mano Súper Dura thirty thousand youth accused of being gang members were arrested between July 2003 and July 2005.[6]

The organizations charged with the implementation of these programs spoke as if they were under siege in much the same way that Homies Unidos had been three years earlier. In fact, I was immediately struck with how these organizations were now navigating the same thorny terrain as had Homies Unidos, and in some cases crossing the same blurred boundaries as the organization had previously. Bear in mind that all of these groups had started to distance themselves from Homies Unidos precisely because of this same difficulty in drawing the line between their program activities and the activities of the gang. Yet despite their status as government- and church-sponsored programs, these groups now found themselves, like Homies Unidos, squeezed between the police and the gangs.

The experience of Pro-Jóvenes is a case in point. Pro-Jóvenes was a temporary project of the European Union with a mandate to strengthen and to provide technical support to the programs of Salvadoran government entities such as the CNSP and the Secretariat of Youth. When I explained to Lisette Miranda, then director of Pro-Jóvenes, that I wanted to see the impact of manodurista policies on the ground, she suggested I follow her rehabilitation team into the field, starting with their projects in the neighborhood and housing projects of La IVU (Instituto de Vivienda Urbana), where there was a very strong clika of the 18th Street Gang. As Miranda explained:

We're there with the Secretariat of Youth experimenting with a small business project . . . that can provide an [alternative] everyday space for the guys. So we're now working with twenty-two youth from 18th Street in a bakery. They've been through four months of training in bread making, and now they're entering the profit-making phase.

This work with the 18th Street clique in La IVU is allowing us to do work inside the schools. Last year there was a 25 percent reduction in student enrollment [and] . . . the school was their recruitment center. So a large part of the school population went over to the other side [the gang]. What we're trying to do now is to ensure that the children who are in kindergarten pass into the next phase of education, and those in sixth grade pass onto seventh grade, et cetera . . . So we're investing considerably in infrastructure. We've recuperated all the sports areas . . . and we're involved in community work all around, but it's also because the gang is letting us.

The intention behind the rehabilitation project was not simply to keep gang members occupied with alternative income-generating projects but also, Miranda explained, "to explore how they might allow us to do our prevention programs in primary schools, that is, [we have to] negotiate [with the gang to get into the communities]."

So I made plans to visit La IVU with Denora, a former gang member who after going through a rehabilitation program herself in 1996 had been working ever since for rehabilitation programs of one sort or another. Denora joined her gang in the early 1990s when three deportees from the United States formed a clique in her barrio. As she explains, all three of the deportees are now dead. In fact, of all the kids who had jumped in when she was initiated, she tells me, "every single one of them" is now dead. "There's not one left, except me and one [guy] who was sentenced to prison for thirty years. Of sixty, only two of us are still living."

I had been to La IVU several times with a community organizer from CNSP in 2003 when the organization was just starting to work with that community. My most vivid memories of the neighborhood were of the basketball court that also served as a soccer field and of the glare of the spotlights that drenched the field at night. At that time, the community council was having difficulty meeting the costs of the resulting electric bills. These sports arenas had become the trademark and the proud centerpieces of CNSP's violence prevention projects. Their staff would give tours for delegations of dignitaries and funders from the European Union to see these jewels, and the visitors would exclaim, "Even Europe doesn't have courts like this!"

When Denora and I pulled up to that much-touted CNSP sports field in my rental car, there was a joint patrol of armed soldiers in green and police in blue walking away from the neighborhood. I had not seen the military in the streets of San Salvador since my first trip to the country during the civil war. My shock of recognition—this was what the remilitarization of the landscape looked liked—was met with Denora's shrugging it off as a visual icon of everyday life now taken for granted in neighborhoods such as La IVU.

The Soldier Cop

Denora and I passed the stalls of street vendors and crossed the street to climb up a steep flight of cement stairs to the top of a short hill. The steps emptied out into a passageway leading to a series of two-story cement apartment complexes. We were headed for the bakery. Before we reached the apartment where the bakery was housed, we were stopped and called to one side by the baker, Sonia, who was the project coordinator. She had decided not to open the bakery that morning because the police and the military (most likely the same group we had just seen leaving the barrio on the street below) had come up into the apartment complex housing the bakery looking for "gang members." Apparently, over the last week the police backed by the military had been stepping up surveillance in this complex by detaining the program participants as they came and went from the bakery to wash the pans or to leave them out to dry. In talking with me about today's incident, Sonia explained:

S: Today in the morning, I was waiting for the guys, and they never appeared . . . I realized they [the police] were here . . . three stationed there, and two here. The others, I didn't see, but afterwards the guys told me that they were posted all around here.

E: Before you were distinguishing between those in blue [police] and those in green [soldiers] . . .
[She only saw "those in blue" this time, who kept coming in and out of hiding.]

S: Look, they [the police and soldiers] are often around here, but this was very strange because it wasn't a normal patrol, rather they were monitoring the bakery. And so she [pointing to another woman] said,

"Let's go see what they're going to do." So we went over there, and a woman told us, "They've gone." "Oh they've gone?" "Yes, but listen, those in green [the soldiers]," she said to me, "had been stationed here and were walking around here, and it wasn't just three, it was much more," she said to me.

And when they left [went down the stairs] she said that they said to the others, "Let's go!" In other words, they weren't patrolling, rather they had come for them [the program participants]. And because of this, before anything else could happen, I decided "better not to make bread today," and so I closed the bakery . . . Why would I open the bakery if they're [the police are] going to hide there?

Denora suggests that now that the police have left I should see the bakery. On the way we pass a young man, Arturo, who had just come out from hiding. He was a participant in the bakery project. Arturo had been deported from Texas about a year ago. He had already suffered from multiple gun wounds, spent time in the *bartolinas* ("like county jails over there [in the United States]") for illicit association, and was lying low in La IVU despite the fact that his family was from another barrio. He said that the bakery project "kept him off the street," but he saw it as a hobby, not as an economic option.[7] He was aiming for jobs that could make use of his bilingual abilities. He listed the litany of transnational enterprises associated with globalization in El Salvador: Dell computer, Federal Express, call centers, and so on.[8] He seemed optimistic, saying that Dell just needed a copy of his criminal background. I didn't say it out loud, but I thought to myself that such documentation was more likely to undo the deal than to close it. I figured he knew as much, since he hadn't followed up with the paperwork. But really, he said, he planned to go back to the States "no matter what happens."

Denora and I go with Sonia to see the bakery. As Sonia speaks about her pedagogical approach to Mano Extendida, another one of the program participants, Pepe, shows up. Bearing all the "phenotypical" and expressive characteristics of a "gang member" as proscribed by Mano Dura (tattoos, shaved head, and baggy pants falling below his boxers), Pepe is clearly a prime target for the police.

P: Today we won't be making bread, right? That's rough, man! They're always robbing us of our tranquility. We can't win either way.

E: Yeah, we came here to observe the bakery in operation.

P: Only God knows if it's going to be like this, the way we planned today or tomorrow . . .

E: What were you going to do today?

P: Today we were going make a fruit tart . . . What a pity!

They start to talk once again about how the guys participating in the program are always dealing with being detained by the PNC. What follows is a recounting of incident after incident of being detained, arrested, harassed, and so on. The two women chime in, reminding him of still more incidents.

B: And on that day, they captured you again.

P: The following day I went out, they captured me again.

B: He was having lunch . . .

D: And the other one too, they were going to take him away from his own business. He was cooking, peeling vegetables to make a soup.

P: . . . me with a chocolate milk and two bread rolls. And they came up to me as if I was robbing a car . . . "Come here right now," he said to me. He took me up the stairs . . . just for being there.

B: They held you for how many days?

P: About four days. Por la *agrupación* [illicit gathering] they said.

B: But they take, let's say, they take one from here and another from there, and they cite them for illicit association.

E: Oh, so they weren't together when they were captured?

B: No. He was drinking his chocolate milk [laughing at the absurdity] there, and the other one was [working] in his business.

P: The other one was taking care of his business, peeling vegetables.

These disruptions by the police were particularly disconcerting given that Pro-Jóvenes had already reached an accord with the police to implement the bakery project. The police had agreed to help with the project, and to give their own violence prevention workshop once a week. Denora and Sonia began to recount another incident with the police, this time at a wake of "a *compañero* (friend) of the guys from another barrio but also from the [same] gang." On the morning before the wake, the police had attended a neighborhood meeting for the first time. When the meeting was over, one of the guys spoke to the deputy inspector, asking if the police could accompany them to the zone where the wake would be held so that they would not be stopped by police on the way. Apparently, the PNC deputy inspector agreed to provide the youth with police protection en route.

S: They [asked] me: "Señora, do you think we could make more bread quickly to take to the wake . . ."

The deputy inspector [had] said okay, yes they could go. "Tell us the number of youth going, the microbus that you're going to go in," he said. "Give us the license plate number and the address of where you're going to be, and go in peace/calmly."

Denora takes over recounting the story:

D: From there they left for the wake . . . at the beginning when they arrived they explained [what they were doing there] and they [the police] didn't say anything, as I understand it according to them . . . They [the police] said that they might come, but they were only going to monitor them . . . [and] they would . . . leave them in peace. So they arrived at the wake content, with the understanding that they had authorization [to be there] . . . and also accepting the backing of the [police] . . .

B: The other [thing] is, these kinds of things go on late into the night . . .

D: Around ten or eleven at night, the police from the anti-riot division came and started mistreating everyone . . . They were held for four hours in the street, everyone, they even took out the corpse and registered it, out of the coffin they took him, yes, the dead man . . . They threw out the flowers, they mistreated children who were there [and the] women . . . who were there sharing the grief of the family of the young man. They had passed four hours held like that . . . in the street. They beat them. OK, so one came back with scrapes everywhere, and with swelling and bruises, and one was beaten with a rifle . . . and another one of the kids, a sixteen year old, had pepper gas sprayed into his face, all over his face . . . After beating them up like this they took them into the PNC station [and] they were there for three days: Wednesday until Saturday.

If the director of the Secretariat of Youth hadn't intervened and asked for a special hearing they would have remained there until Monday. And they [the police] took their earrings, necklaces, cell phones, documents, and their bakery identifications (which gives them official permission to be participating in the program—but the PNC doesn't respect this).

P: Yeah . . . all of us were together looking at the corpse of our friend that the other gang killed. And so, they took everyone out, "Get out everyone! Hurry!" and so we all went outside . . . "This one's already gone to the devil," they [the police said] said pointing to the deceased. Then they handcuffed everyone, with our legs like this . . . But we're not doing anything. We're at a wake. Why would we make trouble at a wake, especially at one of a friend from the same gang? How are we going to mess with the wake of someone who is being honored, like a friend, like someone from the family . . . one could say?

No, man. This is not just, if you understand me . . . They should take me in for what I have done, not for something someone else has done [that is, the other gang in the case]. But this is how the police here [are] . . . They are police like, how can I say it? They're corrupt police . . . All human beings deserve another opportunity . . . no matter who they are, because el Señor Jesus Cristo . . . came to die here so that we could all live. You understand? So, we also are human beings. We also have the right to an opportunity that he gave us. Don't you think so?

The difference is that we go around with tattoos. But this is our thing. It's nothing. It doesn't hurt anyone, nor is it offensive. This not intended to offend. It's something that is . . . you understand . . . something of ours, particular to us. How am I going to tell you [he says, pointing to my jeans] not to wear pants? It's your thing. If you feel good this way, I can't demand that you change this way of being. Maybe this is something el Señor can demand, because he made you. He created you.

Not even our mothers tell us things like these "deeply esteemed" police. Not even our mothers care [about how we dress].

E: So you can't go out?

P: No, I can't go out safely from here to there (he points down the hundred-yard passage leading to the street).

E: So what can you do?

P: Nothing, except go around with great humility, respecting, not them, because if we had guns we'd have killed them already. We're not scared of them. They're humans too, who can have their lives taken away. The difference is the respect that [accrues to] the uniform they wear, not the people. No way, man! Respecting the uniform [of those who are] supposedly, or so they say, guarding the people's security and social order. This is something you can respect. It's good to guard the security of a person, the people, like the kind of people who live here . . . So we respect the uniform, right? For its work. But when the police come and start to beat someone . . . What right does he have to beat someone? Simply because he's an authority?

E: So how do you manage to live here?

P: We live here because God is great, I would say. If we didn't have faith and confidence in the Lord Jesus Christ . . .

E: So it's like being imprisoned in your house?

P: Yes. But it's different here. There're women here [the women laugh uproariously] . . . women!!!! In prison there're only men, and to wake up only to look at the faces of men . . . no! That's the difference!

Then Pepe begins to reminisce about the old days, boasting of his conquests—theft, stabbings, and so on. His posturing did not surprise me, but I was taken aback when both women laughed in concert with him. Did they truly find this funny? Did they feel pressured to play along with him? Were they afraid to show disapproval? Finally, Denora returned to talking about the program.

D: We convened another meeting after this incident and the police didn't show up. We meet every fifteen days with all the community actors . . . there was a representative of the gang there who heard everything that they [the police] said they were going to offer, and in the end it didn't turn out to be the way they said it was going to be in this meeting. And so what we [Secretaría de la Juventud and Pro-Jóvenes] are doing is sending a letter to the subcommissioner who gave the workshop, who approached us, who explained what was the process . . . The idea of the project is to leave them with a small business in the community.

S: Look, for example, the $140 which we had, that we had collected in these seven days . . . was [in the end used] to maintain the guys and to give them food the three days that they were there, in the county jail!

According to Sonia and Denora, the authorities do not provide food in these holding facilities. Families and friends are expected to bring food to the inmates. "So what they had managed to save was used to maintain themselves while imprisoned. The letter [that was sent off this morning] asks . . . We are asking please ask the people [the police] who are patrolling the neighborhood, please don't interrupt this process. The PNC, they won't let them succeed, or us to develop a single program."

As we were leaving, Pepe asked Denora if she could give him a dollar and accompany him down the stairs to the street, so he could eat lunch at one of the stands with our "protection." We were all relieved to see that there was no sign of the police and soldiers we had seen upon our arrival.

I had asked to see the impact of El Plan Mano Dura, and here it was almost too plainly laid out in the same belligerent tactics that I had seen in Los Angeles with Homies Unidos's weekly arts program during the Rampart scandal. While I had already seen this happening to the Homies Unidos San Salvador program in 2003, now it appeared that the police didn't even trust the projects funded and run by and in cooperation with the government, the very programs—few as they were—that comprised the new Mano Amiga and Mano Extendida element of El Plan Súper Mano Dura introduced by President Saca. During the course of my work I was to hear over and over this story of sabotage from one NGO and church group after another.

Spaces of Encounter

Everyone, it seemed, was suspected of providing a front for the gangs—wittingly or unwittingly. And it wasn't just the right-wing government and the police who feared as much. The indistinction between good and evil, violence and peace, was proving difficult for those piloting the rehabilitation programs, few and far between though they were. Miranda herself had acknowledged that while the gang may have allowed them into the community to work with the youth in the schools, they hadn't stopped recruiting. For example, "At four in the afternoon when the bread is ready they meet, right, to eat the bread or to take it to sell . . . And you'll see that there are little homies, really young, who haven't yet tattooed themselves and that don't dress like that . . . and after speaking to them we realize that they are part of the group, not just aspirants but they are in the group." Knowing that Miranda had worked in collaboration with the staff of Homies Unidos in its early days and thus was more than familiar with the group's history, I began to talk about the similarities I had noted. I told her how interesting it was to hear her speak this way about the trade-offs they had to make with active gang members. It was so reminiscent of the very thing that proved problematic for Homies Unidos. As I expressed it to her:

> What I want to ask is this: Homies Unidos's work required that they worked with active gang members, but the line between what was the

work for the prevention of social violence and what was the work for violence was not always easy to determine. The idea was always that the youth themselves were going to work with their own communities or, in this case, neighborhoods and gangs, because obviously they had all been gang members. So given that you have to convince the gangs to let you into their neighborhoods, how are you avoiding confusing your work to provide opportunities to youth who clearly are in need but who are also involved in gangs?

She nods knowingly.

> Yes, I know what you mean, because it happens, they can use you. For ex-ample, on the topic of police, in order to do these kinds of things, like for instance the bakery . . . we also have to coordinate with the police, and to let them know that this is work that we are doing. Now what's the risk that we take on? The space that we are recuperating can serve other ends. Similarly, how will they use what they earn from the bakery? Who can guarantee that they aren't buying up an arsenal with what they are earning from the bakery? Or that the space of the bakery is being used to organize because the police do not allow them to meet formally? [T]he only way that we can control or diminish the margins [of error], let's say, with which we will never have absolute guarantees, and I think that in this work there is always this mutual advantage.

What does Miranda point to as the only way of controlling or diminishing the margins? Follow-up? By whom? She replies, "What I can say to you . . . is through follow-up. For example, the guy who is working with them for the Secretariat of Youth, who we are accompanying in his efforts, is an ex-gang member, but we can't just leave it with him, and this is something we learned from Homies. In other words, the follow-up cannot be left to just him. He is not the only one responsible. Rather, a *técnico* [a trained program evaluator] goes there with him."[9] This is not the by, for, and of model of self-empowerment or consciousness-raising of Homies Unidos. And on what is the técnico going to base his or her evaluation?

> Look, it's really difficult. While they're making the bread they're listen-ing to their music . . . the music of the gang . . . and the first time this left me shocked because it was the first time that I had heard [that kind of music]. So I tell them, "You are taking a risk. If anyone hears this [music],

they'll say, 'No one else but the gang could be playing this . . .' So choose the music, but choose something else."

We call them by their names [not their gang names], but for us this is really difficult. Between them it's not like that. For example they came to me on Monday saying, "Look, after we made the bread on Sunday we stopped off at a café to drink some sodas. The police came and took four of us." What were they doing? Why did they take the four? "No, *nothing*, we were just standing there and they took four of us!" Do you think they were doing nothing? I don't. It's possible that they weren't doing anything, but the margin that they were doing something is fifty-fifty. I can't say that they weren't doing anything.

True, I think to myself, but then again, what would they have to have done in order to be arrested under manodurista policies? Be tattooed? Be hanging out with other members of the neighborhood? In other words, given these new criminal categories, the margin that they were doing something "illegal" is 100 percent, not fifty-fifty as Miranda suggests.

Nonetheless, Miranda cannot simply ignore the requests that her rehabilitation team brings to her from the field. Switching into the role of her field assistants, she describes her dilemma this way:

"Miranda, speak to the subdirector of public security," Señor Landaverde, who had helped us a lot, "to see what's happening." Why did they take them? Look [the police] are generating a feeling of disappointment in the youth . . . there were twenty-two, now only two are coming [to the bakery] because they're frightened to go out . . . But they could be toying with you too. We don't know. Really, in this world we are not going to enter.

You can see, for example, how they move among one another, taking turns. One week comes one, the next week another, because they're out on missions. They have different roles, and one role in the gang is this, to be in [the bakery] . . .

Some of them have good intentions with the bakery. A few, maybe three out of the twenty-two. I could say to you, this one, this one, and this one. The rest of them, no. The rest are just passing time . . . tomorrow they'll find something else. And this is during the day. At night to illustrate in some way . . . they don't live for that [the bakery], they live for this [the gang].

But we are friends, we're fine, we understand each other, and we know that in the building they control us, that they know when we come and when we go, and just as we distrust them, they distrust us because they associate us with the government and also with the police. We know that we have this relationship of "good friends."

Among the measures they are taking is strengthening ties with human rights associations or programs like ours. We know that this is possible. But the thing is that we *have* to do it because we have to think in terms of costs and benefits. How much to invest in this? What does it imply to work with [them]? Of course, we don't so do with our eyes closed.

So both sides (and I would venture to say, the police too) play off each other, come at each other from this mutual advantage: "Good friends" but not allies, using one another, strangely enough to seemingly the same end: space to maneuver; a base of operation inside the now militarized space of the barrios. Miranda continues:

In La IVU, the neighborhood association doesn't have much tolerance for the gang, which is very interesting considering that its people have grown up there, and the guys who belong to the gang are guys who have grown up there, and more than that, that have been friends all their lives, they're all friends, family really, and also neighbors—this one's the son of *fulano* ["so and so"], and this one of [someone else] . . . and yet there's very little tolerance for the gang. So what are we doing, for example, with the [playing] field . . . we've arranged it so that the gang uses it at a particular time. They take turns. But we are also succeeding in getting the community to open up a formal space, systematic space to the gang too, which can become a space of encounter. It's a very interesting space of encounter. But this is formal more than anything, no one's going to change their way of life from this.

One could say that these projects were about opening up spaces of encounter, spaces for the gang inside the community, spaces for Pro-Jóvenes inside the schools, and space for youth in general. But one might also think of these projects—the bakery and the basketball court and soccer field—as extortion money, the price that the CNSP, Pro-Jóvenes, and the Secretariat of Youth had to pay the gang to enter the community. This program of "re-insertion" was clearly two pronged: not only to "insert" the gang into society but also to "insert" Pro-Jóvenes into the community.

But even the lines between "the gangs" and "the community" seemed blurred. As in Los Angeles, the language of "community" in El Salvador is unstable and contested. Studies of gangs in both places invariably hold that gangs fill in for the absence of a sense of belonging to a community and function as a fictive kinship network. Miranda went so far as to suggest that the gang has surpassed being a network of young men and women. Now, she argued, the family was a fundamental part of that network. In other words, the gang is no longer a *substitute* for the family but has *subsumed* it. As she put it:

Everyone always says that the problem of the gangs is "*la familia, la familia, la familia* [the family, the family, the family]!" But it's the same family that enables these things. Really, you can see these kids in the communities with their families intact, and how the family has been converted into a space, one can't say of stimulus but of support for the same guy, no? . . . All of those who leave the prisons [after visiting their sons, husbands, brothers] . . . the same family serves to carry messages from one to another [gang member]. They are the ones who are facilitating their passage from one space to the next. It's like a mafia.

For me the theme of gangs has surpassed being a form of socialization, we could say, to have a utilitarian character. They live from this and the family is part [of it] . . . They also live from this [*vivirse*]. You can see, for example, when the person responsible for collecting extortions is locked up, who goes to collect the rent in their place? The girlfriend or wife, because she, in reality, also has to respond to the demands of the clika or the gang. And so, it's a form of life by which they maintain themselves. It's long past having a more subjective character, [being] more about identity the way it was in the beginning, the thing that was so attractive about it. I think it also has something to do with all the doors that have been shut, all the omissions or all the decisions that weren't taken in time.

Something that should have been . . . how can I say it? Something transitional. We have all been young, and all of us have passed through [that difficult phase of identity construction], but then it's over and we take life seriously . . . [But] the doors are all so closed, and they have all been left behind, so that its been transformed into a whole way of life.

And all of . . . the interior dynamic has been transformed. Before, for example, to have a new leader was much more difficult, you had to pass

I don't know how many tests. Now, one gets taken in to prison, immediately in five minutes you have the replacement. The one who is going to assume command and be in communication with [the now-imprisoned leader] inside. The dynamic has changed.

Remember that gang members consider themselves to be "soldiers" in battle. In the aftermath of manodurismo yet another line had been blurred. The distinction between the "soldiers" in the gangs and the "civilians" in the neighborhoods had become increasingly murky.

In an interview with me, the Salvadoran researcher Marlon Carranza pointed to the ways in which manodurista policies had also transformed what he termed la famosa renta (the infamous rent) imposed by gangs as a countervailing system of local taxation. As he put it: "[Súper] Mano Dura has radically altered the terms and stakes of la famosa renta—for example, the "tax" that gangs would impose on bus drivers for using routes through their neighborhoods. Once a quarter or a dollar, these extortions are now in the hundreds and thousands of dollars. Gangs are responsible for the upkeep of their incarcerated members as well as their families. The burden of providing economic assistance to the network has increased enormously with the mass incarceration of young men." It was, he argued, most ironically the need to support all the "homies" inside and their families outside that had turned the prison leadership inside into something more akin to and enabled links with organized crime.

According to Carranza the gangs used to have a certain level of respect for institutions such as the church, the school, and the police. He suggested that since Súper Mano Dura the incidence of gang attacks on the police had increased notably. Even the schools were no longer off limits. While I was in El Salvador, gangs had started to impose extortions of up to five thousand dollars on school principals, threatening to go after students if their demands were not met. In one incident in San Marcos, a school principal who did not cooperate was assassinated.

From Deportation to Extortion

One morning during this visit I receive a call from Weasel, who says he needs to ask for my help with something. He wants to know if we can meet somewhere, and I invite him to breakfast. Sitting at the table, he starts to recount his "story" to me, or as he translates it, with a more than wary laugh, "I've got the scoop!" The cultural cafe and bar where he is working as a tattoo artist, he tells me, has been "taxed." So the wave of gang extortions had reached him. The owner of the bar "got a call from inside and they told him, 'I'm such and such person, and somebody's going to come on this day to pick it up.'" They had already made their first monthly payment. "It affects me a lot because . . . I'm there all the time . . . alone sometimes . . . because I'm the most responsible one. The other guys are younger . . . I don't do it because it's like a hobby. I do it because I *gotta* do it because of my kids . . . and they're not even at school [yet] y'know. And I can't afford to have the people at the bar like scared you know, to open the place up, because it affects me you know."

The week before this meeting, I had met up with Weasel at his rooftop studio above the bar. I had been anxious to catch up with him to see how he was faring since his second deportation from the United States back to El Salvador nine months earlier. While we talked on the rooftop patio he seemed fairly at ease, even though his gaze was, as always, darting back and forth. Wondering if he was concerned for his safety here, I asked him if he wanted to sit facing the stairs while we were talking. "Na, I know everybody here. It's cool." He was excited at the prospect of contributing to the expansion of the cultural cafe end of the bar. The owner was really into it, and he was looking forward to maybe being able to go into some sort of partnership if it worked out. I was relieved. Perhaps he had been right in not going to a third country, say Costa Rica or Spain, upon his return. He had been urged to do so by many people, myself included. We were all deeply worried about his safety upon his return to El Salvador.

But just a week after our reunion, his tone had changed dramatically. The imposition of a monthly "rent" of two hundred dollars on the bar has him worried. Is it because *he* is working there? Is it his fault? He is also scared for his safety, and for his wife and kids (his wife has a little boy from a former union). They know where he lives. I try to comfort him, saying that it had just been a matter of time: the taxation on the business was likely to have happened without his presence. "Yeah. It [the extortion racket] is going on everywhere . . . It's really violent here. Silly to say, but man, people are acting like it's medieval days, or even in the cave man days, where force is what matters, and power and violence . . . It's just how this country is, man, if people know that they can push you around, they're going to do it. But with a little resistance, they think twice about it, you know." Weasel becomes introspective. He is worried that he will be drawn back into this cycle of violence despite all his efforts over the last few years to live by a creed of nonviolence.

Man, Elana, I tell you that's one of the worst battles that I have, like, is myself. Being the person that I am, the knowledge that I've acquired in prison and . . .'cause you can acquire principles and values in prison, you know. Respect. Talking the truth when you have to. Being faithful. Certain things like that. And then finding God in prison you know, and really kinda like, not dedicating myself fully, fully, because I try to, but as much as I try to 100 percent, I couldn't, you know. And then getting out and having to sort of like gain respect from everybody else again, establish my status of respect again, 'cause I've heard a lot of people say like "man, you've changed, man, like you're not the same person anymore. What's wrong with you man. How you gonna let that go by? Why you gonna let that pass?" And I'm just thinking, "Fuck, man, you don't know what it's like to be in jail, 'ey." . . . Man, I don't want nobody dying because of me. I don't want nobody to get hurt because of me . . . But it's like the more you try to avoid this, the more you get sunk into it . . . There's a saying in Spanish, and it's funny and it kind of makes sense, you know. I'm going to tell it to you in Spanish: "Dijo, 'Al perro más seco, se le pegan las pulgas.'" The skinniest dog, the fleas stick to him the most. In other words, they were trying to say, even though you're not doing anything, like you're the new skinny dog in town, you know. But if people start mentioning your name, shit starts falling on you . . . They want to keep you down, or they want you to be responsible for this, you know . . . I'd hate to be the one they're going to make an example of, you know, because I'm the one that everybody knows . . . They know where I live . . . so that's why I'm going to reconnect with people I know [in Guatemala] . . . to make some room for me . . . till I find some means to bring my kids.

Weasel's mood was very reminiscent of that difficult period in 2002 and 2003 right before he decided to try to make it back to the United States. Now two years later Weasel is back in El Salvador, speaking of taking a bus to Guatemala to see if he might set himself up as a tattoo artist in a tourist town up there, and then come back to get his family. My heart sinks again that he has decided not to fight his immigration case so as to petition for Withholding from Removal under the Convention Against Torture Act while in detention in the United States. Like Alex Sanchez, Weasel would have had much expert testimony and many letters of reference and support to draw upon.

So many others fight their cases with little or no resources. After serving more than six months in INS detention and fourteen months in a federal prison for aliens convicted for "illegal reentry" (run by the private security company Corrections Corporation of America), Weasel is considering fleeing once again, but this time to Guatemala. This time he does not want to risk reimprisonment in the United States. I worry for him. Death does seem so close. Here he is, caught between deportation and extortion.

> E: I was worried this was going to happen to you if you were returned to El Salvador. That's why I wanted you to fight your case.
> W: Yeah, but there's got to be another way to go about it than just being locked up [in INS detention while the case is pending] . . . Man, there's got to be another way of, of going about it than just being locked up.[10] I don't know what's the solution to all of this [the situation of the gangs].
> E: Do you think it's real jobs, that that would be the solution? That's what people are saying now.
> W: I think it's welfare. They should have like a welfare system here.

So Weasel sees la famosa renta as substituting for the lack of state support. His analysis resonates with Miranda's earlier claim that the gang and its economic operations had become a way of life and means of survival, not simply for the fictive kin of the gang but also for the biological and the legal family. Like remittances, extortions were fundamental to survival within El Salvador's postwar neoliberal political economy where the state was no longer actively engaged, however modestly, with the social reproduction of its population.

Mass incarceration, it seems, had only increased the stakes of these informal—licit and illicit—economic networks. I wanted to know what Weasel thought of Carranza's thesis. Did he think that the policy of Súper Mano Dura had brought la famosa renta to this next level?

> Exactly, plus I said this, I said this, I'm not lying, man, I foresaw the future, I said: "This guy [Flores] is full of ah . . . crap, because what's gonna happen is because man, I've lived it. In Los Angeles CRASH was hitting on us every day, bam, taking us to jail, and what did we start? We started meeting in other places and instead of just hanging out in the neighborhood and, you know, walking around, doing what we did, you know. We started hanging out in people's houses, other homies. We sat

down saying [he whispers], "Oh, man, we've got to make some money man." You can imagine. They created their own monster, you know.

As with the deportation of Salvadoran immigrant gang-affiliated youth based in Los Angeles, the adoption in El Salvador of the zero-tolerance gang-abatement strategies of the United States had also reinscribed the landscape of the barrios populares. The microphysics of the gang injunction and its logic of enclosure and exclusion in Los Angeles had once again reconfigured the political geography of San Salvador's barrios—albeit in conjunction with the particular conditions in El Salvador. Granted, unlike the gang injunction, Mano Dura is not localized within a proscribed territory. The whole nation (small as it may be) is up for grabs—at least its poor neighborhoods. Neither does manodurismo require a court injunction specifying the borders of the territory to be policed and the particular individuals who would be placed on the injunction. Rather, all marginal barrios and all youth and young adults are subject to these restrictions on their presence in the barrio and their freedom to associate. They are also subject to the police staging their "illicit association," as well as being extensively documented by the police. Even corpses as they lie in coffins at community wakes are photographed and registered.

The Fashion Police

One could argue, and many do, that with gang youth this generalized suspicion has some ground. However, like racial profiling in the United States, manodurista policies are extended to other youth who have no association to gangs. Take, for example, the testimony of one young man, Luis Alonso Argueta. His case speaks both to the heights of absurdity that profiling based on fashion or style can go and to the ways in which zero-tolerance strategies can lead to the abuse of youth in general. Argueta was a high school student who worked in agriculture and was a participant in the Committee against AIDS in the community of Santa Marta in the state of Cabañas. On September 9, 2006, Argueta went to the town Sesuntepeque, the capital of Cabañas, to turn in some documentation to Asociación de Desarrollo Económico Social (ADES, or Association for Economic and Social Development), an NGO with which he had done some work. He then went to a bank to cash a check, but was detained by the police as he left the bank. They asked to see his documents, and they also asked him if he was a member of a gang.

He said no, as he was not. But as he later wrote on September 20, 2006, in a mass e-mail message:

> They told me that I was a *marero* because I was dressed in that style. I answered that it was the fashion, and anyway I was wearing baggy pants and a shirt, the kind with buttons.[11] I wasn't dirty or drunk. I had bathed that day and was engaged in my work. Then I asked, "What's the problem if I dress in this manner if it's our system that makes these [the clothes he was wearing]." They told me to put my belt through the loops of the pants, which I did.
>
> There were three police officers, one of them told the other, "Cut that belt!" At that moment, he took out a knife and with it in his hand he said the same thing, and then threatened me. "Put that belt on properly, if not, I'm going use the knife," and he made a gesture as if he were going to put the knife in my stomach.
>
> Then they said to me: "You think you're so bad that you can intimidate us . . . we're going to make you shit [in your pants], son of a bitch," and they ordered me to the left side of the Banco Agricola [a Salvadoran bank] to register me. I did what they told me. On top of all of this, they had taken my bag and my documents from me. While they were searching me, one of them was insulting me. He gave me two kicks and wanted me to admit that I belonged to a gang. When I answered, looking at them, that I didn't belong to any gang, they told me not to look them in the face.
>
> As they were finishing searching me and ordering me to go, one of them kicked me as I turned around. So I said to them: "You more than anyone know the rights of people, and you know what you are doing is an injustice." As a citizen that pays my taxes so that they can have a salary, I have the right to ask them for their identification numbers, and I did this. I took out a notebook that I had on me and I started to write down the number of the license plate of their car. In that instance . . . they handcuffed me and they took my things from me once again and my identification.
>
> They took me and beat me all the way to the PNC station, and then threw me in *las bartolinas* [the local jailhouse].

The story of abuse continued when Argueta's coworkers and his mother came to inquire about him and ask the reason for his detention. In response to their inquiries they were verbally abused and threatened with imprisonment by the chief of the PNC station. His mother was accused of being irresponsible. Argueta's aim in writing the message, he says, is "for all those who have been beaten and haven't had the courage to write about it and make it known, and for all those who believe that these problems can be changed." How is it, he asks, "that our system, that speaks so much about liberties, reprimands us for the way we dress, in ways that the same system promotes in its publicity and advertising?" Indeed, Salvadoran youth were being fed a steady diet of hip hop fashion and rap music as they wandered through El Salvador's new mega shopping malls.[12] This was the other face of the "Americanization" of the Salvadoran landscape, accompanied as it was by the proliferation of gated communities on the edges of the metropolitan areas.[13]

The police were often barely literate in the semiotics of youth culture. Take, for example, Weasel's first attempt to cross back into the United States at the end of 2003 when he was turned back in Mexico because of his clothing. He read this event through postmodern eyes. We laughed uproariously when he told me why he was the one picked out of everyone on the bus as an undocumented Central American immigrant passing through Mexico. When he asked the *federale* (officer) who apprehended him, "Why me?" the man explained that it was because he was wearing old-fashioned clothes that no Mexican wore anymore. Weasel was wearing, as he put it, "a very stylish [1970s style] retro shirt," and as such he was dressed in the height of urban youth fashion.

And, in fact, in the time since Weasel's second deportation he had only become trendier. Style was always foremost to Weasel, and he was obviously relieved to be out of his prison sweats and to be able to shave his head again. While gang members were removing their tattoos with the consent of the gang, and new gang members were prohibited from getting tattoos, Weasel's colorful tattoos had crept up over his collar and across his neck. An extension (a circular earring) lined the inside of the enlarged hole in his earlobe. I asked him if the cops stopped him for his tattoos. "Yeah, they are always stopping me at Metro Centro," the shopping mall he likes to frequent, and the one where he used to work as a tattoo artist in a surfer's shop before he left for the United States. But when the cops stopped him they didn't take him in. After three years of picking up tens of thousands of youth for hanging out with each other and for bearing tattoos, the police were finally able to discern the class-specific gang and prison tattoos from the sort that Weasel now bore. Or at least Weasel made sure they knew the difference. Before the announcement of Mano Dura he had already started to get color tattoos instead of the black-and-grey prison tattoos. He had done so both to hide the prison origins of his tattoos and because his sense of style was changing. After hanging out with middle-class youth (namely the crowd who hung out at La Luna, the cafe discussed in chapter 4), Weasel was increasingly drawn to the colorful iconography of his Mayan origins as they mixed with elements of reggae, "tribal," and anarchist visual culture. His tattoos had warped into yet another alternative politics of fashion.

Before Weasel fled back to the United States at the end of 2003, he was director of Homies Unidos's arts program in San Salvador. He was working with a colleague of mine to implement a project, funded by a Swiss program, which he had entitled "Art Shield." The timing of the program could not have been more ironic and yet prescient in terms of the dangers in criminalizing the expressive practices of hip hop youth culture. The idea behind it had been to use the expressive culture associated with gangs as a way to soften the social stigma attached to gang youth and the prejudice toward them. Weasel and my colleague had the task of putting this program into effect at the height of Mano Dura's war against the gangs through their expressive practices.

Not only did Mano Dura outlaw and criminalize the wearing of tattoos that designate gang or criminal affiliation but the initial proposal for the plan included a provision requiring tattoo artists to keep a registry of each of the tattoos they made, including a description of the tattoo and the name, address, age, and signature of the client receiving the tattoo. These tattoo registries were to be subject to inspection by the Ministry of Health. It was in this context that Weasel fled El Salvador at the end of 2003, abandoning Art Shield to a friend who had been involved with tagging groups in the United States and who was not affiliated with Homies Unidos. Now he was back, this time struggling to keep a low profile from the fiasco of El Plan Súper Mano Dura and the monsters unleashed by it.

If transnational youth gangs have their origins in the result of failed criminal justice policies in the United States, why did those policies become a model for countries like El Salvador? If Mano Dura led to an increase in violence, why was it extended through Súper Mano Dura? In each case, repression had been productive of the very violence it purportedly aimed to diminish.

While most argue that manodurista policies have been a complete failure, others argue quite the opposite. Indeed, zero-tolerance policies have proved highly productive in the Foucauldian sense. According to some, rather than being a fiasco Súper Mano Dura was a success precisely because it increased the level of violence in El Salvador, thereby justifying the need not only for zero-tolerance policies but also the remilitarization of society, and with it the return of the warlords. One Spanish Catholic priest, Padre Antonio Rodríguez, or Toño (who at one point had to flee the country after giving a controversial sermon), put it in these stark, albeit conspiratorial, terms:

> Mano Dura has been very successful for the purpose it was created. Mano Dura was not created to resolve the problem of youth gang violence. It was created to generate a phantasm in the population of fear, or terror, that would be converted into two dreams:
>
> The first to increase migration . . . to push people out [of the country]. . . . Second, . . . to increase the wave of violence in the population . . . to justify the militarization of the country and the [passage of] the anti-terrorist law.
>
> . . . They militarized the airport . . . they placed them [the military] in the communities, there [he says gesturing to the window and to the street outside] you will see soldiers walking about . . . they come out on this street. The people are frightened . . . They [ARENA] achieved all the objectives of Mano Dura.

For Padre Toño, therefore, Súper Mano Dura not only produced a carceral and surveillance state but also marked the return to El Salvador of the low-intensity warfare of the 1980s and with it the military state. "The government wanted us to think that we had one problem. Their discourse—that we had only one problem—penetrated the population. That was the problem of violence . . . Violence is productive for the power of the executive, at the expense of the judiciary and the legislature. The greatest achievement of free trade is the exportation of people. What are Salvadorans going to export? Pupusas? Not even Pollo Campero . . ."[14]

Padre Toño was not immune to the productive power of this phantasm of fear. His tone was desperate. He feared his days in El Salvador were numbered. He was frightened and emotionally exhausted. He hadn't felt safe at night in the barrio since 2003 and before Mano Dura was launched. He no longer worked in his office late at night and or walked back to his house after dark. He was waiting to see if he would be granted a year's sabbatical to rest, but he feared "what was going to come out at the psychological level."

I've seen so many dead bodies in three years. Many. Here, outside, I saw someone who had been stabbed . . . Psychologically speaking it's really tough, really tough. I received a death threat. The Spanish embassy got me out in six hours. It was for something I said in my sermon.

. . . I was in a meeting with the 23rd Street Gang, after which I returned to my house. At midnight they killed two of the kids with whom I had been meeting. In a bus, a bullet here and another there (pointing to his body). I buried them. . . . The violence has really increased. The other day, they killed a little boy. I have his photo here. He was a kid who I helped build a house with his mother. Two days later, they killed a mother with her son of twenty-two years in a *tortillera* [a place where tortillas are made and sold]. Just fifteen days ago. Yesterday, they killed another here. Yesterday, a boy of twenty, who lived here. I was at his wake last night. The other day—the sister of a kid in our youth parish, nineteen years old. They kidnapped her. They asked for five hundred dollars and because the family didn't have it, the next day there was a wake in their house, the girl dead. The violence here is really grave . . . It's a complete disaster, a disaster for *us* [not the government].

It wasn't the objective to eliminate violence. A country like this one, with a government like this one, needs this [kind of] population, and needs to generate a violent population. If not, the system can't be maintained. The system won't be maintained [otherwise]. The system is maintained with this [violence], unfortunately, right?

Mano Dura was a success. It did what it intended to do . . . They managed to convince the society that they had one problem and that was the gangs . . . this boiling pot has its escapes and its phantasms.

Does this return of the military to policing functions in El Salvador suggest a simple return to the past and the collusion between the military, the police, and the ruling elite? In a conversation with me in September 2006 Roberto Burgos, a constitutional attorney at the University of Central America's Institute for Human Rights (IDHUCA), pondered the question this way:

I have my opinion and it's this. The armed forces and the police never really separated . . . The army never really withdrew from the public security functions.[15] So for me, it's a little difficult to say to you that we are returning to the past. It's that we never left or got rid of all of it. So it makes it impossible for me to say whether it's a new model, because in practice, we've never had a totally new model. Nor can I lie in saying that the security forces are the same as the past. They have changed and there have been some advances. . . . The problem is that these small gains are now seen as an obstacle to fighting delinquency. But the reality is that the armed forces never abandoned its public service work.

Even so, Burgos worried that Plan Súper Mano Dura was distorting the role of the military in contemporary El Salvador.

The military now say, "Look, now we have deployments . . . [so] we need a larger budget. We need the United States to send new transport vehicles, we need new arms, we need more aid, more uniforms because we're in a military campaign against the gangs or the thieves. And if this mounts up—I know perhaps [that this] doesn't pertain [directly] to your question—the fact that the armed forces are participating in the campaign in Iraq, it distorts not only the role of the police that needs a guard to protect them so that he can protect me, but also the role of the military. The military regains their profile.

We have a minister of defense who opines over the death penalty, who offers his opinion about public security . . . the environment . . . The military leaders that we had, los Señores de la Guerra, as we called them in the conflict in the eighties, feel once again [that they have a political voice] . . .

The UMO, these anti-riot units that were formed by France, lately have started to be trained [using] the helicopters of the air force . . . in simulating rescues . . . But who's going to guarantee me that this anti-riot unit will not use the air transport training to repress a protest rally? I have the right to worry because of the history of my country . . .

The United States, of course, had played a central role in that history. And there was considerable concern that its newly opened International Law Enforcement Academy for Latin America (ILEA) in San Salvador might repeat that history. The self-proclaimed mission of the program was to combat international crimes, such as drug trafficking, organized crime, and terrorism, by providing high-quality training to members of law enforcement agencies throughout the world. Originally established under Bill Clinton in 1995, ILEA has additional training facilities in Hungary, Botswana, and the United States. The United States and the Salvadoran government had signed a bilateral agreement to establish ILEA San Salvador on September 21, 2005. Most Salvadoran human rights organizations opposed the agreement, saying that say ILEA was the new School of the Americas, which was the training ground for many of the Salvadoran military officers accused of gross human rights violations during the civil war.[16] In fact, the primary reason I had met with Burgos was to discuss his organization's controversial collaboration with ILEA. Here the role of IDHUCA was particularly delicate given the history of this Jesuit university not only as ardent defender of human rights during the civil war but also because of the then still unresolved case of the murder of six Jesuits priests and their housekeeper on the UCA campus by the Salvadoran military during the final FMLN offensive in 1989.

Burgos, however, argued that ILEA was the last hope to realize the Peace Accord's goal of a civilian police force truly independent of the military and thus counteract state tyranny. It was, after all, the ineffectiveness of the PNC that had been leveraged to launch joint patrols with the military. As such, IDHUCA along with then police chief Ávila (ARENA's presidential candidate for 2009) pointed to the need for better technical training for the police. Burgos was adamant that bad management of crime scenes, the inability to bring technical proof to court hearings, and poor expertise in ballistics and forensic medicine and the like "generates more impunity and more suffering."

Burgos concluded: "What is our option? Do we permit the armed forces to train the police . . . or do we get behind an initiative that really would give us a professional civil police? Besides, we asked for guarantees that they will not train anyone from the military section . . . and that the history of the students from the region be impeccable."

The fear of participation by the United States was, of course, not unfounded. Burgos acknowledged that many of the worst violators of human rights in El Salvador had passed through the School of the Americas, were trained by the FBI, and were stationed at Fort Benning in Georgia and Fort Bragg in North Carolina for training in the infantry or military intelligence. As Burgos put it:

[During the last years of the war] . . . everyone would go around with their blue ICITAP [International Criminal Investigative Training Assistance Program] folder, even though they didn't know what it was, but were in reality very proud of it! But given the role of the United States in training our military and security forces during the war . . . it seems very logical to me with the Peace Accords the first attempt was . . . to say, okay, we're going to try to distance ourselves a bit from the United States in the training of the new units . . .

After the Peace Accords there was a clear intent to train the police based in parameters of the European Union, including, you know, the uniforms of the police, the form in which they march . . .

I interject, "But the United States has now returned as the dominant model?" To which Burgos responds, "They've returned, clearly."

PART III

**A DISTURBANCE IN
TIME AND SPACE**

In the frame of my camera, a member of the youth group of the Farabundo Marti National Liberation Front (FMLN) is painting a red star, the insignia of the FMLN, on the cheek of Pájaro, a deported Salvadoran immigrant and La Mara Salvatrucha (MS) gang member from Los Angeles. The campaign slogan "Juntos somos el cambio" (Together we are the change) is emblazoned on the back of the FMLN youth's T-shirt. This snapshot, taken in 1996 during the municipal campaigns in a small town in eastern El Salvador, joins these two disparate figures of resistance: the transnational street youth gang and the leftist guerrilla group turned political opposition party.

I have another photograph of Pájaro taken the day before. In it he and his homeboys Perol, also from MS in Los Angeles, and Marcus, from the Tooner youth gang (a lesser-known Chicano gang in Glendale, California), are posing showing off their tattoos and gesticulating in gang signs. All three have had their encounters with the criminal justice system in the

United States. Although Perol and Marcos have taken off their shirts to show off their tattoos, Pájaro keeps his long-sleeved oversized athletic shirt on. Shortly after his deportation, he was attacked and stabbed in the chest seventeen times. He'd rather not expose his wounds to the camera, he explains. It's not clear whether these are the signifying scars of gang or death squad violence—of retribution or social cleansing.

At the time the photos were taken Pájaro was twenty-four years old. Born in El Salvador, he had lived the better part of his young life, nineteen years, in Los Angeles. He returned to his hometown of Santa Elena after serving a prison term at the California State Penitentiary for his involvement in an armed robbery. He claims he left the United States voluntarily, but he is in fact a deportee who consented to sign a "voluntary" departure form. From the time he was ten years old, Pájaro was involved with MS.

I call this dialectical image of Pájaro in leftist political drag "La Mara Salvatrucha in FMLN face." But couldn't it be the other way around: the FMLN in the face of the gang—the legacy and the history of it? What are we to make of this dialectical image of the gang (MS or 18th Street) with the guerrilla (FMLN) and the transference of the red star, the stain of the FMLN, onto Pájaro's cheek, whose body bears the stain of his gang's insignia in black ink? Is "La Mara Salvatrucha in FMLN face" an image of an incipient solidarity borne of a youthful impulse to find correspondences with, and so recognize themselves in, the revolutionary consciousness of the previous generation and their utopian project? The photograph certainly appears to offer a vision of inclusiveness: Juntos somos el cambio. But merely fusing these elements, MS and the FMLN, into a harmonious perspective would be to work against the principles of the dialectical image. Such a straightforward identification between these elements erases the gap between the sign and referent by fusing them into a deceptive totality. The dialectical image, on the other hand, interrupts the context into which it is inserted, thereby leaving the image's ideational elements in productive suspension and setting its semiotic content into question.[1]

Doble cara (two-faced), the Salvadoran trope for this fragmented gaze, is at play in a number of dialectical figures throughout the book, namely: homeboys deported from the immigrant barrios of Los Angeles claiming the streets of Salvadoran cities and towns; deported gang members turned transnational peace activists; cops turned criminals, immigration agents and soldiers. This chapter opens with yet another image, the gangster as guerrilla, and it ends with the gangster as terrorist. Ending this volume with these particular figures enables us to consider the history obscured in the contemporary obsession with transnational youth gangs—a history that takes us back to the beginning of the book and to the wane of the cold war and the end of the Salvadoran civil war. Up to this point, the chapters of this volume have appeared in a fairly straightforward chronology from 1992 through 2006. In this chapter, however, I suspend that chronology, ironically enough, in order to bring time back into the production of transnational space. But I use a very particular notion of time that focuses on "spectral" or "spiritual" moments that are not docile to either time or space. The ethnographic events in this chapter disjoin "the living present from the instituted order of the calendar,"[2] and from its immediate and literal United States or Salvadoran geography.

What follows is a montage of interlocking images and imaginaries, which dwell in and beyond the frame of a particular criminal type—be it communist, gangster, or terrorist—and a particular moment or war. These images bear marks of the future and of the past in a present moment that is not quite either, but yet is uncannily familiar. Together they point to the productivity of that which is repressed in U.S.-Salvadoran security relations, and its continual return: the reproduction of the terrorist, and with it the refugee who has, fifteen years after the signing of the Salvadoran Peace Accords, reappeared as a repetitive type in U.S. immigration courts. This book closes, then, with a consideration of how the securityscapes resulting from the globalization of gangs and gang-abatement strategies have been grafted onto the War on Terror. In this light, the War on Terror appears as a disturbing continuation of the past in the present made visible in hauntingly familiar forms, and El Salvador and the United States emerge as a dense hall of mirrors, an endlessly refracted and warped time and space of connection and contact.

From Political to Social Violence

As described in chapter 6, despite post–civil war reforms El Salvador was troubled by the specter of old and new forms of violence. Efforts sponsored by the state and NGOs to identify the source, direction, and subject of this violence distinguished the political from the social, and constructed the latter as postpolitical. The "political" violence of El Salvador's authoritarian and revolutionary past had (according to the local discourse) given way to "social" violence. There was even a strange nostalgia for the managed violence of the war—its predictability and political logic. This was "a war with-out sense," "without barracks." And as violence without a discernible logic or form, the country was consumed with anxieties over it.[3]

But El Salvador was, in fact, a veritable hall of mirrors where the "real of violence" was open to interpretation.[4] The "Case of Rosa N.," which erupted in the Salvadoran media in December 2002, was a case in point. As noted in chapter 5, the head of an unknown young woman between the ages of fifteen and seventeen was discovered in a black backpack in Parque Libertad, a park in the center of San Salvador. Within hours, a thigh was found at a bus termi-nal, and later that same week part of a human torso was discovered floating in a river. All of these parts belonged to the same unidentified corpse, whose forehead was tattooed with the number "18."

That case was just one in a series of macabre mutilations and decapita-tions of young women attributed to members of the 18th Street Gang. In re-sponse to the Rosa N. case, the director of the National Civil Police (PNC), Mauricio Sandoval, launched a major media campaign around these decapi-tations and mutilations, conducted mass arrests of gang members, and called for the passage of special anti-gang laws modeled on U.S. legislation. Most of the gang members originally accused of these beheadings were, it seems, picked up for "illicit associations"—a vague and all-encompassing infraction based on public nuisance and vagrancy laws—and not for any di-rect evidential links to the crimes. The alleged ringleaders of the Rosa N. case were released after documentation was produced to corroborate their claims that they had been in PNC custody during the period in which the crime was said to have taken place. However, El Viejo Lin, a member of the 18th Street Gang and deportee from Los Angeles who was the purported intellectual author of these crimes, remained in custody on other charges. Meanwhile, new cases of decapitations and mutilations continued to surface and more gang members were arrested by the police. The national newspaper El Diario de Hoy began to call MS "La Mara Satánica" (the Satanic Gang) and to sug-gest that the number "18" tattoo stood for 666, the sign of the devil.

Media coverage of these monstrous events was infused not only with talk about satanic cults and the killings as sacrificial rituals to build group solidarity, but also with conspiracy theories and the reemergence of death squads of the 1980s and of La Sombra Negra (the Black Shadow) of the 1990s. The PNC uncovered a store of grenades, and Chief Sandoval posed in front of the cache accusing El Viejo Lin of plotting to assassinate him. Apart from his alleged status as the national leader of the 18th Street Gang in El Salvador, El Viejo Lin was now also said to have been an FMLN guerrilla combatant during the civil war. El Viejo Lin in turn accused Sandoval of using him as a scapegoat to gain popularity for his bid as presidential candidate for ARENA in the 2004 elections. And because of the coincidence of the decapitations with mayoral and national legislative electoral campaigns, conspiracy theories abounded about the role of police and the right wing in the murders. "Intimidation tactics," as one former FMLN combatant put it: "What they want is a timid society." And as Lonly, one of the gang members accused in the Rosa N. case but later released, proclaimed: "It's a clandestine group pretending to be gang members."

Indeed, these accusations became fused with a resurgence of killings of political candidates and activists around the time of the elections. The head of the FMLN, Shafik Handal, held a press conference decrying what he saw as the return of the death squads. In the papers there was a bizarre convergence between the counterposed, purportedly unrelated opposites of social and political violence. Gang members, said to be political activists for the Right or the Left, were now picked up as suspects in the murders of political candidates and activists. The PNC attributed these crimes to "personal vendettas" (again, social not political violence) and the election campaigns played on—but not without more bizarre convergences.

In San Salvador, MS youth joined a march in the FMLN's campaign-closing ceremonies. A cameraman took pictures of them, shouting that their presence was proof that there was no difference between gangsters and guerrillas. In response the gang members tackled him and confiscated his film, and were subsequently charged with assault. In Soyapango, a cadre of 18th Street Gang members sporting ARENA T-shirts was sighted at the party's campaign-closing ceremonies. An ARENA assemblyman accused the FMLN of sending the gang members to discredit the Right. After a gang member, El Crazy, escaped from prison with the help of a PNC officer, accusations spread that the police were working in collaboration with the gangs. Some of the police, it was rumored, were tattooed with symbols of the 18th Street Gang.

In a move reminiscent of the Salvadoran intelligence agency efforts to uncover the guerrilla's clandestine operations during the civil war, the PNC released maps of the supposed command and cell structure of the gangs. These maps together with the gang members' *placas* or noms de guerre—Zorro, Crazy, Lonly, Baby, Skyny, Slayer, Pato, Vampi, and Drimer—were printed alongside their birth names in national newspapers as a kind of a public outing of El Salvador's most wanted. What kind of unveiling was this? In a country where newspapers once published death threats against the political opposition, would such intelligence incite further violence, be it gang or vigilante?

In this dizzying dramatization of doble cara, representations of gang violence are constantly disrupted by the return of the repressed—political violence in forms that are familiar and yet strange. The Left and the gangs suspect the government and police of organizing the killings (be they mutilations of women or the murder of political candidates) to look like gang killings. Yet both mutilations and murders also look like something else. They are strangely reminiscent of another production of violence, namely the elimination of the opposition through the macabre extrajudicial-style killings that took place during the war years. Are the death squads copying a fantasy of gang rape? Could it be the gangs acting out a fantasy by copying the death squad–style killings of the civil war period?[5]

This disorganized mimesis generates surplus meaning that eludes representation and demands that we rethink the connection between representation and what is represented.[6] Both state and nonstate actors are similarly caught up in a recurrent, mirroring dynamic of suspicion and fantasy, which flourishes by means of rumor woven finely into webs of magical realism.[7] Moreover, while gang violence is presented as a new post–civil war (and therefore postpolitical) phenomenon, the stories surrounding it are haunted by cultural formations of meaning and modes of feeling attached to that war.

The Production of a Culprit

El Viejo Lin, the poster boy for Sandoval's campaign against gangs, offered me his take on what he invokes as "reality" and his version of what had been repressed by his representation as a most-savage other. Lin begins his testimony, which he offers to me as "the truth, and nothing but the truth," by situating himself in history—a short and fantastic history of El Salvador's recent past imbricated as it is with the United States.[8] His narrative is filled with political intrigue, ghostly plots, and conspiratorial twists, which might, to quote Lin, "seem unimaginable to you but not to me." Set as it is between El Salvador and Los Angeles from the late 1970s to the present, Lin's narrative is embedded in a transnational geography peopled by a theater of ghosts.[9] I want here to consider how Lin directs our gaze through the looking glass, or the mirror of doble cara.

Lin leverages the well-worn plot of the Left's political imaginary where the state is the obscure hand behind these killings. He does so in order to deconstruct his "production as culprit."[10] According to Lin, the new structure of the postwar formation, the National Civil Police, is governed by the same forces behind the pre–Peace Accords structure and by the same intelligence apparatus of El Salvador's dirty war.[11] His case has, in his words, been "simulated" or manufactured by DECCO, the Elite Division to Combat Organized Crime. He has been isolated from those who could help him, his brother, his only alibi, was assassinated, and his wife arrested. He likens himself to Oswald in the Kennedy assassination case. He is a scapegoat for the larger state affairs of Sandoval's bid for presidency and the need to deflect international attention away from a contentious and violent strike over the privatization of healthcare.

Then Lin turns doble cara upon himself. He grew up in Pico Union in Los Angeles, where he joined the 18th Street Gang. His sister, on the other hand, followed in the footsteps of their activist parents (both members of the Salvadoran teachers union, ANDES 21 de Junio) and became involved with refugee assistance organizations and the solidarity movement.[12] Lin says he came back to El Salvador during the war with his sister's husband, a journalist, to film documentaries in the mountains of Guazapa and on other guerrilla fronts across the country. These documentaries, of a "cultural political character," were to be shown to solidarity committees in the United States. While in Guazapa, however, Lin joined the guerrillas:

> I stayed for a year in the mountains . . . took up my weapon [gun] and was caught with a cassette, a videocassette that we had filmed in the guerrilla camps there. I was a political prisoner for two years, you understand . . . After that I returned from where I had come [Los Angeles and the 18th Street Gang] . . .
>
> I am an ex political prisoner . . . Whatever you may make of my appearance . . . [gesturing toward his facial tattoos and shaved head]. Don't believe that things are as they seem.

I press him on this. How is it he was gang member and guerrilla, criminal and political prisoner? He looks at me: "One assumes perhaps, people of principle [that is], that one thing can't combine with another . . . but this is how it is." Lin's challenge to me, a so-called person of principle, takes me full circle to that FMLN *mitin* (political rally) where I first saw, and captured on film, an assimilation of those contraries—gang and guerrilla—in Pájaro's face. Only here, El Viejo Lin refashions himself as "18th Street Gang in FMLN face." Or, once again, is it the other way around? Is it the FMLN, its history, its legacy, in the face of the gang?

Gangster in Guerrilla Face

Let's return to the FMLN mitin. With a red star on his cheek and a red bandana around his head Pájaro has joined the crowd gathered by the stage. He nods to me from a crowd of people adorned with red face paint clapping and swaying to the classics of *la nueva canción* (the new song)—the quintessential musical form of the Latin American revolutionary struggles of the 1970s and 1980s. The lyrics mix strangely with the memories in my head of the sounds of hardcore rappers from South Central Los Angeles alongside heavy metal of the 1970s, the usual background music to my meetings with Pájaro.

I am surprised to see Pájaro here at the mitin. He has never expressed any formal political leanings to me or any memory of the Salvadoran civil war. Rather, when speaking of history he tells of the history of MS, and when speaking of politics he refers to gang politics inside U.S. prisons. Does Pájaro know of the brutal massacre of university students and teachers for their presumed association with the guerrillas, which took place in this very square? Does he discern the historical continuities and discontinuities between the present and the past, particularly as it resonated with youth?

Don Orlando, a teacher at the local high school, did not think today's youth had any real concept of the political struggle of the past. Several days before the mitin I stopped by his house to speak with him about the effects of migration on the attitudes among youth in Santa Elena, but he preferred to explain those attitudes in relationship to revolutionary struggle. An old recording of the now iconic "Poema de Amor" (Love Poem) by the Salvadoran revolutionary poet Roque Dalton played in the background. The culprit for youth delinquency was, as far as Don Orlando was concerned, something other than migration. "The difference with the youth today is that they have no social memory of the war, and no political conscience. There is no collective political project," he lamented.

After speaking to Don Orlando, I set off to join Amanda, a local high school student, at an evening concert sponsored by the FMLN in anticipation of the rally the next day. Like Pájaro, Amanda had also been marked and branded by her migration to Washington, D.C.—albeit with a gendered difference. After she became pregnant, her mother had sent her back to El Salvador to live with her father and his new wife. Amanda and I sat together listening to El Salvador's best known la nueva canción band playing their renditions of Silvio Rodríguez, Mercedes Sosa, and the like. For many of my compañeros in Los Angeles and in San Salvador, who had given the better part of their youthful energies to the FMLN, this music had become associated with a painful nostalgia of the failed promise of la nueva patria (the new country)—the elusive promised land of the revolution. Some of them had withdrawn from the FMLN after the party agreed to sign an amnesty rather than demand a full accounting of the human rights abuses of the war and the prosecution of those responsible for them. Others had felt betrayed by the concessions made by the FMLN to the neoliberal reforms of the ARENA government. I was taken aback by the huge response that the music evoked in the crowd singing along. I say that I was taken aback because at the time, by all accounts coming to me out of El Salvador, a country to which I had not been to in the three years since the 1994 election, the FMLN was not a political force with which to be reckoned. Moreover, by all theoretical accounts during the same period, there was no viable alternative platform to neoliberalism being expressed, at least in traditional leftist formations such as the FMLN.

Amanda, who was singing along with youthful emotion, did not know that I already knew these songs, and so started to translate the lyrics for me. "It's important that you understand these lyrics," she explained earnestly. "These songs, they speak a lot of truth." Amanda was only twelve when the war ended, and she had left for the United States shortly before. In 1996, most middle-class youth were listening to the Beatles, who were making a big comeback in Latin America. Yet it would appear that, at least through the poetics of la nueva canción, the memory of the revolutionary project continued to reside within Amanda, as well as in the crowd surrounding her.[13]

Pájaro had not attended the concert but he was at the mitin the next day, nodding to me from the crowd of people adorned with red face paint and clapping and swaying to the classics of la nueva canción. The well-worn lyrics blur into each other: "Todo, todo cambia [Everything, everything changes] . . . puedo imaginar una cultura diferente [I can imagine a different culture] . . . Si no creyera en la locura [If I didn't believe in the madness]" and then,

"El pueblo unido jamás será vencido [The people united will never be defeated]."

On stage, Don Francisco, a return migrant from Los Angeles and Virginia, spoke in his capacity as a member of the local FMLN's candidate advisory council. He was part of the reason I was in Santa Elena conducting a study on youth. Up until the start of the campaign, Francisco had been the president of the local branch of CASE, the El Salvador–based counterpart to a network of four United States–based committees of Tabudos (the self-designated term for people from Santa Elena) living in the United States (Los Angeles, San Francisco, Washington-Virginia, and Houston). Founded in California four years earlier, CASE is by its own definition a nonpartisan community service organization, although within the literature on migration CASE would be described as an immigrant hometown association, or HTA.[14] Once the campaign was in full swing though, Francisco withdrew from the presidency in order to run as a council member on the local FMLN mayoral candidate's ticket.

Francisco was flanked by Shafik Handal (who is now deceased but then was the national party chair of the FMLN) as well as by the candidate for state legislature and by Tony, the local FMLN mayoral candidate. Francisco answers attacks made by the incumbent mayor, Nelson Funes, who was from the ruling right-wing party, ARENA. Nelson Funes, who had previously labeled CASE as an FMLN front group, had recently accused CASE of funding the FMLN campaign. In an effort to debunk these accusations, Francisco read a letter from Los Angeles: "Los Angeles, 8th of March, 1992. There are many miles that separate us from one another. Yet the love of our roots, our people and our town obliges us to always be close to you . . . The solution [for Santa Elena] is not the exodus of her people, but the installation of the FMLN in Santa Elena. . . ." The letter was signed by "a group of Tabudos in a foreign land," all of them members of the "FMLN International Diplomatic Commission of Santa Elena." Francisco explained that it was not CASE but rather this commission of Tabudos living in the United States that had underwritten 90 percent of the local FMLN campaign expenses.

At the end of the rally, I turned and said good-bye to Pájaro before approaching the stage to ask Francisco about the letter and the commission. Francisco gave me the contact information for Adan, the author of the letter. Later I would meet up with Adan in Los Angeles, where he worked as room service captain in a hotel downtown. Adan, I would discover, was a student activist during the war. His parents had sent him out of the country shortly after the massacre that had taken place in this very town square, although he would not be recognized by the United States as a refugee.

The Reproduction of a Refugee

La Mara Salvatrucha in FMLN face, the dialectical image with which I began this chapter, suggests a transference between MS and the FMLN. Pájaro, the MS gang member, employs the red star iconography of the FMLN, but as what? Is it a tribute to the historical heroics of political resistance? Does he see there something akin to his own status as "soldier" for the gang, or his own alienation as refugee turned deportee? I am not here making any claims about Pájaro's participation in the FMLN mitin. Indeed, as a deported gang member himself, Pájaro appears as a packed and displaced sign that refuses easy representation. Just as he won't show his scars and can't or won't say what they represent, he could not or would not articulate the reasons for his presence at the rally. He is no Viejo Lin, who (whether or not he might be the national leader of the 18th Street Gang and a former FMLN combatant) is a translator between these generations and these projects.

Rather than illuminating the relationship between these rebellious projects, the dialectical image of La Mara Salvatrucha in FMLN face, re-worked through doble cara, asks us to pose another question: What makes these things appear different and discrete so that they seem to be copying each other and feeding off of each other's correspondence? Whatever claims are made in contemporary El Salvador for drawing clear analytic distinctions between political and criminal violence, derived as they are from the peri-odization of the civil war (before, during, and after), that war refuses his-torical boundaries and functions as a past ever present.

By the early 2000s, as if to demand a fuller accounting of the past as it in-flects the present, the Salvadoran civil war refugee of the 1980s made a some-what ironic comeback as the refugee escaping the gang war. The gang war refugee, another dialectical image, has become a curious social formation and legal subject in U.S. immigration courts. I am not invoking this term as an established legal category or in reference to a homogenous class of refu-gee. Rather, I am using the term to refer to two broad categories of appli-cants. The first group includes undocumented Salvadoran immigrant youth and young adults without a criminal record who claim to have fled forced recruitment into gangs and to have a well-founded fear of becoming targets of gang violence in El Salvador. The second group includes documented and undocumented immigrant gang members with criminal histories, including arrests for their illegal reentries into the United States after being deported back to Central America, who are seeking "withholding of removal, on the grounds that they will be targets of the gangs and death squads and that the government is unable or unwilling to protect them upon their return to El Salvador. Both groups argue that deportation back to El Salvador is tantamount to a death sentence.

By 2003, Homies Unidos in Los Angeles was inundated with requests from attorneys and families to provide information on country conditions in El Salvador and to identify expert witnesses — so much so, that they launched a human rights project called Libertad Con Dignidad (Liberty with Dignity). In 2008, the Washington Office on Latin America launched its Gang Related Asylum Project, and the National Immigration Project identified gangs as a focus area of its immigration enforcement and raids program, for which it established a Web site with legal decisions related to these asylum cases. In light of the increasing number of these asylum claims, the United Nations High Commissioner for Refugees (UNHCR) released a guidance note clarifying the circumstances under which victims of criminal gangs or activities warrant international protection under the 1951 Convention relating to the Status of Refugees and its 1967 Protocol.[15] While UNHCR's guidelines do recognize age, gender, and social status as innate and immutable characteristics of individuals who resist forced recruitment into gangs or oppose gang practices, the success rate of these cases in U.S. immigration courts thus far has been less than 1 percent. As of 2008, only five petitioners had been granted the asylum for which they petitioned, one of whom was Alex Sanchez. Another one of the successful cases was denied upon appeal by the government to the Federal Board of Immigration Appeals. Two further decisions involved a brother and a sister in the same case. The brother expressed anti-gang sentiment in El Salvador and openly confronted the gang for sexually assaulting his sister. Both he and his sister received asylum in the United States. One other case was granted in 2004. All of the successful cases were unpublished opinions and therefore could not be used as precedent for subsequent cases. Moreover, the only published precedent cases were both denied on appeal to the Federal Board of Immigration Appeals.[16] In both cases, the court denied the applicants' claim to membership in a "particular social group" that made them vulnerable to persecution by gangs. In another more recent case, although the petitioner was granted withholding from removal he was not released but rather assigned indefinite detention. At the same time, in the wake of the regional turn to manodurista policies and with the increase in extortions and homicides in El Salvador, the number of Central American political asylum claims in the United States almost doubled from 7,000 in 2004 to 13,999 in 2007. In 2005, only 700 claims were granted.[17]

Thus once again, not unlike during the civil war in the 1980s when only 2 to 3 percent of U.S. political asylum cases were granted to Salvadorans and Guatemalans, it is almost impossible to win asylum as a "gang war refugee." To grant asylum to these petitioners would be to acknowledge the failure of U.S. immigration and law enforcement policy, not to mention the failure or lack of will on the part of the Salvadoran state to protect Salvadoran citizens. This ironic twist at work in the emergence of deported gang members alongside unaffiliated youth as a new, albeit unlikely, class of refugee brings us back full circle to the 1980s and to the return of the repressed in more than one way: the ongoing participation of the United States in the production and reproduction of violence in El Salvador.

The Reproduction of a Terrorist

While in the post-9/11 political climate it was almost impossible to meet the standards of proof required for asylum and for withholding of removal, it was considerably easier to inadvertently pass for something else—namely a terrorist. Indeed, as attorneys and immigrant and youth rights groups began advocating on behalf of "the gang war refugee," yet another criminal type was surfacing, "the gangster as terrorist." Salvadoran youth and young adults, already caught between the intersection of immigration and criminal law, were to become vulnerable to anti-terrorist law—both in the United States and in El Salvador.

In the United States, the intersection between crime and terrorism was at first made only obliquely. The California Street Terrorism Enforcement Protection Act (STEP) of 1986 translated gang-related activities into the language of terrorism. After the 9/11 attacks, William Bratton, former police chief of the New York Police Department and a key figure in the globalization of Broken Windows and Zero Tolerance, played up this linguistic resonance further. When Bratton assumed the post of chief of the Los Angeles Police Department in 2002, he began his term by conflating the language of STEP with that of the War on Terror. He called for "an all-out assault" against "street terrorists," STEP's preferred name for gang members, and against "homeland terrorism," his preferred term for gang activity. Bratton had launched his campaign against gangs by drawing implicit links between crime and terrorism. As a result, LAPD was able to tap into Homeland Security money.

Interestingly, like the intersection between criminal and immigration law, this contemporary link between crime and terrorism also has its origins in 1996 with the passage of the Anti-Terrorist and Effective Death Penalty Act (AEDPA)—and as such, well before 9/11 and Bush's War on Terror. Because AEDPA explicitly links crime and terrorism, the current War on Terror's "state of exception" derives considerable force from this earlier moment in legislative history.[18]

Many legal scholars argue that legislators took advantage of the fears surrounding the World Trade Center bombing of 1993 and the Oklahoma City bombing of 1994 to use AEDPA to gut legal protections for prisoners. In so doing they point to the fact that those implicated in the bombings were tried and convicted successfully prior to the passage of AEDPA.[19] Indeed, critics contended that AEDPA had more to do with preventing state prisoners from exercising their constitutional rights to due process than with preventing terrorism.[20] Previous legislation had already limited legal protections for those facing trial: the Violent Crime Control and Law Enforcement Act of 1994, otherwise known as the Crime Bill or "The Beast," had allowed the use of evidence acquired through illegal search and seizures to be included in criminal proceedings. It sanctioned these warrantless searches under the "good faith" rule that is used in cases in which the police think they could have obtained a warrant in drug-related crimes. In so doing, it severely limited civil remedies for illegal searches.[21] In addition, AEDPA further undercut due process and habeas corpus by mandating the number of times a prisoner on death row could appeal his or her death sentence. Given that habeas corpus has direct links to the history of racial and ethnic disadvantage before the law,[22] it should come as no surprise that AEDPA's gutting of habeas corpus was just as rooted in attacks against the racially marked poor and immigrants through the War on Crime.

Only after 9/11, however, did explicit links between gangs and terrorists begin to circulate in the media, on the Internet, in policy circles, and in the courts.[23] The case of José Padilla was the first. Padilla, at one point a member of the Chicago-based gang the Maniac Chicago Disciples, had converted to Islam and was accused of collaborating with terrorists. Then, starting in November 2004, a spate of articles published on the Internet and in newspapers such as in the *Boston Herald*, *Los Angeles Times*, and *Washington*

Post insinuated links between La Mara Salvatrucha and Al Qaeda. Take, for instance, the language of this Internet intelligence news source article entitled "Criminals, Jihadists Threaten U.S. Border: Unholy Alliance of Terrorists, Gangs, Revolutionaries Pose New Security threat." The article begins as follows: "What would happen if criminal gangsters, revolutionaries and Islamic terrorists all got together in a common goal of overthrowing governments of America's neighbors and smuggling operatives into and out of the United States? Some senior police and intelligence sources [say] . . . that is just what is happening in Central America today."[24] A *Boston Herald* article claimed that U.S. intelligence had informed them that they had located members of Al Qaeda in MS in El Salvador, and the *Washington Post* published information that a member of Al Qaeda, Adnan G. el Shukrijumah had met with leaders of the gang in Honduras.[25] Police and intelligence officials here and there subsequently denied any evidence of such links, but the implicit was made explicit, if only through rumor and innuendo. The official negation of these rumors did not stop Newt Gingrich from hosting an hour-long special on Fox News channels devoted to exploring these hypothetical links, where he placed gang-abatement strategies at the center of the War on Terror.[26]

Aired in June 2005, the documentary, entitled "American Gangs: Ties to Terror?" was publicized as follows:

The one-hour special report will focus on how international gangs such as Mara Salvatrucha—or MS 13—pose not just a risk to our personal security, but our national security as well.

"Fueled by the global nature of the drug trade, gangs are increasingly international operations," said Speaker Gingrich. "With the infrastructure in place to move and distribute drugs across the border, the danger exists that they will use their network to, for the right price, traffic terrorists and weapons into the country."

"After all, why wouldn't two groups—one driven by greed and the other by hatred—collaborate to further their goals," Gingrich added.[27]

The documentary, which followed on the heels of the Fox News hour and coverage of Iraq, Al Qaeda, Afghanistan, and the Taliban, opens with footage from the attacks on the Twin Towers and with Gingrich's opening lines: "September 11, 2001, brought new terror to our land . . . but have we missed a dangerous threat inside our borders, inside our towns? . . . Experts warn these gangs could also have ties to foreign terrorist groups . . . with their enterprising antics of drug trafficking [and] smuggling people and possibly weapons of mass destruction across our borders. Government officials at Homeland Security say drastic measures are needed to strike down these gang networks." While the language throughout is tentative, the imagery is not. As experts are brought in to demonstrate the structural analogies between gangs and terrorists and their potential mutually convenient and profitable arrangements, Gingrich's production team makes these hypothetical connections visible to us by splicing the screen in half with jihadists aiming rifles on one side and tattooed youth using spray paint cans on the other. The documentary literally splices footage from both worlds together in a montage of images. In a style reminiscent of MTV music videos, the screen shifts back and forth frenetically between footage of turbaned jihadists and tattooed gang members—both heavily armed and with machine guns aimed. These images are interspersed with those of people scrambling through the gullies of the U.S.-Mexico border or climbing the walls that now run between the two countries; pages of Arabic script (possibly from the Koran); violent gang initiations; and youth gesticulating wildly with bandanas covering their faces and pointing guns to their own heads. Gangster and terrorist are brought together in nightmare of free association.

Gingrich concludes his documentary by arguing that these possible links between immigration, gangs, and terrorism clearly support first bringing law enforcement and immigration agencies together, and second bringing national security and law enforcement into one unified effort—"for if not, our very civilization maybe at risk." It comes as no surprise, perhaps, that Fox News and Gingrich would be the conduit for popularizing links between gangs and terrorists and feeding our imaginations with alarmist reportage. But this "gang–crime–terrorism continuum" and the justification of the United States as a security state also became a legitimate topic of debate among military strategists.[28] In a special report to the Web site for Defense and National Interest, Gary Wilson and John Sullivan advocated applying "third generation street gangs (3G2), netwar, and fourth generation warfare (4GW) . . . to investigate typologies and relationships of third generation street gangs and terrorist groups."[29] They too argued that the division between gangs as a law enforcement concern and terrorists as a military concern could no longer be maintained where distinctions between war and crime are becoming increasingly blurred.[30] Their publication followed on previous works that argued that gangs, as a mutated form of "urban insurgency," posed a serious challenge to state sovereignty. As such, gangs were both political and criminal in nature and thus required police and military forces to provide collective security and stability.[31]

Moreover, the use of terrorism discourse entered criminal proceedings in state courts. After the September 11, 2001, terrorist attacks, thirty-six states added terrorism-related laws to their criminal codes, using them to enhance sentences that, in some cases, now include the death penalty. In a *Washington Post* article, the journalist Michelle García explored how these new laws have provided prosecutors with new opportunities, and she noted somewhat wryly that in 2005 "the newest face of an alleged terrorist wears a goatee, stands about five feet tall, dresses in baggy clothes and resides in the Bronx." Ironically, the gang member Edgar Morales, aka "Puebla," was among the first people ever charged under New York's state terrorism laws. Gregory Mark, a former prosecutor who became a legal historian at Rutgers, commented on this ever-expanding definition of the term "terrorism" in the context of the Morales case, "Language is plastic . . . As new situations arise and the imagination of prosecutors is stimulated, the statutes which were clearly intended for one purpose are expanded."[32] "Terrorism" was clearly operating here as a "free-floating signifier" and within the realm of the imagination.[33]

Wilson and Sullivan, the authors who theorized the "gang–crime–terrorism continuum," argued the point that Gingrich acknowledged throughout his broadcast, namely that "despite law enforcement's vigilance in looking for interaction between transnational criminal organization or gangs (transnational or otherwise) and international terrorist groups within the United States few investigators have identified any tangible direct association in open sources. Those who have, described the connections as speculation supported by little evidence."[34] However, the investigators concluded that the failure to make these links was "not an intelligence failure but a failure of imagination."[35] There was certainly no lack of imagination in Gingrich's graphic rendering of his speculative thesis. As Richard Hofsteader notes, "What distinguishes the paranoid style is not the absence of verifiable fact but rather a curious leap in imagination."[36] Even if hypothetical, terror and its deterrence evoke intense fear. The manipulation of frames for purposes of creating collective terror has to be directed to the imagination. There is no sense of the "untrue" or "unreal," say Zulaika and Douglass, "when one is submerged in dream or fantasy."[37]

One gang in particular captured the media's imagination like no other in the post-9/11 climate. With Gingrich's version of this "gang–crime–terrorism continuum" thesis vividly in place, he turns his focus to La Mara

Salvatrucha—MS 13. MS, we are told, is "known for its extreme violence," and has become the target of a national effort between law enforcement and Immigration and Customs Enforcement (ICE) of Homeland Security. That effort went under the name of Operation Community Shield. The operation was launched on March 14, 2005, in seven cities across the country with the arrest of 103 purported members of MS.[38] In the documentary we see a photograph of an MS gang member who has made the ICE Most Wanted list. Law enforcement's biggest fear is, according to Gingrich, that "MS 13 has already begun working with international terrorists."

National Geographic Channel picked up on this focus on MS 13 in a documentary, *World's Most Dangerous Gang*, which first aired in February 2006. In the film the correspondent Lisa Ling explains that MS "rules over four miles of Los Angeles, but that's just the beginning." We are told that MS is a "huge multinational, deeply organized crime group" and has spread "like a virus" across the country, invading thirty-three states and six countries from El Salvador to Canada, and from Alaska to Spain. With ten thousand foot-soldiers, the gang "crosses the border at will." In fact "the gang started to grow so fast that a federal task force was created to deal specifically with MS." Ling is referring to the aforementioned Operation Community Shield campaign.

The National Geographic documentary begins and ends with the murder of sixteen-year-old Brenda Paz, an MS member turned FBI informant. After divulging considerable information about MS—recorded footage that is included—Ling tells us that Paz was drawn "back into the gang, and that the news she was a rat leaked out." Paz, who was pregnant, was stabbed twelve times. The location, suburban Virginia, and the murder weapon, a machete, provoked considerable anxiety. Paz's body was found in the wooded outskirts of Virginia, in an area not previously associated with gang violence. This signals that the suburbs are no longer lily white or middle class, and that MS may appear in a "neighborhood near you." A similar message had also been circulating on Internet blogs. An article from Police E MAG, featured on a private blog called somewhat misleadingly the Homeland Security National Terror Alert,[39] refers to a case in suburban Nassau County, New York, where two murders were attributed to MS. The message is that MS has "moved into the upper middle-class enclaves of [Long] Island, into the kinds of communities where the locals assume that crime is somebody else's problem."[40]

Interestingly, the machete that was used to kill Paz was interpreted by the media as a sign of the particular savagery of MS. In commenting on the documentary, Kevin Pranis of the Justice Policy Institute notes: "While I'd consider a machete a far less lethal weapon than a gun, the coverage has suggested that somehow machetes are an even more savage sort of weapon than any weapon previously conceived and that machete-wielding gangsters should cause more fear than 15-year olds with machine guns."[41] The irony here is that this is a reversal of the anxieties of the 1980s attached to the replacement of knives by guns. Perhaps the image of the machete resonated with the gruesome videos in circulation at the time of hostages being beheaded by Islamic jihadists.

At the same moment, the figure of the machete-wielding Salvadoran gangster came to be featured in the popular FX television series The Shield. A Salvadoran gang, "Salvas," made its debut in the show's sixth season through the mass killing of rival gang members. The killers, another rival Mexican gang, were "instructed to do it jungle style" so it looked like the doings of the Salvadoran gangs. The show is filled with gruesome scenes of hacked up and bloody body parts, and the grenade alongside the machete become the distinguishing features of Salvadoran criminality.

As the journalist Bob Garfield notes in the opening to his radio interview with Pranis, the terror surrounding MS is linked to a larger set of anti-immigrant politics:

> If you're a politician seeking to demonize illegal immigrants, there's nothing to make you feel righteous quite like MS-13. The Salvadoran gang, also known as Mara Salvatrucha, has grown from its Los Angeles roots in the '70s to infiltrate and terrify a growing number of U.S. communities, where heavily tattooed gang-bangers have engaged in crimes as petty as vandalism and as gruesome as machete dismemberments and murder.
>
> The largest part of the terror, however, has lived in the headlines as the press fixates on the Latin menace . . .
>
> Various politicians have come into Newark, New Jersey, to decry the murders of three young students there by perpetrators allegedly including two illegal immigrants, who may or may not have had gang connections, and have not only connected them to MS 13 but to Muslim terrorists and God knows who all.

In responding to Garfield's suggestion that MS 13 really stands for the political demonization of Latino immigrants in general, Pranis concurs that MS has been conflated with national security issues:

Absolutely, and that's why the murder of—which was a gruesome murder—of Brenda Paz near Washington, D.C., is so important, because it happened so close to the Capitol. I think that was either MS 13's greatest success or greatest mistake, depending on whether you want the gang to grow.

They got the attention of federal lawmakers. That got the attention of the national media. And so MS 13 has become the poster child for the dangers of immigration, if you listen to the anti-immigrant advocates . . .

But unfortunately our obsession with MS 13 as the peril from south of the border, coming wielding machetes and with their, you know, incredibly tight-knit political and criminal organization, is really unfortunately distorting the debate.[42]

Pranis's Justice Policy Institute was part of a coalition of United States and Central American organizations seeking to intervene in that debate and to advocate for alternatives to repressive zero-tolerance strategies.

The national police campaign Operation Community Shield has since extended its focus on MS to include all gangs,[43] but MS 13 served as a powerful hieroglyph for the production of the gangster as terrorist—and as yet another threat to our national security. The unsubstantiated sightings of MS with Al Qaeda, recognized as hypothetical, are nonetheless portrayed as inevitable if we do not make the necessary conceptual leaps to recognize the interrelationship of the wars against criminals, immigrants, and terrorists.

We see once again the extraordinary productivity of media and the law in the production of a culprit, and of the fictional economy of representation.[44] As news reportage, the documentaries by Fox and National Geographic deploy the generic traditions of fiction: the horror movie and the melodrama that together warn of the monsters among us and that depict a society on the brink of chaos and dissolution. Gingrich's poetic techniques of splicing footage of gangs and terrorists together not only heightens the impact of his message, but the play-like frames allow him to forgo all pretense of distinguishing fact from fabrication. And these are only two of an explosion of documentary films on Central American gangs. Even the string of independent productions can't seem to relinquish the excited and the frenetic pace of crime cinema, or to resist the generic seepage between progressive documentary and action movie—lured by the same glamour as the youthful recruits that crowd in front of their cameras.

My point here is not that gangs and terrorists are mere figments of our imagination or that the violence that they inflict is not of grave concern. Rather, I am troubled by the enabling capacities of these fictional realities about gangs and terrorists, not simply because they unleash the coercive apparatus of the security state but also because they enable and reproduce the very enemy they seek to eradicate.

Some would argue that thanks to the media hype around the gang, MS 13 became arguably more of a brand than an organization. Certainly, the proliferation of movie-like coverage made it "the most exciting gang to be a part of." Pranis, who argues that the gang had been publicized too much, worries over these enabling fictions: "I talked to someone who'd gone to El Salvador and met a bunch of MS 13 members who'd basically recruited themselves from media coverage" rather than through an existing clique.[45]

The Changing Face of the Gang

The Salvadoran media is certainly no less complicit than the U.S. media in leveraging gang youth obsessed with "representing" their neighborhoods for the camera. Gang youth have eagerly sought out the limelight of the camera, just as the camera has courted them. Consequently, their performance—posing, posturing, throwing signs, and baring tattoos—had been a regular feature of Salvadoran media coverage since the mid-1990s, when the war against the "communists" shifted to a war against "criminals."[46] But in 2007, something strange appeared to be happening in the realm of representation in El Salvador: the tattooed gangster, that ubiquitous post–civil war criminal type, was no longer at the front and center of Salvadoran headline news.

This recent disappearance of gangs from the newspapers and television news might suggest that Mano Dura and its sequel Súper Mano Dura were successful in reducing violence. But we have already seen that they failed miserably on that count. What, then, accounts for this disturbance in representation? Was it embarrassment on the part of the state, contrition on the part of the media for its active coproduction of the spectacle,[47] or the gang's growing resistance to representation? I would suggest that it was a result of all these things, but for now I want to explore the role of the gang itself. In previous chapters, I described the ways in which the criminalization of gang expressive practices and visual culture is at the core of manodurista policies. The tattoo became, in and of itself, grounds for arrest.

As I discussed in chapter 6, three years after the implementation of mano-durismo I returned to El Salvador to track its effects. Seeking various ways back into the now militarized and radicalized barrios, and upon the advice of a Salvadoran colleague, I sought out an evangelical pastor. When I reached him on his cell phone, he suggested we meet at Mr. Donut (a Salvadoran chain restaurant) in a shopping center in a middle-class neighborhood in San Salvador, and thus on relatively neutral ground. The pastor was much younger than I expected, but he wore the uniform well: black slacks, white long-sleeve shirt tucked in, clean-cut hair, black leather briefcase, and, of course, a Bible. We had not been speaking for very long, however, when the pastor began to morph into something else. There was a trace of something under his skin in the corner of his eye—the trace of tears, tattooed tears. The mark of a gangster? Perhaps the pastor noticed my puzzled gaze change to one of recognition, because he turned his conversation about his mission-ary work with youth in the barrios as evangelical pastor to his former work recruiting youth from those barrios as a founding member of one of the 18th Street cliques in San Salvador. He had been deported, he explained, from Los Angeles in the 1990s. The pastor's costume could not hide the barely visible, yet startling, trace of tears, once tattooed and now removed. It was not so much a removal as a fading or a shading, but a shading into what?

Early the next morning, the pastor was dragged from his house and shot. He bled to death before reaching the hospital. I cannot speak for the pas-tor's status as reformed gang member. Was he "playing with God's word," something that is not treated lightly by gang members? Or had his death been staged to look like a gang killing at the hand of death squads? The pas-tor knew, he had said, that he could only do this work "by the grace of God," and that he would live only "as long as [his] work was God's will." I could not know if rather than unmasking, the trace underneath his skin was yet another form of masking.[48]

The changing face of the gang and its morphing into something else emerged as a theme in the following weeks. Gang leaders, it seemed, were discouraging any more tattoos and were telling their members to stop dress-ing like gang members so that they could pass for *civiles* (civilians) and go undercover, so to speak, as *fulano zoutano* (*futano del tal*; "so and so"). Gang members were seeking out tattoo removal programs in growing numbers and with the consent of their leaders. Many suggested that the expressive cul-ture of the gang that had been such an attractive part of this youth identity-making project was, in fact, only disappearing as a measure of self-defense, that is, as a strategic move on the part of the gang. Indeed, as my Salvadoran colleague Lisette Miranda, who coauthored the first study of youth gangs in El Salvador when she was working for UNICEF in the early days of this so-called phenomenon, exclaimed to me: "In the end, if you look over it, what has been the result of El Plan Mano Dura and El Plan Súper Mano Dura, La Ley Anti-Mara? . . . The most tangible result has been the transformation of the dynamic of the gang. Now the gang is much more clandestine." A doctor working at a tattoo removal clinic found herself inadvertently aiding this move to go underground: "The participation of the gangs in the CNSP tattoo removal program for example, has to do with this new dynamic." Some have even told me: "I'm not changing them [erasing my tattoos] to rehabilitate myself, I'm changing with the authorization of the gang . . . as part of a tactic to be able to continue [with the gang]. It's incredible!" The researcher Marlon Carranza had a similar analysis. He suggested that the proud public performance of the gangster identity embodied in the hand gesture and the strut, worn on and bleeding through the skin in the form of the tattoo, the costume-cum-uniform, and the battle scars exposed—all claiming loudly "Soy pandillero!" "This is what I am!" "Here I am!"—had become muted because of the repression. This provocation, this lust for social recognition that had filled the front pages of Salvadoran newspapers, the visuals for nightly news, and one foreign documentary project after another, was now, as a result of manodurismo, going underground. The rules were changing: "Don't dress like a gang member. Dress like the rest. Don't bring attention to yourself."

As much of it as I had encountered, I had never really given the gang tattoo its due in my research. Perhaps it was my concern as an anthropologist with the politics of the gaze and my reticence to exoticize gangs. Certainly, my ambivalence had much to do with my ongoing solidarity with Latino immigrant rights activists in the United States who felt that the focus on youth culture was "a boutique issue" that distracted from and undermined more far-reaching legalization and citizenship efforts. My methodology involved "hanging out" with gangs and gang peace activists, not asking them to pose or to perform before a camera. If anything, I was interested in observing how gangs and media worked together to produce particular stories, representations, and effects. Needless to say, gang members would ignore me when there was a photographer of any sort around. My rarely used point and shoot camera held no allure for them. They had their priorities straight—photo opportunities to represent their neighborhoods and to build their reputations, their fame, and their "street cred," which national and international news outlets were hard at work broadcasting.

The tattoo clearly calls for a detailed analysis of its form, the biography and geography of which it speaks, and the practices surrounding tattooing—not the least of which being the deep desire of gang members to be looked at and displayed, or their "to be looked-at-ness."[49] Mark Blanchard expounds on this phenomenon well when he says, "The tattoo is about revealing, being revealed and gazing upon the revealing. The tattooed subject focuses the public gaze on his or her own body or part of the body while also delighting himself or herself as both exhibitionist and voyeur of his or her own spectacle, in a ritual of intense specularity."[50]

In the post–civil war era, the gang tattoo had become a crucial mark in the process of creating new categories that remade difference in a purportedly ethnic and racially homogeneous El Salvador. In a moment when indigenous Salvadorans, who after the massacre of 1932 had hidden their true selves in order to be free of persecution,[51] were making an unexpected reappearance, youth were themselves actively engaged in creating a fiction of ethnic singularity. By marking themselves with tattoos, a phenotypical marker, youth from different neighborhoods made themselves into others to one another and beyond. In the absence of discernible differences, the tattoo distinguished one group from another with what Arjun Appadurai might term "dead certainty."[52]

What interests me here, however, is the tattoo in reverse—that is, its removal. What is this "trace" beneath the skin? Is this purported morphing into society at large an unmasking or a further masking, a form of camouflage? Susan Phillips in her work on tattoo removal clinics in East Los Angeles examines tattoo removal as a redemptive process wherein a new self counters a former self, and where the new self repents or has a change of heart. Tattoo removal in this context releases people from the bind of their previous material choices and enables a "rematching of hearts and skins" so that the skin no longer portrays the old self. Phillips sees the ability to erase tattoos as an empowering process, a "social and bodily realignment," that directly counters social exclusion.[53] But is this morphing from "street" to "decent" and blending back into society through tattoo removal always an act of redemption, or can it be a cleverly crafted disguise, a resistance of the gaze?[54] The tattoo, which marked which barrio one was from and thus one's territorial identification, had after all become a powerful instrument of state power.

Perhaps it's not surprising then that these disturbances in representation converged with a disturbance at another level: namely, in the boundary systems of the gang and the configuration of neighborhoods. Expressive cultural practices and urban space are two interrelated means through which social inequality is reconfigured.[55] As a result of the mass arrests of gang members, made in large part solely on the basis of the tattoo, the boundary system of the neighborhoods was in flux once again. I say once again because, as I discussed in chapter 4, in the mid-1990s Salvadoran geography had been rewritten (or its political boundaries redistricted) by U.S. inner-city politics and the deportation of gang members. The territorial identifications of these neighborhoods had been reshaped according to divisions between barrios in cities such as Los Angeles.

Now, as a result of Mano Dura, the gangs' operations seemed to be increasingly independent from a particular barrio. The territory of the barrio had been radically transformed, and the local geography of the neighborhood was no longer the central space of identification or operation for the gang. In response to Súper Mano Dura, gangs had become much more fluid and mobile.[56] So, for instance, it was not uncommon to find youth from Soyapango hiding out in El IVU, where they would not be recognized. Padre Toño, the Spanish priest mentioned in the last chapter who had headed the local parish in the neighborhood of Mejicanos, described the transformation to me this way: "The gang was much more visible [before Mano Dura]. We knew who they were. We were friends with them. [Now] we've lost all contact with the clique of the community. They're in prison or in hiding. Now they're moving their people around to take care of their territory. It's almost as if they're changing personnel around. Now you don't know who's who. It causes great insecurity and a level of anguish that is intolerable." Like deportation, this incarceration or arrested mobility had ironically produced new modes of transgressive mobility and with it a new set of anxieties.

Thus an effect of these disturbances, both in representation and in urban space, was to turn the gang into a ghostly presence. This growing invisibility of the gang was accompanied by greater social insecurity and profound doubts about who exactly were among the "we" and who were among the "they." Difference went underground as gang members donned masks of everydayness.[57]

If Mano Dura was a success it was to blur the very categories from which it had derived its logic—a visual logic. After all the forums, the documentation, the reports, the documentaries, and the intelligence gathering, "the gang" now exceeded and eluded strategies of institutional knowledge. "It is super, super dynamic!" exclaimed an exasperated Salvadoran researcher. What new logic would emerge in its place? Or better put, what new subjects would be hailed into being by that logic? Interestingly, as the gang member retreated from the news headlines in El Salvador, something else seemed to be coming into representation (and I might even argue, back into representation). The trace on the evangelical pastor's face that ostensibly marked his conversion from one doctrinal certainty to another, like a Derridean stain, marks "the future and the past in a present moment which is neither."[58] The same month that the pastor was killed, El Salvador passed its anti-terrorist law, which capitalized on this moment of epistemic murk to label both gangsters alongside activists against neoliberal policies alike as terrorists. The gang member had filled a slot for the state, but the ruling right-wing in El Salvador had never relinquished that slot's premiere occupant, the communist, who is at times also an Indian and also a gangster, but always a communist.[59]

HALL OF MIRRORS ———— **CONCLUSION**

A confrontation on July 5, 2006, between university students and the Salvadoran National Police arguably marked the passage from social to political violence. Two police officers in the PNC's anti-riot unit were killed outside the National University of El Salvador during a protest against increased bus fares. Certainly ARENA latched onto the killings as signs of the reradicalization of the Left; much was made of the fact that the alleged killer, Mario Belloso, was a low-level member of the FMLN. This incident, together with an overall increase in violence, ensured the passage of the Anti-Terrorist Law later that year.

For many Salvadorans, the introduction of the Anti-Terrorist Law, even though it was based on a similar law in Cuba, harkened back to the repressive history of El Salvador.[1] Roberto Burgos, the constitutional lawyer who I had consulted about the U.S.-run International Law Enforcement Academy, expressed his fears of the potential consequences of the new law this way:

"The problem with this new concept of security that is being applied in Latin America after 9/11 [is that] we are hearing things once again that aren't new. Look, I very much respect that 9/11 changed the lives of people in the U.S. and they started to see terrorism as a daily problem, but to speak of terrorism and the measures to counter terrorism here in Central America, we don't hear this as something good. It was the excuse to repress whatever political opposition, and so it seems very natural to me that people are resistant." And events were to prove Burgos right. A year later on July 3, 2007, the law was leveraged to arrest sixty protestors who had blocked the roads into the town Suchitoto in a rally against the privatization of water. President Saca was scheduled to give a speech that day, but the protestors succeeded in preventing him from entering the town. In the end, they were arrested and charged as "terrorists." After considerable domestic and international pressure to free the protestors, the charges against them were eventually dropped. However, the connection between terrorism and social movements protesting neoliberal policies had been made explicit by ARENA, which indicated that the protestors were "all from the Left." Saca even asserted that the protests in Suchitoto were all part of Mario Belloso's plans.

Poised as El Salvador now was between the threat of gangs and socialists, the country had become once again strategically placed within U.S. interests — albeit this time with recourse to the dominant paradigm of the War on Terror. The gang–crime–terrorism continuum had served its purpose. Even those willing to distinguish between the training at the new U.S.-led police academy and the training of murderous soldiers at the School of the Americas worried over the double-edged nature of support from the United States. As Burgos put it, "In the end it's always 'What is the world that the U.S. wants, and what . . . is convenient for the U.S., given its vision of its internal security? .' . . . This is undeniable. They are the ones paying for the party. It is they who elaborate the program." The ruling right-wing party, ARENA, was eager to go along with the program and to throw its lot in with the Bush administration's war in Iraq. While largely a symbolic presence, as of November 2008 El Salvador was the only Latin American country in Bush's Coalition of Willing, which had dwindled from forty-five nations to five.[2] While the country's participation had long been unpopular among Salvadorans, its newspapers proudly published images of Salvadoran immigrants dressed in the uniform of the U.S. military and bound for Iraq, and those inside and outside the nation who had been killed were lauded as national heroes. For its part, the United States gratefully acknowledged Salvadoran support. Six

Salvadoran Special Forces soldiers were awarded the Bronze Star for their service in Iraq. The tiny isthmus of El Salvador was, once again, among the top recipients of U.S. military largesse. Immigrant soldiers fallen in battle were granted posthumous U.S. citizenship that then extended to their surviving families.[3] And the American dream was extended to Iraq through yet another Salvadoran labor migration for jobs with American private security companies such as Triple Canopy and Blackwater in Iraq.[4] Once again, El Salvador became a player in the U.S. "protection racket" and its "global military-gift economy" with a vengeance.[5]

The ARENA government also capitalized on the so-called Pink Tide—the renewal of the Latin American Left in countries like Bolivia and Venezuela—to reaffirm its commitment to the next phase of the United States neoliberal economic agenda in El Salvador and to the Dominican Republic–Central American Free Trade agreement (DR–CAFTA was ratified by the Salvadoran government in March 2006). Moreover, ARENA consistently held the power of the United States in the region over the heads of Salvadoran voters. So in the 2005 presidential election, for instance, ARENA argued that if Shafik Handal, the FMLN candidate that year, was elected then the United States would discontinue temporary protected status for Salvadorans living abroad and so end the flow of family remittances. The Bush administration supported this strategy. It objected to Handal's leftist ties: he was formerly the head of the Salvadoran Communist Party and was a staunch and vocal critique of neoliberalism. Much was made over Handal's relations with the Venezuelan president Hugo Chavez and the Bolivian president Evo Morales. In violation of Salvadoran sovereignty, the U.S. ambassador openly warned Salvadorans in newspaper headlines that the election of Handal would have a serious and negative impact on U.S.-Salvadoran relations. And in 2006, after ARENA was once again assured the presidency, the Bush administration proposed $13 million in military aid to El Salvador.

While problematic, it was not surprising that Handal's ties would be criticized. However, ARENA painted the FMLN's center-left and reformist candidate Mauricio Funes, a longtime television journalist critical of the ARENA government, in much the same light to its United States supporters. El Salvador's Minister of Foreign Affairs, Marisol Argueta, spoke on September 18, 2008, before the conservative American Enterprise Institute in Washington, D.C. Her speech included a direct appeal for the United States to concern itself with the possibility of an FMLN victory in the upcoming elections. In stating that members of the FMLN had ties to the terrorist organizations Euskadi Ta Askatasuna or Basque Homeland and Freedom (ETA) and Fuerzas Armadas Revolucionarias de Colombia—Ejército del Pueblo or Revolutionary Armed Forces of Colombia—People's Army (FARC), Minister Argueta argued that "losing El Salvador will be a dangerous proposition for both the security and the national interests for both El Salvador and the United States." This could send El Salvador back thirty years to "a time of turmoil." "The security of the United States is at stake in El Salvador," she added, quoting Ronald Reagan. She also asserted that Latin America faces a threat from a wave of neosocialism from groups that take power through democratic elections and populist appeals. "If power goes to the wrong hands, El Salvador may well be the next populist failure in the hemisphere."[6]

While it is clear that the interests of the ARENA and Bush administrations in both countries were aligned, it also seemed that they were locked in a dynamic that exceeded the strategic manipulation of foreign policy or the rational technologies of policing strategies. Fantasy proves a useful heuristic with which to probe the irrational and excessive dimensions of the political here.[7] One might say that fantasy glues together the United States and El Salvador psychically. Take, for instance, Newt Gingrich's role in his Fox TV media construction of the moral panic around the rumor of the fantastic kinship between Salvadoran gangbangers and Islamic jihadists. In brandishing what he admits are scantly even facts, Gingrich makes great leaps into discursive fantasy. He knows what he is doing but he cannot do otherwise.[8] He is compelled to repeat the trauma of U.S. intervention in El Salvador in the name of the War on Terror. The symptom of suspicion thus persists and reorganizes around a new set of enemies.

Fantasy produces subjects and subjectivities.[9] As Padre Toño concluded about El Salvador, "This boiling pot has its escapees [émigrés] and its phantasms [gangs]." A politics of paranoia—be it about illegal aliens, gangs, or terrorists—relies on fictional realities to drive draconian agendas at the same time as it brings those fictions into being. It feeds into the proliferation of the very monsters it seeks to eliminate. The gang MS is marketed as an international brand and its international reach grows. Youth basking in the limelight of the camera become more sophisticated and go underground. They become phantasmatic figures in the neighborhoods they once openly claimed, and yet the violence explodes beyond its already shocking levels.

In writing about 9/11, Begoña Aretxaga argued that those attacks were the materialization of a fictional reality, a displacement of terrorism from the screens of movie theaters onto the screens of the television newscast.

We have, she argued, "at the level of political imaginary, [been] aiding the discursive and military construction of Terrorism with a capital T."[10] Like terrorism, in the post-9/11 era, the so-called transnational gang crisis has also proved to be a fertile site for political, media, and research imaginaries in the United States and Central America and beyond. In 2006, reports began coming in from new and unexpected quarters. "La Mara Salvatrucha Expands Its Reach into Spain," the headlines read. Seemingly unaware of the fact that these youth gangs were actually offshoots of the Latin Kings in New York and were, by and large, either ethnically Puerto Rican or Ecuadorian, the Spanish called in the Salvadoran gang experts for consultation. One Salvadoran researcher who was invited explained how she arrived only to find "the whole Salvadoran mafia" there, referring to the small group of Salvadoran researchers, program directors, government officials, and so forth working on the "transnational gang crisis."

In the last few years, the production of studies, documentaries, and articles on the subject of transnational gangs in the region has been prolific, to say the least. It is a struggle to keep apace with this veritable industry. How might we, the authors of those publications, have contributed to the production of these neoliberal securityscapes, wittingly or unwittingly, aggressively or reticently? As one Salvadoran researcher, looking back at her decade-long involvement with the topic of gangs and youth violence, remarked to me ruefully: "Look, all of us who have worked on and conceptualized the theme are also responsible [for the current situation] because [after all] we are the ones who have conceptualized [the issue] and given it structure and form." Even community activists who field requests from researchers, funders, media producers, policymakers, and so forth are no less implicated in the production of this spectacle—as are the gang members or "wannabes" who seek the limelight of the camera or neighborhood walls as billboards. The players in this complex of forces (police, immigration officers, the military, media, policymakers, and indeed academic experts, myself included) have enabled the reproduction of that which they purportedly set out to undo—the "transnational gang crisis." Moreover, that crisis feeds into the larger regional and global agendas of neoliberal trade agreements and counterterrorist strategies.

As I describe in chapter 7, the representation of the "transnational gang crisis" within the idiom of "terrorism" coincided with the return of the figure of the "communist," often labeled a "terrorist." Moreover, it seems that this proliferation of interlocking images of terrorists and criminals also guides the reproduction of U.S.-Salvadoran relations and thereby plays into the actual production of transnational gangs. This mirroring paranoid dynamic has proven to be a fundamental structure underlying transnational life between the United States and El Salvador. Criminal deportees reemerge as refugees, military advisors as civil police consultants and then homeland security advisors, guerrillas as gangsters, cops as criminals, and activists or advocates as scholars. Dislocations wrought by forced migration in the 1980s recur through forced repatriation in the 1990s, and both combine in the return of yet another repressed figure: the Salvadoran refugee. Relations between El Salvador and the United States are refracted through these transnational "mirrors of production"—intensive mimetic interactions across former borders between North and South. Clearly, the border between the United States and El Salvador, albeit structured through an imperialistic rather than a formal colonial relation, has been "punctured porous" first by war and migration and now by democratization and neoliberal trade and security agreements.[11] The Transnational Anti-Gang Unit (TAG) and the federal Interagency Taskforce on Gangs propose that the United States and its allies like El Salvador take mutual responsibility for their regional security and support one another's efforts to suppress gangs through cooperation and collaboration. Both enable cross-border policing and the easy flow of intelligence information between countries. Together, these initiatives formalize the inter-American neoliberal securityscapes that have been the central focus of this book.

The disappearance of the communist challenge and with it the triumph of neoliberalism as the dominant order between the United States and El Salvador coincided with the signing of a new social contract in El Salvador. Indeed, the appearance of the gang member as a "new criminal type" in the immediate post–civil war period bears a particular relationship to the emergence of "democracy" in El Salvador as the form and discourse of political legitimacy.[12] In *Violence and the Sacred* René Girard argued that the loss of distinction between former enemies leads to a "mimetic crisis." This structural crisis, he says, can only be resolved through a unanimous antipathy toward a common enemy. A scapegoat, then, is always necessary to the beginning of a system. Across their entwined histories, it seems that El Salvador and the United States have both needed an other—a "contemporary savage"[13]— against which to redefine themselves, be it the figure of the native, the communist, or in this case, the gangster. However, zero-tolerance strategies, or what Allen Feldman terms "securocratic wars of public safety," cannot resolve the crisis precisely because they emulate the sacrificial form itself and are therefore subject to "compulsive repetition disorder." Not unlike gang warfare itself, these state wars against gangs lead to redundant violence, and to a "politics on autopilot" that fails to move society beyond crisis to "a new historical stage."[14] Contrary to the assertion that securityscapes work to entrench the state rather than to deterritorialize it,[15] this book has illustrated how securityscapes effectively undermine the very sovereignty they set out to defend and the very peace they seek to establish. Our criminal obsessions with transnational gang youth mark a ritual repository par excellence of this violent transnational history from the wane of cold war to the rise of the War on Terror. We only bleed further into one another.

IMPRESSIONS FROM A POLITICAL PRESENT ——— **EPILOGUE**

Inauguration: 1569, from Fr. inauguration "installation,
consecration," from L. inaugurationem (nom. inauguratio)
"consecration, installment under good omens," from in-
augurare "take omens from the flight of birds, consecrate
or install when such omens are favorable," from in- "on,
in" + augurare "to act as an augur, predict" (see *augur*).

—Online Etymology Dictionary

On January 21, 2009, Barack Hussein Obama was sworn in as the forty-fourth president of the United States of America, and the first African American president, as a sign that, in his words, "all are equal, all are free and all deserve a chance to pursue their full measure of happiness," and that U.S. Americans "reject as false the choice between our safety and our founding ideals."[1] For the briefest moment, there was a sense that the country had been cleansed of its original and most recent sins. In Los Angeles, anger gave way to an unfamiliar calm.

The politics of recognition at work in what promoters and cynics alike called "the Obama Brand" was astounding. Obama's subject formation was unlike that of any other U.S. president. It spanned Kansas, Hawaii, Kenya, and Indonesia; it was biracial but nurtured by middle-class Anglo Americans; in later years it was married with radical and reformist African American political, religious, and cultural traditions; and it brought together community activist, constitutional law professor, and politician. The Republican ex-Secretary of State General Colin Powell endorsed Obama over John McCain in recognition that the Democratic candidate had the capacity to cross ethnic, racial, and generational lines, and as such was a "transformational figure" who represented a new generation coming onto the stage of U.S. and world politics.[2] People all over the world watched and celebrated Obama's inauguration in recognition of what had been accomplished, and in hopeful anticipation of the end of the Bush regime's global War on Terror.

Obama had called for a transformational politics based on hope and generosity rather than on fear and greed. Certainly, in Latin America Obama's victory brought widespread expectations of a dramatic shift in Washington's approach to the region.[3] Obama, speaking during his electoral campaign from Miami, declared that his election would usher in a "new chapter in the story of the Americas," as well as signal the end of U.S. unilateralism in Latin America—a welcome break from the revival of the cold war–inspired policies of the Bush administration.[4]

On June 1, 2009, in San Salvador, Mauricio Funes, the candidate for the leftist opposition party the FMLN, was sworn in as president of El Salvador. Secretary of State Hilary Clinton was in attendance. Her smile radiated the Obama administration's support of this affirmation of the democratic process that had brought to power the former guerrilla army considered "terrorist" by previous administrations. Clinton's red dress echoed the sea of red flags, T-shirts, and caps at FMLN celebrations across the country and in the diaspora. The Latin American leftist presidents Hugo Chavez, Evo Morales, and Daniel Ortega were all noticeably absent. However, Cuba's Vice-President Estéban Lazo, the first official Cuban visitor since 1962, received a standing ovation to the roar of "Cu-ba, Cu-ba, Cu-ba!" hours before the Funes administration "correct[ed] a historic error," by renewing diplomatic relations between the two countries.[5] Brazilian president Luiz Inácio Lula da Silva, with whom Funes had taken care to publicly align himself, was also present.

Dubbed by many, including Funes himself, as El Salvador's Obama, the incoming Salvadoran president had come to victory promising a new politics of the Left and with the support of a surprising coalition of forces. Both the right-wing and private sectors could be counted among "friends of Mauricio Funes." Not only had the Funes election ended twenty years of uninterrupted rule by ARENA, Funes was also the first president from the Left since the founding of the modern Salvadoran state. His election was, in his words, "the night of the greatest hope in El Salvador." For a moment, the disillusionment and cynicism of the postwar years had subsided.

Like Obama, Funes inherited a daunting financial crisis. His crisis, however, was further exacerbated by the loss of remittance income from Salvadoran immigrants in the United States. Salvadorans were out of work at home and abroad. In both countries, the magic of casino capitalism and its emperors had lost some of the incredulity and adulation, if not actual power, that they had enjoyed and fed off of over the past two to three decades. In the United States, Wall Street and Main Street alike demanded the renewed presence and forceful intervention of the state, albeit on different terms. In El Salvador, Funes—invoking the slain Archbishop Romero as his "teacher and the spiritual guide of the nation"—promised that alongside his continued commitment to CAFTA and dollarization his government would have "a preferential option for the poor, for those who need a robust government to get ahead and to be able to compete in this world of disequilibrium under fair conditions." "The Salvadoran people are watching," he declared, and "Archbishop Romero will be the final judge."

In the concluding chapter of this book, I argued that the so-called transnational gang crisis between the United States and El Salvador revealed that the two countries were locked in a mirroring paranoid dynamic that served to reproduce old and new forms of violence. With the unraveling of the Republican-ARENA alliance, it seemed that this account might close much as it had opened in 1992 with another potentially hopeful and heady historical juncture—the Salvadoran Peace Accords and the election of Bill Clinton. What would this current moment, this reeling present—always already in the past—portend for the issues of concern in this book? In what ways might these transnational politics of hope—condensed in the dialectical image of the "Obama–Funes inauguration" and the chants of "Yes, we did" in the United States and "Sí se pudo" in the United States and El Salvador—reconfigure the web of relations and field of forces that undergird the neoliberal securityscapes mapped out in the foregoing chapters? Could these developments signal the beginning of the end of neoliberalism, or at least the most vulgar and predatory expressions of its logic? Where would questions of security policy—local, regional, and global—fall in this moment of potential, of seeming emergence?[6] Would El Salvador and the United States remain locked in the same terrible dance with each other? Or would these "transformational" politics usher in, as Obama promised, a new chapter in U.S.-Latin American relations?

. . .

> What presents itself as progress . . . can soon show itself to be the perpetuation of
> what was presumably overcome . . . [We need to] formulate an idea of progress that
> is subtle and resilient enough not to let itself be blinded by the mere appearance
> . . . of emancipation."[7]
>
> —Jürgen Habermas

As in 1992, this politics of possibility was quickly forestalled. In the midst of writing this epilogue as an acknowledgment of the always unfinished nature of ethnographies of the contemporary, I received an urgent message. Alex Sanchez of Homies Unidos Los Angeles had that morning been arrested in his home in Bellflower, California, in front of his wife and three children by twenty or so armed FBI agents. The activist network—formed after Sanchez's first arrest by Rampart police officers in 2000 and expanded well beyond that over the years through his work with Homies Unidos— was immediately activated through phone, e-mail, Facebook, and Twitter. Responding to the call in the message, I set this epilogue aside and rushed to the Federal Court Building in downtown Los Angeles where Alex was to be arraigned that afternoon. Sanchez stood accused of leading a double life, of wearing two faces. The well-known and much-loved gang intervention worker was allegedly still an active shot caller for MS 13. He was charged with conspiracy to murder under the federal Racketeer Influenced and Corrupt Organizations Act (RICO).[8]

Specifically, Sanchez was charged with ordering a gang member, Juan Bonilla (a.k.a. Zombie), to kill Walter Lacinos (a.k.a. Camaron) in El Salvador. Lacinos had been deported to El Salvador after imprisonment, shortly before his death. But the defense attorney Kerry Bensinger argued that the prosecution had, in fact, got the wrong Zombie. Bensinger's primary argument was that LAPD officer Flores had confused two people, each of whom went by the moniker Zombie. Sanchez had spoken to a Zombie, but his legal name was Ricardo Termino Hernandez.[9] It turns out that the Zombies were everywhere.[10]

The indictment, which included twenty-three other allegedly active members of MS 13, was based on a three-year secret investigation by the FBI and the LAPD with substantial assistance from the U.S. Bureau of Prisons and the U.S. Department of Justice Criminal Division's Gang Unit, and the cooperation of, among others, the U.S. Immigration and Customs Enforcement (ICE) and the Salvadoran National Police (PNC)—a coalition of forces articulated in the transnational security agreement of 2007 to create the Transnational Anti-Gang Unit (TAG).[11] Sanchez's many supporters argued that, at best, the arrest was proof of how these overreaching laws draw in the innocent with the guilty, and at worst, a retaliation for Alex's role in exposing the impact of the Rampart scandal on immigrants and for successfully facing off deportation proceedings in 2000. Moreover, Alex had been a vocal opponent of Operation Community Shield and the Transnational Anti-Gang Unit, and had served as an expert witness for the defense in several RICO cases—the law under which he was now charged.

The RICO law is the most recent state of exception leveraged against gang members, be they actively, formerly, or allegedly affiliated. As Alex put it to me during our first meeting after his release, "RICO is the new gang injunction. It's just another case of guilt by association." Being back in jail reminded him that the "prisons are just a tool to continue the enslavement of our young men and women in violence and poverty. . . . There is no rehabilitation in incarceration." Under RICO, the burden of proof rests with the defense rather than the prosecution. The prosecution need only show a "preponderance of evidence" rather than prove "guilt beyond a reasonable doubt."[12] Defendants are presumed to be guilty until proven innocent. Even if the conspiracy to murder charge were to be dropped, Alex Sanchez could still be found guilty of the lesser charge of "conspiracy." He could be facing a life sentence or deportation after a lengthy incarceration.

Certainly Sanchez's ongoing communication and association with active gang members in his capacity as gang peace activist continued to make him vulnerable to charges of "conspiracy" with a criminal organization despite the growing recognition for that work by the City of Los Angeles, if not the LAPD, the FBI, or ICE. Alex was, in fact, among those who wrote the language for the city specifying the role of the "gang intervention worker" in arbitrating and diffusing disputes between neighborhoods. The prosecution argued that the Sanchez supporters, who pulled together 120 character reference letters and two million dollars in bond and sureties, were all well-meaning dupes unaware of Alex's double life. For Tom Hayden, Alex's arrest reflected a "throwback to the pre-Rampart mentality," and proof of LAPD's ongoing "two-track approach, a velvet glove toward the public and an iron hand toward the underclass."[13]

On June 27, 2009, three days after Alex's arrest, the president of Honduras, Manuel Zelaya, was ousted by the Honduran military when troops arrested him in his pajamas and sent him into exile in Costa Rica. President Funes put his troops on alert at the Salvadoran-Honduran border. Initially, President Obama joined the rest of the world in condemning Zelaya's ousting as an illegal coup and a disturbing throwback to a pattern characteristic of earlier authoritarian regimes in Latin America. But in this first test case of Obama's promise for a new chapter in U.S. foreign policy in Latin America, the position of the United States would waver in the coming months and Zelaya would not be reinstated. The United States would, instead, endorse the results of an election that the majority of Hondurans boycotted and that lacked, according to the U.N Secretary General, the Organization of American States, and the Carter Center, conditions for a free and fair election.[14]

Back in Los Angeles, at the advice of the independent monitor Michael Cherasky, U.S. District Court Judge Gary Fees lifted the Federal Consent Decree that had been imposed on the LAPD since the Rampart scandal. During the scandal, Cherasky's risk management company, Kroll Associates, was awarded a five-year $11 million contract to monitor reforms in the LAPD.[15] Shortly after Fees's decision, Cherasky formed Altegrity Inc., a new holding company for his expanding security business that would provide "global security solutions and specialized law enforcement training" to its clients.[16]

With the consent decree lifted, police chief William Bratton declared his mission to reform the LAPD accomplished. Three weeks later, on August 5, 2009, Bratton announced that he would be returning to the realm of the private security industry as chairman of Altegrity Risk International, a newly established subsidiary of Cherasky's Altegrity Inc. This was not the first time Cherasky and Bratton had worked together, some might say, as accomplices. In the wake of the Rampart scandal, and immediately preceding his tenure as LAPD chief, Cherasky hired Bratton to serve as a key member of his team monitoring the police department. Tom Hayden pointed out, during an airing of KCRW's Which Way LA on August 5, 2009, the potential conflict of interests here: "That [Bratton] would be close personally and institutionally to the person chosen to do the monitoring . . . and then go [back] into business with that person . . . [is] a story that should be pursued."[17] Nonetheless, Bratton's impending departure was met with glowing evaluations of his contributions to reforming the LAPD on most fronts. Lifting the consent decree was a tacit endorsement of Bratton's emphasis on increasing the number of stops, frisks, and arrests for minor crimes in inner-city neighborhoods and of his aggressive anti-gang war tactics.

Meanwhile in El Salvador, gangs, crime, and violence were back in the headlines. In 2005 and again in 2007, the United Nations Development Programme's project Towards a Society without Violence gathered Salvadoran media outlets to sign a public accord "Medios Unidos por La Paz" (Media United for Peace) in which media agreed to reduce sensationalist coverage of violence.[18] This agreement, however, unraveled after the inauguration of El Salvador's new president.[19] The media frenzy only picked up when on September 2, 2009, the French-Spanish photojournalist and documentary filmmaker Cristian Poveda was killed as he was leaving Tonacatepeque, an 18th Street barrio ten miles outside San Salvador and the neighborhood where he had filmed his recently released documentary La Vida Loca. The film is an intimate portrait of gang life and death, as well as a scathing attack of ARENA's zero-tolerance policies. Poveda had just returned to El Salvador from a European tour of his documentary, and he was in Tonacatepeque purportedly to make advance arrangements for a French fashion magazine to do a story, perhaps a fashion layout, with the women featured in the documentary. Rumors abounded as to who killed Poveda and why.

In the following weeks, a police officer and five members of the 18th Street Gang were arrested by the PNC and charged with killing Poveda. Had the leadership of the gang changed? Did the new leadership not approve of the film and the way in which the gang was portrayed? Had Poveda broken an agreement not to screen or sell the film in El Salvador? Did they think that he had profited from them with his tour of international film festivals or his distribution agreements? How had pirated copies of La Vida Loca found their way to the black market in the streets of San Salvador? Had rumors been spread insinuating that Poveda was collaborating with the PNC? Had he interfered or inadvertently impacted personal relationships or gender politics in the gang? Or were these gang members the hired gunmen of other forces? Had Poveda's strong leftist critique of ARENA's Súper Mano Dura made him a target of the right wing? Was this an attempt by ARENA to destabilize the Funes administration? Had the macho bravado of this photojournalist, who had covered the Salvadoran civil war and many other wars, finally pushed him too far? Regardless of these questions, El Salvador was once again in the international news headlines with stories of gangs and violence.

I had arrived in El Salvador just two days before Poveda's murder. I was there not to conduct new research but to meet with the various people cited in this book to confirm in person before sending the manuscript off for publication that they were comfortable with my analysis and with the use of their names. Regardless of the actual reason for Poveda's murder, many of the researchers, advocates, and activists cited in this book were stunned and thrown into doubt as to what the implications might be for the future of their work.

In response to the mounting critique from the Right that violence had only increased in the first few months of his presidency, Funes was now calling for the continued and expanded role of the Salvadoran military in civil policing. Under manodurismo, the military had been limited to patrols with the police. Funes suggested that there may be a need to change some laws to enable the military to make arrests and to pursue criminals. The military answered that it was ready and willing to take on the new role. More than 40 percent of the entire army was put on standby awaiting orders from the president. As El Salvador's defense minister, General David Munguia Payes, said in mid-October: "We're prepared to operate anywhere in the country. If the president decides to involve the armed forces in the fight against crime, he can give us certain powers that we don't have at this moment to be able to act as police."[20] Clearly, the military's political profile had not weakened under the new FMLN administration.

Stranger still, in California Governor Arnold Schwarzenegger, seeming to invoke the language of activists against the prison industrial complex long disregarded by Republicans and Democrats alike, promised to submit a constitutional amendment to ensure that "never again do we spend a greater percentage of our money on prisons than on higher education."[21] His solution, however, was not to reform sentencing laws or decriminalize or defelonize nonviolent crimes, despite the ruling in February 2009 by three federal judges that the California prison system must reduce overcrowding by as many as 55,000 inmates within three years.[22] Instead, Schwarzenegger proposed accelerating the construction of privately owned and run prisons, or better yet, building and operating prisons in Mexico to house undocumented felons who were currently imprisoned in California as a cost-saving measure to generate more revenue for education. Prison reform, it seemed, would not mean fewer prisons or prisoners.

The United States deported a record number of 20,406 Salvadorans in 2009. In responding to the criticisms of immigration advocates of the conditions under which over 320,000 detainees were being held,[23] Obama promised an overhaul of the detention system and to transform it from a criminal to a "truly civil detention system."[24] The changes called for were extensive, including holding the government accountable to its own detention standards and fundamental human rights. While ICE was still drafting the new standards, Corrections Corporation of America offered to "soften the look" of one of their facilities with hanging plants, flower baskets, new paint colors, and different bedding and furniture free of charge.

President Obama's plans for Comprehensive Immigration Reform, postponed until 2010, met fierce opposition in Arizona with the passage of SB1070. The state law empowered police to stop and question people about their immigration status and to detain those unable to produce legal documentation. While Obama opposed the law, he also announced that he would send an additional twelve hundred National Guard troops to the border, boasting that there were "more boots on the ground near the Southwest Border than at any time in our history."[25]

The belief that the most heinous aspects of the Bush administration's antiterrorism tactics would disappear with the election of Obama proved to be a "facile illusion." Rather, those tactics were institutionalized as a "new species of security state formation."[26] While U.S. troops were withdrawn from Iraq, actions heated up on the Pakistani and Afghani fronts. Iran remained a potential next target in the pursuit of elusive weapons of mass destruction. Guantanamo had not been closed. Rather, much work went into establishing a legal basis for continuing indefinite detentions.

. . .

> Optimism and hope are different. Optimism tends to be based on the notion that there's enough evidence to allow us to think things are going to be better. . . . Whereas hope looks at the evidence and says it doesn't look good at all, but we're going to go beyond the evidence to create new possibilities.[27]
> —Cornel West

As this book was going to publication, the political landscape in and between the United States and El Salvador shifted, or so it seemed. The unrelenting weight of political depression lifted for the Left and progressive liberals in both countries, if only for a moment. The dialectical image of the Obama and Funes inaugurations revealed, in a lightning flash of history, alternative futures rooted in past liberation struggles—African American and African and Latin American. As yet, however, there is very little evidence that our political present will redeem those past commitments to build a more equitable and just future.

In the immediate afterglow of regime change in the United States and El

Salvador the securityscape has only thickened, the politics of simultaneity speeded up, and the farcical tragedy still plays to captive audiences on the transnational stage. Both countries remain in a "permanent state of exception," and neoliberal logics still dominate despite of and indeed through the discourses of financial crisis and disaster and their affective insecurities.[28]

Obama and Funes, of course, came to power as figureheads of fragile regimes and unstable configurations of forces.[29] Not surprisingly, the politics of hope that so many dared read into those political events must be played out in the interstices of these precarious coalitions and alliances. Whereas the destabilizing potential of the dialectical image of the Obama and Funes inaugurations seems to have been quickly reabsorbed into familiar plots of criminality, terrorism, and scarcity, we must continue to attend to areas where ideational elements remain in productive tension, or rather insist that they remain so. The contemporary moment is, after all, always a constellation of different temporalities—dominant, residual, and emergent.[30] All three are "always constitutive of the present as a dynamic phenomenon."[31]

It seems appropriate to signal the presence of ongoing, reemerging, and new counterpublics here, most particularly within a new generation of scholars from El Salvador and among the children of Central American immigrants who are the counterpart to Obama's Joshua Generation (the inheritors of the Moses Generation), in this case the inheritors of the Salvadoran liberation, solidarity, and sanctuary movements.[32] The constituencies of support around the Alex Sanchez case, for example, evidence the larger national and transnational social movements of which Homies Unidos is now an integral part. The formation of the Union Salvadoreña de Estudiantes Universitarios (USEU) between students in El Salvador and the children of Salvadoran immigrants in U.S. colleges and universities is another generative space.[33] Grassroots activism against Pacific Rim Mining Corporation's El Dorado project in Canbañas, El Salvador,[34] and the Venezuelan- and Cuban-initiated Alianza Bolivariana para los Pueblos de Nuestra América (Bolivarian Alliance for the Peoples of Our America, or ALBA) represent ongoing projects against neoliberalism from below and above respectively.

This epilogue is not, however, the place to set up the impossible narrative of what comes next, or even to begin to track the effects of contemporary restructurings. The present—not to be mistaken for progress—reels on. Although things do not look good, it is far from obvious where we are going.[35]

ACKNOWLEDGMENTS

The long list of people I wish to thank far outweighs the scope of this book—ambitious as its transnational reach may be. I only hope that the pages of this volume are worthy of so much kindness and generosity.

Special thanks must go to the many remarkable people I met through Homies Unidos in San Salvador and in Los Angeles without whom this book would and could not have been written. I owe more than I can say to Magdaleno Rose-Ávila, Alex Sanchez, Silvia Beltrán, José William Huezo Soriano, Luis Ernesto Romero, Rocio Santacruz, Mirna Solozono, Claudia Hernandez, Edgar Ramirez, and to those Homies who are no longer with us: Marvin Novoa Escobar, Gato, Sigfredo Rivas, and to so many others for their deep insights into the underside of neoliberal globalization. Thank you all for the opportunity to write and to act in solidarity with you in your difficult and dangerous work to build peace in the streets of Los Angeles and San Salvador. To the Sanchez family—Señor and Señora Sanchez, Delia, Melly, Oscar, Alvin, Elba, Alex Jr., Marlon, and Melissa—who continue to bear on a daily and most intimate basis the burden of the neoliberal securityscape discussed in this book, may your son, husband, brother, and father receive a fair trial and be vindicated once and for all.

My Salvadoran and "North American" compas, whom I first met in Los Angeles and with whom I had the pleasure and the pain of working in Los Angeles and in solidarity with El Salvador during that remarkable period between the Fenastras bombing and FMLN offensive in 1989 and the Los Angeles riots in 1992, include Sonia Baires, Oscar Andrade, Rosanna Perez, Kay

Eekhoff Andrade, Susan Kandel, Eduardo Gonzales, Linda Garrett, Sarah Stephens, Yadira Arévalo, Ann Mello, Ceclia Grail, Francisco Rivera, Salvador Sanabria, Mayron Payes, Alba Escobar, Nubia Magaña, and Todd Howland. I thank you all for believing (or at least conceding to others) that I had something worthwhile to contribute to your struggle for social and economic justice in the Americas. Needless to say, you all changed my thinking and future path irrevocably.

Other Central American Angelenos who offered me their insights include Omar Corleto, Roberto Lovato, Carlos Vaquerano, Carlos Ardon, and Héctor Tobar. My understanding of immigration and criminal law and the politics of law enforcement and gangs has been profoundly influenced by Tom Hayden, Niels Frenzen, Susan Alva, Greg Simon, Robert Foss, Alan Diamante, Judy London, Tom Parker, Jorge González, Shan Potts, and Sushma Raman.

To the Comite de Amigos de Santa Elena (CASE) and the Tabudos — Matilde Celaya, José Antonio Aparicio, Omar Corleto, Jose Eliazar Cordova, Ricardo and Morena Rodríguez, Beatriz de Lizama, Carmen and Mario Ernesto Zapata, Celina Yamileth Martínez, Marcos Velásquez, and Amalia and Nora Granados — thank you for all that you taught me about Los Angeles through the lens of your *querido pueblito*. My thanks here also go to the CORO Foundation for my first privileged access to the richly contentious territory of Southern California, and to Kate McDermott, Marie Unini, and Jesse Lerner for early poetic insights into the cityscapes — material, imagined, local, and global — of Los Angeles.

The Department of Anthropology at the University of Texas was a remarkable space in which to take stock of my own migration story and political commitments, to develop a research agenda grounded in those commitments, to be held to the demands of rigorous social and cultural theory, and to learn to let ethnography lead theory even as the politics and practice of the method are themselves subject to interrogation and theorization. I owe so much to my dissertation advisor Kathleen Stewart for blowing my mind open with her wild thinking and for seeing me through difficult times with her unswerving support and encouragement. Ted Gordon and Charlie Hale were important role models for combining scholarship and activism and for grounding theory in the realpolitik of Central American and U.S. social justice movements. The late Begoña Aretxaga's strong influence in my postdoctoral work on violence belies the brevity of our encounter. This surely is the sign of the truest teacher — an absent but powerful interlocutor. My thanks here to James Brow, Polly Strong, Joseba Zulaika, Kay Warren, and Yael Navarro-Yashin, who worked with great love and respect in putting together a memorial panel, a journal special issue, and an edited volume of Begoña Aretxaga works, thereby enabling me to extend and deepen my connection to her powerful and insightful prose.

Conversations with José Limón, Barbara Harlow, Bob Fernea, James Brow, Doug Foley, and Michael Hanchard at the very earliest stages of this project helped me begin to lay important groundwork for the story I would later tell. Wayne Lesser and the late Elizabeth Fernea were so kind to remember me from my undergraduate days with them and to support my return to the university as a graduate student nearly a decade later. To my partners in crime in the graduate program—Liz Lilliott, Chantal Tetreault, Vânia Cardoso, Scott Head, Carol Cannon, Halide Velioğlu, Apen Ruiz, Louise Meintjes, David Samuels, Susan Lepselter, Guha Shankar, John Bodinger, Mark Anderson, Marc Perry, Julio Cesar Tavares, Galio Gurdián, Ben Chesluk, and Moira Killoran among many others—thank you all for the essential play of ideas and the strong sense of intellectual community.

At the University of California, San Diego, I have been so fortunate to find a rich interdisciplinary home not only in a wonderfully eccentric Department of Communication but also with like-minded colleagues in and across many departments and centers. I am most grateful for the generous counsel and support of my current and former UCSD colleagues, including Vince Rafael, Robert Horwitz, Val Hartouni, Dan Hallin, Michael Schudson, Roberto Alvarez, Ramón Gutiérrez, Teresa Caldeira, Jim Holston, Charles Briggs, Clara Mantini-Briggs, David Pellow, Lesley Stern, Jeffrey Minson, Lisa Cartwright, Gary Fields, Mike Cole, Olga Vásquez, Carol Padden, David Serlin, Joel Robbins, Ricardo Dominguez, Natalia Molina, Christine Hunefeldt, and Misha Kokotovich. To the scattered seeds of the Pomegranates—the closest I've ever come to belonging to a "gang"—a thousand thanks for your camaraderie and consolation during boot camp at UCSD: Nancy Postero, Roberto Tejada, Tom LePere, Esra Özyürek, Marc Baer, Keith McNeal, Jody Blanco, Marivi Blanco, and Sofia Blanco, Nayan Shah, and Ken Foster. The university has also provided me with important material and institutional support through the Center for Global California Studies (formerly the California Cultures in Comparative Perspective Program), the Center for the Study of Race and Ethnicity's Summer Faculty Fellowships, the Faculty Career Development Grant Program, and the Hellman Fellowship.

I would like to gratefully acknowledge the Global Security and Cooperation Project of the Social Science Research Council for generously funding my postdoctoral research in San Salvador through a grant from the MacArthur Foundation. Subsequent workshops with various SSRC initiatives and collaborations were all exceedingly productive venues in which to stretch my thinking and to engage with a wonderful group of interdisciplinary and international scholars. These include the Translocal Flows in the Americas project and the collaborating institutions Instituto Tecnológico y de Estudios Superiores de Occidente and the Rockefeller Foundation, the Youth, Globalization and the Law project, and the Youth in Organized Violence project and the collaborating institutions Institute for Security Studies in Pretoria, South Africa, and the Harry Frank Guggenheim Foundation. Special thanks here go to John Tirman, Itty Abramson, Marcial Godoy-Anativia, Rossana Reguillo, Tomás Ibarra Frausto, Ron Kassimir, Sudhir Vekatesh, Raúl Villa, Alcinda Honwana, Jean and John Comaroff, Sasha Abramsky, John Hagedorn, Renato Rosaldo, and Philip Bourgois. My work also benefited greatly from a wonderfully inspired workshop with a group from the Cultural Agency in Americas project at the Rockefeller Center in Bellagio and discussions with Doris Sommer, Juan Flores, Mary Louise Pratt, Benedict Anderson, and Marvette Pérez.

Many U.S.-based scholars of El Salvador and Central America, U.S.-bound Latin American migration, and Latino studies have provided to me both inspiration and important sources of feedback. Nick De Genova, Roger Rouse, Laura Lomas, and Brandt Peterson were extremely generous with their time in reading and commenting on my work at various stages. I also benefited greatly from conversations with Cecilia Menjívar, Ellen Moodie, Sarah Mahler, Nora Hamilton, Norma Chinchilla, Cecilia Rivas, Beth Baker-Cristales, Luis Plascencia, Donna DeCesare, Luis Guarnizo, Patricia Landolt, Héctor Perla, Alfonso Gonzales, Eric Popkin, Gaku Tsuda, David Pederson, Magalí Muria, and Cecilia Rivas.

In El Salvador, I have been fortunate to work alongside and to engage with a number of researchers, advocates, and activists who opened up rich ethnographic spaces to me and were important interlocutors in an extended transnational dialogue. I owe an enormous debt to the generosity and intellectual courage of the late Mario Lungo, José Miguel Cruz, Kay-Andrade Eekhoff, Sonia Baires, Jeanette Aguilar, Lissette Miranda, María Santacruz Giralt, Marcela Smutt, Marlon Carranza, Roxana Martel, Lorena Cuerno,

América Rodríguez, Ingrid Olivio, Marta González, Gilma Pérez, Roberto Burgos, Silvia Guillen, Miguel López, Jesus Aguilar, Vicki Rodríguez, Kristin Rosecranz, Father Antonio Rodríguez, Jeanne Rikkers, Yesenia Ramírez, and Carlos Ramos. Thank you all for the work that you do and for the invaluable insights that you shared with me over the years.

The Foundation for National Development in El Salvador (FUNDE), the Department of Architecture and Urban Planning at the University of Central America, the Permanent Forum on Migrants in El Salvador, and the United Nations Development Project's program Hacia una Sociedad sin Violencia (Towards a Society without Violence) were all important institutional bases in one way or another for me as I conducted fieldwork in El Salvador.

Several people who held posts in government agencies related to law enforcement and security issues were also exceedingly generous with their time in helping me understand issues from an institutional perspective. Included here are Augusto Cotto, Hugo Ramírez-Menjívar, Carlos Ponce, and Subcommissioner Caseres, all of the National Civil Police; Eduardo Linares, the former chief of the San Salvador Metropolitan Area police; Oscar Bonilla, the former director of the National Council for Public Security; Luis Cobarrubias, the former director of ICITAP in San Salvador; and René Dominguez, the former vice minister of security.

This book could not possibly have reached fruition without enlivening conversations with and steady commentary from my dear friends Sonia Baires, Nancy Postero, and Roberto Tejada; developmental editor extraordinaire Laura Helper-Ferris; and the writer's anthropologist-cum-psychoanalyst, Ken Wissoker, editor-in-chief of Duke University Press. I owe Ken an added debt not only for his patient support of this book project over the longue durée but also for selecting two outstanding readers who have both made themselves known to me since this book was approved for production. I cannot thank Susan Coutin and George Marcus enough for their deep engagement with both drafts of my manuscript and for their very provocative and productive suggestions.

Notwithstanding the order here, my first thanks will always be to my parents, whom I love and respect. To my late mother, Dorene Golin Zilberg, thank you for always having my back. Your memory lives on strong. I remain grateful to my father, Bernard Zilberg, for his continued intellectual passion, honesty, and pragmatism. To my partner Matthew Elgart, who joined me on the last but long leg of this project, a thousand thanks to you for your love, company, and cooking through the pleasure and pain of writing; for allowing me to transform your precious music studio into a writer's study; and for your patience and flexibility with my living between cities and, at times, two countries.

To my large "extended family" in El Salvador, California, and Texas, thank you all for showing me the warmth of community in my various sojourns: La familia Baires—the late and much loved Doña Alicia, philosopher and storyteller Don Beto, and their marabunta ("las niñas" Laura, Gloria, Sonia, and Gladys, and los muchachos Tati, Tito, and Benji)—for being my guardian angels and regular interlocutors in El Salvador; adopted sisters Martha, Kat, and Liz Henry, along with Rachel Feit, Janine Bergin, and their good men, Bill Breaux and Paul Wintle, for friendship, shelter, and sustenance always appreciated, never forgotten; the Texas landslayt—the Caplans, Morrises, Lackmans, Altmans, and Crystals, for giving me peace of mind from a distance knowing that my father was in your good company; and the newest branch of my family, the Elgart-Pacht-Seigel contingent, for the warmest of welcomes and for all your patience, love, and support during these very demanding years. I am also very grateful to Arlene Young, Judy Riley, and Jean Paul for taking me in on the San Diego end of the congested commute from Los Angeles.

. . .

Earlier and partial versions of some chapters appeared in the following publications:

"Inter-American Ethnography: Tracking Salvadoran Transnationality at the Borders of Latino and Latin American Studies," in *Companion to Latino Studies*, ed. Juan Flores and Renato Rosaldo. Oxford: Blackwell, 2007.

"Refugee Gang Youth: Zero Tolerance and the Security State in Contemporary US-Salvadoran Relations," in *Youth, Law and Globalization*, ed. Sudhir Venkatesh and Ronald Kassimir. Stanford: Stanford University Press, 2007.

"Gangster in Guerilla Face: The Political Folklore of Doble Cara in Post-Civil War El Salvador," *Anthropological Theory* 7, no. 1 (March 2007): 37–57.

"Fools Banished from the Kingdom: Remapping Geographies of Gang Violence between the Americas (Los Angeles and San Salvador)," *American Quarterly* 56, no. 3 (2004): 759–79.

"A Troubled Corner: The Ruined and Rebuilt Environment of a Central
American Barrio in Post-Rodney King Riot Los Angeles," *City and Society*
14, no. 2 (2002): 31–55.

"Falling Down in El Norte: A Cultural Politics of the ReLatinization of Los
Angeles," *Wide Angle* 20, no. 3 (1999): 182–209.

NOTES

INTRODUCTION *Neoliberal Securityscapes*

1 Robinson, *Transnational Conflicts*, 88–89.

2 I use the term "youth" to refer to both minors and young adults. I do so because, while gang-affiliated Salvadoran immigrants should only be deported for criminal offenses committed as adults, they are generally brought into the criminal justice system while they are still minors. In addition, although adulthood begins at age eighteen in the United States, the United Nations General Assembly has defined "youth" as those persons falling between the ages of 15 and 24 years, inclusively. Within the category of "youth" they distinguish between teenagers (13–19) and young adults (20–24). Individual countries use slightly different variations of this age range. For instance, in El Salvador the planning group for the Youth Law (discussed in chapter 5) was age 30.

3 Menjívar and Rodríguez, *When States Kill*, 3–27.

4 For a discussion of the first point, see Weldes et al., *Cultures of Insecurity*. For an exploration of militarism, see Gusterson, *People of the Bomb*, xxi.

5 I use the term "Salvadoran (immigrant) youth" to refer to both those who have and have not immigrated to the United States. My use of the word "friction" alludes to Anna Tsing's work in *Friction: An Ethnography of Global Connection*.

6 See Pratt, "Why the Virgin of Zapopan Went to Los Angeles." Globalization and transnationalism are still both highly contentious terms and concepts. Anna Tsing in her essay "The Global Situation" offered one of the most cogent early critiques of this turn to the global and the seduction of what she terms "global futurism." She rightly argued that we should not accept globalization as a definitional characteristic of an era without examining and locating these global dreams and projects ethnographically (342). Exasperated with the quickness by anthropologists to adopt David Harvey's teleology of capitalism and its contemporary cul-

tural logic through, among others, the metaphor of time-space compression and its attendant imagery of flows, circulation, and interconnection (Harvey, *The Condition of Postmodernity*), she asked us to examine critically "how . . . we know the shape of time and space" (341). Tsing insisted that if anthropologists want to make the link that Harvey insinuates between political economy and cultural formations, they must locate those links ethnographically. This inter-American ethnography is my effort to locate from the ground the compression of time and space between the United States and Central America.

7 See Van Schendel and Abraham, *Illicit Flows and Criminal Things*, for a discussion of how these terms—legal and illegal, licit and illicit—better theorize the state-centric term "criminal." For a similar critique, see Nordstrom, *Global Outlaws*.

8 For a discussion of deportation and state sovereignty see De Genova and Peutz, *The Deportation Regime*. See Mbembe, "Necropolitics," for a discussion of disposable subjects (27). For a discussion of immobilized subjects see Zilberg, "Fools Banished from the Kingdom" and Peutz, "Embarking on an Anthropology of Removal."

9 While the term "neoliberalism" was generally used to describe Latin America before it was used for the United States, in this volume, I insist on looking at neoliberal structural adjustments as processes taking place simultaneously in El Salvador and the United States, and even suggest that, while the term itself may not have been invoked, the neoliberal economic and social policies were initiated in the United States before they were in El Salvador (see chapter 2 for a more detailed discussion of the effects of neoliberalism in Los Angeles during the 1980s and the early 1990s).

My own periodization differs from these latter studies in so far as I see the effects of neoliberal structural adjustments occurring in El Salvador and the U.S. simultaneously, and in some cases, in the U.S. earlier.

10 I am grateful to Nancy Postero for her excellent summary of neoliberalism and the various contemporary positions on it in her essay "Revolution and New Social Imaginaries in Postneoliberal Latin America." Part of this summary is revisited in her article, "The Struggle to Create a Radical Democracy in Bolivia."

11 As a political philosophy, neoliberalism originates with Freidrich Hayek's critique of the then dominant common sense that the Great Depression and Second World War were the result of insufficient regulation of the market. He argued instead that it was central planning by the state that led to the rise of the authoritarian regimes of Hitler, Mussolini, and Stalin. For Hayek the system of private property was the most important guarantee of freedom because it reduced the amount of power the state could exercise over individuals (Hayek, "The Road to Serfdom"). His ideas were echoed by the economist Milton Friedman, who trained a whole generation of economists at the University of Chicago. Nonetheless, it was Key-

nesian economics that dominated the post–New Deal and postwar period up until the economic crisis of the 1970s. Although neoliberalism was first introduced by the United States in Chile under Pinochet, it was not until the late 1970s and early 1980s under the neoconservative regimes of first Thatcher and then Reagan that neoliberalism—as we currently understand it, market democracy—emerged as the dominant economic and political model. That said, as Nikolas Rose argues, neoliberalism as a new rationality of government, characterized by privatization, marketization, individual autonomy, and self-governance, "is not merely the vicissitudes of a single political ideology—that of neoliberal conservatism" but "underpins mentalities of government from all parts of the political spectrum precisely because it was the Right, rather than the Left, that . . . managed to articulate a rationality of government consonant with this new regime of the self" (Nikolas Rose, "Governing 'Advanced' Liberal Societies," 60). Thus it was in the absence of an alternative political rationality from the Left that both the Democratic Party in the United States and the Labor party in the United Kingdom came to power in the 1990s having embraced the philosophy, political project, and rationality of neoliberalism (ibid.). David Harvey argues that neoliberalism was a political project "to re-establish the conditions for capital accumulation and to restore the power of the economic elite" after the crisis in capitalism at the end of the 1960s, as the industrialized world faced inflation, the oil embargo, fiscal crises, and high unemployment (A Brief History of Neoliberalism, 19).

12 See, for example, Mandel, Late Capitalism; Lash and Urry, The End of Organized Capitalism; and Harvey, The Condition of Postmodernity.

13 Omi and Winant, Racial Formation in the United States, 14.

14 Or what was then referred to as "devolution" of the welfare state.

15 Welfare reform also found its way into the Illegal Immigration and Immigrant Responsibility Act of 1996, which also targeted immigrant access to social services and welfare, regardless of legal status or age.

16 For a discussion of the ways in which the contemporary Western and indeed now the global financial system has come to resemble a vast casino where players place bets on the future with high-risk stakes, see Strange, Casino Capitalism; Comaroff and Comaroff, "Millennial Capitalism"; and Klima, Funeral Casino.

17 Robinson, Transnational Conflicts, 87–101.

18 See Lungo, Migración internacional y desarollo; and Funkhouser, "Remittances from International Migration."

19 United Nations Development Program, Informe sobre dessarollo humano El Salvador 2005. This abysmal economic situation was not simply an ongoing "third world" condition. Rather, the austerity programs and structural adjustment policies of the 1990s had increased and deepened poverty. While there were, as William Robinson notes, "social compensation funds" attached to those programs "puta-

tively intended to 'target' the poor," they "isolat[ed] poverty from the process of capital accumulation and economic development" (*Transnational Conflicts*, 246). In so doing, they treated poverty as an individual pathology rather than as a consequence of the socioeconomic exclusion immanent in the economic system itself.

20 See Comaroff and Comaroff, *Law and Disorder in the Postcolony*, for a discussion of this phenomenon in South Africa.

21 Foucault, *The Birth of Biopolitics*, 256.

22 Walpin, "The New Speed-up in Habeas Corpus Appeals," n.p.

23 See Ruth Gilmore's *Golden Gulag* for a critique of the position that the prison-industrial complex has become a profitable industry for the private sector. As she states, "With the exception of a few privately managed 500-bed facilities, [California's 90 prisons] are wholly public: owned by the state . . . , financed by Public Works Board debt, and operated by the California Department of Corrections" (8). Gilmore's claims are based on 2005 figures. See Sasha Abramsky's *American Furies* for an alternative view of the privatization of prisons. Privatization, however, is more pronounced in prisons devoted to holding immigrants serving out their sentences for illegal reentry. Regardless, prisons involve the private sector at the level of construction, food, and cleaning contracts.

24 For a discussion of this issue, see Abramsky, *American Furies*; and Gilmore, *Golden Gulag*.

25 Corrections Corporation of America, http://www.correctionscorp.com/about.

26 Bernstein, "City of Immigrants Fills Jail Cells with Its Own."

27 Denis Childs, presentation at Critical Resistance event, University of California, San Diego, January 21, 2010.

28 For more on this notion, see Simon, *Governing through Crime*.

29 See Abramsky, *American Furies*.

30 For further examination of these prisons, see Dow, *American Gulag*.

31 For an examination of the negative structures of feeling, see Cortez, "Estetica del cinismo"; Moodie, "'It's Worse than the War'"; Kokotovich, "Neoliberal Noir"; Zilberg, "Gangster in Guerilla Face"; and Nelson, *Reckoning*. An evaluation of El Salvador's transition to democracy is discussed in Call, "Democratization, War and State-Building," 829, 848; and in Grandin, *Empire's Workshop*, 198.

32 See Villalobos, *De la tortura a la proteccion ciudadana*.

33 Call, "Democratisation, War and State-Building: Constructing the Rule of Law," 842–43.

34 On this, see LeFebvre, *The Production of Space*, 74; and on power, see Foucault as examined by Soja in *Postmodern Geographies*, 16–21.

35 The term "gang intervention worker" is more current and commonly used in Los Angeles (for more on this issue, see the epilogue).

36 LeFebvre, *The Production of Space*, 376.

37 Ibid., 36–46.

38 De Certeau, *The Practice of Everyday Life*, 117–22.

39 See Rouse, "Thinking through Transnationalism," 1.

40 See Herbert, *Policing Space*.

41 Blanchard, "Lost in America," 502.

42 For more on this notion, see Conquergood, "Homeboys and Hoods," 47; and Phillips, *Wallbangin'*, 117–66.

43 See Zilberg, "Fools Banished from the Kingdom."

44 Smutt and Miranda, *El fenomeno de las pandillas de El Salvador*, 30.

45 Cruz, "Los factores associados a las pandillas juveniles en Centroamérica," 685–86.

46 Ibid., 37.

47 See Cruz and Portillo, *Solidarid y violencia en las pandillas del Gran San Salvador*, 51–52.

48 Barnes, "Transnational Youth Gangs in Central America, Mexico and the United States," 8–9. Sponsored by the Center for Inter-American Studies and Programs at the Instituto Tecnológico Autónomo de México, the Ford Foundation, and the Kellogg Foundation, 2007.

49 See Balmaceda, "Maras y pandillas."

50 For an expansion of this view, see Hagedorn, "Making Sense of Central America Maras."

51 E. P. Thompson, an important figure in "critical criminology," notes that studies that emerged from the Birmingham School of Cultural Studies in Britain argued that researchers "cannot simply take over the definitions of those who own property, control the state and pass the laws which 'name' what shall be crimes" (*Whigs and Hunters*, 193–94).

52 Caldeira, *City of Walls*. See also Marroquin Parducci, "Indiferencias y espantos"; and Fernández de Castro and Santamaría, "Demystifying the Maras."

53 On "critical gang studies," see Mike Davis's foreword to Hagedorn, *A World of Gangs*, xv. Gangs are seen variously as the result of "multiple marginality" (Vigil, *Barrio Gangs*); a channel for economic survival in communities abandoned by the larger society (Venkatesh 2006 and 2008); and a form of political resistance to an established order (Hagedorn, *A World of Gangs*; Gordon, "Cultural Politics of Black Masculinity"; Davis, *City of Quartz*; and Vargas, *Catching Hell in the City of Angels*). Others argue that gangs should be treated from a social-movements perspective (Brotherton and Barrios, *The Almighty Latin King and Queen Nation*); or that they fill in for the vacuum left behind by failed social movements and the primacy given to waging military wars rather than investing in communities (Hayden, *Street Wars*). Also see Conquergood, "Homeboys and Hoods"; Conquergood and Seigel, *The Heart Broken in Half*; Vigil, *A Rainbow of Gangs*; Phillips, *Wallbangin'*; and De Genova, "American Abjections."

54 See Tilly, "War Making and State Making as Organized Crime," 169.

55 On structural violence, see Galtung as analyzed in Bourgois, "The Continuum of

Violence in War and Peace," 246; and on symbolic violence, see Bourdieu as cited by Bourgois in the same volume, 302.

56 The tendency to ignore or footnote questions of gender is common to youth studies in general and gang studies in particular. That said, the focus on male immigrant youth and male deportees in this volume is due in part with how "criminality" is differently gendered. Although girls do join gangs, and the number of women in prison is on the rise, my own ethnographic data suggested that in the United States, girls and young women are criminalized, albeit not incarcerated, for their inappropriate reproduction, and the subsequent burden they are said to pose for the state and the taxpayer. While some of these young women are gang members, and do enter the criminal justice system, they do not go to prison at the same rate as their male counterparts. This is, in many cases, due to the fact that when young women have children they tend to leave the gang or at least cease being active in the gang. As a result, they are not deported to El Salvador at the same rates as their male counterparts.

57 De Genova, "Migrant 'Illegality' and Deportability in Everyday Life," 423.

58 In my usage here I allude to Siegel, A New Criminal Type in Jakarta.

59 As Stuart Hall et al. note in their study of the figure of the "black mugger" in postcolonial immigrant communities in Britain, every trope or stereotype has a "career" or a prehistory (Policing the Crisis, 3–28). I do not mean to imply that the "looter" chronologically precedes the "hoodlum" and so on. I am rather thinking along the lines of de Certeau and his discussion of how techniques or procedures within a discursive configuration take turns, if you will, hiding out and coming to the fore (The Practice of Everyday Life, 45–49).

60 See de Certeau, The Practice of Everyday Life, 118.

61 See Appadurai, "Disjuncture and Difference in the Global Cultural Economy."

62 For a discussion of the use of the term "riot" as opposed to "uprising" or "rebellion" and so on, see chapter 1.

63 For a discussion of the racialization of the riot as black, and the relative silence of Latino voices in the media coverage, see Valle and Torres, Latino Metropolis, 45–66. For a discussion of blacks as "event insiders," see Hunt, Screening the Los Angeles "Riots." Also see Smith, "Transmitting Race." For a discussion of the racialization of the riots as a black vs. Korean event, see Abelman and Lie, Blue Dreams; and Cho, "Korean American vs. African American," 196–211.

64 Barthes, "Myth Today."

65 On the notion of "moral entrepreneurs," see Cohen, Folk Devils and Moral Panics.

66 For a discussion of allegorical readings as an act of political poesis, see Stewart, "An Occupied Place," 143–44; and Agee and Evans, Let Us Now Praise Famous Men.

67 Reality, as Begoña Aretxaga (drawing on Lacan) reminds us, is a "play of surfaces," and "the really real is always somewhere else, always eluding us" ("Violent Specters," 33). Aretxaga urges us not to settle for representations of reality but

rather to look for its emergence in "the disturbance of representation, [and in] the eruption of what is repressed by representation" (27).

68 See Benjamin as examined in Buck-Morss, *The Dialectics of Seeing*, 67–77, 219.

69 Indeed, as Joseph Masco argues, the "newness of the War of Terror is an invention" and we need to "historicize these logics as long-standing American Cold War strategies . . . to demonstrate the foreign and domestic costs of allowing officials to define the United States [and I would add, its allies] as 'counterterrorist state[s]'" ("Active Measures," 298). Masco echoes Benjamin's philosophy of history, which debunks the "phantasmagoria of progress" and constructs a counterdiscourse that exposes progress as the fetishization of modern temporality as an "endless repetition" of the "new" as the "always the same" (Benjamin in Buck-Morss, *The Dialectics of Seeing*, 56).

70 For more on this notion, see Grandin, *Empire's Workshop*.

71 For discussions of the "Salvador Option," see Grandin, *Empire's Workshop*; and Lomas, "The War Cut Out My Tongue."

72 See Loxton, "Imperialism or Neglect."

73 Manwaring, "Street Gangs," 13. For a more detailed discussion of Manwaring's thesis, see chapter 7.

74 See Wilson and Sullivan, "On Gangs, Crime, and Terrorism."

75 Alan Klima in *The Funeral Casino* (7, 13), his ethnography of Thailand's gift economy, speaks of the passing of one world order to another in terms of the old global military-gift economy and the new liberal free-market economy. My particular use of the term "protection racket" draws from Charles Tilly, "War Making and State Making as Organised Crime"; William Stanley, *The Protection Racket State*; and Margaret Huggins, *Political Policing*. Whereas Tilly introduced the term to refer to the analogy between organized crime and State-sanctioned wars in general, Stanley deployed the term to describe the particular collusion between elites and the military in El Salvador. The 1992 Salvadoran Peace Accords succeeded in breaking this protection racket. As Stanley notes, "[t]he story of intra-elite politics and state violence in El Salvador is also a story of actively harmful measures by the United States" (6–8). Huggins extends the role of the protection racket to include foreign police forces. Support and training of police in Latin American authoritarian regimes put the U.S. at the center of the "protection racket" in so far as they served to buttress U.S. foreign policy and economic interests. While Stanley's and Huggins's "protection rackets" are associated with bygone regimes, I suggest that these new market democracies also involve "protection rackets" insofar as U.S. aid and technical assistance is now tied to cooperation in its wars against drugs, gangs, and terrorists.

76 As Begoña Aretxaga notes in conversation with Diane Taylor's *Disappearing Acts*, "this mirroring paranoid dynamic often takes the form of powerful identifications and obsessive fascination as when the state engages in terrorist or criminal

practices in order to appropriate the power it attributes to its enemies, criminals, subversives, or terrorists." "Maddening States," 402.

77 The "messy texts" (Marcus and Fischer, *Anthropology as Cultural Critique*, 8) produced by this "multi-sited research imaginary" (Marcus, "Ethnography in and of the World System") are made so, Marcus suggests, by their attempts to "*fictionalize the effect of simultaneity*" ("Imagining the Whole," 26; my emphasis). The simultaneity in my own text is more than a writing strategy or the privileged view of an anthropologist.

78 Marcus, "Ethnography in and of the World System," 106–11; de Certeau, *The Practice of Everyday Life*, 100. Both de Certeau's vocabulary of travel itineraries–spatial trajectory, vectors of direction, geographies of action, and velocity (117–22), and the previously mentioned work of Henri LeFebvre on microphysics of the social production of space—representations of space, spaces of representation, and spatial practices (*The Production of Space*, 74)—also proved exceedingly useful to me in constructing my methodology.

79 Indeed, these narratives are strangely reminiscent of recent continental or pan-American literature that challenges the "limiting set of tacit assumptions that result from perpetual immersion in the study of a single American culture" and demands that we retheorize the very premises upon which the concepts of "American hermeneutics, alterity, history and historiography rests" (Saldívar, *The Dialectics of Our America*, 3–4). Ironically enough, an inter-American ethnography of deported Salvadoran gang youth joins in Martí's political project to make the Americas whole again. But this project is not merely "the belated expression of out-of-touch Bolivarian desires" but is rather "one of the possible mappings or articulations demanded by already existing sociocultural processes" (Poblete, *Critical Latin American and Latino Studies*, xxii–xxiii).

80 For a discussion of borderlands theory, see, among others, Alvarez, "The Mexican–United States Border"; Anzaldúa, *Borderlands*; Heyman and Campbell, "Recent Work on the U.S. Mexico Border"; Kearney, "Borders and Boundaries of State and Self at the End of Empire"; Paredes, "*With a Pistol in His Hands*"; Saldívar, *Border Matters*; Velez-Ibañez, *Border Visions*; and Vila, *Ethnography at the Border*.

81 See Smith's "Can You Imagine?" and *Transnational Urbanism* for a discussion of migration and the politics of simultaneity.

82 Marcus, "Imagining the Whole," 60.

83 See Haraway, "Situated Knowledges"; and Foucault, *Power/Knowledge*.

84 Hale, *Engaging Contradictions*, 11.

85 Ibid. Also see Gordon, *Disparate Diasporas*; Vargas, *Catching Hell in the City of Angels*; and Gilmore, *Golden Gulag*, for an example of ethnographic scholarship grounded in direct political engagements.

86 Ibid., 13.

87 Regarding the notion of contamination, Kathleen Stewart distinguishes between

"constructive" social-scientific theorizing that "see[s] its object from a decon-taminated distance" and "contaminated cultural critique" that "disrupts the dis-tance between observing subject and the 'real' world of objects; it mixes with its object and includes itself as an object of its own analysis. The two are dialectically related in such a way that each mode must interrupt the other in order to consti-tute itself ("On the Politics of Cultural Theory," 395). Contaminated cultural cri-tique is not the same as simply recognizing that the subject is socially constructed. Rather, it considers "notions of the analyst embedded in conventions of academic discourse—such as the practice of taking distance from one's 'object' of analysis, practices of self-control and transcendence, and particular ways of making judg-ments and choices which have come to signify . . . intellectual victory over other possible interpretations or finding." Contaminated critique "put[s] the analyst on a par with her 'objects' of analysis." Modes of knowing and being in the world "out there" and in academe (both postmodern and modernist modes of critique) are all the stuff of cultural politics (Stewart quoted in Molino, *Culture, Subject, Psy-che*, 139).

My use of the term "complicity" draws from both Renato Rosaldo's and George Marcus's critique of the function of "rapport" in the "ideologies of field-work." Rosaldo politicizes the complicity form to explore the unequal relations of power between the ethnographer and his or her informants and to situate the knowledge produced from that unequal encounter within the broader colo-nial context (Rosaldo, "Imperialist Nostalgia," in *Culture and Truth*, 68–89). Like Rosaldo's encounter with the Ilongots of the Philippines, mine with Salvadorans both in the United States and El Salvador was enabled by U.S. imperialism as well as my privileged racial—although not always class—positioning. Marcus extends the notion of complicity to consider how the changing conditions of fieldwork demand a more complex sense of ethnographer-subject relations. Here, the infor-mant does not simply occupy a subordinate role in relationship to the researcher (and may in fact occupy a position of dominance). Regardless, the informant has his or her own agenda, set of interests (which include the "outside world" of the researcher), and complex affiliations. Complicity also "goes beyond the sense of 'partnership in an evil action' to a sense of being complexly involved through a relationship to a third interest/party/object." It is a "more generative and more ambiguous morality" than imperialist nostalgia, precisely because it places the researcher in a much more complex and often "disturbing relation" to his or her informant, and considers how the researcher serves knowingly, wittingly, and re-luctantly as an informant to projects not of his or her own making and design. Complicity provides a way of recognizing how the ethnographer is "always on the verge of activism, of negotiating some kind of involvement beyond the distanced role of the researcher" (Marcus, *Ethnography through Thick and Thin*, 122–23).

88 Fortun, *Advocacy after Bhopal*, 23.

89 Ibid.

90 On the notion of strategic duality, see Sjoberg as discussed in Hale, *Engaging Contradictions*, 11.

CHRONOLOGY *The Divided Ends of Peace*

1 See William Robinson, *Transnational Conflicts*, 89.

2 See Alvarez, Dagnino, and Escobar, *Cultures of Politics, Politics of Cultures*. Some have described this development in post-conflict societies as an infatuation with civil society (Comaroff and Comaroff, "Millennial Capitalism," 292).

3 The name La Mara Salvatrucha has many possible meanings. The word *mara* in El Salvador is used to refer to a group of people. Some argue that it is taken from Caliche, the Salvadoran vernacular Spanish that bears the traces of Colonial Spanish and the indigenous language Nahuat. In Caliche, *marabunta* refers to colony of a fierce type of ant. *Salva* is drawn directly from Salvadoran, but like its namesake El Salvador it also shares the word "savior" as its root. *Trucha*, also Caliche, literally means trout, a fish that has to swim upstream against the current in order to reproduce. *Trucha* can also mean "streetwise" or "alert." Some argue that in the United States, Mara Salvatrucha simply stands for "Salvadoran neighborhood."

4 For a more detailed account of the gang's origins, see Hayden, *Street Wars*, 206–10.

5 For a treatment of the conscription of minors into the Salvadoran army, see the film *Voces Inocentes/Innocent Voices* (2004).

6 I also collaborated with WINDS, an international women's collective focused on working in solidarity with women's groups in El Salvador. It was an offshoot of the Washington office for COMADRES, an organization of Salvadoran mothers who kept records of their disappeared family members and protested for their release.

7 See Perez and Ramos's *Flight to Freedom* for personal accounts of Salvadoran political exiles.

8 For a discussion of Salvadorans as refugees, see Aguayo, *El éxodo centroaméricano*; Coutin, *The Culture of Protest*; Montes and Vasquez, *El Salvador 1987*; Ward, *The Price of Fear*; and Zolberg, Suhrke, and Aguayo, *Escape from Violence*. After the war, the scholarship tended to propose a framework that could account for a dialectical relationship between the terms refugee and immigrant (see Hamilton and Chinchilla, "Central American Migration"; and Menjívar, *Fragmented Ties*).

In her critical essay about the framing of the study of displacement, and of the refugee as an epistemological object and a particular kind of object of knowledge, Liisa Malkki quotes Hein in noting that with "minimal conceptual elaboration, immigration constituted an economic form of migration, and refugees a political form." She added that "mass migrations are frequently employed as foreign policy tools and refugees become instruments of warfare and military strategy" ("Refugees and Exile," 496, 504–5). This could not be more true than in the Salvadoran case. The term "calculated kindness" comes from Ong, "Cultural Citizenship as Subject-Making," 742.

9 See Perla, "Si Nicaragua Venció, El Salvador Vencerá," for a discussion of the defining role that Salvadoran refugees and political activists played in the development of this movement.

10 These individuals include, among others, Jane Fonda, Ed Asner, Richard Gere, Edward James Olmos, Eli Morales, Jackson Brown, and Mike Farrell.

11 The Sanctuary Movement was an ecumenical religious and political movement that actively defied U.S. immigration policy by sheltering Central American refugees from Immigration and Naturalization Service authorities. The Sanctuary Movement was seen by many as a modern-day "underground railroad." Several of these activists were indicted by the Department of Justice for smuggling aliens, among other charges. The defense claimed that these "illegal" actions were justifiable to save the lives of people who would otherwise be killed as a result of U.S. military funding. For more detailed discussions of the Sanctuary Movement, see Coutin, *The Culture of Protest*; and Perla, "Si Nicaragua Venció, El Salvador Vencerá."

12 This transition was documented in a community survey by the Santa Chirino Amaya Refugee Committee in 1991, and was corroborated that same year by a poll taken by the *Los Angeles Times*.

13 The belated recognition of Salvadorans as war refugees by the passage of TPS in 1990 was further bolstered by the settlement of the American Baptist Church case that same year. Under the settlement, the State Department and INS agreed to review 150,000 formerly denied political asylum claims and to reopen the process to thousands more Salvadorans and Guatemalans. Given the temporary nature of the TPS and the uncertain outcomes of political asylum cases, legal service organizations debated over whether to encourage Central Americans to come out of the shadows and make their presence in the United States known by filing for these programs. Many, however, argued that those who did not file would not be included in any subsequent legalization and citizenship drives.

14 See Funkhouser, "Remittances from International Migration"; Lungo and Kandel, *Transformando El Salvador*; Orozco, "From Family Ties to Transnational Linkages" and "Remittances and Markets"; Pedersen, "American Value"; and Katherine Andrade-Eekhoff, "Asociaciones salvadoreñas en Los Angeles y las posibilidades de desarrollo en El Salvador," 11–44.

15 On the night of March 2, 1991, Rodney King and two passengers in his car were pursed by California Highway Patrol officers. According to those officers, in the subsequent freeway chase King reached speeds of more than one hundred miles per hour (Court TV, *The Rodney King Case*). King refused to pull over because he knew that a DUI would be a violation of the conditions of his parole for an earlier robbery conviction (Cannon, *Official Negligence*, 43). Several LAPD officers and a helicopter joined in the pursuit, and finally caught up with King. George Holiday,

a passerby, filmed the subsequent events and the video was taken as proof by most that the LAPD officers had used excessive force. On April 29, 1992, an all-white jury in Simi Valley judged officers Koon, Powell, Wind, and Briseno not guilty. In 1993, the investigation was reinstated by the U.S. Department of Justice. Officers Powell and Koon were found guilty; Wind and Briseno were acquitted.

The Watts riots broke out in Watts, an African American neighborhood, on August 11, 1965, after a California Highway Patrol officer pulled over and arrested Marquette Frye for drunken driving. When the officer refused to let Frye's brother drive the car home but insisted on impounding it instead, a crowd gathered and a struggle ensued when the officer decided to take in Frye's brother and mother too. This incident was the immediate catalyst for the riot, but racial tensions were already rife.

16 This was the Los Angeles of Mike Davis's *City of Quartz* and *Ecology of Fear* (where one would encounter signs of carceral architecture and the effects of the exclusionist and defensive social policies of the "Not In My Backyard!" or NIMBYist movement); of Ruben Martínez's *The Other Side* (where you could be South in the North and North in the South at the same time); and of Héctor Tobar's *Tattooed Soldier* (where you reencountered on the streets of Los Angeles the enemies you had fled from in Guatemala).

17 See Central American Refugee Center (CARECEN), "Report on Civil Rights and Human Rights Violations"; Mike Davis, "Beyond Blade Runner," 369; and Hayden, *Street Wars*, 210–11.

18 American Civil Liberties Union, "Civil Liberties in Crisis," 7.

19 Betancur, Figueredo Planchart, and Buergenthal, "From Madness to Hope."

20 Popkin, *Peace without Justice*, 11.

21 Cristiani in May, "Review of *From Madness to Hope*."

22 Popkin, *Peace without Justice*, 10.

23 Omi and Winant, *Racial Formation in the United States.*

24 See Robinson, *Transnational Conflicts*. As Robinson notes, U.S. funding was aimed as much at transforming the landed oligarchy (supported as it was by the military) as it was at defeating the popular insurgency. Indeed, the great majority of U.S. funds actually went to stabilizing the Salvadoran economy in the midst of the civil war and to promoting a new elite that would collaborate in instituting neoliberal reforms and integrating El Salvador into the new global economy once that war was won. While 30 percent of U.S. aid went to the Salvadoran military, increasing its size by 400 percent, Robinson argues that the military was, ultimately, sacrificed in this U.S.-directed regime change (88–89, 99).

25 These post–civil war economic transformations would eventually be formalized with the passage in 2005 of the Dominican Republic–Central American Free Trade Agreement (DR–CAFTA).

26 The truce was actually negotiated before the riots (Hayden, *Street Wars*, 93–94).

27 House Bill HR 666.

28 See Federman, "Who Has the Body?"

29 Coutin, *Legalizing Moves*, 143–61.

30 Coutin, *Nation of Emigrants*, 21.

31 Although my focus here is on gang-affiliated and alleged youth, the law had tremendous consequences for other sectors of the immigrant population. For instance, upon submitting their citizenship applications, some adults with U.S.-born families, and who owned businesses and homes in the United States, found themselves in deportation proceedings for minor offenses committed years previously but deemed felonies retroactively.

32 See Brown, "Legislating Repression."

33 See DeCesare and Montaigne, "Deporting America's Gang Culture."

34 The language "forced out" is derived from a photographic exhibit and book by C. Kismaric entitled *Forced Out: The Agony of the Refugee in Our Time*. I use the term with reference to the deportee in order to draw a relationship between the *forced depatriation* of the refugee and the *forced repatriation* of the deportee. The linguistic resonance highlights, I hope, the political nature of deportation as against the tendency to read it as the natural result of an individual's criminal record.

35 Working as I had been with Salvadorans in Los Angeles I was certainly aware of the phenomenon, and I knew of the photojournalist Donna DeCesare, who just started exhibiting her work on Salvadoran gangs in Los Angeles and San Salvador.

36 See Zilberg and Lungo, "Se han vuelto haraganes?"

37 For a discussion of levels of violence in El Salvador during this period see Cruz and González, "Magnitud de la Violencia en El Salvador," and Villalobos, *De la tortura a la proteccion ciudadana*. The PNC subsequently revised the figures on which this analysis was based, admitting that the annual homicide rate had been closer to two thousand rather than eight thousand. While this homicide rate was still alarming, the earlier claim that people were being killed at greater rates after than during the civil war was incorrect (Villalobos, 136). The accuracy of statistics on violence in El Salvador are notoriously difficult to verify, and each source uses different criteria by which to measure violence (Cruz, Argüello, and González, *El crimen violento en El Salvador*, 11–54). Regardless of the actual figures, Salvadorans felt the threat of violence acutely. For an early discussion of perceived violence, see Moodie, "It's Worse than War." While it is important not to take statistics at face value, or to confuse perception with actual incidences of violence, none of this obviates the inordinate levels of violence in El Salvador (see United Nations Development Program, "Informe Sobre Desarrollo Humano Para América Central 2009-2010").

38 For a discussion of La Sombra Negra and death squad activity in the postwar period see United Nations, "Report from the Joint Group for the Investigation of Illegal Armed Groups with Political Motivation in El Salvador," 568–74, and Amnesty International, "The Spectre of Death Squads," 3.

39 See Nelson, *Reckoning*, for a discussion of "duping" in the Guatemalan case. For a discussion of postwar disillusionment in El Salvador, see Silber, "Mothers/Fighters/Citizens"; Cortez, "Estética del cinismo"; Kokotovich, "Neoliberal Noir"; and Zilberg, "Gangster in Guerrilla Face."

40 See Popkin, *Peace without Justice*.

41 A year after the new laws went into effect, Minister of Public Security Hugo Barrera describes the new codes as "the principal public security problem, as they give exaggerated protection to criminals," and he blames the codes for the failure to adequately control common crime. In May 1999, 77.57 percent of El Salvador's prison population of 7,027 is still awaiting trial, and only 1,576 are actually serving sentences (Popkin, *Peace without Justice*, 16–17).

42 On April 1, 1991, Mayor Tom Bradley appointed Warren Christopher to investigate the LAPD. The commission was created to conduct a full and fair examination of the structure and operation of the LAPD, including its recruitment and training practices, internal disciplinary system, and citizen complaint system.

43 Hayden, *Street Wars*, 227–28.

44 See Glover and Lait, "Ex-Chief Refuses to Discuss Rampart."

45 See Poole, "Rampart Scandal." I say "purportedly" because the investigation was stalled by then LAPD Chief Bernard Parks.

46 Siems, *Between the Lines*, 71.

47 The U.S. Supreme Court issued decisions that restricted the right of the U.S. government to order deportation of non-U.S. citizens convicted of felony crimes, and to indefinitely detain aliens who had been ordered to be deported from the United States but who are not accepted by their countries of citizenship. This decision meant that the decision made in 1996 could no longer be applied retroactively to crimes committed before 1996, and it restored the right of judicial review to foreigners facing deportation. See Marquis, "Ashcroft Seeks Return of Criminal Immigrants"; Taylor, "INS Stuck over What to Do with Detainees"; Sachs, "Second Thoughts"; Greenhouse, "Justices Place Limits on Detention in Cases of Deportable Immigrants"; Lane, "Justices Decide Immigrants Have Right to Review"; and Greenhouse, "Justices Permit Immigrants to Challenge Deportations."

48 The concept of reducing crime by attending to the smallest of offenses such as broken windows was introduced by George Kelling and James Wilson. Under this law enforcement model, it is as important to police nonviolent and noncriminal behavior as it is to address violent crime. Police patrol neighborhoods on foot and root out "disorderly . . . disreputable, obstreperous, or unpredictable people: panhandlers, drunks, addicts, rowdy teenagers, prostitutes, loiterers, and the mentally disturbed" (Kelling and Wilson, "Broken Windows," available at www.theatlantic.com). Under Giuliani, this translated into zero tolerance of all minor infractions in order to achieve what Kelling and Wilson term "order maintenance."

49 According to its official Web site, ICE "protects national security and upholds public safety by targeting criminal networks and terrorist organizations that seek to exploit vulnerabilities in our immigration system, in our financial networks, along our border, at federal facilities and elsewhere in order to do harm to the United States. The end result is a safer, more secure America" ("About ICE," http://www.ice.gov).

50 See Berrigan and Wingo, "US Military Involvement in Latin America."

51 See Seper, "Al Qaeda Seeks Tie to Local Gangs."

52 See Associated Press, "Officials: Al Qaeda, Latin Gangs Not Linked."

53 See "Investigations: Community Shield," http://www.ice.gov.

54 For an ethnography of the SOA, see Gill, The School of the Americas.

55 See Postero, Now We Are Citizens.

ONE Latino Looter

1 For a discussion of cultural interagency, see Said, Culture and Imperialism; Berger, A Seventh Man; and Papastergiadis, Modernity as Exile.

2 I am grateful to Scott Sterling and Jesse Lerner for access to this footage.

3 Reginald Denny was a truck driver who was nearly beaten to death by a group of black assailants who came to be known as the "L.A. Four." The attack was captured by a Los Angeles news service helicopter and the video was broadcast live on U.S. national television.

4 Lucia Artal Ramos, one of hundreds of undocumented immigrants, was stopped by police, told that she was going to get "a free ride back to [her] country," and handed over to Immigration and Naturalization Services (see Mydans, "Criticism Grows over Aliens Seized during Riots").

5 Rosenberg, "King Case Aftermath."

6 For discussions of the racialization of the riots as black, see Smith, "Transmitting Race"; Zilberg, From Riots to Rampart; Hunt, Screening the Los Angeles "Riots"; and Valle and Torres, Latino Metropolis. Valle and Torres argue that "coding the cast black and white according to a socially constructed discourse that preceded the event itself—trapp[ed] the interpretation of the event in a circular racializing logic. . . . The two societies, one black, one white, [a] separate and unequal dichotomy made famous by the Kerner Commission[,] could not contain a multicultural riot in which villains and victims defied racial typecasting" (Latino Metropolis, 45–46, 53).

7 Hunt, Screening the Los Angeles "Riots," 45.

8 On the post-Fordist programs and globalization, see Valle and Torres, Latino Metropolis, 47.

9 Valle and Torres, Latino Metropolis, 50, 54.

10 Frenzen and Acosta, Los Angeles Times, "Immigrant's Roundup Was a Dirty Trick."

11 I interviewed Tobar in Los Angeles in September 1999. Tobar absorbed his journ-

alistic coverage of the riots into the last chapter of his 1998 novel *The Tattooed Soldier*.

12 The first quote is derived from Rand Corporation, "Report on the Los Angeles Riot"; and the second is from U.S. Attorney General Williams P. Barr, quoted in Brimelow, "Time to Rethink Immigration," 46.

13 This depiction of the riots, while more inclusive, does not account for the placement of Korean immigrants and Korean Americans in the riots. There is considerable overlap in South Central, Pico Union, and Koreatown between African American, Latino, and Korean populations. For discussions of the riots as a Korean event, see, among many others, Abelman and Lie, *Blue Dreams*; Cho, "Korean American vs. African American"; and Kim, "Home Is Where the Han Is." See also the documentary *Sa-I-Gu*, directed by Dai Sil Kim-Gibson and Christine Choy.

14 Miles, "Blacks vs. Browns," 67.

15 Brimelow, "Time to Rethink Immigration," 45.

16 Dumm, "The New Enclosures," 178–95.

17 See Hall et al., *Policing the Crisis* for a discussion of national moral panics in reference to the "black mugger."

18 See chapter 3 for a discussion of IIRAIRA. Proposition 187 was a ballot initiative in 1994 designed to deny illegal immigrants social services, health care, and public education. It was introduced by Assemblyman Dick Mountjoy (Republican from Monrovia, California) as the "Save Our State" initiative. It passed with 58.8 percent of the vote but was overturned by a federal court.

19 I borrow the term "visible, if silenced" from Valle and Torres, *Latino Metropolis*, 53. See chapters 3 and 4 for an extended discussion of the practices and cultural politics of incarceration and deportation.

20 Valle and Torres, *Latino Metropolis*, 55.

21 On "the law of place," see de Certeau, *The Practice of Everyday Life*, 118.

22 See Valle and Torres, *Latino Metropolis*, 55.

23 Economist, "Pull Together?"

24 Ruben Navarrette Jr., "Should Latinos Support Curbs on Immigration?"

25 Ibid.

26 Ibid.

27 Ibid.

28 A version of this section of the chapter was previously published in the special issue of *Wide Angle* titled "City Scapes II," edited by Clark Arnwine and Jesse Lerner (20, no. 3 [1999]: 182–209). My thanks to journal editor Ruth Bradley and guest editors Clark Arnwine and Jesse Lerner for their invaluable editorial assistance and for allowing me to include the material here in my book.

29 For a discussion of psychic disturbances, see Bergson, *Matter and Memory*. For a discussion of space-time-being, see Harvey, *The Condition of Postmodernity*, 201–10.

30 Film director Schumacher employs an array of filmic devices to produce an awe-

some schizophrenic accumulation of energy in his protagonist (and indeed, in his audience)—it is the sort of madness born of late capitalism's excess. The opening scene described here is a graphic evocation of what Fredric Jameson, drawing upon Lacan's theorization of the connection between linguistic malfunction and the psyche of the schizophrenic, argues is central to the postmodern condition: "The breakdown of the signifying chain . . . into a rubble of distinct and unrelated signifiers" ("Postmodernism, or The Cultural Logic of Late Capitalism," 71–73).

31 For a discussion of "structures of feeling," see Williams, *Marxism and Literature*, 128–34. In relation to the European Economic Community, Nadia Serementakis poses the question, "At what levels are the economic and social transformations of regional integration being felt?" (*The Senses Still*, 3).

32 For a discussion of "place panic," see Casey, *Remembering*. For a discussion of "insecurity of territory," see Virilio, *Essai sur l'insecurite du territoire*.

33 For a discussion of the way in which the sewer represented the grotesque social body in Victorian Britain, see Stallybrass and White, *The Politics and Poetics of Transgression*, 80–124.

34 For a discussion of "spatial apartheid," see Goldberg, *Racist Culture*, 185–202.

35 Davis, "Los Angeles Was Just the Beginning," 14. In this regard, the film counters another post-riot release—Studio City's newest theme park and mall, City Walk. Unlike the cityscape in *Falling Down*, City Walk is a tame simulation of heterogeneous Los Angeles for the tourist industry, endangered by the fallout of bad post-riot press: "The best features of Olvera Street, Hollywood and the West Side synthesized in easy, bite-sized pieces for consumption by tourists and residents who don't need the excitement of dodging bullets in the Third World country that Los Angeles has become" (Davis, "Los Angeles Was Just the Beginning," 18). By mounting the concrete barrier that separates the highway from the lived spaces hidden on the other side, D-Fens brings into view precisely those elements that City Walk keeps at bay. In this respect, the film engages precisely those elements that *City Walk*'s facile celebration and commodification of multiculturalism holds at bay: the Los Angeles landscape as it "socially and physically erodes into the 21st century" (2).

36 See Klein, *The History of Forgetting*, 107, for critique of the film's grasp of "urban reality."

37 See Bakhtin, *Problems of Dostoevsky's Poetics*, 122–23, for the critical potential of the carnivalesque in bringing people who are in life separated by impenetrable hierarchical barriers into free and familiar contact with each other and the reverse sides of their worlds. Similarly, in their discussion of capitalism and schizophrenia in *The Anti-Oedipus*, Deleuze and Guattari argue that "the schizophrenic out for a walk is a better model than a neurotic lying on the analyst's couch." The "schizo" out for a stroll is an effect of the "awesome . . . accumulation of energy or charge" produced by capitalism. This charge, conceived of as desire, carries with it revo-

lutionary potential, and so must continually be repressed by the very forces that induce its unleashing (34).

38 For a discussion of genre as an ideological orienting framework, see Bauman, "'Genre' and 'Performance,'" 53.

39 The Korean immigrant inner-city convenience store owner was another much-maligned figure in the Los Angeles riots. This social type was accused of taking advantage of the relative lack of amenities and the lack of market competition in low-income neighborhoods by overpricing its inventory. The fatal shooting of Natasha Harlins, a fifteen-year-old African American customer, by store owner and Korean immigrant Soon Ja Du the previous year served as a powerful political text for this negative characterization of Korean merchants in the inner city. For a compelling counter-narrative see the previously referenced documentary, Sa-I-Gu.

40 See Soja, Postmodern Geographies, 24.

41 Ibid., 222–48.

42 The critical and parodic elements of film noir and the desolation epic are absorbed into Western adventure, only to be contained within a detective-cop genre and its law-and-order narrative. This generic ordering speaks to ideological and power relations underlying the production and consumption of discourse (Bauman and Briggs, "Genre, Intertextuality and Social Power," 131–32).

43 Central American Refugee Center, "Report on Civil Rights and Human Rights Violations during the Post–Los Angeles Riot."

44 "Normal" conditions in the inner city of Los Angeles are a particularly good example of what Walter Benjamin insisted was a chronic "state of emergency" (the "inner city crisis") (Illuminations, 275).

45 Davis, "Los Angeles Was Just the Beginning," 6.

46 On the apartheid urban order, see Goldberg, Racist Culture, 190. The reference to the sewers that serve as tunnels for smuggling undocumented immigrants into the United States is drawn from the film El Norte (1983).

47 American Civil Liberties Union, "Civil Liberties in Crisis," 7.

48 Limbaugh, "Falling Down," 108.

49 Davis, Magical Urbanism, 156–57.

TWO Street Hoodlum

1 By "rebuilt" I do not mean literally rebuilt on the same corner. However, Jack in the Box made quite a display of the fact that they were the first to return to the inner city to invest, and they did, in fact, literally build on the site of a burned facility in South Central Los Angeles.

2 Note that unless otherwise indicated, all Rebuild Los Angeles quotes are drawn from the Rebuild LA Collection, 1992–1997, archive, which is housed in the Re-

search Center for the Study of Los Angeles Archives and Special Collections, Charles Von der Ahe Library, Loyola Marymount University.

3 *Los Angeles Times*, "Why Ueberroth and Rebuild Los Angeles Must Not Fail." A "neglected area" was defined by RLA as a census tract in which 20 percent or more of residents lived below the poverty line. This discussion of development in the undeveloped inner city is reminiscent of James Ferguson's discussion in *The Anti-Politics Machine* of the "less developed country." In this context, the undeveloped, isolated inner city comes to serve as the focus of intensive care by a host of government task forces, social service agencies, private foundations, and community-based organizations, and, in the aftermath of the riots, private corporations. Indeed, one is tempted to meddle with the order of the discourse a little and refer to the underdeveloped inner city as an ICU (intensive care unit).

4 See Katz, *The Undeserving Poor*.

5 Ferguson's discussion in *The Anti-Politics Machine* of the "law of governmentality" is also a useful analytical construct here, although it operates in reverse. Whereas in the spatial cultural discourse of "third world" development the "less developed country" is a result of government neglect, in the absence of government planning in the ICU the problem arises precisely from the counterproductive interference of the welfare state.

6 Nikolas Rose, in "Governing 'Advanced' Liberal Democracies" (155), critiques Stuart Hall's argument that the neoconservative political regimes of Thatcher's government (and by extension the Reagan administration) were underpinned by a coherent and elaborated political rationality that they then sought to implement. He suggests instead that the advanced liberal mentality of government that came to be termed neoliberalism involved a gradual organization of diverse skirmishes. While I agree with Rose, I nonetheless find it useful to juxtapose these two documents given that they were released after and in response to the Los Angeles riots.

7 The Washington Consensus, as proposed by John Williamson, identified ten reforms: fiscal discipline, reordering public expenditure priorities, tax reform, liberalizing interest rates, a competitive exchange rate, trade liberalization, liberalization of foreign investment, privatization, deregulation, and property rights.

8 Without enough support from Democrats to defeat Republican opposition, Clinton had to back off from these programs.

9 The same point that Saskia Sassen notes in "Whose City Is It?" about the continuing and integral role that the state does in fact play in globalization through legislating the terms of capital flows holds true for the role of the state in privatization.

10 Harvey, *The Condition of Postmodernity*, 122.

11 *Los Angeles Times*, "Why Ueberroth and Rebuild Los Angeles Must Not Fail."

12 See Christian Zlolniski, *Janitors, Street Vendors and Activists*, for a discussion of Justice for Janitors in Silicon Valley.

13 For a discussion of Walter Benjamin's treatment of consumers as a dreaming collective, see "Dream World of Mass Culture" in Buck-Morss, *The Dialectics of Seeing*, 253–86.

14 The Los Angeles historian Mike Davis has accounted for this aspect of the riots as follows: "The riot arrived like a magic dispensation. People were initially shocked by the violence, then mesmerized by the televised images of bi-racial crowds in South Central LA helping themselves to mountains of desirable goods without interference from the police . . . Thousands immediately interpreted this as a last call to participate in the general redistribution of wealth in progress . . . The looting crowds were governed by a visible moral economy. As one middle-aged lady explained to me, 'Stealing is a sin, but this is like a television game show where everyone in the audience gets to win'" ("LA Intifada," 2).

15 This visual access is akin to what Benjamin speaks of as the "perceptual acuity" and "optical unconscious" afforded by new techniques of production (Benjamin in Buck-Morss, *Dialectics of Seeing*, 267–68).

16 Indeed, the technical reproduction of the riot is a particularly striking example of the human reappropriation of new technology anticipated by Benjamin. Of course, it is not the photograph or radio but rather video and television that represent the "new nature" here. Benjamin believed that technical reproduction would give back to humanity the capacity for expression that technical production threatens to take away (Buck-Morss, *Dialectics of Seeing*, 268). The response of the "dreaming collective" of the mass television audience in Los Angeles represented the capacity for the inventive reception based on mimetic improvisation (264), which perhaps went beyond even Benjamin's wildest imaginings.

Whereas there is ground for rescuing the liberatory potential from mass media, with the rise of fascism Benjamin modified his romantic notion of the new technology and mimesis. Indeed, the Rodney King case is, from start to finish, a profound example of the ways in which electronic media is Janus-faced, with its potential for both liberation and repression. Whereas the video of the Rodney King beating captured the victim's oppressors on tape with a "seeing is believing" clarity, the subsequent Simi Valley verdict demonstrated how even home video's indexical relationship between sign and signifier can be deconstructed and reconstructed semiotically to re-present the victim as the oppressor. Video has certainly provided what Benjamin termed a "new schooling for mimetic powers" (267), but not necessarily to liberatory ends.

The Reginald Denny beating, which followed the verdict, is itself a perverse mimetic improvisation of the video of the Rodney King beating. Taking on the role of LAPD officers, these young men reenact the trauma of the Rodney King beating on the body of Reginald Denny. This incident did not help turn a racially motivated beating into blows against racism but instead only added fuel to the criminalization of young black men as well as money to the burgeoning prison industry. The footage of the looting during the Rodney King riot was used against individuals and their criminal prosecutions and, finally, against Latinos as a group by fueling xenophobia and nationalism.

Given these repressive consequences, I would add Foucault's notion of repression as a positive production and the new nature/video as another means of surveillance to Benjamin's more utopian conceptions thereof. The liberatory and repressive potential appear in the same medium and can take the same form.

17 In 1957 various avant-garde groups in Europe came together to form the Situationist International (SI). Over the next decade the SI developed a critique of modern society. Its methods of agitation were influential in the revolt in France in May 1968. Although the SI itself was dissolved in 1972, Situationist theses and tactics have been taken up by radical currents in different parts of the world.

18 Situationist International, "Theory of the Dérive," 155–57.

19 Miles, "Blacks vs. Browns," 42.

20 Buck-Morss, The Dialectics of Seeing, 164, 159–91.

21 Bohanan in Appadurai, The Social Life of Things, 25.

22 Buck-Morss, The Dialectics of Seeing, 16, 72.

23 At the time of this campaign, the successful bargaining of unionized janitors for wage increases still paled in comparison to the 1970s wage scale for the equivalent work. In other words, even after its victories, the union had not restored the salaries and benefits of previous contracts, since broken, between labor and the private sector.

24 Mahler, American Dreaming, 83.

25 Cannon, Official Negligence, 359–72.

26 Hayden, Street Wars, 4.

27 Regarding STEP, see California Penal Code, Section 186.2. For an extremely useful summary of the STEP Act provisions and the larger context in which it was enacted see Gilmore, Golden Gulag, 107–9.

28 See Dunn, The Militarization of the U.S.-Mexico Border, 1978–1992; and Nevins, Operation Gatekeeper.

29 Lopez and Connell, "Troubled Corner."

30 Jean and John Comaroff examine how this sort of appropriation of the licit operations of the market and the rule of law and the "recommission of their substance" is part of a more "troubled dialectic . . . of law and dis/order framed by neo-liberal mechanisms of deregulation . . . [It is] the pas de deux in which norm and transgression, regulation and exception, redefine each other" (Introduction to Law and Disorder in the Postcolony, 5).

31 Bohannan in Appadurai, Social Life of Things, 25–27.

32 Dumm, "The New Enclosures," 276. In his discussion of the representational schema of African American transgressive mobility, Dumm footnotes Brenda Bright's insightful treatment of Mexican American mobility in her ethnography of

Los Angeles low riders. Referring back to the Rodney King incident, Bright notes that having a car does not necessarily give a man the mobility he desires. Latinos and African Americans have long been subject to strict surveillance and delimited mobility. In exploring the car as a site of domination and resistance, Bright examines how the cultural practice of low riders allows for the reworking of these limitations of mobility placed on racialized cultures in the United States. This is especially true for Los Angeles, with its legacy of surveillance and conflicts between racial minorities and the police, and to continual reinforcement of racial boundaries as criminal boundaries ("Remappings: Los Angeles Low Riders," 90–91). The image of the freeway as a sign of free circulation brings us back to chapter 1 and to the sudden flight by the film character D-Fens from the clogged arteries of the Los Angeles freeways that once represented individual freedom and mobility—for the Anglo-American male at least. The discussion of mobility in relationship to a male subject, be he white, black, or brown, is deeply tied to questions of space.

33 Foucault, *Discipline and Punish*, 195–200.

34 See American Civil Liberties Union (ACLU), "False Premises, False Promise."

35 For the border, see Dunn, *The Militarization of the US–Mexico Border*; and for South Africa, see Goldberg, *Racist Culture*.

36 El *vacil*, or hanging out in the streets, bears a relationship to the Situationist International's notion of *dèrive*, or drifting, and Walter Benjamin's *flânerie*, or prowling. See chapter 5 for an elaborated discussion of el vacil.

37 Ironically, City Walk became a popular hangout for inner-city youth and gang youth precisely because of its effort to mimic the pedestrianism of a city street. My use of the quoted term in this sentence is from Holston, "The Modernist City and the Death of the Street."

38 See Sorkin, *Variations on a Theme Park*.

39 Davis, *Magical Urbanism*, 51–57. In his impassioned survey of how Latinos in Miami, New York, and Los Angeles are "reinvent[ing] the US big city," Davis argues that Latin American immigrants, who are "transforming dead urban spaces into convivial social places" (55), are the most important constituency for the preservation of our urban communities, and that "all of Latin America is now a dynamo turning the lights back on in the dead spaces of North American cities" (57). Similarly, Margaret Crawford's introduction to the edited volume *Everyday Urbanism* draws upon LeFebvre's notion of "spaces of representation" and Soja's idea of "third space" to argue that in Los Angeles women, immigrants, low-level employees, and teenagers are restructuring urban spaces according to an "alternative logic of public space" (28–29).

40 While I would not argue that the injunction is a pure example of Foucault's panopticism (it is hardly economical or efficient) it does share certain features, including spatial partitioning through the penetration into, and regulation of, the smallest details of everyday life. And while the mini-mall at Alvarado and Pico is

not on the postmodern technological order of Mike Davis's "smart building," it is an integral figure in the redevelopment of the barrio as "carceral city" (Davis, *City of Quartz*, 221–64). This reengineering at the street level is further perfected by another key figure (which perhaps is at a formal level truer to Foucault's notion of panopticism), namely that of the omnipresent helicopter and its night scope, which swoops back and forth along the streets and alleys of the barrio, peering into the windows of the apartment buildings where these gang members are, so to speak, under house arrest.

Unlike the newscopter, the policecopter is a purer example of panopticism, since the two-way vision of synopticism enabled by live coverage or reality TV is absent. The blinding light of the policecopter is a vivid metaphor for this one-way visual perception. For a discussion of panopticism versus synopticism, see Andrejevic, *Reality TV*, 1–17.

41 For a discussion of gang injunctions, see Klein and Maxson, *Street Gangs Patterns and Policies*, 220. In theory, community policing takes the view that the police and citizens are coproducers of police services and are jointly responsible for reducing crime and improving the quality of life in local neighborhoods. According to the philosophy of community policing, local police should provide citizens with formal access to the department's decision- and policymaking processes, initiate frequent personal contacts with community members on their beats, and interact in an attentive, friendly, and compassionate manner. Enforcing the law and fighting crime remain important elements of policing, but community policing recognizes that, in reality, most police work is oriented toward non-enforcement tasks such as maintaining order and providing social services (see Eck and Rosenbaum, "The New Police Order"). For an analysis of the politics of community policing and the struggle over what it constitutes, see Lyons, *The Politics of Community Policing*.

42 As Malcolm Klein and Cheryl Maxson note, a study of southern California injunctions found few indicators of direct community participation in the selection of targeted gang members in the development of the evidence for the lawsuit or in its enforcement. The injunction, they argue, is "largely a one-man show, and that man was the police" (*Street Gangs Patterns and Policies*, 220–21).

43 See O'Malley, "Containing Our Excitement."

44 A coalition of groups, including the Labor Community Strategies Center, AGENDA, a South Central organization, and Coalition Against Police Abuse (CAPA), led a successful citywide campaign to defeat the federal Weed and Seed Program by arguing that "Weed and Seed attempted to control social service agencies by placing their funding under the authority of the Justice Department and criminalizing inner-city black and Latino youth through 'target zones' that allowed them to be arrested and convicted under even more repressive federal statutes" (Mann, "Building the Anti-Racist, Anti-Imperialist United Front").

45 See Chesluk, "Visible Signs of a City Out of Control" and *Money Jungle*.

46 *Los Angeles Times*, "Why Ueberroth and Rebuild Los Angeles Must Not Fail."

47 O'Malley, "Containing Our Excitement," 182.

48 Hayden, "Fruits of War," 5–6.

49 See Rose, "Governing 'Advanced' Liberal Democracies."

50 Ibid., 157.

51 Borrowing from Claude Lefort's *Democracy and Political Theory*, Rosalind Deutsche invokes that marvelous image of "the empty space of the social" and the ways in which the "guardians of public space" attempt to occupy, fill up, and take possession of that empty place, which in democratic society is the locus of power— namely, The People (*Evictions*, 273–79).

THREE *Criminal Cop*

1 Cannon, "LAPD Confidential," 62.

2 See chapter 5 for a discussion of the founding of Homies Unidos in San Salvador.

3 There was some overlap here with the Wilshire division.

4 For a discussion of the inception of this gang as expounded by Alex Sanchez, see Hayden, "Fruits of War," 206–9. See also Vigil, *A Rainbow of Gangs*, 131–45.

5 A *pupuseria* is a street-front restaurant named for the Salvadoran national dish the *pupusa*, which is to El Salvador as the hamburger is to the United States. The pupusa is made up of a thick corn tortilla filled with combinations of pork, beans, a hard white cheese, and a green vegetable called *loroco*.

6 Reverend James Lawson worked with Dr. Martin Luther King Jr. and was a leading theoretician and tactician of nonviolence within the American civil rights movement. He continues to be involved in training activists in nonviolence. Connie Rice is a prominent civil rights attorney and is co-director and co-founder of the Advancement Project in Los Angeles. Angela Oh is also a well-known civil rights attorney, who became more widely known for her advocacy on behalf of Korean Americans in the aftermath to the riots in 1992 and was later appointed by President Bill Clinton to the President's Initiative on Race.

7 For a discussion of "dangerous classes" see Simon in O'Malley, "Containing Our Excitement," 162.

8 The conflict between Left and Right might be construed thus: Who gets to pacify these "dangerous classes" and what does that pacification entail? While I do not locate community-level resistance within this body per se, I do agree with O'Malley's contention that the very existence of competing discourses of criminology is indicative of resistance ("Containing Our Excitement," 164).

9 See O'Malley, "Containing Our Excitement," for a discussion of this hard side of neoliberalism and its punitive technologies, 172.

10 This was true for the African American gangs, the Bloods, and the Crips, but not

so for the Latino immigrant gangs 18th Street and MS. In fact, the war between 18th Street and MS began in 1992.

11 Until fairly recently, street vending was an illegal practice in Los Angeles. It is now possible to apply for health-code certification and tax licenses. However, many vendors cannot afford these fees or lack the technical expertise needed to navigate the complex set of laws governing vending. Moreover, vendors must move their trucks every hour. For details on street vending in Los Angeles county, see the Web site for the Coalition for Humane Immigrant Rights of Los Angeles, Street Vending Committee at http://www.chirla.org. Also see Crawford, "Contesting the Public Realm," 6–7, among others.

12 Hayden, "Fruits of War," 223–25.

13 For a discussion of the space of the street as a space of cultural resistance, see Bourgois, In Search of Respect, and as a space of community activism, see Gregory, Black Corona, 110–38. For a discussion of the street as a space of contagion, fear, and fascination, and a key site for the formation of the modernist split between the savage and civilized other, see Stallybrass and White, The Politics and Poetics of Transgression.

14 The discussion of "third space" in this particular context is drawn from Chase, Crawford, and Kaliski, Everyday Urbanism, 29. For earlier and additional discussions of "third space," see Anzaldúa, Borderland/La Frontera; Bhabha, The Location of Culture; and Soja, Thirdspace.

15 Dumm, "The New Enclosures," 29.

16 Statement made by Warren Olney during his daily radio talk show This Way LA, KCRW, September 9, 1999.

17 See Aretxaga, "A Fictional Reality," for a discussion of how the Basque police operated as both "the law and its transgression" (60).

18 Cannon, "LAPD Confidential," 34.

19 The CAL/GANG list is a database containing a list of 160,000 individuals meeting the so-called gang profile. That profile includes a list of "tell-tale" traits or signs of gang membership. An individual need only exhibit three out of about sixteen traits to give an officer "probable cause" to stop him or her.

20 Cannon, "LAPD Confidential," 34.

21 See Rivera, "Scandal Stirs a Grim Specter of Emotions."

22 See Herbert, Policing Space, for a discussion of how the spatial practices of both the LAPD and gangs draw from the same "adventure/machismo normative order." Herbert's ethnography of the LAPD shows that police officers and gang members share many traits such as enjoyment of the thrill of danger, the rush of adrenaline, and the destructive power of the gun. Indeed, he finds that police officers actually seek out antagonism from gang members intentionally in order to experience "the excitement of trying to enact territoriality in dangerous and challenging circumstances" (88–89).

23 Simon quoted in O'Malley, "Containing Our Excitement," 162.

24 Perez quoted in Cannon, "LAPD Confidential," 66.

25 For a theorization of the dialogical or reciprocal nature of violence, see Girard, *Violence and the Sacred*, 143.

26 Taussig, *Mimesis and Alterity*, 78.

27 Sullivan, "The Murder of Notorious B.I.G."

28 See Taussig, *Defacement* for a discussion of "public secrets." In Begoña Aretxaga's work, which explores how the state plays at being the savage other, she argues that the interiorization of a fantastic enemy characterizes counterinsurgency and anti-terrorist thinking and is fundamental to the logics of political transgression (Aretxaga, "A Fictional Reality," 54). See chapter 7 and the conclusion of this book for a discussion of how these same logics operated between the United States and El Salvador in the post-9/11 period.

29 Homies Unidos in San Salvador, on the other hand, was initially founded on the "union" of the two major rival gangs 18th Street and MS.

30 Dwight Conquergood, in his long-term ethnographic work with the Latin Kings in Chicago, describes the gang neighborhood as "a subterranean space of life-sustaining warmth, intimacy and protection" ("Homeboys and Hoods," 47).

31 Nichols, *Blurred Boundaries*, 46.

32 Girard argues that when two desires converge on the same object, they are bound to clash, and that mimesis, coupled with desire, leads automatically to conflict (Girard, *Violence and the Sacred*, 146).

33 O'Malley, "Containing Our Excitement," 160.

34 See Edmund T. Gordon's "Cultural Politics of Black Masculinity" for an alternative interpretation of black male practice as active politics of accommodation and resistance. In his discussion, Gordon takes issue with the culture of poverty thesis, which pathologizes all nonconformist, non-middle-class behavior. He calls for a more nuanced understanding of the African American male cultural process that, rather than couching the black male "crisis" in psychological terms, rethinks these problems in political terms. In so doing, African American males' active denial of authority and the legitimacy of the state and its institutions, the deliberate violation of the precepts of capitalist ownership, and the rejection of the social and moral norms of Anglo civil society also speak to their political resistance to an established order. Similarly, Dwight Conquergood argues that the Latin Kings were "keenly aware of class difference in communication style, and are critical of what they take to be the tepid, distant, interpersonal mode of the middle class" ("Homeboys and Hoods," 47).

35 This is not the actual language used by the organization, but is rather derived from O'Malley, "Containing Our Excitement," 164.

36 In this sense, the position of Homies Unidos supports David Brotherton and Luis

Barrios's thesis in *The Almighty Latin King and Queen Nation* that gangs can be approached from a social movements perspective. Brotherton and Barrios argue that gangs are political entities that have, through their individual and collective practices, the potential to resist, transform, or transcend society's structures.

37 This was the first of two such protests outside the Rampart station not mentioned in the *New York Times Magazine*. The second was held in conjunction with the Y2K protests around the Democratic National Convention. See Hayden, *Street Wars*, for a discussion of both protests.

38 The custody and immigration status of a young Cuban boy, Elián González, were at the center of a heated controversy in 2000 involving the Cuban and United States governments, Elián's father and family in Cuba, and the anti-Castro Cuban American political organizations and the boy's relatives in Miami. However, after the appeals by the Miami relatives met several rejections by the 11th Circuit Court of Appeals in Atlanta, and a refusal to hear the case by the U.S. Supreme Court, Elián returned to Cuba with his father, Juan Miguel González, on June 28, 2000.

39 The Bus Riders Union, a project of the Labor/Community Strategy Center, is a progressive civil rights and environmental justice membership organization focused on the mass transit and public health needs of transit-dependent communities in Los Angeles (see http://www.busridersunion.org).

40 O'Connor, "INS Probes Its Role in Rampart Case."

41 See chapters 4, 5, and 6 for a detailed discussion of conditions in El Salvador.

42 See chapter 5 and 6 for a discussion of zero-tolerance gang abatement strategies in El Salvador.

43 O'Connor, "Suit Alleges Harassment of L.A. Gang Peace Group."

44 Javier Ovando's immigrant status was not a pressing issue in the Rampart investigation. The crime for which Ovando was framed would have kept him in prison and thus out of the deportation pipeline for a good twenty-three years.

FOUR *Criminal Deportee*

1 According to Immigration and Naturalization Services and U.S. Citizenship and Immigration Services statistical yearbooks, the average number of individuals deported to El Salvador from 1996 to 2005 was 4,686, which is almost double the average number deported annually between 1980 and 1995. By 2009, the number of deportees climbed to 20,406, a weekly average of 1,700 (Coutin, *Nation of Emigrants*, 24).

2 This quote is excerpted from "Radio Diaries" on *This American Life*, National Public Radio (May 21, 1999). The show was produced by Joe Richman and narrated by José Huezo Soriano (a.k.a. Weasel).

3 Boyer, "Bad Cops," 71. However, of the three thousand cases under investigation,

Garcetti determined that the lowest priority was to be given to people who had been deported as a result of a conviction and may be impossible to find (Weinstein, "Rampart Probe May Now Affect Over 3,000 Cases").

4 For a discussion of the dialectical tension between the barrio as a community enabling and disabling space, see Villa, *Barrio-Logos*, 1–18.

5 Barrios populares or marginales here refer to working class, poor, and marginal neighborhoods.

6 As noted in the introduction to this book, this is not a linguistic study. However, I have chosen not to "clean up" the transcription of Gato's English in order to leave the mixture of languages in his speech visible.

7 As I will discuss at length in the next two chapters, in El Salvador the tattoo is taken as a sign of criminality. Those bearing tattoos can be barred from attending school, for example, and the presence of a tattoo has been used as grounds for failing to provide timely medical attention to the wounded in hospital emergency rooms, resulting in unnecessary deaths from bleeding. The discrimination can be so fierce that even the most innocuous tattoos can be misconstrued. For instance, one deportee I knew used to wrap a bandage up the length of his arm before he left for classes in a private college. This, he explained to me, was to avoid conflict with the local gangs and the police and to enable him to enter the college. His tattoo, the source of so much discrimination and danger, was simply the name of his youngest daughter who lived in Los Angeles. He had tattooed her name into his arm so that "she would always be close" to him.

8 Magdaleno Rose-Ávila had just come from Los Angeles, where he was Amnesty International's West Coast regional director. He'd had significant experience in Central America as a Peace Corps director in Nicaragua and then Guatemala in the 1980s. As a renegade and a would-be Catholic priest, Rose-Ávila began his political activism in the Chicano movement with *Teatro Campesino* (the street theater group formed by playwright and director, Luis Valdez) and working for Cesar Chavez's Farm Workers Union in the 1970s. As the son of Mexican farm workers himself, he grew up in Denver, Colorado, where he, alongside many of his contemporaries, struggled with drugs and violence.

9 Cruz and Peña, *Solidarid y violencia en las pandillas del Gran San Salvador*.

10 Güera means light-skinned. The alternative spelling of Huera's name is in and of itself a sign of the Americanization of Salvadoran Spanish as well as the influence of Spanglish.

11 See Vigil, *Barrio Gangs*; Phillips, *Wallbangin'*; and Villa, *Barrio-Logos*, among others, for the centrality of space and place in Chicano culture and gangs as a hyper-intensification of place attachment.

12 The urban planner Kevin Lynch in his oft-cited study of cognitive mapping takes up the problem of spatial alienation wrought by modernization and urbanization (*Image of the City*). Drawing on Lynch's work, Fredric Jameson suggests that

"the alienated city is above all a space in which people are unable to map (in their minds) either their own positions or the urban totality in which they find themselves" and that "disalienation in the traditional city . . . involves the practical reconquest of a sense of place" ("Postmodernism," 89). The spatial alienation and fettered mobility of these deported immigrant gang youth, however, result from very different conditions than those affecting the middle-class city dwellers, tourists, and business travelers in Lynch's and Jameson's respective works.

13 See Smith's "Can You Imagine" and *Transnational Urbanism* for a discussion of migration and the politics of simultaneity.

14 See Harvey, *The Condition of Postmodernity*.

15 The term *coyote* is a slang term used in Central America, Mexico, and the United States for someone who helps smuggle migrants across borders. Coyotes are distinguished from human traffickers because the migrants have actively engaged their services. In describing these cases where people who transformed from recipients of remittances to providers of remittances, I do not want to suggest that the journey involved in that transformation is a hop, skip, and a jump, or that it is not an undertaking of considerable financial and physical risk. Two months later, this young woman's youngest sister arrived in Los Angeles, but she had been raped along the way while crossing through Mexico. Moreover, many people lose their money, and never make it across. Doña Leti herself tells the story of her first entry into the United States overland, and how she stood her ground against her coyote, who made the mistake of thinking she would just give in to his advances.

16 Tabudos is the name that people from Santa Elena have coined for themselves.

17 At the time, girls were selected as queen, not based on looks but rather, how much money they could raise for the organization.

18 In the post-9/11 era, joining the military became an increasingly common alternative occupation for Latino immigrant youth. For a discussion of the aggressive recruitment of Latinos for the War on Terror, see Amaya, "Dying American"; Mariscal, "Homeland Security, Militarism, and the Future of Latinos and Latinas in the United States"; Perez, "Discipline and Citizenship"; Plascencia, "Citizenship through Veteranship"; and chapter 7 in this book.

19 For a discussion of this "return migration," see chapter 6.

20 Williams, *Marxism and Literature*, 128–35.

21 In *Culture and Imperialism*, Edward Said sets out to demonstrate how the imperial power and its colonies were produced in relation, or counterpoint, to each other. He argues that the nineteenth-century British novel, the quintessential genre of British cultural production and expression of British identity, is intimately related to and dependent upon the social space of empire. National identity is thus worked out through the relationship between home and abroad, the metropole and its colonies. Others have discussed how the postcolonial era has been, in turn, marked by a reversal in this cultural production of identity. The "periphery"

emerges at the "center" in the form of the now-well-known trope "the empire strikes back." See Centre for Contemporary Cultural Studies (CCCS), *The Empire Strikes Back*.

22 Grosfoguel, Maldonado-Torres, and Saldívar justify using the term "colonial" for Latino immigrants even though they were never directly colonized by the metropolitan country to which they migrated. Nonetheless, because they are "racialized" in similar ways to the "colonial/racial subjects of empire" upon arrival in the United States, and because many have actually fled the results of direct U.S. military intervention in their countries of origin, these authors argue that the lack of a notion of "coloniality" is precisely the dimension lacking in much of the transnational literature (*Latin@s in the World-System*, 6–11).

23 On the notion of "representational ambivalence," and living life "off the hyphen," see Arias, "Central American–Americans," 185 and 171.

FIVE *Gang Peace Activist*

1 On police reforms, see Call, "Policing the New World Order," "From Soldiers to Cops," and "Democratization, War and State-Building"; Call and Stanley, "Protecting the People"; Costa, *La Policía Nacional Civil de El Salvador*; Stanley, "Protectors or Perpetrators?"; and Ziegler and Nield, "From Peace to Governance." On judicial reforms, see Popkin, *Peace without Justice*. For more on gang-abatement strategies, see Aguilar, "El manodurismo y las 'politicas' de seguridad"; ERIC et al., *Mara y pandillas en Centroamérica*; Fundación de Estudios Para la Aplicacíon del Derecho (FESPAD), *Informe annual sobre la justicia penal juvenil, El Salvador*; Catholic Relief Services, "Gangs in Central America"; Cruz and Carranza, "Pandillas y politícas públicas"; USAID, "Central American and Mexico Gang Assessment"; Zilberg, "Refugee Gang Youth"; Coutin, *Nation of Emigrants*; and International Human Rights Clinic, "No Place to Hide."

2 Indeed, the organization and its members were the realization of Homi Bhabha's "hybrid"—a hybridization of forms—perhaps beyond even his wildest imaginings (see *Nation and Narration*).

3 As noted in the introduction, while the female prison population has been on the rise in the United States, it was more common for young Latina women to be policed by what was left of the welfare state, for their reproductive functions. Moreover, Latina youth also tended to leave gang life earlier to care for their children.

4 See chapter 4 for a discussion of these Internet cultural practices.

5 Cruz and Peña, *Solidaridad y violencia en las pandillas del Gran San Salvador*, 207.

6 Ibid., 59.

7 Santacruz and Concha-Eastman, *Barrio adentro*, 111.

8 On transgressing the line, see Foucault, "A Preface to Transgression."

9 Michel de Certeau distinguishes between the "strategies" of so-called more formal politics and the "tactics" of everyday life in the so-called "informal arena" (*The Practice of Everyday Life*, xix).

10 In de Certeau's language, Homies Unidos could be described as sitting on that "borderline," which its members constantly "manipulate" through the "tactics" of "everyday practices (talking, walking, shopping . . .)," and the "clever tricks of a hunter's cunning [which can be] poetic as well as warlike" (*The Practice of Everyday Life*, xix).

11 Ibid.

12 For a more detailed discussion of doble cara, see Zilberg, "Gangster in Guerrilla-Face" and chapter 7 in this book.

13 See Fraser, "Rethinking the Public Sphere," for a discussion of structurally ordained spaces (14).

14 My intention here is not simply to settle with an analysis of these ideologically saturated discourses and their conflation in the contemporary Salvadoran "folk devil" (Cohen, *Folk Devils and Moral Panics*; Hall et al., *Policing the Crisis*) of the deported gang member. Above and beyond discourse analysis, I want here to think through Homies Unidos's silent, visibly uncomfortable, but ubiquitous presence in this Habermasian public sphere and its idealized speech community where formerly suspect, banned, and exiled political forces now sit at the table with representatives of the right wing.

15 The Foro had a prehistory. It was the latest constellation of groups that had during the 1980s organized around the forced migration of Salvadorans fleeing the war and political violence. The nature of "the migrant" question had shifted away from its original focus: the United Nations High Commission on Refugees (UNHCR), the camps for refugees fleeing the civil war in neighboring Honduras, and the subsequent repatriation of those refugees back to El Salvador (see Zolberg, Suhrke, and Aguayo, *Escape from Violence*; Cagan and Cagan, *This Promised Land*; and Silber, "Mothers/Fighters/Citizens"). The Foro was a mixture of old and reorganized forces, but it had a new focus: no longer the refugee but rather the *hermano lejano*, the *retornado*, and the *deportado*. Moreover, that focus had switched from the United Nation's role in the Central American region to the Salvadoran state's role in and with respect to the Salvadoran expatriate in or returning from the United States.

16 See Zilberg and Lungo, "'Se han vuelto haraganes'?"

17 For a discussion of CARECEN, see chapters 1 and 3.

18 See chapter 7 for a discussion of political versus social violence.

19 As I discuss in the next chapter, it wasn't until 2004 that these proposals received some recognition through the establishment of the Secretariat for Youth as a response to critiques of El Plan Mano Dura's sole emphasis on repression.

20 Esseveld and Eyerman in Lucero, "On Feuds, Tumults, and Turns," 8.

21 Alvarez, Dagnino, and Escobar, *Cultures of Politics, Politics of Cultures*, 6.

22 The person was referring to, among others, the three deported gang members who had been arrested in the much-publicized case La Tormenta Tóxica (The Toxic Storm). That case revolved around a private beachside rave party that the police attempted to turn into a major drug bust around the time of President George W. Bush's visit to El Salvador. Fifteen people, mostly middle- and upper-middle-class youth, one the son of a state assembly member, were arrested. All were released except for the three deportees, who over a year later were still in prison awaiting trial.

23 See chapter 7 for a further discussion of the case of Rosa N.

24 Caldeira, *City of Walls*, 341.

25 Villalobos, *De la tortura a la proteccion ciudadana*, 184.

26 Caldeira, *City of Walls*, 339–42.

27 The exception here being the successful campaign mounted against kidnappings of prominent family members.

28 Costa, *La Policía Nacional Civil de El Salvador*, 27–28.

29 See Betancur et al., *From Madness to Hope*, chapter 2, "National Civil Police."

30 See Gill, *The School of the Americas*.

31 The self-described mission of ICITAP is as follows: To "serve as the source of support for United States criminal justice and foreign policy goals by assisting foreign governments in developing the capacity to provide professional law enforcement services based on democratic principles and respect for human rights." It was created by the Department of Justice in 1986 to respond to a request from the Department of State for assistance in training police forces in Latin America. Since then, ICITAP's activities have expanded to encompass two principal types of assistance projects: (1) the development of police forces in the context of international peacekeeping operations, and (2) the enhancement of capabilities of existing police forces in emerging democracies. Assistance is based on internationally recognized principles of human rights, rule of law, and modern police practices (http://www.usdoj.gov/criminal/icitap). For a critical discussion of ICITAP's history in Latin America, see Huggins, *Political Policing*.

32 IUDOP, "Delincuencia y opinion pública."

33 See California Penal Code Section 186.20–186.23.

34 Quoted in Hidalgo, "Transforming L.A.—El Salvador's Gang Connection."

35 Due to all of the people who were willing to write letters on behalf of Weasel, he received a relatively light sentence. At the time, "Illegal Reentry" could result anywhere from a five- to fourteen-year sentence.

SIX *Soldier Cop*

1 See Aguilar, "El Manodurismo y las 'politicas' de seguridad."

2 See Moodie, "'It's Worse than the War.'"

3 Even the National Association of Private Enterprise (ANEP), the Salvadoran Foun-

dation for Social and Economic Development (FUSADES, the conservative think tank set up during the war years by the United States and the new Right in El Salvador), and the newly reinstalled chief of the PNC, Rodrigo Ávila, all concurred with this assessment of manodurismo. Rodrigo Ávila had also served as the first chief of police of the newly created PNC, and he would become ARENA's presidential candidate in the 2009 elections.

4 My translation of "los señores de la guerra" as "warlords" does not imply the common meaning associated with the latter term. Rather, warlords here refers to the commanders in the official state military. A more literal translation would be "masters of the war."

5 See Robinson, *Transnational Conflicts* (87–102), for a discussion of how the Peace Accords involved sacrificing the Salvadoran military alongside the power of those among the landed oligarchy who had not adjusted to the new neoliberal agenda introduced by the United States via the new right in El Salvador, represented then by the new ruling political party, ARENA, and such U.S.-sponsored think tanks as FUSADES.

6 Cruz and Carranza, "Pandillas y políticas públicas," 25.

7 The idea of the bakery as a potential cottage industry in El Salvador was fraught with contradiction. With the exception of only the very largest operations, one local bakery after another was closing its facilities as a result of being unable to compete with foreign imports because of the neoliberal restructuring of trade policies.

8 See Rivas, "Imaginaries of Transnationalism," for a discussion of this growing transnational communications industry in El Salvador.

9 This chapter focuses on how manodurista policies undermine efforts as prevention and intervention. It is also often the case, however, that these programs themselves are poorly conceived, are executed by people with little training, and are not subject to proper evaluation. I sought out Pro-Jóvenes and Lisette Miranda in particular precisely because of their resources, combined technical know-how, and experience.

10 Weasel was not wrong to fear further detention. The most recent request granted for Withholding from Removal for a former gang member came with a high price: permanent detention.

11 The term used in the e-mail was "bangui," not "baggy." Although there is a brand of clothing called Bangui, none of the teenagers and young adults I asked had heard of it, and they generally thought that Argueta must have intended to write "bagui" as a transliteration for "baggy."

12 See Rivas, "Imaginaries of Transnationalism," for a discussion of the mega-mall industry.

13 See Baires, "Socio-Spatial Urban Transformations, Social Exclusion and Internal Borders in Central America."

14 Pollo Campero is a Guatemalan fast-food chain specializing in fried chicken and popular in Central America. It was common for Central Americans to fly back to the United States with bags of Pollo Campero as gifts. As a result, the chain opened up branches in Los Angeles to cater to Central Americans living there. There was even a branch in the Glendale Galleria shopping mall.

15 Burgos was referring to certain postwar security plans for coffee cultivation such as Grano de Oro and Plan Caminante. He argues that Mano Dura and Súper Mano Dura have their antecedents in the postwar transition.

16 See Gill, *The School of the Americas*, for an ethnography of the SOA.

SEVEN *Gang–Crime–Terrorism Continuum*

1 Benajmin in Buck-Morss, *Dialectics of Seeing*, 67–77.

2 See Derrida, *Specters of Marx*, for a discussion of this notion of time (xix–xx).

3 For a discussion of the distinction and continuum between political and social or criminal violence see Cruz, "Los factores posibilitadores y las expresiones de la violencia en Los Noventa"; Ramos, *Violencia en una sociedad en transicion*; Scheper-Hughes and Bourgois, *Violence in War and Peace*; Zilberg, "Gangster in Guerilla Face." See Moodie, " 'It's Worse than the War,' " for a discussion of nostalgia for the war in the face of postwar crime.

4 On the "real of violence," see Aretxaga, "Violent Spectres."

5 Drawing on Zulaika and Douglass, Aretxaga argues that what is copied is not terrorism but a fantasy of terrorism. Like the savage, the terrorist exists in a fantasized form as the "other" of an imaginary relation, which is to say as a collective representation ("A Fictional Reality," 60). Fantasy, in its Freudian sense, is not a purely illusory construction but is a form of reality in its own right, a scene whose structure traverses the boundary between the conscious and the unconscious (Aretxaga, *States of Terror*, 106). Fantasy has no "owner" or subject—it is a technique of The Real irrupting into the Symbolic order.

6 Horkheimer and Adorno use the term "organized mimesis" to think about the co-optation of mimesis as a function of alterity by fascism; that is, not as outright repression but as organized control of mimesis (*Dialectic of Enlightenment*, 148). Building on this notion of "organized mimesis," Aretxaga speaks of the "disorganized and fantastic character of organized mimesis" to discuss "the organized copy of terrorism by the state to eliminate terrorism" ("A Fictional Reality," 60).

7 The cultural argument unleashed by the Rosa N. case is a perfect example of what Aretxaga explored as a "mirroring paranoid dynamic," where the accusations do not face in one direction ("Maddening States," 399–402). For a discussion of the role of the relationship between rumor and magical realism in violence in Colombia, see Taussig, *Shamanism, Colonialism, and the Wild Man*, 8.

8 Like Anderson's use of "imagined," in my use of "fantastic" I do not mean "un-

real." Aretxaga speaks of the "structure of fantasy" as a reality that transcends a concrete individual to become a social fact to demarcate the space of the real ("Violent Specters," 12). That said, neither am I presenting the details of Lin's testimony as fact. Indeed, I rather suspect Lin had me pegged and told me his story in terms he knew I would understand. Truth or fantasy, honesty or manipulation, what is of interest here are the forms of emplotment by which Lin structures his narrative.

9 As Derrida notes, "Every age has its scenography" and its own "theatre of ghosts" (*Specters of Marx*, 119).

10 For a discussion of the "production of a culprit," see Aretxaga, "Violent Specters," 28–32.

11 These are the structures that were supposedly dismantled under the conditions of the Peace Accords of 1992. See chapter 5 for a discussion of the disbanding of the extant public security system.

12 The teacher's union, ANDES, was an important political formation of the Left in the period leading up to the civil war. It remains active in contemporary El Salvador.

13 When I last saw Amanda she was living in San Salvador and had become a committed evangelical Christian. Amanda had always been a bit of a rebel and critical of society around her. She said that her conversion to Christianity helped her with her earlier frustrations and finally had given her some peace.

14 For studies of Salvadoran immigrant hometown associations, see Lungo and Kandel, *Transformando El Salvador*; Landolt, Autler, and Baires, "From Hermano Lejano to Hermano Mayor"; Baker-Cristales, *Salvadoran Migration to Southern California*; and Hamilton and Chinchilla, *Seeking Community in a Global City*.

15 UNHCR, "Guidance Note on Refugee Claims Relating to Victims of Organized Gangs."

16 WOLA, *Central American Gang-Related Asylum Guide*.

17 Aizenman, "More Immigrants Seeking Asylum Cite Gang Violence."

18 I allude here to Agamben, *State of Exception*.

19 See Cole and Dempsey, *Terrorism and the Constitution*.

20 Brown, "Legislating Repression," 6.

21 See Federman, "Who Has the Body?"

22 Ibid., 323.

23 The one exception is the purported recruitment of a Chicago gang by Libya in September 1989 to shoot down U.S. airliners with shoulder-fired missiles.

24 Farah, "Criminals, Jihadists Threaten U.S. Border."

25 McPhee, "Eastie Gang Linked to Al-Qaeda"; Seper, "Al Qaeda Seeks Tie to Local Gangs."

26 Gingrich, "American Gangs—Ties to Terror?"; Hayden, "Gingrich/Fox Invent Gangs/Terror Link."

27 Gingrich, "American Gangs—Ties to Terror?"

28 See Wilson and Sullivan, "On Gangs, Crime, and Terrorism."

29 Wilson and Sullivan, "On Gangs, Crime, and Terrorism," 1. The stated aim of Defense and the National Interest is to "foster debate on the roles of the U.S. armed forces in the post–Cold War era and on the resources devoted to them. The ultimate purpose is to help create a more effective national defense against the types of threats we will likely face during the first decades of the new millennium. Contributors to this site are, with a few exceptions, active/reserve, former, or retired military. They often combine a knowledge of military theory with the practical experience that comes from trying their ideas in the field. As you browse our site, please pay particular attention to the e-mails from our deployed forces in such places as Kosovo, Bosnia, Afghanistan, Iraq and other Middle Eastern Countries" (http://d-n-i.net).

30 Wilson and Sullivan, "On Gangs, Crime, and Terrorism," 13.

31 See Manwaring, "Street Gangs."

32 García, "N.Y. Using Terrorism Law to Prosecute Street Gang."

33 On the "free-floating signifier," see Zulaika and Douglass, Terror and Taboo.

34 Wilson and Sullivan, "On Gangs, Crime, and Terrorism," 2.

35 Ibid., 16.

36 Hofstader in Marcus, Paranoia within Reason, 1.

37 Zulaika and Douglass, Terror and Taboo, 30.

38 See United States Immigrations and Custom Enforcement, "Operation Community Shield."

39 NationalTerrorAlert.com describes itself as "a private homeland security blog and not affiliated with any government agency" that archives and comments on "homeland security related news items from a variety of news sources, as well as provide[s] immediate updates on breaking stories, bulletins and any change in status to Homeland Security advisory."

40 Domash, "America's Most Dangerous Gang."

41 Garfield, "Gang Scare."

42 This show followed the release of a study by the Justice Policy Institute in July 2007. The study, entitled "Gang Wars: The Failure of Enforcement Tactics and the Need for Effective Public Safety Strategies," counters the prevailing common sense about the rise of gang membership, the racial makeup of gangs, the degree to which gangs are involved in the drug trade and responsible for the national crime rate, as well as the permanence of gang membership (Greene and Pranis, Gang Wars).

43 Since its inception, ICE agents across one hundred field offices, working in conjunction with hundreds of federal, state, and local law enforcement agencies nationwide, have arrested a total of 7,655 street gang members and associates,

representing over 700 different gangs (United States Immigrations and Custom Enforcement, "Operation Community Shield").

44 Jean Comaroff and John Comaroff study what they call the South African "fictional economy of representation." A similar "metaphysics of disorder" that feeds "criminal obsessions" in the South African postcolony ("Criminal Obsessions") also appears to be at work in both El Salvador and the United States.

45 Garfield, "Gang Scare."

46 For analysis of Salvadoran media coverage of gangs, see Marroquin, "Indiferencias y espantos"; Martel, "Las maras salvadoreñas"; and Moodie, "Wretched Bodies, White Marches, and the *Cuatro Visión* Public in El Salvador."

47 In 2007, Salvadoran media outlets signed a public accord, "Medios Unidos por La Paz" (Media United for Peace), agreeing to reduce sensationalist coverage of violence in recognition of the media's role in generating more violence. Interestingly, in 2009 after the FMLN candidate Mauricio Funes was sworn in as the first Salvadoran president, media coverage of violence and gangs increased significantly. While it would take a serious content analysis of the Salvadoran media to corroborate such a claim, many on the Left felt that this was an intentional effort of the part of the right-wing-owned media to undermine Funes popularity with the Salvadoran public.

48 This was not the first time someone who I knew had been killed. But the proximity of our first meeting and his murder was particularly agonizing. After three years of grappling with the timing and meaning of his death, I learned from sources close to him that by the time he was killed, the pastor had, it seemed, resumed his activity in the gang when he was killed. Whether his activity was a desperate attempt to replace the funding for the project he had been working on which had come to an end or whether it was an indication that he had only masqueraded as a pastor in order to receive those funds, or something else altogether, I cannot say.

49 See Mulvey, *Visual and Other Pleasures*.

50 Blanchard, "Post-Bourgeois Tattoo," 295.

51 See Peterson, "Remains Out of Place."

52 Tattoos can be mobilized as marks of "predatory identities whose social construction and mobilization require the extinction of the other" (Appadurai, *Fear of Small Numbers*, 53).

53 Phillips, "Make It Last Forever," 15, 36.

54 On "street" to "decent," see Anderson, *Code of the Street*.

55 See Caldeira, "Remaking Walls and Inequality."

56 Marlon Carranza, interview with the author, September 2006.

57 Thus, in working to highlight the differences between them and us, Súper Mano Dura inaugurated "a new economy of slippage and morphing" (Appadurai, *Fear of Small Numbers*) and "an abundance of shadows" (Ferguson, *Global Shadows*).

58 Derrida, *Specters of Marx*, 116.

59 I am grateful to Brandt Peterson for his insights into Mano Dura through the lens of the events of 1932 and with it the echoes between *el indio* and *el marero* despite their considerable divergences.

CONCLUSION *Hall of Mirrors*

1 Many people assume that it was based on the USA PATRIOT Act. Presumably, ARENA knew that they would minimize the resistance to the law if they drew upon a model from a communist country. That said, there is a great deal in common between Cuban and U.S. antiterrorist legislation (Hernandez-Reguant, "The Migrant as Terrorist").

2 According to *The Board*, a blog by the editorial writers of the *New York Times*, even though the Bush administration reported forty-nine nations, there were actually only forty-five (*New York Times* Editorial Board, "President Bush's 'Coalition of the Willing'").

3 See Lovato, "The War for Latinos"; Mariscal, "Homeland Security, Militarism, and the Future of Latinos and Latinas in the United States"; Flores, *A Piece of the American Dream*; and Amaya, "Dying American."

4 See Harman, "Firms Tap Latin America for Iraq," for a discussion of how Salvadoran police are leaving their jobs to take higher-paying positions in private security in Iraq with American contracting firms.

5 See n. 80 in the introduction to this volume for a discussion of "the protection racket" and the "global military-gift economy."

6 Tim's El Salvador Blog, "Election Meddling."

7 See Rose, *States of Fantasy*.

8 For a useful discussion of "doing in spite of knowing," see Navarro-Yashin's study of the role of cynicism in Turkish politics. As Navarro-Yashin notes, Slavoj Žižek borrows from Lacan's psychoanalytic symptom to explore the question of why, in spite of its interpretation, the symptom does not dissolve but rather persists (Žižek, *The Sublime Object of Ideology*, 74; Navarro-Yashin, *Faces of the State*, 159–60).

9 Indeed, fantasy is productive in the Foucauldian sense—this despite Foucault's focus on the rationality of the disciplinary apparatus and governmentality to the exclusion of fantasy (see Aretxaga, *Shattering Silence*).

10 Aretxaga, "Maddening States," 145. This eerie sensation of reality invaded by fictional portrayals has been explored at length in Hollywood movies about the Arab terrorist. Aretxaga argues that we are in a moment of what Derrida (*Specters of Marx*) has called a "phantomatic mode of production"—a mode in which we are caught between the production and actualization of mirroring phantoms (Islamist and Western terrorisms), where fantasies organize reality as fear and thrill. In speaking of the footage of the attacks on the Twin Towers, she states: "The very

familiarity of the scene, already seen in popular Hollywood disaster movies, made reality unreal and shocking. It was not that a terrorist attack on the United States was unimaginable, it had in fact been imagined to satiety in films like *Independence Day*" (*States of Terror*, 270–75). See also Davis, who argues in "Flames of New York" that the attacks were a perfect example of Freud's "uncanny effect" which is produced "when the distinction between imagination and reality is effaced, as when something that we have hitherto regarded as imaginary appears before us in reality" (Freud in Davis, 38).

11 On "punctured porous," see Taussig, *Mimesis and Alterity*, 251.

12 I allude here to Siegel, *A New Criminal Type in Jakarta*.

13 Aretxaga, "A Fictional Reality," 64.

14 Feldman, "Securocratic Wars of Public Safety," 330, 346–48, and *Formations of Violence*, 191.

15 See Weldes et al., *Cultures of Insecurity*.

EPILOGUE *Impressions from a Political Present*

1 Obama, "President Obama's Inaugural Speech."

2 Sweet, "Colin Powell Endorses Barack Obama on NBC's 'Meet the Press.'"

3 Ayuso and Hursthouse, "¿Cambio? Latin America in the Era of Obama."

4 See Hursthouse and Ayso, "¿Cambio? The Obama Administration in Latin America."

5 See Garrett, "The Funes Inauguration."

6 Williams, "Dominant, Residual, Emergent" in *Marxism and Literature*, 121–27.

7 Habermas, "Consciousness-Raising or Redemptive Criticism," 56–57.

8 Enacted in 1970 as part of Richard Nixon's Crime Bill, RICO was first intended to root out the Mafia, but its application has since become considerably more widespread.

9 The defense also noted that Flores's testimony leaves out the portion of the transcript in which one of the MS gang members on the phone call tells Alex to "stay out of it" since he "is not active" any more. Upon cross-examination, Flores explains to the defense that he did not find this relevant to his determination that Alex was a "shot caller" for the gang.

10 Hayden, "At the Alex Sanchez Trial, a Window onto the Global War on Gangs."

11 Federal Bureau of Investigation, "Twenty-Four Defendant Indictment Names Members and Leaders of Notorious MS-13 Gang."

12 See Anderson and Jackson, "Law as a Weapon."

13 This analysis was subsequently published in an article by Hayden entitled "Has Bratton's LAPD Really Reformed?"

14 Pine, "Honduras' Porfirio 'Pepe' Lobo."

15 Hayden, "Bratton's exit opens the door to questions of conflict of interest."

16 See Altegrity's Web site, http://www.altegrity.com/.

17 See also Hayden, "Bratton's exit opens the door to questions of conflict of interest."

18 See Mittrany, "Medios de El Salvador unidos contra la violencia."

19 While it would take a serious content analysis study of the Salvadoran media to
corroborate such a claim, many on the Left felt this was an intentional effort on
the part of the right-wing-owned media to undermine Funes's popularity with the
Salvadoran public. Certainly the incoming president Funes and the outgoing president Saca occupied very different positions with respect to mainstream media in
El Salvador: Funes had been fired for his investigative, hard-hitting current affairs
TV show; the outgoing president, Antonio Saca, was a prominent media mogul.

20 Witte-Lebhar, "El Salvador."

21 During Schwarzenegger's term as governor, the California prison population increased from 160,000 in 2004 to 170,973 in by the end of 2009. The corrections
budget grew from 5 percent of the general fund to more than 10 percent during
the same period (Petersila, "A Retrospective View of Corrections Reform in the
Schwarzenegger Administration," 148–53).

22 A federal judge installed a receiver in 2006 to oversee inmate health care in California state prisons, finding that substandard care led to the death of about one
prisoner per week (Moore, "Court Orders California to Cut Prison Population").

23 Tumlin, Joaquin, and Natarajan, "A Broken System," vi.

24 Roberts, "Immigration Detention Facilities to Become Less Like Prisons." Undocumented entry into the United States is a civil not criminal offense; three-
fifths of detainees have no criminal record.

25 Obama, "Remarks by the President on Comprehensive Immigration Reform," n.p.

26 See De Genova, "Antiterrorism, Race, and the New Frontier."

27 Cornel West in Smith, Twilight, 105.

28 Funes did not support the FMLN's position that El Salvador should join Alianza
Bolivariana para los Pueblos de Nuestra América (the Bolivarian Alliance for the
Peoples of Our America, or ALBA), the Venezuelan- and Cuban-initiated alternative to neoliberal trade agreements. In 2004, Venezuela and Cuba initiated the now
eight-member ALBA group to create a mechanism of international trade based on
mutual benefit and cooperation rather than profit and the free market. Current
member states include Bolivia, Cuba, Nicaragua, and Venezuela. In October 2009
leaders from ALBA agreed to create an autonomous regional currency, much like
the Euro. This unit, the sucre, was due to be implemented in 2010.

29 For a discussion of the respective "power blocs" or cross-class coalitions brought
together under Obama and Funes, see Winant, "Just Do It"; and Garret, "The
Funes Inauguration."

30 I allude here to Williams, "Dominant, Residual and Emergent" in Marxism and Literature.

31 James Faubion on Raymond Williams (Rabinow and Marcus, *Designs for an Anthropology of the Contemporary*, 93–94).

32 The "Joshua Generation," as Howard Winant notes, is a term invoked by Obama in a convocation address he gave to students at Howard University in 2007: "Everyone in this room stands on the shoulders of many Moseses. They are the courageous men and women who marched and fought and bled for the rights and freedoms we enjoy today. They have taken us many miles over an impossible journey. But you are members of the Joshua Generation. And it is now up to you to finish the work that they began. It is up to you to cross the river" (Obama in Winant, "Just Do It," 50).

33 See Portillo, "Although I Wasn't There, I Remember."

34 Pacific Rim Mining Corporation is a Canadian company with subsidiaries in the United States and El Salvador, including Pac Rim Cayman LLC, Pacific Rim El Salvador, S.A. de C.V., and Dorado Exploraciones, S.A. de C.V. In June 2008, more than one thousand protestors shut down Pacific Rim's El Dorado gold mining project by arguing that it would divert thirty thousand liters of water from surrounding agricultural communities. The murders of six environmental activists, although as yet unprosecuted, were widely thought to be linked to gold mining in the region (CISPES, NACLA, and Upside Down World, "The 2009 Salvadoran Elections").

35 Kathleen Stewart speaks of the need for a speculative and concrete attunement in order to discern not whether things are "going well" but that things "*are* going": "The world is still tentative, charged, overwhelming, and alive" (*Ordinary Affects*, 128).

Abelmann, Nancy, and John Lie. *Blue Dreams: Korean Americans and the Los Angeles Riots.* Cambridge: Harvard University Press, 1995.

Abraham, Itty, and Willen van Schendel. "The Making of Illicitness." In *Illicit Flows and Criminal Things: States, Borders, and the Other Side of Globalization*, ed. Willen van Schendel and Itty Abraham, 1–37. Bloomington: Indiana University Press, 2005.

Abramsky, Sasha. *American Furies: Crime, Punishment and Vengeance in the Age of Mass Imprisonment.* Boston: Beacon, 2007.

Adorno, Theodor W. *Aesthetic Theory.* Trans. C. Lenhardt. London: Routledge and Kegan Paul, 1984.

Agamben, Giorgio. *State of Exception.* Trans. Kevin Attell. Chicago: University of Chicago Press, 2003.

Agee, James, and Walker Evans. *Let Us Now Praise Famous Men.* Boston: Houghton Mifflin Company, 1941.

Aguayo, Sergio, Agustín Irigoyen, and Miguel Angel Velásquez. *El éxodo centroaméricano: consecuencias de un conflicto.* Mexico D.F.: Secretaría de Educación Pública, 1985.

Aguilar, Jeanette. "El manodurismo y las 'politicas' de seguridad." In *El plan mano dura y la ley antimaras (Discusión no. 20)*. San Salvador: Asociación Bienestar Yek Ineme, 2004.

Aizenman, N. C. "More Immigrants Seeking Asylum Cite Gang Violence." *Washington Post*, November 15, 2006.

Alberto Amaya, Edgardo. "Security Policies in El Salvador, 1992–2002." In *Public Security and Police Reform in the Americas*, ed. John Bailey and Lucía Dammert, 132–47. Pittsburgh: University of Pittsburgh Press, 2006.

Alvarenga, Patricia. *Cultura y etica de la violencia: El Salvador 1880–1932.* San Jose: Director General de Editorial Universitaria Centroamericana (EDUCA), 1996.

Alvarez, Robert. "The Mexican–U.S. Border: The Making of an Anthropology of Borderlands." *Annual Review of Anthropology* 24 (1995): 447–70.

Alvarez, Sonia E., Evelina Dagnino, and Arturo Escobar, eds. *Cultures of Politics, Politics of Cultures: Re-Visioning Latin American Social Movements*. Boulder, Colo.: Westview Press, 1998.

Amaya, Hector. "Dying American, or The Violence of Citizenship: Latinos in Iraq." *Latino Studies* 5 (2007): 3–24.

American Civil Liberties Union. "Civil Liberties in Crisis: Los Angeles during the Emergency." Los Angeles: ACLU Foundation of Southern California, 1992.

———. "False Premises, False Promise: The Blythe Street Gang Injunction and Its Aftermath." Los Angeles: ACLU Foundation of Southern California, 1997.

Amnesty International, United States of America. "Torture, Ill-Treatment and Excessive Force by Police in Los Angeles." Amnesty International, AMR 51/76/92, May 1992.

Amnesty International. El Salvador. "The Spectre of Death Squads." Amnesty International, AMR 20/015/96, December 1996.

Anderson, Benedict. *Imagined Communities: Reflections on the Origin and Spread of Nationalism*. Revised edn. London: Verso, 1991.

Anderson, Elijah. *Code of the Street: Decency, Violence and the Moral Life of the Inner City*. New York: W. W. Norton, 1999.

Anderson, Thomas. *Matanza*. Willimantic, Conn.: Curbstone Press, 1992.

Anderson, William L., and Candice E. Jackson. "Law as a Weapon: How RICO Subverts Liberty and the True Purpose of Law." *Independent Review* 9, no. 1 (summer 2004): 85–97.

Andrade-Eekhoff, Katherine. "Asociaciones salvadoreñas en Los Angeles y las posibilidades de desarrollo en El Salvador." In *Migración Internacional y Desarollo*, ed. Mario Lungo, 11–44. Vol. 2. San Salvador: Fundación Nacional para el Desarollo (FUNDE), 1997.

———. "Las asociaciones salvadoreños en Los Angeles y su rol para el desarrollo nacional." In *Migración internacional y desarollo*, ed. Mario Lungo. Vol. 2. San Salvador: Fundación Nacional para el Desarollo, 1997.

———. "Migración y capital social en El Salvador: Reflexiones con respecto a estado de la nación." In *Equidad y desarrollo social de informe de desarrollo humano en El Salvador*. San Salvador: Programa de Naciones Unidas para el Desarrollo, 2001.

Andrejevic, Mark. *Reality TV: The Work of Being Watched*. Lanham, Md.: Rowman and Littlefield, 2004.

Anzaldúa, Gloria. *Borderlands: The New Mestiza = La Frontera*. San Francisco: Spinsters/ Aunt Lute, 1987.

Appadurai, Arjun. "Disjuncture and Difference in the Global Cultural Economy." *Public Culture* 2, no. 2 (1990): 1–24.

———. *Fear of Small Numbers: An Essay on the Geography of Anger*. Durham: Duke University Press, 2006.

———. "Global Ethnoscapes: Notes and Queries for a Transnational Anthropology." In *Recapturing Anthropology*, ed. Richard Fox, 191–210. Seattle: University of Washington Press, 1991.

———. *Modernity at Large: Cultural Dimensions of Globalization*. Minneapolis: University of Minnesota Press, 1996.

———. "Patriotism and Its Futures." *Public Culture* 5, no. 3 (1993): 411–29.

———, ed. *The Social Life of Things: Commodities in Cultural Perspective*. Cambridge: Cambridge University Press, 1988.

Applebaum, Richard P., and William Robinson. *Critical Globalization Studies*. New York: Routledge, 2005.

Arana, Ana. "How the Street Gangs Took Central America." *Foreign Affairs* 84 (May/June 2005): 98–110.

Aretxaga, Begoña. "A Fictional Reality: Paramilitary Death Squads and the Construction of State Terror in Spain." In *Death Squad: The Anthropology of State Terror*, ed. Jeffrey A. Sluka, 46–69. Philadelphia: University of Pennsylvania Press, 1999.

———. "Maddening States." *Annual Review of Anthropology* 32 (2003): 393–410.

———. "Playing Terrorist: Ghastly Plots and the Ghostly State." *Journal of Spanish Cultural Studies* 1, no. 1 (2000): 43–58.

———. *Shattering Silence: Women, Nationalism, and Political Subjectivity in Northern Ireland*. Princeton: Princeton University Press, 1997.

———. *States of Terror: Begoña Aretxaga's Essays*, ed. Joseba Zulaika. Reno, Nev.: Center for Basque Studies, 2006.

———. "Terror as Thrill: First Thoughts on the 'War on Terrorism.'" *Anthropological Quarterly* 75, no. 1 (Winter 2002): 138–50.

———. "Violent Specters, or The Scene of Political Fantasy in a Small Place along the Pyrenees." Paper prepared for Fantasy Spaces: The Power of Images in a Globalizing World, Amsterdam, August 27–29, 1998.

Arias, Arturo. "Central American-Americans: Invisibility, Power and Representation in the US Latino World." *Latino Studies* 1 (2003): 168–87.

———. *Taking Their Word: Literature and the Signs of Central America*. Minneapolis: University of Minnesota Press, 2007.

Associated Press. "Officials: Al Qaeda, Latin Gangs Not Linked." February 24, 2004.

Ayuso, Tomás, and Guy Hursthouse. "¿Cambio? Latin America in the Era of Obama: An Early Reading on the Administration," February 3, 2010. Council on Hemispheric Affairs, http://www.coha.org.

Baires, Sonia. "Socio-Spatial Urban Transformations, Social Exclusion and Internal Borders in Central America." *Revista Centroamericana de Ciencias Sociales* 6, no. 1 (2008): 5–34.

Baker-Cristales, Beth. *Salvadoran Migration to Southern California: Redefining El Hermano Lejano*. Gainesville: University Press of Florida, 2004.

Bakhtin, Mikhail. "Epic and Novel." In *The Dialogic Imagination: Four Essays*. Ed. Michael Holquist. Trans. Caryl Emerson and Michael Holquist, 3–40. Austin: University of Texas Press, 1981.

———. "The Problem of Speech Genres." In *Speech Genres and Other Late Essays*. Ed. Michael Holquist and Caryl Emerson. Trans. Vern W. McGee, 60–102. Austin: University of Texas Press, 1986.

———. *Problems of Dostoevsky's Poetics*. Ed. and trans. Caryl Emerson. Minneapolis: University of Minnesota Press, 1984.

Balmaceda, Gema Santamaría. "Maras y pandillas: Límites de su transnacionalidad." *Revista Mexicana de Política Exterior*, no. 81 (2007): 101–23.

Banks, Gaby. "The Tattooed Generation: Salvadoran Children Bring Home American Gang Culture." *Dissent* (Winter 2000): 22–29.

Barnes, Nielan. "Transnational Youth Gangs in Central America, Mexico and the United States." Report. Sponsored by the Center for Inter-American Studies and Programs at the Instituto Tecnológico Autónomo de México, the Ford Foundation, and the Kellogg Foundation, 2007.

Barthes, Roland. "Myth Today." In *Mythologies*, 109–58. New York: Hill and Wang, 1972.

Basch, Linda, Nina Glick Schiller, and Cristina Szanton Blanc. *Nations Unbound: Transnational Projects, Postcolonial Predicaments, and Deterritorialized Nation-States*. Langhorne, Pa.: Gordon and Breach, 1994.

Baudrillard, Jean. *The Mirror of Production*. St. Louis: Telos Press, 1975.

Baudrillard, Jean, and Charles Levin. *For a Critique of the Political Economy of the Sign*. St. Louis: Telos Press, 1981.

Bauman, Richard. "Genre" and "Performance." In *Folklore, Cultural Performances, and Popular Entertainments: A Communications-Centered Handbook*, 41–49, 53–59. New York: Oxford University Press, 1992.

Bauman, Richard, and Charles L. Briggs. "Genre, Intertextuality, and Social Power." *Journal of Linguistic Anthropology* 2, no. 2 (1992): 131–72.

———. "Poetics and Performance as Critical Perspectives on Language and Social Life." *Annual Review of Anthropology* 19 (1990): 59–88.

Bauman, Zygmunt. *Globalization: The Human Consequences*. London: Verso, 1998.

Benjamin, Walter. *The Arcades Project*. Ed. Rolf Tiedemann. Trans. Howard Eiland and Kevin McLaughlin. Cambridge: The Belknap Press of Harvard University Press, 1999.

———. *Illuminations*. Ed. Hannah Arendt. Trans. Harry Zohn. New York: Schocken Books, 1969.

———. "Paris of the Second Empire in Baudelaire." In *Charles Baudelaire: Lyric Poet of High Capitalism*, 9–106. London: New Left Books, 1973.

————. *Reflections: Walter Benjamin, Essays, Aphorisms, Autobiographical Writings*. Ed. Peter Demetz. Trans. Edmund Jephcott. New York: Schocken Books, 1978.

Berger, John. *A Seventh Man: Migrant Workers in Europe*. New York: Viking Press, 1975.

Bergson, Henri. *Matter and Memory*. Trans. Nancy Margaret Paul and W. Scott Palmer. New York: Zone Books, 1988.

Berlant, Lauren. "Nearly Utopian, Nearly Normal: Post-Fordist Affect in La Promesse and Rosetta." *Public Culture* 19, no. 2 (2007): 273–301.

————. *The Queen of America Goes to Washington City: Essays on Sex and Citizenship*. Durham: Duke University Press, 1997.

Bernstein, Nina. "City of Immigrants Fills Jail Cells with Its Own." *New York Times*, December 26, 2008.

Berrigan, Frieda, and John Wingo. "US Military Involvement in Latin America: Guns, No Butter." *Signs of the Times in the Americas* 1, no. 1 (spring 2006): http://www.sicsal-usa.org.

Betancur, Belisario, Reinaldo Figueredo Planchandt, and Thoma Buergenthal. "From Madness to Hope: The 12-Year War in El Salvador. Report of the Truth Commission for El Salvador." New York: United Nations Publications, 1992.

Bhabha, Homi. *Nation and Narration*. New York: Routledge, 1990.

Blanchard, Marc. "Lost in America." *Cultural Anthropology* 7, no. 4 (1992): 496–507.

————. "Post-Bourgeois Tattoo: Reflection on Skin Writing in Late Capitalist Societies." In *Visualizing Theory: Selected Essays from V.A.R., 1990–1994*, ed. L. Taylor. New York: Routledge, 1994.

Bohannan, Paul. "Some Principles of Exchange and Investment Among the Tiv." *American Anthropologist* 57 (1955): 60–70.

Bourdieu, Pierre. *Distinction: Social Critique of the Judgement of Taste*. Trans. Richard Nice. Cambridge: Harvard University Press, 1984.

————. *Outline of a Theory of Practice*. Trans. Richard Nice. Cambridge: Cambridge University Press, 1977.

Bourgois, Philippe. "The Continuum of Violence in War and Peace: Post-Cold War Lessons from El Salvador." In *Violence in War and Peace: An Anthology*, ed. Nancy Scheper-Hughes and Philippe Bourgois, 425–34. Oxford: Blackwell, 2004.

————. *In Search of Respect: Selling Crack in El Barrio*. Cambridge: Cambridge University Press, 1995.

Boyer, Peter. "Bad Cops." *New Yorker*, May 21, 2001, 60–77.

Bran, Sergio. "Violencia, cultura, inseguridad publica en El Salvador." *Realidad: Revista de Ciencias Sociales y Humanidades* 64 (1998): 100.

Brenner, Neil, and Nik Theodore. *Spaces of Neoliberalism: Urban Restructuring in North America and Western Europe*. Oxford: Blackwell, 2003.

Bright, Brenda. "Remappings: Los Angeles Low Riders." In *Looking High and Low: Art and Cultural Identity*, ed. Brenda Jo Bright and Elizabeth Bakewell, 89–123. Tucson: University of Arizona Press, 1995.

Brimelow, Peter. "Time to Rethink Immigration: The Decline of the Americanization of Immigrants." *National Review* 44 (1992): 30–46.

Brotherton, David C., and Luis Barrios. *The Almighty Latin King and Queen Nation: Street Politics and the Transformation of a New York City Gang.* New York: Columbia University Press, 2004.

Brown, C. Stone. "Legislating Repression: The Federal Crime Bill and the Anti-Terrorism and Effective Death Penalty Act." In *Criminal Injustice,* ed. Elihu Rosenblatt, 100–107. Cambridge, Mass.: South End Press, 1996.

Brown, Wendy. "Neoliberalism and the End of Liberal Democracy." *Theory and Event* 7, no. 1 (2003): 1–21.

Browning, David. *El Salvador: Landscape and Society.* Oxford: Clarendon Press, 1971.

Buck-Morss, Susan. *The Dialectics of Seeing: Walter Benjamin and The Arcades Project.* Cambridge: MIT Press, 1993.

Bürger, Peter. "Benjamin's Concept of Allegory" and "Montage." In *Theory of the Avant-Garde,* 62–82. Minneapolis: University of Minnesota Press, 1984.

Cagan, Steve, and Beth Cagan. *This Promised Land: El Salvador.* New Brunswick: Rutgers University Press, 1991.

Cahn, Michael. "Subversive Mimesis: Theodor W. Adorno and the Modern Impasse of Critique." In *Mimesis in Contemporary Theory: An Interdisciplinary Approach,* ed. Mihai Spariosu, 1:27–64. Philadelphia: John Benjamin's Publishing Company, 1984.

Caldeira, Teresa. *City of Walls: Crime, Segregation, and Citizenship in Sao Paulo.* Berkeley: University of California Press, 2000.

———. "'I Came to Sabotage Your Reasoning!' Violence and Resignification of Justice in Brazil." In *Law and Disorder in the Postcolony,* ed. Jean Comaroff and John L. Comaroff, 102–49. Chicago: University of Chicago Press, 2006.

———. "Remaking Walls and Inequality: Graffiti and Pichações in São Paulo." Paper presented at the annual meeting of the American Anthropological Association, Washington, D.C., November 28, 2007.

Calhoun, Craig, ed. *Habermas and the Public Sphere.* Cambridge: MIT Press, 1992.

Call, Charles. *Constructing Justice and Security after War.* Washington: United States Institute of Peace, 2007.

———. "Democratization, War and State-Building: Constructing the Rule of Law in El Salvador." *Journal of Latin American Studies* 35, no. 4 (2003): 827–62.

———. "From Soldiers to Cops: 'War Transitions' and the Demilitarization of Policing in Latin America and the Caribbean." Ph.D. dissertation, Stanford University, 1999.

———. "Policing the New World Order." *Strategic Forum* 84 (October 1996): 1–4.

Call, Charles, and William Stanley. "Protecting the People: Public Security Choices after Civil Wars." *Global Governance* 7, no. 2 (2001): 151–71.

Campbell, Greg, and Joel Dyer. "Death by Deportation: A Denver Judge Denied a

16-Year-Old's Political Asylum Application—and Sentenced Him to Death." *Boulder Weekly*, May 27, 2004.

Cannon, Lou. "LAPD Confidential: America's Most Infamous Police Department Is in Trouble Again, Devastated by This Corrupt Cop's Confessions." *New York Times Magazine*, October 1, 2000, 32–66.

———. *Official Negligence: How Rodney King and the Riots Changed Los Angeles*. Boulder, Colo.: Westview Press, 1999.

Caraval, Doreen. "Salvador Helps Refugees Filing for Asylum in U.S." *New York Times*, October 27, 1995.

Carpignano, Paolo, Robin Andersen, Stanley Aronowitz, and William DiFazio. "Chatter in the Age of Electronic Reproduction: Talk Television and the 'Public Mind.'" In *The Phantom Public Sphere*, ed. Bruce Robbins, 93–120. Minneapolis: University of Minnesota Press, 1993.

Casey, Edward S. *Remembering: A Phenomenological Study*. Bloomington: Indiana University Press, 1987.

Central American Refugee Center (CARECEN). "Report on Civil Rights and Human Rights Violations during the Post–Los Angeles Riot." Los Angeles: CARECEN, 1992.

Centre for Contemporary Cultural Studies (CCCS). *The Empire Strikes Back: Race and Racism in 70's Britain*. London: University of Birmingham, 1983.

Chambers, Ian. *Migrancy, Culture, Identity*. London: Routledge, 1994.

Chambers, Ross. *Room for Maneuver: Reading (the) Oppositional (in) Narrative*. Chicago: University of Chicago Press, 1991.

Chase, J., M. Crawford, and J. Kaliski. *Everyday Urbanism*. New York: Monacelli Press, 1999.

Chavez, Leo. *The Latino Threat: Constructing Immigrants, Citizens, and the Nation*. Stanford: Stanford University Press, 2008.

Chavez, Leo, Richard Flores, and Marta Lopez-Garza. "Migrants and Settlers: A Comparison of Undocumented Mexicans and Central Americans in the United States." *Frontera Norte* 1 (1989): 49–75.

Chesluk, Ben. *Money Jungle: Imagining the New Times Square*. New Brunswick: Rutgers University Press, 2007.

———. "Visible Signs of a City Out of Control: Community Policing in New York City." *Cultural Anthropology* 19, no. 2 (2004): 250–75.

Chinchilla, Norma, Nora Hamilton, and James Louckey. "Central Americans in Los Angeles: An Immigrant Community in Transition." In *The Barrios: Latinos and the Underclass Debate*, ed. Joan Moore and Raquel Pinderhughes, 51–78. New York: Russell Sage Foundation, 1993.

Cho, S. K. "Korean American vs. African American: Conflict and Construction." In *Reading Rodney King / Reading Urban Uprising*, ed. Robert Gooding-Williams, 196–211. New York: Routledge, 2000.

CISPES, NACLA, and Upside Down World. "The 2009 Salvadoran Elections: Between Crisis and Change." North American Congress on Latin America, January 2009. http://nacla.org.

Clifford, James. "Diasporas." *Cultural Anthropology* 9 (1994): 302–38.

———. *Routes: Travel and Translation in the Late Twentieth Century.* Cambridge: Harvard University Press, 1997.

———. "Spatial Practices." In *Anthropological Locations: Boundaries and Grounds of a Field Science*, 185–222. Berkeley: University of California Press, 1997.

———. "Traveling Cultures." In *Cultural Studies*, ed. Lawrence Grossberg, 96–116. New York: Routledge, 1992.

Clifford, James, and George Marcus, eds. *Writing Culture: The Poetics and Politics of Ethnography.* Berkeley: University of California Press, 1986.

Cohen, Stanley. *Folk Devils and Moral Panics: The Creation of the Mods and Rockers.* New York: St. Martin's Press, 1972.

Cole, David, and James Dempsey. *Terrorism and the Constitution: Sacrificing Civil Liberties in the Name of National Security.* New York: New Press, 2002.

Comaroff, Jean, and John L. Comaroff. "Criminal Obsessions, After Foucault: Postcoloniality, Policing, and the Metaphysics of Disorder." In *Law and Disorder in the Postcolony*, ed. Comaroff and Comaroff, 273–98. Chicago: University of Chicago Press, 2006.

———. Introduction to *Law and Disorder in the Postcolony*, ed. Comaroff and Comaroff, 1–56. Chicago: University of Chicago Press, 2006.

———, eds. *Law and Disorder in the Postcolony.* Chicago: University of Chicago Press, 2006.

———. "Millennial Capitalism: First Thoughts in a Second Coming." In "Millenial Capitalism and the Culture of Neoliberalism," special issue of *Public Culture* 12 (2000): 291–343.

Conquergood, Dwight. "Homeboys and Hoods: Gang Communication and Cultural Space." In *Group Communication in Context: Studies of Natural Groups*, ed. Larry Frey, 23–55. Hillsdale, N.J.: Lawrence Erlbaum, 1993.

Conquergood, Dwight, and Taggart Seigel. *The Heart Broken in Half.* Portland, Ore.: Collective Eye Distribution, 2007.

Cordova, C. B. "Central American Migration to San Francisco: One-Hundred Years of Building a Community." Paper presented at the conference Central Americans in California: Transnational Communities, Economies, and Cultures, sponsored by the Center for Multiethnic and Transnational Studies, University of Southern California, 1996.

Coronil, Fernando. "Transcultural Anthropology in the Américas (with an Accent)." In *Cuban Counterpoints: The Legacy of Fernando Ortiz*, ed. Mauricio A. Font and Alfonso W. Quiroz, 139–59. Lanham, Md.: Lexington Books, 2005.

Cortez, Beatriz. "Estética del cinismo: La ficción centroamericana de posguerra." *Ancora: Suplemento Cultural de La Nación*, March 11, 2001. http://www.nacion.com.

Costa, Gino. *La Policía Nacional Civil de El Salvador (1990–1997)*. San Salvador: Universidad Centroamericana José Simeón Cañas, 1999.

Court TV. *The Rodney King Case: What the Jurors Saw in California vs. Powell*. Oak Forest, Ill.: Court Television Network, 1992.

Coutin, Susan. "Cultural Logics of Belonging and Movement: Transnationalism, Naturalization, and U.S. Immigration Politics." *American Ethnologist* 30, no. 4 (2003): 508–26.

———. *The Culture of Protest: Religious Activism and the U.S. Sanctuary Movement*. Boulder, Colo.: Westview Press, 1993.

———. *Legalizing Moves: Salvadoran Immigrants' Struggle for U.S. Residency*. Ann Arbor: University of Michigan Press, 2000.

———. *Nation of Emigrants: Shifting Boundaries of Citizenship in El Salvador and the United States*. Ithaca: Cornell University Press, 2007.

———. "Suspension of Deportation Hearings: Racialization, Immigration, and 'Americanness.'" *Journal of Latin American Anthropology* 8, no. 2 (2003): 58–95.

Crawford, Margaret. "Contesting the Public Realm: Struggles over Public Space in Los Angeles." *Journal of Architectural Education* 49, no. 1 (September 1995): 4–9.

———. Introduction to *Everyday Urbanism*, ed. John Chase and John Kalisli, 8–35. New York: Monacelli Press, 1999.

Cruz, José Miguel. "Los Factores associados a las pandillas juveniles en Centroamérica." *ECA: Estudios Centroamericanos* 685–86 (2005): 1155–82.

———. "Los factores posibilitadores y las expresiones de la violencia en Los Noventa." *ECA: Estudios Centroamericanos* 52 (1997): 978–92.

———. *Street Gangs in Central America*. San Salvador: University of Central America Press, 2007.

———. "Violencia, democracia y cultura en America Latina." *ECA: Estudios Centroamericanos* 55 (2000): 511–25.

Cruz, José Miguel, Alvaro Trigueros Argüello, and Francisco González. *El crimen violento en El Salvador*. San Salvador: Instituto Universitario de Opinión Pública, 2000.

Cruz, José Miguel, and Marlon Carranza. "Pandillas y políticas públicas: El caso de El Salvador." In *Juventudes, violencia y exclusion: Desfíos papa las politicas públicas*, ed. Javier Moro. Guatemala: Magna Terra Editores, 2006.

Cruz, José Miguel, and Luis A. Gonzalez. "Magnitud de la Violencia en El Salvador." *ECA: Estudios Centroamericanos* 52 (1997): 953–66.

Cruz, José Miguel, and Portillo Peña. *Solidaridad y violencia en las pandillas del gran San Salvador: Más alla de la vida loca*. San Salvador: University of Central America Press, 1998.

Dávila, Arlene. *Barrio Dreams: Puerto Ricans, Latinos, and the Neoliberal City*. Berkeley: University of California Press, 2004.

Davis, Mike. "Beyond Blade Runner: Urban Control. The Ecology of Fear." *Open Magazine Pamphlet Series*, no. 23 (1992).

———. *City of Quartz: Excavating the Future in Los Angeles*. London: Verso, 1990.

———. "Flames of New York." *New Left Review* 12 (November–December 2001): 34–50.

———. "LA Intifada." *Social Text* 33 (1992): 19–33.

———. "LA Was Just the Beginning: Urban Revolt in the U.S." *Open Magazine Pamphlet Series*, no. 20 (1992).

———. *Magical Urbanism: Latinos Reinvent the US City*. London: Verso, 2000.

Dear, Michael. *The Postmodern Urban Condition*. Malden, Mass: Blackwell, 2000.

———. "The Premature Demise of Postmodern Urbanism." *Cultural Anthropology* 6, no. 4 (1991): 538–52.

Debord, Guy. "Theory of the Dérive." In *Situationist International Anthology*, ed. K. Knabb, 50–54. Berkeley: Bureau of Public Secrets, 1981.

de Certeau, Michel. *The Practice of Everyday Life*. Berkeley: University of California Press, 1984.

DeCesare, Donna. "The Children of War: Street Gangs in El Salvador." NACLA *Report on the Americas* 32, no. 1 (1998): 21–29.

DeCesare, Donna, and Fen Montaigne. "Deporting America's Gang Culture." *Mother Jones* (July 1, 1999), 44–51.

De Genova, Nicholas. " 'American' Abjection: 'Chicanos,' Gangs, and Mexican/Migrant Transnationality in Chicago." *Aztlan: A Journal of Chicano Studies* 33, no. 2 (Fall 2008): 141–74.

———. "Antiterrorism, Race, and the New Frontier: American Exceptionalism, Imperial Multiculturalism, and the Global Security State." *Identities* 17, no. 6 (2010): 613–40.

———. "Migrant 'Illegality' and Deportability in Everyday Life." *Annual Review of Anthropology* 31 (2002): 419–47.

———. "The Production of Culprits: From Deportability to Detainability in the Aftermath of 'Homeland Security.' " *Citizenship Studies* 11, no. 5 (2007): 421–48.

De Genova, Nicholas, and Nathalie Peutz, eds. *The Deportation Regime: Sovereignty, Space, and the Freedom of Movement*. Durham: Duke University Press, 2010.

De La Garza, R., Manuel Orozco, and Miguel Baraona. "Binational Impact of Latino Remittances." Los Angeles: Tomás Rivera Policy Institute, 1997.

Deleuze, Gilles, and Félix Guattari. *Anti-Oedipus: Capitalism and Schizophrenia*. Trans. Robert Hurley, Mark Seem, and Helen R. Lane. Minneapolis: University of Minnesota Press, 1983.

DeSipio, L. "Sending Money Home . . . For Now: Remittances and Immigrant Adaptation in the United States." Working paper. Washington: Inter-American Dialogue; Austin: Tomás Rivera Policy Institute, 2000.

Derrida, Jacques. *Specters of Marx: The State of the Debt, the Work of Mourning and the New International*. Trans Peggy Kamuf. New York: Routledge, 1994.

Deutsche, Rosalind. *Evictions: Art and Spatial Politics*. Chicago: Graham Foundation for Advanced Studies in the Fine Arts; Cambridge: MIT Press, 1996.

Dirlik, Arif. *The Postcolonial Aura: Third World Criticism in the Age of Global Capitalism*. Boulder, Colo.: Westview Press, 1997.

Domash, Shelly Feuer. "America's Most Dangerous Gang." *Police Magazine*, March 1, 2005. http://www.policeone.com.

Dow, Mark. *American Gulag: Inside US Immigration Prisons*. Berkeley: University of California Press, 2004.

Dumm, Thomas L. "The New Enclosures: Racism in the Normalized Community." In *Reading Rodney King / Reading Urban Uprising*, ed. Robert Gooding-Williams, 178–95. New York: Routledge, 1993.

Dunkerley, James. *Power in The Isthmus: A Political History of Modern Central America*. London: Verso, 1988.

Dunn, Timothy. *The Militarization of the U.S.–Mexico Border, 1978–1992: Low-Intensity Conflict Doctrine Comes Home*. Austin: Center for American Studies, 1996.

Durand, J. E., A. Parrado, and D. S. Massey. "Migradollars and Development: A Consideration of the Mexican Case." *International Migration Review* 30 (1996): 423–44.

Durham, William. *Scarcity and Survival in Central America: Ecological Origins of the Soccer War*. Stanford: Stanford University Press, 1979.

Eck J., and D. Rosenbaum. "The New Police Order: Effectiveness, Equity, and Efficiency in Community Policing." In *The Challenge of Community Policing: Testing the Promises*, ed. D. Rosenbaum, 3–23. Thousand Oaks, Calif.: Sage, 1994.

Economist. "Pulling Together?" May 9, 1992.

Equipo de Reflexión e Investigación (ERIC), Instituto de Encuestas y Sondeos de Opinión (IDESO), Instituto de Investigaciones Económicas y de Desarrollo (IDIES), Instituto de Opinión Pública (IUDOP). *Maras y pandillas en Centroamérica*. Vol. 1. Managua: UCA Publicaciones, 2001.

———, eds. *Maras y pandillas en Centroamérica*. Vol. 2. Managua: UCA Publicaciones, 2004.

ERIC, IDIES, IUDOP, and NITLAPAN-DIRINPRO, eds. *Mara y pandillas en Centroamérica: Political juveniles y rehabilitación*. Vol. 3. Managua: UCA Publicaciones, 2004.

Fagen, Patricia Weiss. "Central American Refugees and U.S. Policy." In *Crisis in Central America: Regional Dynamics and U.S. Policy in the 1980s*, ed. Jeffrey Frieden, Nora Hamilton, Linda Fuller, and Manuel Pastor. Boulder, Colo.: Westview Press, 1988.

Fairness and Accuracy in Reporting, Los Angeles. "Race, Lies and Videotape: Media Coverage of the Los Angeles Rebellion." Los Angeles: FAIR, 1992.

Farah, Joseph. "Criminals, Jihadists Threaten U.S. Border: Unholy Alliance of Terrorists, Gangs, Revolutionaries Pose New Security Risk." Joseph Farah's G2 Bulletin, January 17, 2005. http://www.worldnetdaily.com.

Federal Bureau of Investigation. "Twenty-Four Defendant Indictment Names Members and Leaders of Notorious MS-13 Gang, Alleging Federal Racketeering

Violations, Including Multiple Murders." Press release, June 24, 2009. http://
losangeles.fbi.gov.

Federman, Cary. "Who Has the Body? The Paths to Habeas Corpus Reform." *Prison Jour-nal* 84, no. 3 (September 24, 2004): 317–39.

Feldman, Allen. *Formations of Violence: The Narrative of the Body and Political Terror in North-ern Ireland.* Chicago: University of Chicago Press, 1991.

———. "On Cultural Anesthesia: From Desert Storm to Rodney King." *American Eth-nologist* 21, no. 2 (1994): 404–18.

———. "Secureaucatic Wars of Public Safety." *Interventions* 6, no. 3 (2004): 330–50.

Ferguson, James. *The Anti-Politics Machine: "Development," Depoliticization and Bureaucratic Power in Lesotho.* Cambridge: Cambridge University Press, 1990.

———. *Global Shadows: Africa in the Neoliberal World Order.* Durham: Duke University Press, 2006.

———. "Of Mimicry and Membership." *Cultural Anthropology* 17, no. 4 (2002): 551–69.

Ferguson, James, and Akhil Gupta. "Spatializing States: Toward an Ethnography of Neoliberal Governmentality." *American Ethnogologist* 29, no. 4 (2002): 981–1002.

Fernandez, James. *Persuasions and Performances: The Play of Tropes in Culture.* Bloomington: Indiana University Press, 1986.

Fernández de Castro, Rafael, and Gema Santamaría. "Demystifying the Maras." *Ameri-cas Quarterly* 1, no. 2 (fall 2007). http://www.americasquarterly.org.

Flores, Juan. "Latino Studies." In *Critical Latin American and Latino Studies*, ed. Juan Po-blete, 191–205. Minneapolis: University of Minnesota Press, 2003.

Flores, Paul. "A Piece of the American Dream" (video). http://jorgemariscal.blogspot.com.

Fortun, Kim. *Advocacy after Bhopal: Environmentalism, Disaster, New Global Orders.* Chicago: University of Chicago Press, 2001.

Foucault, Michel. *The Birth of Biopolitics: Lectures at the Collège de France, 1978–1979*, ed. Michel Snellart. New York: Palgrave Macmillan, 2007.

———. *Discipline and Punish: The Birth of the Prison.* Trans. Alan Sheridan. New York: Vintage Books, 1979.

———. *Power/Knowledge: Selected Interviews and Other Writings, 1972–1977.* Ed. and trans. Colin Gordon. New York: Pantheon Books, 1980.

———. "A Preface to Transgression." In *Language, Counter-Memory, Practice: Selected Essays and Interviews*, ed. Donald F. Bouchard, trans. D. Bouchard and Sherry Simon, 29–55. Ithaca: Cornell University Press, 1977.

Fraser, Nancy. "Rethinking the Public Sphere: A Contribution to the Critique of Actu-ally Existing Democracy." In *The Phantom Public Sphere*, ed. Bruce Robbins, 1–32. Minneapolis: University of Minnesota Press, 1993.

Freemon, Celeste. "View from Parker Center: A One-on-One with Police Chief Bill Bratton." *LA Weekly*, January 10–16, 2003.

Freire, Paulo. *Pedagogy of the Oppressed*. Trans. Myra Bergman Ramos. New York: Herder and Herder, 1970.

Frenzen, Niels, and Frank Acosta. "Immigrant's Roundup Was a Dirty Trick." *Los Angeles Times*, May 11, 1992.

Friedberg, Anne. *Window Shopping: Cinema and the Postmodern*. Berkeley: University of California Press, 1993.

Friedman, Jonathan. *Cultural Identity and Global Process*. Thousand Oaks, Calif.: Sage, 1994.

Fundación de Estudios para la Aplicacíon del Derecho (FESPAD). *Informe annual sobre la justicia penal juvenil, El Salvador*. San Salvador: FESPAD, 2005, 2006.

Funkhouser, E. "Remittances from International Migration: A Comparison of El Salvador and Nicaragua." *Review of Economics and Statistics* 7, no. 1 (1995): 137–46.

García, Michelle. "N.Y. Using Terrorism Law to Prosecute Street Gang." *Washington Post*, February 1, 2005.

García Canclini, Nestor. *Consumers and Citizens: Globalization and Multicultural Conflicts*. Minneapolis: University of Minnesota Press, 2001.

———. *Transforming Modernity: Popular Culture in Mexico*. Austin: University of Texas Press, 1993.

Garfield, Bob. "Gang Scare." On the Media from NPR, August 24, 2007. http://www.onthemedia.org.

Garret, Linda. "The Funes Inauguration." Center for Democracy in the Americas, trip report, May 31–June 3, 2009. http://www.democracyinamericas.org.

Geertz, Clifford. "Deep Play: Notes on the Balinese Cockfight," 412–54. In *The Interpretation of Cultures*. New York: Basic Books, 1973.

Gill, Lesley. *The School of the Americas: Military Training and Political Violence in the Americas*. Durham: Duke University Press, 2004.

Gilmore, Ruth Wilson. *Golden Gulag: Prisons, Surplus, Crisis, and Opposition in Globalizing California*. Berkeley: University of California Press, 2007.

Gingrich, Newt. "American Gangs—Ties to Terror?" *Fox News*, July 3, 2005.

Girard, Renee. *Violence and the Sacred*. Trans. Patrick Gregory. Baltimore: Johns Hopkins University Press, 1977.

Glick-Schiller, Nina, and Georges Fouron. "Everywhere We Go, We Are in Danger: Ti Manno and the Emergence of a Haitian Transnational Identity." *American Ethnologist* 17, no. 2 (1990): 329–47.

Glover, Scott, and Matt Lait. "Ex-Chief Refuses to Discuss Rampart." Street Gangs, August 23, 2003. http://www.streetgangs.com.

Goldberg, Theo. *Racist Culture: Philosophy and the Politics of Meaning*. London: Blackwell, 1993.

Goldstein, Daniel. *The Spectacular City: Violence and Performance in Urban Bolivia*. Durham: Duke University Press, 2004.

Gómez-Peña, Guillermo. *Warrior for Gringostroika*. St. Paul, Minn.: Graywolf Press, 1993.

Goodale, Mark. "Introduction to 'Anthropology and Human Rights in a New Key.'" *American Anthropologist* 108, no. 1 (2006): 1–8.

Gooding-Williams, Robert, ed. *Reading Rodney King / Reading Urban Uprising*. New York: Routledge, 1993.

Gordon, Edmund T. "Cultural Politics of Black Masculinity." *Transforming Anthropology* 6, nos. 1–2 (1997): 36–53.

———. *Disparate Diasporas: Identity and Politics in an African-Nicaraguan Community*. Austin: University of Texas Press, 1998.

Gramsci, Antonio. *Selections from the Prison Notebooks*. New York: International Publishers, 1992.

Grandin, Greg. *Empire's Workshop: Latin America, the United States and the Rise of the New Imperialism*. New York: Metropolitan Books, 2006.

Greene, Judith, and Kevin Pranis. *Gang Wars: The Failure of Enforcement Tactics and the Need for Effective Public Safety Strategies*. Washington: Justice Policy Institute.

Greenhouse, Linda. "Justices Permit Immigrants to Challenge Deportations." *New York Times*, June 26, 2001.

———. "Justices Place Limits on Detention in Cases of Deportable Immigrants." *New York Times*, June 29, 2001.

Gregory, Derek. *Geographical Imaginations*. Cambridge, Mass.: Blackwell, 1994.

Gregory, S. *Black Corona: Race and the Politics of Place in an Urban Community*. Princeton: Princeton University Press, 1998.

Grosfoguel, Ramón, Nelson Maldonado-Torres, and José David Saldívar. *Latin@s in the World-System: Decolonization Struggles in the 21st Century U.S. Empire*. Boulder, Colo.: Paradigm, 2005.

Guarnizo, Luis. "The Emergence of the Transnational Social Formation and the Mirage of Return Migration among Dominican Transmigrant." *Identities* 4, no. 2 (1996): 281–322.

———. "Going Home: Class, Gender, and Household Transformation among Dominican Return Migrants." In *Caribbean Circuits: New Directions in the Study of Caribbean Migration*, ed. Patricia Pessar, 13–60. New York: Center for Migration Studies, 1997.

Gupta, Akhil, and James Ferguson, eds. *Anthropological Locations: Boundaries and Grounds of a Field Science*. Berkeley: University of California Press, 1997.

———. "Beyond Culture: Space, Identity and the Politics of Difference." *Cultural Anthropology* 7, no. 1 (1992): 7–23.

Gusterson, Hugh. *People of the Bomb: Portraits of America's Nuclear Complex*. Minneapolis: University of Minnesota Press, 2004.

Habermas, Jürgen. "Consciousness-Raising or Redemptive Criticism: The Contemporaneity of Walter Benjamin." *New Left Review*, no. 17 (Spring 1979): 30–69.

Hagedorn, John. "Making Sense of Central America Maras." *Air and Space Power Journal*, May 27, 2008. http://www.airpower.maxwell.af.mil.

———. *A World of Gangs*. Minneapolis: University of Minnesota Press, 2008.

Hale, Charles R. "Cultural Politics of Identity in Latin America." *Annual Review of Anthropology* 26 (1997): 567–90.

———, ed. *Engaging Contradictions: Theory, Politics, and Methods of Activist Scholarship.* Berkeley: University of California Press, 2008.

Hall, Stuart. "Culture, Community, Nation." *Cultural Studies* 7, no. 3 (1993): 349–63.

———. "Gramsci's Relevance for the Study of Race and Ethnicity." *Journal of Communication Inquiry* 10 (1986): 5–27.

———. "The Local and the Global: Globalization and Ethnicity." In *Culture, Globalization and the World System: Contemporary Conditions for the Representation of Identity,* ed. Anthony King, 19–40. Binghamton: Department of Art History, State University of New York, 1991.

———. "New Ethnicities." In *Black Film, British Cinema (ICA Documents),* ed. Kobena Mercer, 27–31. London: Institute of Contemporary Arts, 1988.

———. "Old and New Identities, Old and New Ethnicities." In *Culture, Globalization and the World System,* ed. Anthony King, 41–61. Binghamton: Department of Art History, State University of New York, 1991.

———. "The Toad in the Garden: Thatcherism among the Theorists." In *Marxism and the Interpretation of Culture,* ed. Cary Nelson and Lawrence Grossberg, 35–57. Urbana: University of Illinois Press, 1988.

Hall, Stuart, Chas Critcher, Tony Jefferson, John Clarke, and Brian Roberts. *Policing the Crisis: Mugging, the State, and Law and Order.* New York: Holmes and Meier, 1978.

Hamilton, Nora, and Norma Stoltz Chinchilla. "Central American Migration: A Framework for Analysis." *Latin American Research Review* 26, no. 1 (1991): 75–110.

———. *Central Americans in California: Transnational Communities, Economies and Cultures.* Los Angeles: Center for Multiethnic and Transnational Studies, University of Southern California, 1996.

———. *Seeking Community in a Global City: Guatemalans and Salvadorans in Los Angeles.* Philadelphia: Temple University Press, 2001.

Haraway, Donna. "Situated Knowledges: The Science Question in Feminism and the Privilege of Partial Perspective." *Feminist Studies* 14, no. 3 (Autumn 1988): 575–99.

Harman, Danna. "Firms Tap Latin Americans for Iraq." *USA Today.* March 3, 2005. http://www.usatoday.com.

Harvey, David. *A Brief History of Neoliberalism.* Oxford: Oxford University Press, 2005.

———. *The Condition of Postmodernity: An Enquiry into the Origins of Cultural Change.* Oxford: Blackwell, 1989.

———. *Spaces of Global Capitalism: Towards a Theory of Uneven Geographical Development.* London: Verso, 2006.

Hayden, Tom. "At the Alex Sanchez Trial, a Window onto the Global War on Gangs." *Nation,* May 21, 2010.

———. "Bratton's exit opens the door to questions of conflict of interest." Op-ed, *Los Angeles Times,* August 13, 2009. http://articles.latimes.com.

———. "Gato and Alex: No Safe Place." *Nation*, June 22, 2000.

———. "Gingrich/Fox Invent Gangs-Terror Link." *Huffington Post*, June 25, 2005. http.//www.huffingtonpost.com.

———. "Has Bratton's LAPD Really Reformed?" *Nation*, July 7, 2009.

———. *Street Wars: Gangs and the Future of Violence*. New York: New Press, 2004.

Hayek, Friedrich. *The Road to Serfdom*. Pleasantville, N.Y.: Reader's Digest, 1944.

Herbert, Stephen. *Policing Space: Territoriality and the Los Angeles Police Department*. Minneapolis: University of Minnesota Press, 1997.

Hernandez-Reguant, Ariana. "The Migrant as Terrorist: US/Cuban Patriot Acts in the Elian Era." Paper presented at the conference Homelands, Borders, and Trade in Latin America: Freedom, Violence, and Exchange after 9–11, Center for Iberian and Latin American Studies, University of California, San Diego, February 25, 2005.

Heyman, Josiah, and Howard Campbell. "Recent Work on the U.S. Mexico Border." *Latin American Research Review* 39, no. 3 (October 2004): 205–20.

Hidalgo, Ellie. "Transforming L.A.—El Salvador's Gang Connection." *Tidings Online*. August 22, 2003. http://www.the-tidings.com.

Holston, James. "The Modernist City and the Death of the Street." In *Theorizing the City: The New Urban Anthropology Reader*, ed. Setha Low, 101–36. New Brunswick: Rutgers University Press, 1999.

Holston, James, and Arjun Appadurai. "Cities and Citizenship." *Public Culture* 8, no. 2 (1996): 187–204.

Horkheimer, Max, and Theodor W. Adorno. "The Culture Industry: Enlightenment as Mass Deception." In *Dialectic of Enlightenment*, 120–167. New York: Herder and Herder, 1972.

Huggins, Martha. *Political Policing: The United States and Latin America*. Durham: Duke University Press, 1998.

Hunt, D. M. *Screening the Los Angeles "Riots": Race, Seeing, and Resistance*. Cambridge: Cambridge University Press, 1997.

Hursthouse, Guy, and Tomás Ayso. "¿Cambio? The Obama Administration in Latin America: A Disappointing Year in Retrospective." Council on Hemispheric Affairs, January 26, 2010. http://www.coha.org.

Inda, Jonathan Xavier, and Renato Rosaldo, eds. *The Anthropology of Globalization: A Reader*. Oxford: Blackwell, 2002.

Instituto Universitario de Opinion de Pública (IUDOP). "Delincuencia y opinion pública." *ECA—Estudios Centroamericanos* 599 (1998): 785–802.

International Human Rights Clinic. "No Place to Hide: Gang, State and Clandestine Violence in El Salvador." Cambridge: Human Rights Program, Harvard Law School, February 2007.

Jameson, Fredric. 1981. *The Political Unconscious: Narrative as a Socially Symbolic Act*. Ithaca: Cornell University Press.

————. "Postmodernism, or The Cultural Logic of Late Capitalism." *New Left Review* 146 (1984): 53–92.

Justice for Janitors. "Low-Wage Workers March to Demand that Ueberroth and RLA Put People First!" Press advisory. December 1992.

Kahn, R. S. *Other People's Blood: U.S. Immigration Prisons in the Reagan Decade*. Boulder, Colo.: Westview Press, 1996.

Katz, C., and Neil Smith. "Uprising and Repression in L.A.: An Interview with Mike Davis by the Covert Action Bulletin." In *Reading Rodney King / Reading Urban Uprising*, ed. Robert Gooding-Williams, 142–54. New York: Routledge, 1993.

Katz, Michael. *The Undeserving Poor: From the War on Poverty to the War on Welfare*. New York: Pantheon Books, 1989.

Kearney, Michael. "Borders and Boundaries of State and Self at the End of Empire." *Journal of Historical Sociology* 4, no. 1 (1991): 52–73.

————. "From Invisible Hand to Visible Feet." *Annual Review of Anthropology* 15 (1986): 331–64.

————. "The Local and the Global: The Anthropology of Globalization and Transnationalism." *Annual Review of Anthropology* 24 (1995): 547–65.

————. *Reconceptualizing the Peasantry: Anthropology in Global Perspective*. Boulder, Colo.: Westview Press, 1996.

Kelling, George W., and James Q. Wilson. "Broken Windows: Police and Neighborhood Safety." *Atlantic Monthly* (March 1982): 29–38.

Kim, E. H. "Home Is Where the Han Is: A Korean-American Perspective on the Los Angeles Upheavals." In *Reading Rodney King / Reading Urban Uprising*, ed. Robert Gooding-Williams, 215–35. New York: Routledge, 1993.

Kim-Gibson, Dai Sil, and Christine Choy, dirs. *Sa-I-Gu: From Korean Women's Perspectives* (DVD). Produced by Dai Sil Kim-Gibson, Christine Choy, and Elaine Kim. San Francisco: Cross Current Media, 1993.

Kismaric, C. *Forced Out: The Agony of the Refugee in Our Time*. New York: Random House, 1989.

Klein, Malcolm, and Maxson, Cheryl. *Street Gangs: Patterns and Policies*. New York: Oxford, 2006.

Klein, Norman. *The History of Forgetting: Los Angeles and the Erasure of Memory*. New York: Verso, 1997.

Klima, Alan. *The Funeral Casino: Meditation, Massacre, and Exchange with the Dead in Thailand*. Princeton: Princeton University Press, 2002.

Kokotovich, Misha. "Neoliberal Noir: Contemporary Central American Crime Fiction as Social Criticism." CLUES: *A Journal of Detection* 24, no. 3 (2006): 15–29.

Labor/Community Strategy Center. "Reconstructing Los Angeles from the Bottom Up: Long-Term Strategy for Workers, Low-Income People and People of Color to Create an Alternative Vision of Urban Development." Los Angeles: Labor/Community Strategy Center, 1992.

Lacan, Jacques. *The Four Fundamental Concepts of Psycho-Analysis.* New York: W. W. Norton, 1981.

LaFeber, Walter. *Inevitable Revolutions: The United States in Central America.* New York: W. W. Norton, 1984.

Landolt, Patricia. "Salvadoran Economic Transnationalism: Embedded Strategies for Household Maintence, Immigrant Incorporation, and Entrepreneurial Expansion." *Global Networks* 1, no. 3 (2001): 217–41.

Landolt, Patricia, Lilian Autler, and Sonia Baires. "From Hermano Lejano to Hermano Mayor: The Dialectics of Salvadoran Transnationalism." *Ethnic and Racial Studies* 22, no. 2 (1999): 290–315.

Lane, Charles. "Justices Decide Immigrants Have Right to Review." *Washington Post,* June 26, 2001.

Lash, Scott, and John Urry. *The End of Organized Capitalism.* Madison: University of Wisconsin Press, 1987.

Leclerc, Gustavo, Raul Villa, and Michael J. Dear. *La Vida Latina in L.A.: Urban Latino Cultures.* London: Sage, 1999.

Lee, Ben. "Textuality, Mediation and Public Discourse." In *Habermas and the Public Sphere,* ed. Craig J. Calhoun, 402–20. Cambridge: MIT Press, 1992.

LeFebvre, Henri. *The Production of Space.* Trans. Donald Nicholson-Smith. Cambridge: Blackwell, 1994.

Lefort, Claude. *Democracy and Political Theory.* Trans. David Macey. Minneapolis: University of Minnesota Press, 1988.

———. *The Political Forms of Modern Society: Bureaucracy, Democracy, Totalitarianism,* ed. John B. Thompson. Cambridge: MIT Press, 1986.

Lerner, Jesse, and S. Sterling, dirs. *Natives.* New York: Filmmaker's Library, 1991.

Limbaugh, Rush. "Falling Down." *Premiere* 7, no. 1 (September 1993): 108.

Limon, Graciela. *In Search of Bernabé.* Houston: Arte Público Press, 1993.

Limón, José. *Dancing with the Devil.* Madison: University of Wisconsin Press, 1994.

Littledog, P. "Free Trade Blockade." *Texas Observer* (1993): 8–11.

Loach, Ken. *Bread and Roses.* London: Paralax, 1999.

Lomas, Laura. "The War Cut Out My Tongue: Domestic Violence, Foreign Wars and Translation in Demetria Martínez." *American Literature* 78, no. 2 (2006): 357–87.

Lomnitz, Claudio. "Decadence in Times of Globalization, Occasional Essay." *Cultural Anthropology* 9, no. 2 (1994): 257–67.

Lopez, David, Eric Popkin, and Edward Telles. "Central Americans at the Bottom, Struggling to Get Ahead." In *Ethnic Los Angeles,* ed. Roger Waldinger and Mehdi Bozoorgmehr, 279–304. New York: Russell Sage Foundation, 1996.

Lopez, Robert, and Ted Connell. "Troubled Corner." *Los Angeles Times,* November 18, 1996.

Los Angeles Times. "Why Ueberroth and Rebuild Los Angeles Must Not Fail." Op-ed. *Los Angeles Times,* November 2, 1992.

Lovato, Roberto. "Sensenbrenner Under Fire—Does Congressman Profit from Undocumented Labor?" *New America Media*, October 6, 2006.

———. "The War for Latinos." *Nation*, October 3, 2003.

Low, Setha. *On the Plaza: The Politics of Public Space and Cultures*. Austin: University of Texas Press, 2000.

Lowe, Lisa. *Immigrant Acts: On Asian American Cultural Politics*. Durham: Duke University Press, 1996.

Lowell, L., and Rodolfo O. De La Garza. "The Developmental Role of Remittances in U.S. Latino Communities and in Latin American Countries." Austin: Tomás Rivera Policy Institute, 2000.

Loxton, James. "Imperialism or Neglect: The Militarization of US Aid to Latin America Since 9/11." *Security and Citizenship Program Bulletin*, no. 1 (January 2007): 1–7.

Lucero, Jose Antonio. "On Feuds, Tumults, and Turns: Politics and Culture in Social Movement Theory." *Comparative Politics* 32, no. 2 (January 2000): 231–49.

Lungo, Mario, ed. *Migración internacional y desarollo*. San Salvador: Fundación Nacional para el Desarrollo, 1997.

Lungo, Mario, and Susan Kandel, eds. *Transformando El Salvador: Migración, sociedad y cultura*. San Salvador: Fundación Nacional para el Desarrollo, 1999.

Lynch, Kevin. *Image of the City*. Cambridge: MIT Press, 1960.

Lyons, William. *The Politics of Community Policing: Rearranging the Power to Punish*. Ann Arbor: University of Michigan, 2005.

Mahler, Sarah. *American Dreaming: Immigrant Life on the Margins*. Princeton: Princeton University Press, 1995.

———. "Theoretical and Empirical Contributions Toward a Research Agenda for Transnationalism." *Transnationalism from Below* 6 (1998): 64–102.

Malkki, Liisa. "Refugees and Exile: from 'Refugee Studies' to the National Order of Things." *Annual Review of Anthropology* 24 (1995): 495–523.

Mandel, Ernst. *Late Capitalism*. Trans. Joris De Bres. London: Verso, 1980.

Mandoki, Luis, dir. *Voces Inocentes / Innocent Voices*. Lawrence Bender Productions, 2004.

Mann, Eric. "Building the Anti-Racist, Anti-Imperialist United Front: Theory and Practice from the L.A. Strategy Center and Bus Riders Union." Labor/Community Strategy Center, 2008. http://www.thestrategycenter.org.

Manwaring, Max G. "Street Gangs: The New Urban Insurgency." Strategic Studies Institute, March 2005. http://www.carlisle.army.mil.

Marcus, George. "Ethnography in and of the World System: The Emergence of Multi-sited Ethnography." *Annual Review of Anthropology* 24 (1995): 95–117.

———. *Ethnography through Thick and Thin*. Princeton: Princeton University Press, 1998.

———. "Imagining the Whole: Ethnography's Contemporary Efforts to Situate Itself." *Critique of Anthropology* 9, no. 3 (1990): 7–30.

———, ed. *Paranoia within Reason: A Casebook on Conspiracy as a Theory of Explanation*. Chicago: University of Chicago Press, 1999.

————, ed. *Rereading Cultural Anthropology*. Durham: Duke University Press, 1992.

Marcus, George, and Michael Fischer. *Anthropology as Cultural Critique: An Experimental Moment in the Human Sciences*. Chicago: University of Chicago Press, 1986.

Mariscal, Jorge. "Homeland Security, Militarism, and the Future of Latinos and Latinas in the United States." In "Homeland Securities," special issue of *Radical History Review* 93 (fall 2005): 39–52.

Marquis, Christopher. "Ashcroft Seeks Return of Criminal Immigrants." *New York Times*, July 21, 2001.

Marroquin Parducci, Amparo. "Indiferencias y espantos: Relatos de los jóvenes de pandillas en la prensa escrita de Centroamérica." In *Los relatos periodísticos del crime*, ed. German Rey, 55–91. Bogotá: Centro de Competencia en Comunicación. Fundacíon Friedrich Ebert, 2007.

Martel Trigueros, Roxana. "Las maras salavadoreñas: Nuevas formas de espanto y contro social." *Estudios Centroamericanos* 61, no. 696 (2006): 957–79.

Martínez, Demetria. *Mother Tongue*. Tempe, Ariz.: Bilingual Press, 1994.

Martínez, Ruben. *The Other Side: Fault Lines, Guerrilla Saints, and the True Heart of Rock 'n' Roll*. London: Verso, 1992.

Masco, Joseph. "Active Measures; or, How a KGB Spymaster Made Good in Post-9/11 America." In "Homeland Securities," special issue of *Radical History Review* 93 (Fall 2005): 1–12.

May, Roy H. Jr. "Review of *From Madness to Hope: The 12-Year War in El Salvador*." The Christian Century Foundation, August 11, 1993.

Mbembe, Achille. "Necropolitics." *Public Culture* 15, no. 1 (2003): 11–40.

McPhee, Michele. "Eastie Gang Linked to Al-Qaeda." *Boston Herald*, January 5, 2005.

Menjívar, Cecilia. *Fragmented Ties: Salvadoran Immigrant Networks in America*. Berkeley: University of California Press, 2000.

Menjívar, Cecilia, and Néstor Rodríquez. *When States Kill: Latin America, the U.S., and Technologies of Terror*. Austin: University of Texas Press, 2005.

Miles, Jack. "Blacks vs. Browns: Immigration and the New American Dilemma." *Atlantic* 270 (1992): 41–68.

Mitchell, W. J. T. *Landscape and Power*. Chicago: University of Chicago Press, 2002.

Mittrany, Carola. "Medios de El Salvador unidos contra la violencia." Communidad Segura, March 4, 2007. http://www.comunidadesegura.org.br.

Molino, Anthony, ed. *Culture, Subject, Psyche: Dialogues in Psychoanalysis and Anthropology*. Middletown, Conn.: Wesleyan University Press, 2004.

Moodie, Ellen. "'It's Worse than the War': Telling Everyday Danger in Postwar San Salvador." Ph.D. dissertation, University of Michigan, 2002.

————. "Microbus Crashes and Coca-Cola Cash: The Value of Death in 'Free-Market' El Salvador." *American Ethnologist* 32, no. 1 (2006): 63–80.

————. "Wretched Bodies, White Marches, and the *Cuatro Visión* Public in El Salvador." *Journal of Latin American an Caribbean Anthropology* 12, no. 2 (2010): 382–404.

Montes, Segundo. *El Salvador 1989. Las remesas que envían los salvadoreños de Estados Unido: Consecuencias sociales y económicas.* San Salvador: Instituto de Investigaciones, Universidad Centroamericana José Simeón Cañas, 1990.

Montes, Segundo, and Juan José García Vasquez. "Desplazados y refugiados salvadoreños" (preliminary report). San Salvador: Universidad Centroamericana José Simeon Cañas, 1985.

————. *El Salvador 1987: Salvadoreños refugiados en Los Estados Unidos.* San Salvador: Instituto de Investigaciones, Universidad Centroamericana José Simeón Cañas, 1987.

————. "Salvadoran Migration to the United States: An Exploratory Study." Washington, D.C.: Hemispheric Migration Project, CIPRA, Georgetown University, 1988.

Moore, Solomon. "Court Orders California to Cut Prison Population." *New York Times,* February 6, 2010.

Mulvey, Laura. *Visual and Other Pleasures.* Bloomington: Indiana University Press, 1989.

Murray Li, Tania. *The Will to Improve: Governmentality, Development, and the Practice of Politics.* Durham: Duke University Press, 2007.

Mydans, Seth. "Criticism Grows over Aliens Seized During Riots." *New York Times,* May 29, 1992.

National Geographic. "World's Most Dangerous Gang." National Geographic Explorer Series, 2006.

Navarrette, Ruben Jr. "Should Latinos Support Curbs on Immigrants?" *Los Angeles Times,* July 5, 1992.

Navarro-Yashin, Yael. *Faces of the State: Secularism and Public Life in Turkey.* Princeton: Princeton University Press, 2002.

Nelson, Cary, and Lawrence Grossberg, eds. *Marxism and The Interpretation of Culture.* Urbana: University of Illinois Press, 1988.

Nelson, Diane. *Reckoning: The Ends of War in Guatemala.* Durham: Duke University Press, 2009.

Nevins, Joseph. *Operation Gatekeeper: The Rise of the "Illegal Alien" and the Making of the US–Mexico Boundary.* New York: Routledge, 2002.

New York Times, Editorial Board. "President Bush's 'Coalition of the Willing'—or Orwell Comes to Iraq." Op-ed, *New York Times,* November 25, 2008, http://theboard.blogs.nytimes.com.

Nichols, Bill. *Blurred Boundaries: Questions of Meaning in Contemporary Culture.* Bloomington: Indiana University Press, 1994.

Nordstrom, Carolyn. *Global Outlaws: Crime, Money, and Power in the Contemporary World.* Berkeley: University of California Press, 2007.

Obama, Barack. "President Barack Obama's Inaugural Speech." *New York Times,* January 20, 2009.

————. "Remarks by the President on Comprehensive Immigration Reform." Address delivered to the American School of International Service, Washington, D.C., July 1, 2010. http://www.whitehouse.gov.

O'Connor, Anne-Marie. "INS Probes Its Role in Rampart Case." *Los Angeles Times*, February 25, 2000.

———. "Suit Alleges Harassment of L.A. Gang Peace Group." *Los Angeles Times*, June 3, 2000.

Olney, Warren. "The LAPD's Anti-Gang CRASH Unit." *Which Way LA?* KCRW, Santa Monica, California, September 29, 1999.

O'Malley, Patrick. "Containing Our Excitement: Commodity, Culture and the Crisis of Discipline." *Studies in Law, Politics and Society* 13 (1993): 159–86.

Omi, Michael, and Howard Winant. *Racial Formation in the United States: From the 1960s to the 1980s*. New York: Routledge and Kegan Paul, 1994.

Ong, Aihwa. *Buddha Is Hiding: Refugees, Citizenship, and the New America*. Berkeley: University of California Press, 2003.

———. "Cultural Citizenship as Subject-Making: Immigrants Negotiate Racial and Cultural Boundaries in the United States." *Current Anthropology* 37, no. 5 (1996): 737–62.

———. *Flexible Citizenship: The Cultural Logics of Transnationality*. Durham: Duke University Press, 1999.

———. *Neoliberalism as Exception: Mutations in Citizenship and Sovereignty*. Durham: Duke University Press, 2006.

Orozco, Manuel. "From Family Ties to Transnational Linkages: The Impact of Family Remittances in Latin America." Unpublished paper, Latin American Studies Association, Miami, 2000.

———. "Remittances and Markets: New Players and Practices" (working paper). Washington, D.C.: Inter-American Dialogue; Austin: TX: The Tomás Rivera Policy Institute, 2000.

Papadopoulos, Renos, et al. *Violencia en una sociedad en transición*. San Salvador: Programa de las Naciones Unidas para el Desarrollo, 1998.

Papastergiadis, Nikos. *Modernity as Exile: The Stranger in John Berger's Writing*. Manchester: Manchester University Press, 1993.

Paredes, Américo. *"With a Pistol in His Hands": A Border Ballad and Its Hero*. Austin: University of Texas Press, 1958.

Pastor Jr., Manuel. "Latinos and the Los Angeles Uprising: The Economic Context." Los Angeles: The Tomás Rivera Center, 1993.

Pedersen, David. "American Value: Migrants, Money and Modernity in El Salvador and the United States." Ph.D. dissertation, University of Michigan, 2004.

———. "As Irrational as Bert and Bin Laden: The Production of Categories, Commodities, and Commensurability in the Era of Globalization." *Public Culture* 15, no. 2 (spring 2003): 238–59.

———. "The Storm We Call Dollars: Determining Value and Belief in El Salvador and the United States." *Cultural Anthropology* 17, no. 3 (August 2002): 431–59.

Perez, Gina. "Discipline and Citizenship: Latino/a Youth in Chicago JROTC Programs." In *New Landscapes of Inequality: Neoliberalism and the Erosion of Democracy in America*, ed. Jane L. Collins, Micaela di Leonardo, and Brett Williams. Santa Fe: School of American Research, 2008.

Perez, Rossana, ed., with Henry A. J. Ramos, *Flight to Freedom: The Story of Central American Refugees in California*. Houston: Arte Público Press, 2007.

Perla, Héctor. "Si Nicaragua Venció, El Salvador Vencerá: Central American Agency in the Creation of the U.S.–Central American Peace and Solidarity Movement." *Latin American Research Review* 43, no. 2 (2008): 136–58.

Petersila, Joan. "A Retrospective View of Corrections Reform in the Schwarzenegger Administration." *Federal Sentencing Reporter* 22, no. 3 (2010): 148–53.

Peterson, Brandt. "Consuming Histories: The Return of the Indian in Neoliberal El Salvador." *Cultural Dynamics* 18, no. 2 (2006): 163–88.

———. "Remains Out of Place: Race, Trauma and Nationalism in El Salvador." *Anthropological Theory* 7, no. 1 (March 2007): 59–77.

———. "Unsettled Remains: Race, Trauma, and Nationalism in Millennial El Salvador." Ph.D. dissertation, University of Texas, Austin, 2005.

Peutz, Nathalie. "Embarking on an Anthropology of Removal." *Current Anthropology* 47, no. 2 (April 2006): 217–31.

Philip, Kavita, Eliza Jane Reilly, and David Serlin. "Homeland Securities: Editors Introduction." *Radical History Review*, no. 93 (Fall 2005): 1–12.

Phillips, Susan. "Gallos' Body: Decoration and Damnation in the Life of a Chicano Gang Member." *Ethnography*, 2, no. 3 (2001): 357–88.

———. "'Make It Last Forever': Tattoo Removal at an East L.A. Clinic." Unpublished paper, n.d.

———. *Wallbangin': Graffiti and Gangs in Los Angeles*. Chicago: University of Chicago Press, 1999.

Pine, Adrienne. "Honduras' Porfirio 'Pepe' Lobo: Another Disaster for Central American Democracy Waiting in the Wing." *Council on Hemispheric Affairs*, January 26, 2010.

Plascencia, Luis. "Citizenship through Veteranship: Latino Migrants Defend the US 'Homeland.'" *Anthropology News* (May 2009): 8–9.

Poblete, Juan, ed. *Critical Latin American and Latino Studies*. Minneapolis: University of Minnesota Press, 2003.

Poole, Russell (Detective). "Rampart Scandal." PBS Frontline, n.d. http://www.pbs.org.

Popkin, Margaret. *Peace without Justice: Obstacles to Building the Rule of Law in El Salvador*. University Park: Pennsylvania State University Press, 2000.

Portillo, Yesenia. "Although I Wasn't There, I Remember: The Role of History and Memory in the Transnational Organizing of the Salvadoran Diaspora." Honors thesis, University of California, San Diego, 2010.

Postero, Nancy. *Now We Are Citizens: Indigenous Politics in Postmulticultural Brazil*. Stanford: Stanford University Press, 2007.

———. "Revolution and New Social Imaginaries in Post-neoliberal Latin America." Paper delivered at the conference Post-neoliberalism in Latin America, University of California, San Diego, May 2–3, 2008.

———. "The Struggle to Create a Radical Democracy in Bolivia." In "Actually Existing Democracies," special issue of *Latin American Research Review* (2010): 59–78.

Pratt, Mary Louise. "Why the Virgin of Zapopan Went to Los Angeles: Reflections on Mobility and Globality." In *Images of Power: Iconography, Culture and State in Latin America*, ed. Jens Anderman and William Rowe, 271–89. Oxford: Berghahn Books, 2004.

Rabinow, Paul, and George Marcus, with James D. Faubion and Tobias Rees. *Design for an Anthropology of the Contemporary*. Durham: Duke University Press, 2008.

Ramos, Carlos Guillermo, ed. *America Central en los noventa: Problemas de juventud*. San Salvador: Facultad Latinoamericana de Ciencias Sociales (FLACSO), 1998.

———. *Violencia en una sociedad en transicion: Ensayos*. San Salvador: Programa de las Naciones Unidas para el Desarollo, 2000.

RAND Corporation. "Report on the Los Angeles Riot." Los Angeles: RAND Corporation, 1992.

Rebuild Los Angeles. Rebuild LA Collection, 1992–1997. Research Center for the Study of Los Angeles, Archives and Special Collections, Charles Von der Ahe Library, Loyola Marymount University, Los Angeles.

Reguillo, Rossana, and Marcial Godoy Anativia. *Cuidades translocales: Espacios, flujo, representación. Perspectivas desde las Américas*. Tlalquepaque, Jalisco, Mexico: Instituto Tecnológico y de Estudios Superiores de Occidente, 2005.

Ribando, Clare. "Gangs in Central America," CRS Report for Congress. Congressional Research Service, Library of Congress, May 10, 2005.

Rivas, Cecilia. "Imaginaries of Transnationalism: Media and Cultures of Consumption in El Salvador." Ph.D. dissertation. University of California, San Diego, 2007.

Rivera, Carla. "Scandal Stirs a Grim Specter of Emotions." *Los Angeles Times*, March 19, 2000.

Roberts, Michelle. "'Immigration Detention Facilities to Become Less Like Prisons,' Officials Say." *Huffington Post*, June 16, 2010.

Robinson, William I. *Transnational Conflicts: Central America, Social Change and Globalization*. London: Verso, 2003.

Rodriguez, Nestor. "The Real New World Order: The Globalization of Racial and Ethnic Relations in the Late Twentieth Century." In *The Bubbling Cauldron: Race, Ethnicity, and the Urban Crisis*, 211–25. Minneapolis: University of Minnesota Press, 1995.

Romo, Ricardo. *East Los Angeles: History of a Barrio*. Austin: University of Texas, 1983.

Rosaldo, Renato. *Culture and Truth: The Remaking of Social Analysis*. Boston: Beacon Press, 1993.

Rosas, Gilberto. "The Fragile Ends of War: Forging the United States–Mexico Border and Border Consciousness." *Social Text* 91, no. 2 (Summer 2007): 81–102.

Rose, Jacqueline. *States of Fantasy*. Oxford: Clarendon Press, 1996.

Rose, Nikolas. "Governing 'Advanced' Liberal Democracies." In *Foucault and Political Reason*, ed. Andrew Barry, Thomas Osborne, and Nikolas Rose, 37–64. Chicago: University of Chicago Press, 1996.

Rosenberg, Harold. "King Case Aftermath: A City in Crisis: Television: Medium's Influence Sometimes Warps Our Sense of Reality." *Los Angeles Times*, May 2, 1992.

Rouse, Roger. "Mexican Migration and the Social Space of Postmodernism." *Diaspora* (Spring 1991): 8–23.

———. "Mexican Migration to the United States: Family Relations in the Development of a Transnational Migrant Circuit." Ph.D. dissertation. Stanford University, 1989.

———. "Thinking through Transnationalism: Notes on the Cultural Politics of Class Relations in the Contemporary United States." *Public Culture* 7 (1994): 353–402.

Sachs, Susan. "Second Thoughts: Cracking the Door for Immigrants." *New York Times*, July 1, 2001.

Saénz, Mario. *Latin American Perspectives on Globalization: Ethics, Politics, and Alternative Visions*. Lanham, Md.: Rowman and Littlefield, 2002.

Said, Edward. *Culture and Imperialism*. New York: Alfred A. Knopf, 1993.

Saldívar, José David. *Border Matters: Remapping American Cultural Studies*. Berkeley: University of California Press, 1997.

———. *The Dialectics of Our America: Genealogy, Cultural Critique, and Literary History*. Durham: Duke University Press, 1991.

Sanchez, George, and Raúl Villa. *Los Angeles and the Future of Urban Cultures*. Baltimore: Johns Hopkins University Press, 2004.

Santacruz Giralt, Maria L., and Alberto Concha-Eastman. *Barrio adentro: La solidaridad violenta de la pandillas*. San Salvador: Instituto Universitario de Opinion de Pública, 2001.

Sassen, Saskia. *The Global City: New York, London, Tokyo*. Princeton: Princeton University Press, 1991.

———. *Globalization and Its Discontents: Essays on the New Mobility of People and Money*. New York: New Press, 1998.

———. *The Mobility of Labor and Capital: A Study in International Investment and Labor Flow*. Cambridge: Cambridge University Press, 1988.

———. "Whose City Is It? Globalization and the Formation of New Claims." *Public Culture* 8, no. 2 (1996): 205–24.

Scheper-Hughes, Nancy, and Phillipe Bourgois, eds. *Violence in War and Peace: An Anthology*. Oxford: Blackwell, 2004.

Seper, Jerry. "Al Qaeda Seeks Tie to Local Gangs." *Washington Times*, September 28, 2004.

Serementakis, Nadia. *The Senses Still: Perception and Memory as Material Culture in Modernity*. Boulder, Colo.: Westview Press, 1994.

Siegel, James. *A New Criminal Type in Jakarta: Counter Revolution Today.* Durham: Duke University Press, 1998.

Siems, Larry. *Between the Lines: Letters between Undocumented Mexican and Central American Immigrants and Their Families and Friends.* Tucson: University of Arizona Press, 1995.

Silber, Irina Carlota. "Mothers/Fighters/Citizens: Violence and Disillusionment in Post-War El Salvador." *Gender and History* 16, no. 3 (November 2004): 561–87.

Simon, Jonathan. "The Emergence of a Risk Society: Insurance, Law, and the State." *Socialist Review* 95 (1987): 61–89.

———. *Governing through Crime: How the War on Crime Transformed American Democracy and Created a Culture of Fear.* Oxford: Oxford University Press, 2007.

Simon, L. A., dir. *Fear and Learning at Hoover Elementary.* Los Angeles: Josepha Producciones, 1997.

Situationist International. "The Decline and Fall of the Spectacle-Commodity Economy." In *Situationist International Anthology*, ed. Ken Knabb. Berkeley: Bureau of Public Secrets, 153–59.

Smith, Ana Deavere. *Twilight: Los Angeles 1992.* New York: Anchor Books, 1994.

Smith, Erna. "Transmitting Race: The Los Angeles Riot in Television News." In *Press Politics, Public Policy*, 1–18. Research paper R-11. Cambridge: Harvard University, John F. Kennedy School of Government, 1994.

Smith, Michael Peter. *Transnational Urbanism: Locating Globalization.* Malden, Mass.: Blackwell, 2000.

Smith, Michael Peter, and Luis Guarnizo. "Can You Imagine? Transnational Migration and the Globalization of Grassroots Politics." *Social Text*, no. 39 (1994): 15–33.

———. *Transnationalism from Below.* New Brunswick, N.J.: Transaction Publishers, 1998.

Smith, Neil. "Contours of Spatial Politics: Homeless Vehicles and the Production of Geographical Scale." *Social Text*, no. 33 (1996): 55–81.

———. *The New Urban Frontier: Gentrification and the Revanchist City.* London: Routledge, 1996.

Smutt, M., and Jenny Lissette E. Miranda. *El fenomeno de las pandillas de El Salvador.* San Salvador: FLACSO and UNICEF, 1998.

Soja, Edward. *Postmodern Geographies: The Reassertion of Space in Critical Social Theory.* London: Verso, 1989.

———. *Thirdspace: Journeys to Los Angeles and Other Real and Imagined Places.* Cambridge, Mass.: Blackwell, 1996.

Sorkin, Michael. *Variations on a Theme Park: The New American City and the End of Public Space.* New York: Hill and Wang, 1992.

Stallybrass, Peter, and Alan White. *The Politics and Poetics of Transgression.* Ithaca: Cornell University Press, 1986.

Stanley, William. "Protectors or Perpetrators? The Institutional Crisis of the Salvadoran Civilian Police." Washington: Office on Latin America and Hemisphere Initiatives, 1996.

Stewart, Kathleen. "An Occupied Place." In *Senses of Place*, ed. Steven Feld and Keith Basso, 137–66. Santa Fe: School of American Research, 1996.

———. "On the Politics of Cultural Theory: A Case for 'Contaminated' Cultural Critique." *Social Research* 58, no. 2 (1991): 395–412.

———. *Ordinary Affects*. Durham: Duke University Press, 2007.

———. *A Space on the Side of the Road: Cultural Poetics in an "Other" America*. Princeton: Princeton University Press, 1996.

Strathern, Marilyn. "A Community of Critics? Thoughts on New Knowledge." Huxley Memorial Lecture given to the Royal Anthropological Institute, December 8, 2004.

Sullivan, Randall. "The Unsolved Murder of Notorious B.I.G." *Rolling Stone*, no. 870 (June 7, 2001).

Sweet, Lynn. "Colin Powell Endorses Barack Obama on NBC's 'Meet the Press.'" *Chicago Sun-Times*, October 19, 2008. http://blogs.suntimes.com.

Taussig, Michael. *Defacement: Public Secrecy and the Labor of the Negative*. Stanford: Stanford University Press, 1999.

———. *Mimesis and Alterity: A Particular History of the Senses*. New York: Routledge, 1993.

———. *The Nervous System*. New York: Routledge, 1992.

———. *Shamanism, Colonialism, and the Wildman: A Study in Terror and Healing*. Chicago: University of Chicago Press, 1987.

Taylor, Diane. *Disappearing Acts: Spectacles of Gender and Nationalism in Argentina's "Dirty War."* Durham, N.C: Duke University Press.

Taylor, Marisa. "INS Stuck over What to Do with Detainees." *San Diego Union-Tribune*, July 16, 2001.

Thompson, E. P. *Whigs and Hunters: The Origins of the Black Act*. London: Penguin, 1975.

Tilly, Charles. "War Making and State Making as Organized Crime." In *Bringing the State Back In*, ed. Peter Evans, Dietrich Reuschemeyer, and Theda Skocpol, 169–91. Cambridge: Cambridge University Press, 1985.

Tim's El Salvador Blog. "Election Meddling," October 1, 2008. http://luterano.blog spot.com.

Tirman, John. "Introduction: The Movement of People and the Security of States." In *The Maze of Fear*, ed. John Tirman, 1–16. New York: New Press, 2004.

Tobar, Héctor. "Riots' Scars Include 200 Still-Vacant Lots." *Los Angeles Times*, April 21, 1997.

———. *The Tattooed Soldier*. Harrison, N.Y.: Delphinium Books, 1998.

Tsing, Anna Lowenhaupt. *Friction: An Ethnography of Global Connection*. Princeton: Princeton University Press, 2005.

———. "The Global Situation." *Cultural Anthropology* 15, no. 3 (2000): 327–60.

———. *In the Realm of the Diamond Queen: Marginality in an Out-of-the-Way Place.* Princeton: Princeton University Press, 1993.

Tumlin, Karen, Linto Joaquin, and Ranjana Natarajan. "A Broken System: Confidential Reports Reveal Failures in U.S. Immigrant Detention Centers." Los Angeles: National Immigration Law Center; ACLU of Southern California; and Holland and Knight, 2009.

Ungar, Mark. "Crime and Citizen Security in Latin America." In *Latin America After Neoliberalism: Turning the Tide in the Twenty-first Century?* ed. Eric Hershberg and Fred Rosen. New York: New Press, 2006.

United Nations. "Report from the Joint Group for the Investigation of Illegal Armed Groups with Political Motivation in El Salvador, San Salvador, July 28, 1994." In *United Nations and El Salvador, 1990–1995,* 4:568–74. New York: The United Nations Blue Books Series.

United Nations Development Programme (UNDP). *Informe sobre dessarrollo humano El Salvador 2005: Una mirada al nuevo nosotros. El impact de las migraciones.* New York: United Nations, 2005.

———. *Informe sobre desarrollo humano para América Central 2009–2010: Abrir espacios a la seguridad ciudadana y el desarrollo humano.* New York: United Nations, 2009.

United Nations High Commissioner for Refugees (UNHCR). "Guidance Note on Refugee Claims Relating to Victims of Organized Gangs." March 31, 2010, http://www.unhcr.org.

United States Agency for International Development (USAID). "Central American and Mexico Gang Assessment." Washington: USAID Bureau for Latin American and Caribbean Affairs. Office of Regional Sustainable Development, April 2006.

United States Immigrations and Custom Enforcement. "Operation Community Shield." http://www.ice.gov.

Uzell, D. J. "Conceptual Fallacies in the Rural-Urban Dichotomy." *Urban Anthropology* 8 (1979): 333–50.

Valle, Victor M., and Rodolfo D. Torres. *Latino Metropolis.* Minneapolis: University of Minnesota Press, 2000.

Van Schendel, Willem, and Itty Abraham, eds. *Illicit Flows and Criminal Things: States, Borders, and the Other Side of Globalization.* Bloomington: Indiana University Press, 2005.

Vargas, João H. Costa. *Catching Hell in the City of Angels: Life and Meanings of Blackness in South Central Los Angeles.* Minneapolis: University of Minnesota Press, 2006.

Velasquez de Aviles, V. M. *La Seguridad Ciudadana, la Policia Nacional Civil y los Derechos Humanos.* San Salvador: Procuraduria para la Defensa de los Derechos Humanos, 1997.

Velez-Ibañez, Carlos. *Border Visions.* Tucson: University of Arizona Press, 1994.

Venkatesh, Sudhir. *Gang Leader for a Day.* New York: Penguin Books, 2008.

———. *Off the Books: The Underground Economy of the Urban Poor.* Cambridge: Harvard University Press, 2006.

Venkatesh, Sudhir Alladi, and Ronald Kassimir, eds. *Youth, Globalization, and the Law.* Stanford: Stanford University Press, 2007.

Vigil, James Diego. *Barrio Gangs: Street Life and Identity in Southern California.* Austin: University of Texas Press, 1988.

———. *A Rainbow of Gangs: Street Cultures in the Mega-City.* Austin: University of Texas Press, 2002.

Vila, Pablo. *Ethnography at the Border.* Minneapolis: University of Minnesota Press, 2003.

Villa, Raúl Homero. *Barrio-Logos: Space and Place in Urban Chicano Literature and Culture.* Austin: University of Texas Press, 2000.

Villalobos, Joaquin. *De la tortura a la proteccion ciudadana: La policia nacional civil de El Salvador como instrumento de al pacificacion y democratizacion.* San Salvador: Instituto para un Nuevo El Salvador (INELSA), 2001.

Virilio, Paul. *Essai sur l'insecurite du territoire.* Paris: Stock, 1976.

Voloshinov, V. N., L. Matejka, and I. R. Titunik. *Marxism and the Philosophy of Language.* New York: Seminar Press, 1973.

Wallace, S. "You Must Go Home Again: Deported LA Gangbangers Take Over El Salvador." *Harper's Magazine* 30 (2000): 47–56.

Walprin, Ned. "The New Speed-up in Habeas Corpus Appeals." Supplemental readings for "The Execution." PBS Frontline, n.d. http://www.pbs.org.

Ward, Tom. "The Price of Fear: Salvadoran Refugees in the City of Angels." Ph.D. dissertation, University of California, Los Angeles, 1987.

Warren, Kay, ed. *The Violence Within: Cultural and Political Opposition in Divided Nations.* Boulder, Colo.: Westview Press, 1993.

Washington Office on Latin America (WOLA). *Central American Gang-Related Asylum Guide.* Washington: WOLA, 2008.

———. *Youth Gangs in Central America: Issues in Human Rights, Effective Policing, and Prevention.* Washington: WOLA, 2006.

Weinstein, Henry. "Janitors Lash Out at Rebuild L.A. in Rally." *Los Angeles Times,* December 18, 1992.

———. "Rampart Probe May Now Affect Over 3,000 Cases." *Los Angeles Times,* December 15, 1999.

Weldes, Jutta, Mark Laffey, Hugh Gusterson, and Raymond Duvall, eds. *Cultures of Insecurity: States, Communists, and the Production of Danger.* Minneapolis: University of Minnesota Press, 1999.

White, M. "LA Riot-Aliens." 1992.

Whiteford, L. "The Borderland as an Extended Community." In *Migration across Frontiers: Mexico and the United States,* ed. Fernando Camara and Robet Van Kemper, 127–37. Albany: State University of New York at Albany, Institute for Mesoamerican Studies, 1979.

Williams, Raymond. *Marxism and Literature.* Oxford: Oxford University Press, 1977.

Wilson, Gary I., and John P. Sullivan. "On Gangs, Crime, and Terrorism." Special to

Defense and the National Interest, February 28, 2007. Draco Group, http://www
.dracosecurityconsultants.com.

Wilson, Rob, and Wimal Dissanayake, eds. *Global/Local: Cultural Production and the Transnational Imaginary.* Durham: Duke University Press, 1996.

Winant, Howard. "Just Do It: Notes on Politics and Race at the Dawn of the Obama
Presidency." *Du Bois Review* 6, no. 1 (2009): 49–70.

Witte-Lebhar, Benjamin. "El Salvador: President Mauricio Funes Seeks Military Help
to Curb Violent Crime." Latin American Data Base/Latin American Institute.
http://ladb.unm.edu.

Yngvesson, Barbara, and Susan Bibler Coutin. "Backed by Papers: Undoing Persons,
Histories, and Return." *American Ethnologist* 33, no. 2 (2006): 177–90.

Yúdice, George. "Civil Society, Consumption, and Governmentality in an Age of
Global Restructuring: An Introduction." *Social Text* 14, no. 4 (1995): 1–25.

Zeller, James. "Third World Wages Won't Rebuild L.A." *Los Angeles Times*, December 9,
1992.

Ziegler, Melissa, and Rachel Nield. "From Peace to Governance: Police Reform and the
International Community." Washington: Washington Office on Latin America,
2002.

Zilberg, Elana. "Falling Down in El Norte: A Cultural Politics of the ReLatinization of
Los Angeles." In "Film, Architecture and Urban Space," special issue of *Wide Angle*
20, no. 3 (1999): 182–209.

———. "Fools Banished from the Kingdom: Remapping Geographies of Gang Violence between the Americas (Los Angeles and San Salvador)." *American Quarterly*
56, no. 3 (2004): 759–79.

———. "From Riots to Rampart: A Spatial Cultural Politics of Salvadoran Migration
to and from Los Angeles." Ph.D. dissertation, University of Texas, Austin, 2003.

———. "Gangster in Guerilla Face: The Political Folklore of Doble Cara in Post–Civil
War El Salvador." *Anthropological Theory* 7, no. 1 (March 2007): 37–57.

———. "Inter-American Ethnography: Tracking Salvadoran Transnationality at the
Borders of Latino and Latin American Studies." *Companion to Latina/o Studies*, ed.
Juan Flores and Renato Rosaldo, 492–501. Oxford: Blackwell, 2007.

———. "Refugee Gang Youth: Zero Tolerance and the Security State in Contemporary
US–Salvadoran Relations." In *Youth, Law, and Globalization*, ed. Sudhir Venkatesh
and Ronald Kassimir, 61–89. Stanford: Stanford University Press, 2007.

———. "A Troubled Corner: The Ruined and Rebuilt Environment of a Central American Barrio in Post–Rodney King Riot Los Angeles." *City and Society* 14, no. 2 (2002):
31–55.

Zilberg, Elana, and Mario Úcles Lungo. "Se han vuelto haraganes? Jóvenes, migración
y identidades laborales." In *Transformando El Salvador: Migraciòn internacional, sociedad
y cultura*, ed. Mario Lungo and Susan Kandel. San Salvador: Fundación Nacional
para el Desarrollo, 1999.

Žižek, Slavoj. *The Sublime Object of Ideology*. New York: Verso, 1989.

Zlolniski, Christian. *Janitors, Street Vendors, and Activists: The Lives of Mexican Immigrants in Silicon Valley*. Berkeley: University of California Press, 2006.

Zolberg, Aristide, A. Suhrke, and Sergio Aguayo. *Escape from Violence: Conflict and the Refugee Crisis in the Developing World*. New York: Oxford University Press, 1989.

Zulaika, Joseba, and William Douglass. *Terror and Taboo: The Follies, Fables and Faces of Terrorism*. New York: Routledge, 1996.

Street Hoodlums): assumptions of, 98; corruption in, 42–43, 101–2, 106, 113–15, 131, 245; mimesis of gangsterism and, 113–15, 123, 283n22; territory and spatial logic of, 42, 77, 90–99, 195–96. *See also* LAPD (Los Angeles Police Department)

Crawford, Margaret, 280n39

Crazy Riders (gang), 134

CRECEN (Central American Refugee Center), 35, 72, 104, 119, 161

crime: consumerism and, 83–98; deportation as strategic response to, 4; neoliberal conceptions of, 6–10, 71; policing as product of, 9, 90–97; Salvadoran responses to, 9–10, 18, 40–41, 161–62, 167–73, 247–48; terrorism and, 16–18, 207–14, 220; theoretical approaches to, 14–16. *See also* gangs; terrorism and counterterrorism; *specific police departments, governmental agencies, policies, and gangs*

Crime Bill (1994), 8, 35, 220

"Criminals, Jihadists Threaten U.S. Border" (article), 221

Crips (gang), 34, 104

Cristiani, Alfredo, 33

Cuba, 33–34, 233, 242

CV Amigos Westside (gang), 164

Dalton, Roque, 214

D'Aubuisson, Roberto, 17

Davis, Mike, 67, 84, 95, 263n53, 270n16, 278n14, 280nn39–40

Death Row Records, 115

death squads: in contemporary El Salvador, 40–41, 138, 145, 150–51, 208, 211–12, 218, 228, 269n38; in Salvadoran civil war, 17, 32–33

DECCO (Elite Division to Combat Organized Crime), 213

de Certeau, Michel, 11–12, 15, 19, 157

Decesare, Donna, 121, 141

Denny, Reginald, 56, 273n3, 278n16

deportation: as anti-crime U.S. policy, 2–3, 13, 120, 212–13, 285n1; criminal deportee as figure, 15, 129–31, 154; due process exceptionalism and, 36; geographical disorientation and, 129–45, 164, 230; Los Angeles (1992) riots and, 31; neoliberal ideological roots of, 6–10; police corruption and, 111–12; repression of violence and, 4, 13; Salvadoran violence and, 162–69; transnational spaces and, 145–50. *See also* El Salvador; immigrants and immigration; nationalism; United States; zero-tolerance policing strategies; *specific policies and agencies*

Derrida, Jacques, 232, 296n10

dialectical images: criminal cop, 102, 113–15, 117, 131, 238; definitions of, 16–18, 208; gang peace activists, 102–13, 115–18, 156, 174, 187–90; gangster as terrorist, 208, 213–17, 238; in LAPD protests, 86–89; Mara Salvatrucha in FMLN face, 207–8, 217; Obama and Funes inaugurations, 241–42, 249; soldier cop, 178, 181–87, 238

Diamante, Alan, 43, 110, 120–21

El Diario de Hoy (newspaper), 210

Dominguez, René, 172

Doña Leti, 147–48, 287n15

Doña Ofelia, 146–47

Don Bosco (program), 163

Douglass, William A., 223, 292n5

DR-CAFTA (Dominican Republic-Central America Free Trade Agreement), 5–6, 48, 235

drug trafficking, 92–94, 114–15, 202

Dumm, Thomas, 62, 93, 113, 279n16

Ecology of Fear (Davis), 270n16

Economist (journal), 64

Funes, Mauricio, 235, 242–43, 248–50, 297n19, 298n28
Funes, Nelson, 216

Gang Related Asylum Project, 218
gangs: academic studies of, 14, 158, 191; culture of, 39; definitions of, 153; deportation of members of, 11–12, 40, 47, 129–40; FMLN and, 207–8, 210–11, 213–17; mimesis and, 18–21, 113–15, 211–15, 229–30, 247, 283n22; peace activists and, 16–18, 23, 37, 103–13, 115–18; structures and practices of, 11, 94–97, 112–15, 154–55, 196–99, 227–32, 284n34, 286n7; terminological slipperiness of, 38; terrorism tropes and, 45, 48, 151, 209–39; transnational security measures and, 1–2, 44, 129–40, 244–45. *See also* CRASH (Community Resources Against Street Hoodlums); Homies Unidos (organization); immigrants and immigration; space and spatiality; tattoos; zero-tolerance policing strategies; *specific cities, gangs, and nations*
Gang Violence Prevention Task Force (in California), 39
García, Michelle, 223
Garfield, Bob, 225
Gates, Daryl, 58, 71
gender, 68, 71, 154, 264n56, 288n3
Geragos, Mark, 120–21
Gingrich, Newt, 18, 221–24, 226, 236
Girard, René, 238
Giuliani, Rudolph, 45, 97
globalization. *See* El Salvador; immigrants and immigration; nationalism; neoliberalism; United States; zero-tolerance policing strategies
"Global Situation, The" (Tsing), 259n6
Goldstein, Daniel, 9
Gonzales, Alberto, 1
Guardado, Facundo, 161, 169, 172

Guillén, Silvia, 178
Gusterson, Hugh, 3

habeas corpus, 8, 220
Hale, Charles, 21
Hall, Stuart, 79, 277n6
Handal, Shafik, 211, 216, 235
Harvey, David, 260n11
Haugen, Rana, 110
Hayden, Tom, 39, 43, 104–5, 107–10, 117–21, 123, 245–46
Hayek, Friedrich, 260n11
Hernandez, Ricardo Termino, 244
Hoffman, Paul, 123
Hofsteader, Richard, 223
Hollywood, 55, 60
Hombres y Mujeres Inserción Social de El Salvador (HOMIES), 175
Homies Unidos (organization): Campaign to Free Alex Sanchez and, 42–43, 118–24; founding of, 37, 41, 102–3, 153–54; gang structure and mores of, 115–18, 122–23, 153–55, 167, 218; leadership of, 42–43, 45, 48, 123–24; media's relationship to, 167–68; participation of, in California politics, 39–40, 103–13; Salvadoran politics and, 159–69; in San Salvador, 106, 151–60, 173–75, 178–79, 187; spaces of, 103–13, 123–24, 153; transnational alliance of, 13, 43–44, 106–7, 141–44, 152, 174–75; zero-tolerance policing strategies and, 41, 106–13, 116–18, 122, 157, 172, 187. *See also* CRASH (Community Resources Against Street Hoodlums); dialectical images; *specific forums and leaders*
Honduras, 245–46
hoodlum (trope or figure). *See* CRASH (Community Resources Against Street Hoodlums)
Hoover Street Locos (gang), 92

ICE (Immigration and Customs Enforcement), 45, 47, 49, 224, 226, 245, 248

ICITAP (International Criminal Investigation Technical Assistance Program), 171, 290n31

IDHUCA (University of Central America's Institute for Human Rights), 201, 203

ILEA (International Law Enforcement Academy), 48, 202–3, 233–34

Illegal Immigration Reform and Immigrant Responsibility Act, 8, 36, 39, 44–45, 62

IMF (International Monetary Fund), 33–34

Immanuel Presbyterian Church, 104, 124, 161

immigrants and immigration: citizenship and, 30, 35–36, 44, 234–35; consumerism and, 83–90; deportation of "criminal youth" as U.S. policy, 2, 36–37, 40, 43–44, 117, 129–35, 238, 248; legality and illegality issues and, 4, 9, 14–15, 31–32, 38, 122, 135–37, 140–41, 148–50, 217–18; Los Angeles riots (1992) and, 59–64; media narratives and, 15–16, 64, 224–26; military service and, 234–35, 287n15; mobility of, relatively speaking, 3, 19, 62, 77, 103–13, 231; police relations and, 119–20, 130; race's intersections with, 31–32, 35, 61–62, 64–74, 76; refugee status and, 28–30, 35, 47, 268n8, 269n13; Salvadoran civil war and, 26, 37, 269n13; Special Order 40 and, 45, 117–20; terrorism tropes and, 45, 207–30; transgressiveness of, 15, 58, 62, 93. See also El Salvador; space and spatiality; United States; specific policies, agencies, and people

Immigration Act (of 1990), 28

Immigration and Nationality Act (of 1996), 45

Import Substitution Industrialization (economic model), 33

inauguration (definition), 241–42

INS (Immigration and Naturalization Service), 35, 42, 45, 58, 76, 110, 117–20, 124, 174, 195, 269n11

Interagency Task Force on Gangs, 1, 238

Iraq War, 45, 234–35, 249

IUDOP (University Institute for Public Opinion), 142, 172

IVU (Instituto de Vivienda Urbana), 179, 190, 230–31

Jack in the Box (Pico Union), 77, 92, 96–98, 134, 145, 276n1

Jackson, Jesse, 64

Jail Construction Funding Bill, 8. See also prisons

Johnson, Lyndon, 78

Justice for Janitors (project), 81–83, 86, 88–89

Justice Policy Institute, 225–26

Kelling, George, 272n48

King, Rodney, 41, 57, 59–64, 71–72, 81–82, 269n15, 278n16. See also Los Angeles

Knight, Suge, 115

Koon, Stacey, 71

Koppel, Ted, 59

Korean War, 69

Koreatown, 42, 55, 60, 124, 132

Kroll Associates, 45, 246

labor (organized), 81–83, 86–88

L.A. Bridges Project, 121

Lacinos, Walter, 244

La Curacao (building), 123, 161

La Luna (space), 139–40

LAPD (Los Angeles Police Department): corruption and abuses of, 42–43, 62–

63, 71–72, 101–2, 106, 113–15, 131, 245–46; federal funding and, 219–20; immigration law and, 45, 76, 110, 117–20; leadership of, 45, 58, 71; media and, 65–76; pledges of, to work with gangs, 34; protests against, 55–56, 60–61, 86–88, 285n37; Special Order 40 and, 45, 117–20. *See also* CRASH (Community Resources Against Street Hoodlums); gangs; Homies Unidos (organization); Los Angeles; zero-tolerance policing strategies

Latin Kings (gang), 237, 284n34

Latino looter (trope or figure), 15, 31, 54–65, 72, 75, 81–90, 93, 278n14

Lawson, James, 282n6

Lazo, Estéban, 242

LeFebvre, Henri, 11, 280n39

Ley de Juventud, 164–65, 179

Libertad con Dignidad (organization), 218

Limbaugh, Rush, 73

Linares, Eduardo, 121

Ling, Lisa, 224

Los Angeles: anti-gang measures of, 91–97, 280n40; as destination for Salvadoran refugees, 26–28, 35–36, 140–41, 219; gang membership in, 13; media representations and narratives of, 55–74; 1992 riots and, 15, 31–32, 34–35, 41, 54–65, 71–76, 79–80, 84, 97, 264n63, 269n15, 273n6, 276n39; RLA initiative and, 34, 76–90, 95; San Salvador's geography and, 37, 133–35, 138, 143–45, 149, 230; Special Order 40 and, 45, 117–20; Watts riots and, 59–60, 80, 85, 269n15. *See also* CRASH (Community Resources Against Street Hoodlums); gangs; LAPD (Los Angeles Police Department); *specific neighborhoods*

Los Angeles City Club, 90

Los Angeles Times (newspaper), 59–61, 92, 220

Lula, Luiz, 242

MacArthur Park, 27–28, 145

Magical Urbanism (Davis), 95

Mahler, Sarah, 89

Malkki, Liisa, 268n8

Manic Chicago Disciples (gang), 220

Mano Amiga, 179

Mano Extendida, 179, 182

Manwaring, Max, 18

La Mara Salvatrucha. *See* MS (La Mara Salvatrucha)

Marcus, George, 19, 266n87

Mark, Gregory, 223

Marquez, Mario, 106, 122

Marroquin, Werner, 161

Martínez, Carlos, 161

Martínez, Ruben, 270n16

Masco, Joseph, 265n69

McCain, John, 242

media, 55–65, 73–75, 83–84, 220–29, 236–37, 246–47, 278n16, 295n47, 297n19. *See also specific newspapers, journals, and authors*

Meissner, Doris, 119

Menjívar, Cecilia, 2

Mexican American Bar Association, 104

Miguel Cruz, José, 12, 172

Miles, Jack, 61, 85–86

militarization: in El Salvador, 178–204, 235–37, 248; in the United States, 17–18, 220–23, 237, 294n29

Millennium Challenge Corporation (MCC), 48

Miranda, Lisette, 180, 187–91, 195, 229, 291n9

Morales, Edgar, 223

Morales, Evo, 48

Morataya, José Pepe, 163

Mour, Linda, 59

MS (La Mara Salvatrucha): Al Qaeda and, 16, 47, 221, 226; definitions of, 268n3; in El Salvador, 12–13, 131–35, 138, 141–43; FMLN and, 207–8, 212–14; founding of, 27–28; Homies Unidos and, 37, 102; ICE's operations against, 47, 226, 245, 295n43; international policies regarding, 1–2; media accounts of, 210, 220–27, 236; members of, 41; as new criminal type, 15, 102–3, 219, 224–25; style and structure, 11, 28, 94–97, 112–15, 154–55, 196–99, 227–32, 284n34, 286n7; territory of, 27, 244. See also *American Gangs* (Gingrich); CRASH (Community Resources Against Street Hoodlums); Sanchez, Alex; zero-tolerance policing strategies

NACARA (Nicaraguan Adjustment and Central American Relief Act), 39, 47
NAFTA (North American Free Trade Agreement), 5, 33
National Foundation for Development (FUNDE), 37–38
National Geographic Channel, 224–27
nationalism: deportation's role in, 4, 131–32, 144, 149, 239; frailty of, in the face of capitalism, 10, 84–85; territorial transgressions and, 15, 58, 62, 65–75. *See also* crime; immigrants and immigration; terrorism and counterterrorism; United States
Navarrette, Rubén, Jr., 64, 274n124
neoliberalism: consumerism as core tenet of, 77–90, 96–98; criminologies of, 7–9; definitions of, 4–6, 260n9, 260n11; in El Salvador's economic policies, 32–34, 215; RLA projects and, 77–81; triumph of, historically, 232–38, 241–50. *See also* Bush, George H. W.; Hayek,

Friedrich; Reagan, Ronald; Thatcher, Margaret
New York City, 45. *See also* Broken Windows policy (in New York)
New York Times Magazine, 101, 103, 113, 120
Nicaragua, 26, 34
9/11 (event), 17, 44, 223, 236–37
North Korea, 69
la nueva canción (genre), 214–15

Obama, Barack Hussein, 241–43, 246, 248–50
Oh, Angela, 104, 109, 282n6
O'Malley, Patrick, 98, 117
Operation Community Shield (ICE operation), 47, 226, 245, 294n43
Operation Gate Keeper (LAPD), 91
Organized Crime Drug Enforcement Task Force, 120
Other Side, The (Martínez), 270n16

Pacific Rim Mining Corporation, 250, 299n34
Padilla, José, 220
Parks, Bernard C., 122
Patriot Act, 44, 296n1
Paz, Brenda, 224, 226
Penal Code Reform (of El Salvador), 41, 170
Perez, Rafael, 101–2, 104, 113–15, 117–18, 131
Perla, Mirna, 121
Permanente Committee on Youth Violence, 141
Personal Responsibility and Work Opportunity Act, 8–9
Phillips, Susan, 43, 121, 230
Pico Fiesta mini-mall, 92–94, 98
Pico Union (neighborhood): built environment of, 21, 31, 77–78, 91, 123, 134, 276n1; "community" of, 76, 95–96,

98–99, 101–2, 281n41; demographics of, 60; as destination of Salvadoran refugees, 27, 147, 213; LAPD's view of, 92, 94, 97; policing of, 42; riots in, 55; RLA's view of, 77–78, 90, 97, 277n3; in Salvadoran geographical sensibility, 132, 145

Pico Union Neighborhood Watch, 95

Piñeda, Héctor, 106–7

PIPCOM (Community Police Intervention Patrols), 171

El Plan Mano Duro (Salvadoran crime policy), 46, 165, 168–73, 227–32

El Plan Súper Mano Duro (Salvadoran crime policy), 46, 178, 227–32

PNC (National Civil Police of El Salvador): corruption in, 164, 211, 213; crime statistics of, 162, 270n37; deported gang members and, 40; founding of, 26; Homies Unidos and, 166–68; U.S. policy and, 1, 170–71; zero-tolerance policies of, 163, 169–73, 181–87, 210–11, 233, 247, 270n37. See also El Salvador; militarization

"Poema de Amor" (Dalton), 214

police forces. See specific cities, forces, and units

Poveda, Cristian, 247

Powell, Colin, 242

Pranis, Kevin, 225–27

prisons: gang identity and culture and, 28, 134–35, 214; privatization of, 8, 174, 195, 248, 262n23, 298n21; Salvadoran, 41, 170, 178, 192

Production of Space, The (LeFebvre), 11

Progressive Policy Institute (think tank), 78–79

Pro-Jóvenes (group), 179, 183, 186, 190, 291n9

Proposition 13 (California law), 31

Proposition 184 (California law), 35, 37, 107, 171–72

Proposition 187 (California law), 35–37, 62, 73, 107, 274n18

race and racism: class's intersections with, 55–62, 67–69; Los Angeles riots and, 58–61, 64, 80, 85, 264n63, 269n15, 273n6, 276n39; media narratives and, 15–16, 55–65, 83–84; mobility and, 3, 19, 62, 72–73; U.S. crime and immigration laws and, 35, 61–62, 65–74, 76, 84–86. See also Latino looter (trope or figure)

Ramos, Lucia Artal, 273n3

Rampart Division. See CRASH (Community Resources Against Street Hoodlums)

Reagan, Ronald, 5, 236, 260n11

Reebok corporation, 30

refugees (as trope), 28–30, 35. See also El Salvador; immigrants and immigration

repatriation (forced). See deportation; El Salvador; space and spatiality

El Rescate, 28–30, 161

Rice, Connie, 104, 282n6

RICO (Racketeer Influenced and Corrupt Organizations Act), 244–45

RLA (Rebuild Los Angeles), 34, 76–84, 86–90, 95, 98, 277n3

Robinson, William, 6

Rodríguez, Antonio, 200, 231, 236

Rodríguez, Néstor, 2

Rodríguez, Silvio, 215

Romero, Luis Ernesto, 159, 175

Romero, Oscar, 25–27, 243

Rose, Nikolas, 98, 277n6

Rose-Ávila, Magdaleno, 37, 41, 96–97, 105, 118, 121, 141–43, 146, 155, 286n8

Rosenberg, Howard, 59

Rushing, Rocky, 105, 110

"Time to Rethink Immigration" (Brime-low), 61–62

Tiny Locos of Shatto Park (gang), 149

Tobar, Héctor, 60, 83–84, 270n16

Tooner gang, 207

"Torture, Ill-Treatment and Excessive Force by Police in Los Angeles" (report), 72

TPS (Temporary Protected Status), 28–30

Transnational Anti-Gang Unit (TAG), 1, 238, 244–45

Tree People (organization), 119

Triple Canopy (company), 235

Tsing, Anna, 259n6

Ueberroth, Peter, 34, 76–82

UNHCR (United Nations High Commission for Refugees), 29, 218

Union Salvadoreña de Estudiantes Universitarios (USEU), 250

United Nations Development Program, 158, 260n19

United Nations Truth Commission for El Salvador, 32

United States: anti-gang measures of, 1–2, 47, 109; Border Patrol of, 58, 111; citizenship requirements of, 30, 35–36, 44, 234–35; defense industry's retrenchment and, 31, 54–55, 69–70; gangs as contamination of, 39–40; globalization's effects and, 2–3, 12; immigration policies of, 8–9, 11, 28–30, 35–36, 38–39, 43–44, 47, 49, 120–23, 130–31, 135–40, 148–50, 194, 217, 220, 248–49, 269n11, 272n41, 285n1; implication of, in Salvadoran violence, 2, 6, 130, 162–69, 201–4, 208–9, 219, 233–50; Iraq War and, 45, 234–35, 249; neoliberalism's rise in, 4–6; racial politics of, 30–31, 40; Salvadoran policies and, 16, 18–21, 25–26, 28, 37, 40, 54, 70, 130, 170–71, 173, 270n24, 290n3; War on

Crime of, 2, 35, 37; War on Terror and, 17, 20, 44, 209, 220–21, 234, 236, 239, 242, 265n69; zero-tolerance crime policies of, 4, 6–10, 18, 47–48, 130–31, 152, 270n24. See also El Salvador; immigrants and immigration; nationalism; neoliberalism; specific politicians, gangs, cities, and legislative acts

University of Central America, 142, 201, 203

USA PATRIOT Act, 44, 296n1

Vacant Lot Revitalization Project, 77–78, 98

el vacil, 94, 154–56

Vaquerano, Carlos, 77, 80

Venezuela, 17, 48, 235

La Vida Loca (Poveda), 247

El Viejo Lin, 210–14, 217

Villalobos, Joaquin, 169–70

violence: forced repatriation in El Salvador and, 162–69; as media spectacle, 55–65; as returning repressed, 3–4, 9, 14, 18, 70–72, 114, 152, 178–79, 187–89, 199–204, 209–12, 219, 226–27, 231, 245; Salvadoran Civil War and, 32–33. See also death squads; gangs; Los Angeles; space and spatiality; zero-tolerance policing strategies

Violence and the Sacred (Girard), 238

Violent Crime Control and Law Enforcement Act. See Crime Bill (1994)

Violent Gang Task Force (of INS), 35

Walpin, Ned, 8

Washington Post (newspaper), 220–21, 223

Watts riots, 59–62, 80, 85, 269n15

Weber, Max, 21

Weed and Seed (program), 97–98

Westside Los Crazies (gang), 136

Which Way LA (program), 246

Wilson, Gary, 222–23, 294n29

ELANA ZILBERG IS ASSOCIATE PROFESSOR OF
COMMUNICATION AND CULTURE AND ASSOCIATE
DIRECTOR OF THE CENTER FOR GLOBAL CALIFORNIA
STUDIES AT THE UNIVERSITY OF CALIFORNIA,
SAN DIEGO.

. . .

Library of Congress Cataloging-in-Publication data
Zilberg, Elana, 1963–
Space of detention : the making of a transnational gang crisis between
Los Angeles and San Salvador / Elana Zilberg.
p. cm.
Includes bibliographical references and index.
ISBN 978-0-8223-4713-2 (cloth : alk. paper)
ISBN 978-0-8223-4730-9 (pbk. : alk. paper)
1. Gangs—California—Los Angeles. 2. Gangs—El Salvador—San Salvador.
3. Salvadorans—California—Los Angeles. 4. Gangs—Government policy—
United States. 5. Gang prevention—United States. I. Title.
HV6439.U7L7889 2011
364.1′06609794—dc23   2011021967

Made in the USA
San Bernardino, CA
19 December 2018